Comments on *Being a Sport Psych*

'It is refreshing to see a new text on sport p
away from the traditional psychological ski... ....
philosophical and ethical foundations of service to others. Richard Keegan
takes you on a journey from *being* (a psychologist) to *doing* (sport psychology)
in a kind of voyage of discovery.' – **Professor Mark B. Andersen**,
Halmstad University, Sweden

'This book will be an invaluable companion for any young sport psychology
practitioner or graduate student interested in applied sport psychology.
Richard Keegan's model takes you on a journey through all of the important
processes and decisions that come with being a professional and ethical sport
psychologist. A particular strength is his attempt to help practitioners understand their consulting philosophy, and how working practices in consultants
can be differentiated because of their philosophy.' – **Dr Chris Harwood**,
Loughborough University, UK

'*Being a Sport Psychologist* is a text which uniquely offers something to
both the experienced and neophyte practitioner. By taking the reader on a
journey through the consultancy process the key areas of applied practice
are explored and discussed in a manner that allows the experienced to
reflect on their journey and those in training to grow as practitioners
through exploring and developing knowledge in areas that are sometimes
less explored. The integrated case study *Ella's story* brings aspects of applied
practice to life and will resonate with those looking back on their practice
and those engaged in training.' – **Dr Moira Lafferty**, *University of Chester, UK*

'This text has what it takes to shape the field of sport psychology in very
positive ways. Its concise format, targeted topics, and comprehensive scope give
sport psychologists valuable tools that can lead to tangible and long-standing
growth among our athletic clientele.' – **Associate Professor Zella Moore**,
Manhattan College, USA

Being a Sport Psychologist

Richard Keegan

First published 2016 by
PALGRAVE

Palgrave in the UK is an imprint of Macmillan Publishers Limited, registered in England, company number 785998, of 4 Crinan Street, London, N1 9XW.

Palgrave Macmillan in the US is a division of St Martin's Press LLC, 175 Fifth Avenue, New York, NY 10010.

Palgrave is a global imprint of the above companies and is represented throughout the world.

Palgrave® and Macmillan® are registered trademarks in the United States, the United Kingdom, Europe and other countries.

ISBN 978–1–137–30089–8   paperback

This book is printed on paper suitable for recycling and made from fully managed and sustained forest sources. Logging, pulping and manufacturing processes are expected to conform to the environmental regulations of the country of origin.

A catalogue record for this book is available from the British Library.

A catalog record for this book is available from the Library of Congress.

To the things in life that feed the fire yet bring peace and contentment, all at once – family, science and sport.

And to the unnamed, undervalued, skill of 'continuing to think about a problem, long after the possibility of a simple answer has evaporated'.

Contents

List of Illustrations

Figures

Tables

Worksheets

About the author

Richard Keegan is a practising sport and exercise psychologist, registered in both the United Kingdom (HCPC and BPS) and Australia (AHPRA). He also supervises and assesses trainee practitioners in his role as a BASES accredited Sport Scientist. Richard has been teaching at universities for over 11 years, spanning Loughborough, Lincoln and now Canberra. He completed his MSc and PhD at Loughborough University, and before that, a degree in Psychology at the University of Bristol. Richard works with athletes across the full range of levels – from beginners to world champions – and across a wide range of sports. Richard is a published researcher in the area of applied psychology practices, and is devoted to researching, teaching and practising applied sport psychology.

Acknowledgements

Just in case this is the only instance where I (might) do something of note in the world, I need to offer a few thank-yous to those who helped me but cannot receive a regular 'citation'.

Most important of all, thank you to my wife, Sarah, who has both supported and distracted me along the way: both equally important. I hope I can repay the weekends and late nights that I stole to work on this book.

To my son, your role was more inspiration and keeping me grounded ... and sleep-deprived. If there are any typos, I'm blaming you ☺

To my Mum and Dad, as a new(ish) father, I am only just beginning to understand all the support you've given me along the way. But for letting me be that little bit different, and for challenging me when I was being too different – as well as everything else, of course – thank you.

To my training supervisor, Dr Claire Hitchings, you offered the excellent advice to find my own way and not try to imitate another practitioner. I stuck with it, and to some extent, I'm still going! This book is a product of that thinking, so thank you.

There is a man called Dave Piggott, who, I suspect, has read every piece of writing on the philosophy of science ever written: even long-lost tomes and personal handwritten notes. He helped me see the importance of philosophy, and to find a way of understanding it that allowed me to stay sane.

To the mentor who I feel I let down, I am sorry. I suppose we wouldn't be in this job if we didn't believe people could change, and I hope this book shows that I 'get it' a bit more than when I first started out.

To the conference speaker who triggered me to wonder what 'the greatest sport psychologist in the world' might really look like: thank you. The scrawled notes from that session inspired some lengthy reflections and, ultimately, the writing of this book. Sorry I stopped listening to what you were actually saying. And just in case anyone was wondering, no I absolutely do not claim to be the 'greatest' – in the end, this book is about recognizing the gap between where we are and where we want to be.

Academically, I owe a debt of gratitude to Chris Harwood, Chris Spray, Chris Lavallee and Stuart Biddle. They gave me the space and patience needed to persist with some 'hard problems' and ultimately develop myself as a scientist.

There are a host of coaches, managers, mentors, captains and athletes who gave me important opportunities along the way. Confidentiality prevents me from naming those people, but hopefully you know who you are. In no particular order: the people in rugby, football, tennis, hockey, athletics, boccia, cricket, blind cricket, golf, archery, equestrian sports, motor sports all helped me immeasurably. Even though it was my job to help them.

And to each reader, I hope this book gives you what you need – even if that's different from what you want.

Publisher's Acknowledgements

The publisher and the author thank the people listed below for permission to reproduce material from their publications:

American Psychological Association, Barry Schneider and Jim Taylor, for permission to reproduce Worksheet 4.1. From Appendix, pp. 324–325, in Taylor, J., & Schneider, B. A. (1992). The sport-clinical intake protocol: A comprehensive interviewing instrument for applied sport psychology, *Professional Psychology: Research and Practice*, 23(4), 318–325. Copyright ©1992 by the American Psychological Association. No further reproduction or distribution is permitted without written permission from the copyright holders.

John Wiley and Sons, for permission to reproduce Worksheet 6.1. From Page, A. C., Stritzke, W. G. K. and Mclean, N. J. (2008). Toward science-informed supervision of clinical case formulation: A training model and supervision method. *Australian Psychologist*, 43(2), 88–95.

Luke Rodgers, for permission to reproduce and adapt Table 2.1. From Rodgers, L. (2011). *Essay on Ethics* (unpublished work).

Merriam-Webster, Inc. for permission to reproduce a definition from Merriam-Webster's Collegiate® Dictionary, 11th Edition ©2015 (www.Merriam-Webster.com).

Oxford Centre for Staff and Learning Development, for permission to reproduce and adapt Worksheets 2.3 and 4.3. From Gibbs, G. (1998). *Learning by doing: A guide to teaching and learning methods*. Oxford: OCSLD.

Taylor and Francis Ltd., for permission to reproduce and adapt Table 3.2. From Keegan, R. J. (2010). Teaching consulting philosophies to neophyte sport psychologists: Does it help, and how can we do it? *Journal of Sport Psychology in Action*, 1, 42–52 (www.tandfonline.com).

The British Association for Sport and Exercise Sciences, for permission to reproduce Figure 4.2. From Keegan R. J., & Killilea, J. (2006). Entering sport cultures as a supervised practitioner: What am I getting myself into?, *The Sport and Exercise Scientist*, 1(7), 22–23.

Zella E. Moore, for permission to reproduce and adapt Worksheet 2.1. From Moore, Z. E. (2003). Ethical dilemmas in sport psychology: Discussion and recommendations for practice. *Professional Psychology: Research and Practice*, 34(6), 601–610.

A special thank you goes to the anonymous reviewers for their input into the project and, in one case, for kindly granting us permission to quote from the review.

Preface

Sport and Psychology

During the 20th century, numerous advances were made within the world of sport. These advances ranged from the decision to allow training for the Olympics (which was initially considered cheating – Eassom, 1994), up to and including sophisticated modern training programmes encompassing skills coaching; strength and conditioning; nutrition and, of course, psychology. Most of the time, these support activities are implemented as a result of documented benefits: scientific testing; an enhanced understanding of the human body; developments in sporting equipment; and (sport being a world where everything is recorded, scored and compared) *improved performance*. It should also be noted, however, that athletes are highly competitive, and are prepared to try almost anything to get an extra 1% over their competitors. For example, there is no scientific evidence that wearing a 10-year-old pair of socks is actually lucky, but many have tried it! This necessity for improvement places sport at the cutting edge of human endeavours, with perhaps only military operations and space exploration placing more of a demand on human beings to innovate, adapt and develop.

On this demanding frontier, people feel compelled to consider the impact of human psychology, especially as other avenues for enhancement appear to reach exhaustion (e.g., how much can we ever improve a reaction time? How strong can one muscle ever become without damaging the structures around it?). The problem of turning to psychology to demonstrate hard-and-fast results is clear, but often overlooked. Historically, the science of psychology has struggled to deliver concrete 'bet-your-life' results. Every 'law' gains more and more exceptions, until we wonder whether it is really a 'law' at all. Every important theory has several competitors, as well as several substantial 'flaws', and we rarely manage to successfully resolve which of our competing theories is 'best' or 'true'. The human brain is an incomprehensibly complex network of neurons, connections, neuro-transmitters and fibres, which appears in the flesh as a grey, slippery, porridge-like mass. Even when the most sophisticated tools we have allow us to identify regions, for example, language centres or motor cortex, there are often marked differences between individuals (for example, due to handedness, gender or often for no distinguishable reason). These exceptions mean we have to ignore large portions of the population when we confidently declare that 'this region performs a specific function'. In fact, as a good rule of thumb, if someone ever proclaims to know exactly how the human brain works, you can confidently assume they haven't done their homework. Anybody who has studied the area in detail will be much more cautious and nuanced in their claims.

For example, more frequently than we care to admit, psychologists and researchers revert to 'analogue' (or 'proxy') measurements – so rather than measuring the specific thing we want to (e.g., thoughts and feelings), we need to rely on observations of behaviour, questionnaires or interviews. In a recent example, one paper measured distance run and number of spirits in football/ soccer and directly equated this to 'effort' (Weimar & Wicker, 2014). Effort is famously very difficult to measure, and issues of position, fitness, injury, tactics, opposition, etc. could easily break the link between 'effort' and 'distance covered'. If we spend a few moments considering what exactly effort is, and how it might differ from energy, motivation, fitness and other relevant constructs, we begin to both understand that it is difficult to directly measure and that it would unlikely be measured as a distance. However, more frequently than we like to admit, psychologists using analogue measurements forget that we had to use those analogues because *we could not measure the thing we actually wanted to*, and we frequently conflate the two by assuming we *did* measure the right thing after all. This mistake can lead to inaccurate, contradictory or even misleading claims. To be clear though, if practitioners were to stop making hard-and-fast claims, to tone down and qualify their sales pitch, a large part of the problem could be avoided.

In summary, we have a 'client' (the world of sport) that is constantly searching for guaranteed advancements, turning to a service provider (the world of psychology), which almost by definition is not trading in concrete observations, laws or 'results'. The potential to generate a lose:lose outcome is serious – athletes and coaches could be failed, psychologists and the profession of psychology could be made to look like 'hokum' and a lot of people could lose a lot of money. All this begs an immediate question: why even try? Well, once we get past the cutthroat demand to deliver results, sport is an area with almost unlimited potential to gain financial rewards, fame, glory, esteem and satisfaction (sport is responsible for approximately 2% of the global GDP).

Oh, and people love sport.

In fact, if you're a psychologist and you love sport, then 'sport psychologist' seems the perfect job. If you're involved in sport and you believe psychology is an important consideration for performance and welfare, you might also explore sport psychology. Factually, the number of accredited or licenced sport psychologists in countries such as the United States, United Kingdom and Australia is increasing rapidly (cf. Lidor, Morris, Bardoxaglou, & Becker, 2001): an observation supported simply by examining the growth in the online 'consultant finders' and directories of registered psychologists. If we then stretch our definition to include countries where formal regulation is not in place (so numbers are not recorded), we get a bigger number. Further still, if we look at the number of university courses teaching kinesiology and/or sport science, which often now includes sport psychology modules/units, we get an even bigger number. And then, if we include all the people with no formal education in sport science or psychology, but who are involved in sport and want to try some sport psychology, then we end up with a *very* large number of people. People who, one way or another, are delivering sport psychology: *being sport psychologists*. People who are trying to deliver results, in a result-driven business, using a science whose subject matter (the human brain) is famously ineffable, and whose theories and methods are, necessarily, tentative (relative to 'hard' sciences such as physics). Sounds crazy, no?

Why this book, and why now?

This preface begins to explain why I set out to write this book. We have a role that is: (a) incredibly popular (the sport psychologist); (b) with incredible potential to help athletes and coaches; (c) being performed by people with an incredibly wide variety of qualifications and experiences; (d) all set against the backdrop of the above 'crisis of legitimacy' – can sport psychology offer proven, effective, guaranteed results for sport performers? This situation, at the time of writing, remains one of tremendous potential yet equally serious danger. Succeed and both groups benefit immensely: sport and psychology. Fail and an athlete, her coach(es), family and friends could all be 'turned against' sport psychology, and the reputations of both the practitioner and the profession could be damaged. If these failures occur often enough then sport psychology could just as easily suffer 'death by a thousand cuts', rather than proving itself as an invaluable aspect of supporting performance.

Sport psychology's 'war' to win the hearts and minds of athletes, coaches and administrators remains in the balance, with just as many dissatisfying failures as glorious successes. To check this, just find 10 random athletes/coaches and ask what they think of sport psychology – the results can be quite mixed. For example, as part of the 'Winning Edge' initiative in Australia, each sport's national body was required to submit a document outlining their intentions to use sport science services. Only three, out of 29, specifically requested sport psychology support services. When questioned, several stories emerged of having a 'bad experience' of a sport psychologist (cf. Kirsten Peterson, personal communication, 2013). This book will lay out a strategy for avoiding, or at least minimizing, such bad experiences, by delivering a coherent, transparent, effective and ethical service.

Many sport psychology textbooks open with the above-described message that sport psychology is experiencing a 'moment of opportunity' (e.g., Kontos

& Feltz, 2008; Smith & Bar-Eli, 2007), but very few examine the consequences of failing to properly promote and utilize sport psychology. What if it is only a 'window' of opportunity; one that might eventually close? How long before athletes or coaches or entire sports – following bad experiences or in the absence of compelling evidence – decide sport psychology cannot really help them after all? This book sets out to inform, guide and improve the practice of anyone delivering sport psychology services, at any level, in any situation: anyone being a sport psychologist.

I am the greatest sport psychologist in the world

Well not me, but this was a statement used to begin a keynote presentation I once watched from another sport psychologist. In fairness, he did go on to say that he might not be, and that, in his opinion, there was no way of telling. However, I missed the rest of the talk because the statement triggered me to start filling my notebook with ideas for how we might be able to test such a claim. It is a worthwhile exercise to complete: *What would you look for in seeking the best sport psychologist in the world?*

My thinking quickly progressed beyond the obvious, 'heuristic' criteria such as having a world champion as a client. World champions existed before sport psychology came along, and many still win without a psychologist in their entourage. I also reasoned that it must be possible to deliver world-class sport psychology to children or amateurs (something I still believe). What about delivering great performance improvements? Again, I wasn't sure: Elite athletes do have dips in form, and usually regain their former levels one way or another (more often than not!). I remembered a sport psychologist whose marketing materials seemed to, very conveniently, claim he only worked for a particular (famous) client when he was playing well. There is a very long and complex 'causal chain' between psychological support and athletic performance, and if anything we do our profession a disservice by attempting to reduce what we do to performance enhancement. If we 'live or die' by depending on performance outcomes generated by the athletes, teams, coaches, physiotherapists, etc. then our fate is largely in their hands, not our own; individually and as a profession. Top-flight athletes and teams can all fail; underdogs do win occasionally. It's why people love sport and why betting firms make so much money. So do we really want to tie our reputation to the success or failure of our clients? Further, what if substantial performance improvements came at the expense of athlete welfare, or serious ethical 'lapses'. And what if the same sport psychologist couldn't deliver similar improvements with the next athlete? Whilst I was still sitting in the same conference presentation, I had already moved on from outstanding outcomes to *outstanding process*: What does a great psychologist do that others may not?

First of all, I reasoned that a great sport psychologist must be ethical. Managing clients' expectations of the services delivered, never breaching confidentiality, never allowing conflicts of interest to undermine the quality of service (or people's perceptions of it) and leaving behind happy, healthy clients. Second, I reasoned that a great sport psychologist will know exactly what they are doing: never allowing themselves to be caught out, never making inappropriate assumptions and always able to explain exactly what they are doing at any point in their consulting. As far as possible, a great psychologist would never blindly 'hit and hope' when people's psychological well-being is involved. Third, I listed key steps that a sport psychologist always goes through in some capacity: needs analysis, case formulation, choosing an intervention strategy, planning the support and monitoring progress. A series of sketches led to the model proposed in this book, containing all these steps and reasoning that every sport psychologist goes through these steps with every client, just to a different degree. If each step were as good as possible, then we would be looking at a great sport psychologist.

The problem then became how we might observe how well each step is being completed, but the answer was simple. All the qualification processes I knew at the time, as well as the ethical codes (and even laws in some countries), required psychologists to keep good records. In training and supervision, these records are submitted to reviewers as evidence of competence, and post-registration psychologists must keep good records too (for reasons explained in Chapter 2). So if a sport psychologist cannot 'show their workings' – either as objective records or when questioned by a curious client – then we can be fairly sure we are not looking at the world's greatest.

I was also extremely aware that a 'great' sport psychologist, like the world's greatest athletes, should be constantly improving and learning, otherwise s/he will be overtaken by new developments, or a new competitor. To achieve this, a psychologist rarely 'trains' by practising on mock clients, but rather, they are thrown into real-life practice environments and asked to engage in reflective practice, supervision or mentoring and continual professional development. A great psychologist should be able to learn from every experience (good or bad), and thus be able to deal with unexpected challenges and new problems. After a few more sketches and some reflection of my own, I was sat looking at the model used throughout this book and believing that I had answered the question of how to detect a great sport psychologist. Each step/task was too important to overlook, and each clearly informed or supported others. The world's greatest sport psychologist would be the person who completed all of these processes to the highest standard, and who could demonstrate this process at any given moment. It struck me that after 10 years of training, practice, teaching and assessing, nobody had ever actually laid it out in this way. The only thing I could add already mostly encompassed under 'reflective practice' was that a great sport psychologist would fully understand

and appreciate the importance of these tasks and roles, as well as the way they combine to create a highly effective process.

Training world-class sport psychologists

The requirement to not only be an effective and ethical sport psychologist, but also to demonstrate this to other people is exacerbated where statutory regulation is in place. In these countries, trainee sport psychologists must submit records of training/CPD, records of practice (preferably anonymized) and case studies to examiners: whose job it is to assess whether the trainee is ready to finish supervision and 'go it alone'. Having spent several years as one of these examiners – reviewing written applications and conducting viva voce (verbal) exams – it struck me how incredibly difficult it is for trainee psychologists to demonstrate their thought process, ethical standards and levels of competence. In fact, no part of their training (to my knowledge) makes it clear how a sport psychologist (trainee or experienced) should demonstrate these things to a total stranger. I was initially inspired to try and teach these tasks/roles, and ways of evidencing them, to my own students – undergraduate students on the 'Applied Sport and Exercise Psychology' module in Lincoln (UK) between 2009 and 2012. What I discovered in this process is that: (a) the role of a sport psychologist can be broken down into very clear sub-tasks; (b) that these tasks can be clearly and succinctly articulated and described; and (c) that anyone attempting to deliver sport psychology – whether for the first time or as a highly experienced expert – will be carrying out these tasks (deliberately or otherwise). Obviously, this is not a 'concrete' claim – there is no way of testing it (yet) – but let me put it differently. As an assessor of essays and portfolios, whenever applicants were able to clearly demonstrate how each of the specific tasks had been planned, executed, delivered and assessed, it was significantly easier for me (and any other markers/ assessors) to 'sign off' on someone's competence.

We rewrote our mark schemes and taught the new 'tasks' in class, and the grade average increased by 5% for three consecutive years. By the end of this 'trial', we had 20-year-old undergraduates writing better case studies than some applicants with 4 years' postgraduate training and supervised practice. This moment, April 2012, was when I became convinced that I needed to write this book so that *all* sport psychologists could record and demonstrate the effectiveness (or otherwise!) of their practice.

In the first instance, examiners, regulators, litigators, supervisors and mentors could all legitimately ask for 'evidence' of a psychologist's competence. Those who are not fooled by 'Well I once worked for someone really famous ...' will require concrete, documentary evidence: case studies of working with clients, reflective logs of key decisions, accurate records, etc. Such evidence cannot simply be a collection of superficial descriptions and stories: it needs to demonstrate a critical awareness of one's role, boundaries, capabilities, ethics, interpersonal skills and scientific rigour. Your portfolio of evidence needs to demonstrate that you 'get it'. What better way to demonstrate that you 'get it' than to *actually get it?*

The model that was developed for guiding case studies (outlined in Chapter 1) was not simply a formulaic 'template' for writing about one's consulting. It actually allows the psychologist to understand their job as a holistic whole: clearly detailing how different aspects of the role inform each other. For example, the model (unlike many) addresses how different legitimate definitions of 'science' determine what sort of scientific evidence to use, and how. Likewise, the model denotes how these assumptions/preferences impact on how to define success/failure, how to monitor these things and how best to 'market' oneself as a result. I began to reason that a sport psychologist: (a) who knows exactly what they are trying to do, why and how; (b) who deliberately seeks to eliminate any 'blind spots' from their process; and (c) who can communicate at any given moment exactly what they are doing and why (say to a coach or supervisor) is very likely a *better sport psychologist* than one who cannot. They are more accountable, yes, but they are also more self-aware, less likely to make mistakes (yet more able to learn from them), more coherent and deliberate and so – in all likelihood – more effective. Again, we cannot test this yet, but there is a mature literature suggesting that self-aware, reflective and self-critical psychologists tend to be 'better' – in terms of causing less harm, forming better relationships and generating improved outcomes (e.g., Andersen, 1994; 2004; Cropley, Miles, Hanton, & Anderson, 2007; Cropley, Hanton, Miles, & Niven, 2010).

In my career in sport psychology, I had read a lot of sport psychology textbooks, yet I had never come across a single, short book that neatly encapsulated the core tasks of the sport psychologist's job in a clear and accessible manner. Where the job itself is discussed (as opposed to either methods/techniques or broad topic areas) we were normally presented with separate chapters on key ideas (especially mental skills): sometimes allowing overlapping themes and sometimes leaving obvious 'gaps' (case formulation being a notable example). Hence, in most instances, the reader was being asked to bridge the divide between the complex ideas and unusual terminology of the literature, and the real-life experiences from their own practice. This book, *Being a Sport Psychologist*, set out to avoid such a disconnect. All the tasks described in the model of practice are things that any sport psychologist is doing, whether they admit it or not. Certainly, they are things that any assessor, supervisor, client or lawyers (depending how unlucky you are) will, at some point, require you to explain/demonstrate. Ideally, however, any practitioners reading this book will immediately recognize each task from their own consulting, rather than having to 'work' to associate each concept to their own real-life experiences. As such, this book aims to be uniquely accessible, relevant, informative and empowering. My experiences as I became ready to write the book could be compared to 'the scales falling from my eyes' – sometimes uncomfortable, but ultimately enriching. My aim in writing it is to generate a similar experience for the reader without the pain of having to 'learn the hard way'. In a nutshell: *this is the stuff I wish someone had told me when I started out.*

But why doesn't this model look and sound like the other ones?

There is one final point that needs to be made before progressing on with the real content. Of course, people have already written about this topic, sometimes at great length. Other books exist, other models exist. Having been through the training journey, supervised and assessed others, and tried to assist undergraduates in their first experiences of applying sport psychology, I realized there were some genuine issues with what existed around 2012 – when the book was first 'pitched'. These can be reduced to the following three core points. The first problem was that the literature at the time was quite 'messy': lots of associated ideas, all undeniably relevant, but all tossed together and not organized into a coherent whole for the practitioner. If a new book faithfully reflected that atomized and disconnected literature, it would only serve to confuse another generation of trainees, and alienate them from very important considerations within the job (ethics, philosophy, consulting style). As a second issue, the existing literature would often leap straight to a very advanced level: impenetrable terminology and abstract concepts without much grounding in reality. Again, there was rarely any way for a trainee to make the journey from their current knowledge level, *whatever that might be*, into the complex and very foreign 'territory' of philosophy/style considerations. Third, there were problematic consequences to having many different 'schools' and 'styles', all using special and unique language and all claiming to be separate but without saying how/why. It made it impossible to compare and evaluate the different approaches, which seem wholly unscientific. So the sport psychologist is asked to be scientific in their role, but some of the most important decisions s/he could ever make were couched as 'just pick your favourite approach; the one that makes sense to you'. That's unacceptable.

If we accept the arguments made here (and elsewhere – e.g., Hutter, Oldenhof-Veldman, & Oudejans, 2014; Poczwardowski, Aoyagi, Shapiro, & Van Raalte, 2014) that the entire profession would be enhanced by practitioners being more aware of their style, philosophy and approach, then we need: (a) to organize and reinterpret the existing literature into a single meaningful model; (b) to simplify some core ideas and make them accessible so that practitioners have a 'foothold' in an otherwise impenetrable literature; and (c) we need to be able to compare and evaluate different approaches. Perhaps not asking 'Which is best?' but rather 'Which is best for this client, in this moment, with these needs?'. These aims/requirements may lead to the following criticisms: (a) why doesn't this look like this or that other model, and why didn't you cite these or those folks?; (b) you can't simplify this topic, such-and-such important big name would be spinning in her/his grave; and (c) you can't compare apples and oranges, people just need to pick a style or practice however they see fit. In light of the above aims for the book, such criticisms should at least be contextualized, but should really be rebuffed. *This model and this book are different, by design, in order to produce a different outcome to the existing models and literature.*

In which case, where did this model come from?

Well, I am an experienced qualitative researcher. My PhD adopted qualitative methods, and forced me to delve very deep into issues around how we collect, analyse and interpret data. In particular, the issue of how we turn data from numerous sources and of different types into some kind of representation has plagued science for millennia. Fundamentally, every single theory or model in the world was 'made up' by somebody – often in the bath or shower or in bed at night. Such acts of creation, or inspiration, have variously been termed 'bricolage' (Levi-Strauss, 1966), 'bisociation' (Koestler, 1976), emergence (Glaser, 1978) or the 'Horizon of expectations' (Popper, 1969). So what happened is: I read a lot about this area, I practised applied sport psychology at every given opportunity, I taught it to undergraduates, supervised postgraduates and evaluated the final submissions of trainees about to qualify. Based on that data – literature, experience, reflections, etc. – I gradually developed the ideas presented in this book. In the view of Popper (1969) and many others, it actually does not matter where an idea (or model or theory) comes from, so long as we go on to test it, compare to existing ones and evaluate it for usefulness (as a test, see if you can trace back the origins of some classic theories and models in sport psychology, or beyond. Chances are they were not derived explicitly from observations of data, but rather 'moments of inspiration'). The testing of models and theories, in this case, will begin with people's initial judgements of 'face validity' ('Does it make sense to me? Does it fit with my experiences of everyday applied practice?'). However, I actively encourage researchers out there to test this model in more robust ways, teasing out predictions and hypotheses and testing to see if they hold firm. If it fails a little, we can make it better. If it fails a lot, and we can construct a better 'beginning-to-end' model, then we should move on. That's science. Certainly, if I get time in my career I will be testing and refining the model proposed here. I wouldn't go so far as to claim it's perfect first time out. However, in addressing the three problems detailed above, I do think it holds potential to progress the field of sport psychology.

Personal note: On arrogance

Many colleagues, family and friends have reviewed drafts of this book and I am forever indebted to those people for the help and encouragement they provided. One feedback point I have struggled to deal with was beautifully expressed by an anonymous reviewer: "As can be the case with books that advocate such elevated levels of good practice... there is a danger that Richard could come across as somewhat arrogant in: (a) his perception of his own service; and (b) by extension, his views of the service offered by others... I appreciate that it is a tricky balance to get right...".

I completely understand this criticism. It has played on my mind at many points in the planning, writing and editing of the book. For what it is worth, I want to reassure every reader that I am not arrogant, in the sense of assuming my own practice is excellent, nor do I judge the practice of others from a position of 'assumed superiority'. I deeply appreciate how lucky I am to be able to practise sport psychology whilst working within academia: meaning that my salary does not depend on getting clients through the door or out-competing other services. The privileged position I find myself in offers me incredible opportunities to analyse, reflect, evaluate and ponder, safe in the knowledge that my next paycheque depends more on my annual review – incorporating teaching, publications, grant income and 'leadership' – than next week's client list. One key motivation for me is to utilize this privilege for good, and attempt to contribute to the ongoing development of the profession I love.

Further to the above, there is no assumption that my own practice is (or ever has been) perfect. If we refer to philosophies in Chapter 3, my experiences have led me to become evermore 'fallibilist': attempting to avoid making any presumptions, and always critically questioning my own processes as a practitioner. If we pause for a second to consider what type of consulting experiences might lead to such a situation, it soon becomes clear I must have made mistakes along the way. Why else would I have become so careful to try and avoid them? I must have made mistakes and also, they must have really bothered me! So if, at any point, an issue is raised that might feel personally relevant, please be assured it is not a personal attack, and I may even have experienced something similar in order to prompt these reflections. In particular, there are many memories from when I first set out as a trainee that I regret, and that probably lost me the respect of at least one former colleague/mentor. I was too confident, too brash and too headstrong. The caution and high standards that permeate these pages have been impressed upon me following those experiences. If this book helps other trainees avoid a few more awkward moments, or prevents a few lasting regrets, it will have been worthwhile.

As such, I would urge every reader to try and read the words on these pages in the voice of a gentle, helpful friend. Some passages sound pretty horrible when read in a judging/criticizing voice! I often wish I could be more strident and robust, but I have not learned that skill yet – so at the time of writing I don't have it in me to be that way. The whole motivation for this book was to help. To help new trainees, newly qualified practitioners, supervisors, experienced practitioners and even the athletes and coaches who are often our clients. I would be saddened to hear of it being received any other way. The problems we face, as a profession, are extremely difficult: both difficult to define and then to deal with. This book absolutely does not claim to have 'solved' them, nor that there is a single 'correct' answer. Rather this book seeks to make those difficult problems more 'tractable': laid out in a comprehensible manner, with clear footholds, choices and (estimated) consequences to those choices.

Each sport psychologist will develop their own style, which will come with its own consequences. On the one hand, this book does not seek to identify one 'true' style of practice that is always best, nor to influence trainees to adopt a particular approach. On the other hand, understanding the consequences of such important decisions is important, yet difficult – even with the benefits of experience. By offering a terminology, model and analytic framework for understanding our practice, this book seeks to help facilitate the development of coherent, transparent, effective and ethical sport psychology.

1 Introduction and Overview

1.1 What does a sport psychologist do?

In this book, we adopt a very simple definition of sport psychology: the application of the scientific process to the mental aspects of athletes and sport performers. Notably, this can entail performance enhancement, supporting participation, educating groups about sport psychology, supporting psychological well-being and managing transitions (e.g., to the elite level, or into retirement). The particular wording of this definition can entail both research and applied practice because, in reality, it can be quite misleading to try and distinguish between the two. Even the purest of researchers must produce findings with applied relevance, and present their findings in a way that will inform applied practice. Likewise, even the purest of applied practitioners must remain aware of developments in research, and be able to critically evaluate the relevance of research findings before adopting them into applied practice. As such, this definition is a departure from those listed at the beginning of Kontos and Feltz (2008), but is perhaps closest to that of Weinberg and Gould (1995, p. 8): 'The scientific study of people and their behaviour in sport and exercise settings.'

Applied sport psychology services can be provided to an individual athlete or coach, a group of athletes/coaches, a particular team or sporting organization, a university or even a national or global sport governing body. Increasingly, sport psychology can also involve teaching schoolchildren about basic ideas that might help them in sport, or working with parents to foster supportive environments and reinforce key principles. As an important addition, sport psychologists must also be able to work alongside coaches, managers, physiotherapists, physiologists and many other specialists as part of interdisciplinary teams (cf. Abernathy, Kippers, MacKinnon, Neal, & Hanrahan, 1997). The latter point also emphasizes the very broad scope of psychology in sport, ranging through: psychophysiology (e.g., affective states, brain waves); motor learning and control; emotions and moods; cognition (e.g., information processing); social psychology (relationships, group dynamics); and even occasionally sociology (e.g., cultures). As such, the psychologist practising in sport must be fully conversant in all of these areas, and not simply specialized in one (as researchers often are). In this

1

respect, 'the application of the scientific process to the mental aspects of athletes and sport performers' is not as simple as it sounds.

1.2   A brief history of sport psychology

No sport psychology textbook can be complete without a mention of the contributions made by Triplett, Zajonc, Morgan, Griffith and Martens. In 1898, Triplett observed that cyclists appeared to ride faster in the presence of others than when alone. He then replicated the effect in a controlled lab setting, and with children winding a fishing reel (either alone or in pairs). In establishing a psychological variable as a key factor in physical performance, and cycling in particular, Triplett is credited as having conducted the first sport psychology experiment. While Triplett completed the rest of his long career in pursuing other areas, Zajonc (1965) subsequently reinvigorated the concept of 'social facilitation' in sport performance. The effects of crowd size, home advantage, choking under pressure, social loafing in teams and team cohesion can all trace their roots directly to these origins.

Another tradition, perhaps still alive today, was to borrow theories and paradigms from other areas of psychology and apply them to sport (Landers, 1983). This led to extensive attempts to apply personality theories – the idea that humans have fixed and enduring elements in their psychological make-up – to sport (e.g., Morgan, 1980). There remains to this day a common belief that people can be a 'sporty type': drawn to sport by its competitive nature and physical challenges (the 'gravitation hypothesis' – Young, 1990). Likewise, there remains a strong tendency to measure 'traits' in sport psychology, even when we know phenomena such as confidence and anxiety can change very rapidly and so might not be stable over time like a 'personality trait'. Continuing the borrowing theme, important concepts such as self-efficacy (Bandura, 1977) and achievement orientation (Maehr & Nicholls, 1980) were not sport-specific theories by any means. However, they have served a purpose in offering sport psychology researchers a foothold from which to consider the roles of confidence and motivation, respectively, in determining sport performance.

Preceding many of these studies, Coleman Roberts Griffith is credited as developing the first programme of systematic research and training in sport psychology (cf. Gould & Pick, 1995) – even though a similar institute was opened in Germany 5 years earlier. A key contribution of Griffith was to recommend that research in sport psychology should not borrow from other areas, but should be based purely in sport (cf. Weiss & Gill, 2005). Overall, while this aim remains difficult to achieve, Griffith and his team explored many aspects of sport psychology, even including the benefits to a person of participating in sport.

Finally, mirroring Griffith's call for sport psychology to stand on its own and not borrow from other areas, Rainer Martens (1979) criticized the tendency of sport psychology researchers to retreat to controlled lab settings. He argued that this approach prevented research from replicating the pressures and challenges of real sport settings; that is, they lacked 'ecological validity'. Unfortunately, many of the issues identified by authors such as Griffith and Martens appear just as relevant, and prevalent, in modern sport psychology.

Kontos and Feltz (2008) described three 'current issues' in sport psychology, although they may be familiar following the above summary. First, the worlds of sport psychology research and applied practice remain relatively separate, with very little exchange of ideas between the two. This is arguably detrimental to both, as research loses relevance and practice loses its evidence. Second, researchers remain unclear on how to study sport psychology effectively. In a topic area spanning from the physiological to the social and cultural, is it appropriate to adopt a single set of methods and assumptions? Roberts (1989) argued that there would be most value, or more accomplishment, through exclusively adopting a cognitive approach (e.g., individual level processes, often based on questionnaires). In contrast, Landers (1983) and Morgan (1980) argued such a singular approach would be damaging. Overall, sport psychology retains a genuine 'blind spot' for the philosophy of science (i.e., what are we studying and how can we study it?), and this issue is addressed in Chapter 3. Finally, Kontos and Feltz noted the trend for sport psychology research to focus on elite athletes, when this group only represents a tiny proportion of those participating in sport. There is no reason to assume similarities between elite athletes and recreational or amateur athletes, and likewise no reason to assume everybody wants (or needs) to possess the same mental attributes as elite athletes.

This brief history of sport psychology contains one lingering theme: We are a discipline that has consistently experienced, but not resolved, critical issues: serious issues that threaten the very legitimacy of the profession. In linking research and practice, addressing the issues posed by philosophy of science, and in defining 'world-class' practice as something you can do with amateurs or young athletes; this book aims to genuinely resolve some of these persistent and damaging issues once and for all.

1.3 Regulation and accountability

Perhaps linked to the on-going crises, as described above, many countries already have formal regulation of sport psychologists; for example, the Health and Care Professions Council (United Kingdom, in partnership with the British Psychological Society), the American Psychology

Association (Division 47, in partnership with the Association for Applied Sport Psychology) and the Australian Health Professional Registration Association (in partnership with the Australian Psychology Society). Other countries are working towards this, but many others are not. Where there is statutory regulation, technically a sport psychologist should have undergone a minimum amount of education (undergraduate and postgraduate), as well as several years of supervised practice. If these practitioners 'mess up', they could lose their licence/registration and face disciplinary proceedings. The idea is to offer a degree of quality assurance to clients – a minimum level of education and experience – as well as a degree of accountability (e.g., 'if you don't like what s/he does, here's who you can complain to and here's how it will be dealt with'). In both regulated and unregulated countries, if someone is deeply dissatisfied with your service and wants to hold you accountable then they can, of course, sue (at least for their money back, and perhaps for any 'damages' too). More realistically, dissatisfied athletes and coaches will simply tell any others that the practitioner involved, or the profession as a whole, is not worth the money. As such, whether regulated or unregulated, a sport psychologist needs to be able to demonstrate a high degree of scientific rigour, ethical standards, quality assurance and, ideally (as above), effectiveness. They need to be able to provide documentary evidence that procedures have been followed, that due diligence has been carried out and that any advice given was responsible, ethical and, in all likelihood, appropriate (i.e., likely to help). In a world where clients have high expectations that sport psychology will deliver (rather than perhaps treating it as a gamble that may or may not pay off), we might find more and more clients willing to take legal action if their expectations are not met. And whilst the 'culture of litigation' is generally bemoaned as a symptom of modern malaise and entitlement, it might equally act as a metaphorical 'stick' to drive up standards in sport psychology. Obviously, using the 'carrot' would be preferable and, in this instance, that 'carrot' might be the possibility of creating (and being) truly world-class sport psychologists.

1.4   A model of the sport psychologist's 'process'

On the one hand, sport psychology has, throughout its history, almost exclusively been conceptualized as a scientific endeavour, not pseudo-scientific or any other variation: proto-scientific, anti-scientific or unscientific. Whilst Chapter 3 will make an explicit attempt to discuss several different types of science, this book will maintain the emphasis on a scientific process.

On the other hand, however, the 'stereotypical' scientific process – aloof and unbiased observation, impartial theorizing and diagnosing, leading to precise prescriptions for action – can be quite unsuitable to the practice of applied sport psychology. Sport psychology is a profession where service delivery can take place on a team bus, in a changing room, at pitch-/court-/track-/poolside and sometimes you only have minutes to 'make a difference'. Likewise, sport is an area where passion and partisanship are inevitable; in fact, they are highly valued. It may be very difficult to secure a job without being passionate about the sport; so 'impartial' and 'unbiased' science could be a poor combination for working in sport. As such, the model used in this book – a model designed to describe key steps that any sport psychologist must take in delivering their services – is also highly flexible and inclusive of different 'styles'. All the steps in the model are intended to be 'universal' – in that any practising sport psychologist would recognize them from their own practice – as well as demonstrating the ways that science can be used appropriately to inform one's practice. However, each step will be 'unpacked' as we progress through the book, and different ways of achieving each step will be considered. Likewise, the 'cost' of attempting to overlook any step, or pay it insufficient attention, will be considered in relation to the effects on the client, on your effectiveness (and thus, your reputation) and on your ability to report (and/or defend) your actions. The model is outlined below:

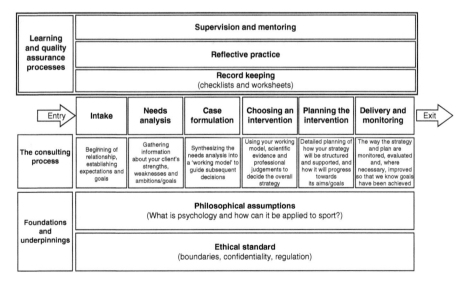

Figure 1.1 *A model of the sport psychology service delivery process proposed in this book. Note that all main boxes are conceptualized as 'universal': applicable to all sport psychology practice – whether explicit or implicit. Steps may not take place in the simple linear order shown, as iterative cycles are quite typical.*

The above model needs to be separated from a theory, a framework or a heuristic. A theory has two specific properties – explanation and falsifiability – that allow us to make predictions, based on known initial conditions (i.e., hypotheses). Our model does not yet facilitate such precision. In addition, theories are usually intended to be 'generalizable' so that they apply to as many instances as possible of the given phenomena. A framework is a set of concepts that is used to understand the world; an interpretive lens through which to look and perhaps see the same phenomenon in a different light (these will be more relevant in Chapter 3). A heuristic can be thought of as a very simple first attempt at apprehending something, a rough guess, mainly used as a basis to ask more relevant questions and perhaps as the starting point for a model. In contrast to all the above, a model is an attempt to represent or illustrate the workings of a complete system, or process. Models can be either descriptive ('this is how we think it works') or prescriptive ('this is what we think should happen'). For now, our model of the applied sport psychology service delivery process is a prescriptive model – this is how I think it should work. If it survives and sticks around, however, it does make testable predictions. For example, that the quality of each step determines the quality of subsequent steps, or that better alignment between philosophy and practice will lead to a better client experience. I would love to see these predictions tested within my own lifetime.

Underpinning principle 1: Ethical standards. Whether you admit it or not, you have an ethical standpoint. It might be that you think 'ethics doesn't matter', or 'I haven't got time to worry about ethics', in which case you are (according to the model in this book) wrong. Ethical considerations are the 'safety net' underpinning any helping profession: protecting the client, the practitioner and the profession as a whole. Ethics involves knowing the limits of your competence, choosing and adhering to a level of confidentiality (from 'none' to 'exclusive'), gaining informed consent (not just consent), ethical marketing, dealing appropriately with child protection and vulnerable populations and establishing personal boundaries. Each of these decisions has very different and *very important* implications for your client, and for you. These issues are important enough to make each decision explicitly so that you can stand by it, rather than allowing it to be made by accident, or even allowing uncertainty to be exploited by less scrupulous individuals. Chapter 2 explores these issues with real-life examples and outlines the importance of explicitly recognizing ethical issues in your practice. Furthermore, the chapter emphasizes the importance of establishing ethical expectations with your client from the very first contact in order to minimize the scope for conflicts. The practice of simply providing the client with the governing body website for ethics is queried and explored, and worksheets for establishing and reviewing one's ethical processes are provided.

Underpinning principle 2: Philosophical awareness. The bad news is that you cannot be a practising psychologist without making philosophical assumptions (again, whether you admit it or not). It is a very rare breed of person that willingly engages with deep philosophical writings, so Chapter 3 provides a rough map of the territory, such that any sport psychologist can at least orient themselves. Even if you have never paid attention to them, you have already made philosophical assumptions (You just don't know it!). As a practising psychologist, one is trying to change something inherently ineffable (e.g., someone's way of thinking/feeling/experiencing) and achieve any number of aims (e.g., performance enhancement, recovery from injury, personal well-being, etc.), with no clear guide on how best to achieve this (e.g., approach/style). This task *requires* a broad range of assumptions to be made in all three of these areas.

Chapter 3 explores and unpacks the core assumptions that any practising psychologist must make, divided into three broad categories: (1) *Overall aims:* What is the purpose of your sport psychology practice: performance enhancement or emotional support? This matters because it determines what you count as a 'win'; (2) *Ontology and epistemology:* these sound horrible but they play a vital role in determining how you act. Fundamentally, we need to consider the very nature of the 'thing' you are studying – because if you try to objectively measure something your client feels is deeply personal and immeasurable, you are doomed to fail (e.g., 'using a psychologist didn't help me at all – he just didn't *get* me'); and (3) *Philosophy of practice:* which refers to the manner in which one attempts to achieve these aims. The way one asks questions, the tools one uses, the nature of the relationship formed, the measures of success and more can all be linked to one's philosophy of practice. Worksheets for uncovering and analysing one's assumptions are included, with a view to at least allowing you to understand your 'position' and the way it may affect your clients. Chapter 3 argues that a coherent and logically consistent set of assumptions leads to an improved experience for the client, increased confidence and assuredness for you as the psychologist and an easier, more transparent, document for assessors and examiners.

1.4.1 The service delivery process

Step 1: Intake. Somehow, a relationship is started. It could be that a coach refers the client to you. It could be that a client calls unexpectedly, having seen you listed on a website. It could be that your lecturer or professor asks you to find a client for your assignment. Alternatively, it could be that you are 'embedded' within a team, with an office on site, and you see the players regularly so they feel comfortable talking to you before they decide to seek psychological support. What we can easily forget is that some vital expectations are established during this initial contact, and that we should pay a lot more attention to them than simply 'getting a client through the door'. At this first contact, the client could reasonably expect you to establish things such as confidentiality expectations (Who will you share information with, and why?); stylistic expectations (Will you be 'hands on' or 'hands off', and why?); and professional boundaries (What will you help to achieve and where will you draw the line? Will you meet socially with clients or interact using social media?). Likewise, you could realistically expect to establish the client's name, age, sport, reasons for seeking help, expectations of you and, importantly, whether you are in fact the right person to offer this help: as a minimum. Further still, all of this information will be constrained by the way you make this first contact: the medium (face-to-face, phone, email) and the context (private practice, embedded, trainee, informal chat).

Chapter 4 will explore this important step in the service delivery process, which by definition *must* be universal, as every working alliance must begin somewhere. The key considerations, their importance and your options for managing them are all reviewed and, in what will form a recurring pattern, the impact of a sport psychologist failing to explicitly consider these issues is discussed and analysed.

Step 2: Needs analysis. A sport psychologist will invariably need some kind of appraisal of their client's 'needs'. This can range from a highly presumptuous 'everybody needs to be better at goal setting' to an extremely sophisticated and detailed understanding of the client, their background, their current mental attributes or 'patterns', their ambitions and their capability for incorporating new advice/initiatives into their life. Likewise, needs analysis can range from a highly uninformed assumption at the beginning of the relationship (as above) right up to something that permeates the entire relationship and forms a key part of the support (or intervention) itself. For example, counselling approaches aim to build the client's own self-awareness *alongside* the practitioner's attempts to understand, which can make the stages between needs analysis and delivery/monitoring highly interrelated and difficult to separate.

Further still, needs analysis can rely on 'instruments' such as questionnaires, performance profiles and checklists, or it can be highly informal and flexible, using interviews, observations and 'contextual awareness', such as coaches' comments or even your own experiences of the sport. Perhaps predictably, different approaches to science will favour different types of needs analysis, and different techniques will generate different types of data, each with their own strengths and weaknesses. Chapter 5 will review these aspects of the needs analysis process, and once again consider the implications of failing to properly consider how they are deployed as a sport psychologist.

Step 3: Case formulation. At some point between meeting a client and offering them help, the psychologist will almost definitely form, hold and work from some sort of model representing the client's inner workings: their psychology. In some cases, this might be a 'universal' model that the psychologist feels is 'true for everyone', or it might simply be that 'everyone benefits from this advice/technique'. Weak models, but models nonetheless.

In contrast, the technical term *case formulation* is originally intended to denote that this 'working model' is a result of drawing together a thorough needs analysis, including different types of data, and trying to ascertain what is going on, and where are the priorities to intervene. At the present time in sport psychology, whilst needs analysis techniques receive a lot of attention, and intervention techniques receive even more, there is very little attention paid to the vital step linking the two. Numerous case studies presented by trainee psychologists can be characterized as: 'I tested some stuff, then I recommended some stuff, but I'm not saying why'. The case formulation stage is *vital* in providing this 'whyness' to one's interventions (or support strategies).

Remembering that there are different approaches to what constitutes 'science', we need to be flexible about what is meant by case formulation. As a good rule of thumb, a strong case formulation should contain the psychologist's best estimate of causes, context, explanations, mechanisms and effects/outcomes. Such a model could be based on scientific theory or on a detailed understanding of the client's own, unique psychological make-up. However, it would be a very dangerous type of psychology that proceeded without any guiding 'model' – in fact, one might question whether it is psychology at all. Chapter 6 will explore in detail the ways that this case formulation process can be approached, and the consequences of paying it too little (or no) attention. Once again, the argument will be made that a sport psychologist is performing this step whenever they deliver their services, whether they admit it or not. Worksheets for evaluating the quality of your own case formulation will also be included with a view to assisting you in your own practice – improving your effectiveness and allowing you to write better, more transparent, case reports.

Step 4: Choosing an intervention. There are a number of intervention approaches available to a sport psychologist, ranging from the potentially under-utilized 'do nothing' (situations often get better without intervention), up to and including the highly over-utilized 'kitchen sink' approach (where athletes are offered a large number of interventions, in the hope that one of them helps). To be clear, the word 'intervention' in this book will refer to any new strategy introduced with the aim of helping the client – including discrete 'methods' and 'techniques', multifaceted strategies, relationship building and more. Assuming a psychologist has reached the decision that s/he is the right person to help, then at some point s/he will be left deciding if/how to help their client. One's choice of intervention is arguably one of the most important steps in the service delivery process: the step where one has a genuine opportunity to help; to make an impact and to prove your worth as a psychologist (as well as to prove the worth of the profession more broadly). Consequently, this step is one where supervisors, assessors, impressed colleagues (on a good day) or lawyers/auditors (on a bad day) will really focus their attention.

Fortunately, if one has conducted clear, justified and coherent processes of intake, needs analysis and case formulation, this step should be a cinch. The detailed and robust 'working model' you have constructed should clearly indicate where it is most important to intervene, and how. If you have used a scientific model from the literature, then it might be worth pausing to check whether it 'holds water'. Likewise, if you have carefully helped to construct a working model that is unique to the client, you might want to pause and double check that it 'fits'. However, generally, the entire point of a good working model is to make predictions about what will work. All that is left then is to check whether your model has suggested a sensible intervention (or support strategy), for example, by carefully reviewing the research that tests it, or reviewing previous times you have used this intervention before (i.e., professional judgement). Unfortunately, case studies from experienced practitioners and undergraduate students alike often fail to explain *why* a strategy was chosen for the client – and *yet a strategy was chosen*. For example: '[Written in a report] The client complained of lacking confidence. I recommended goal setting ... [Quiet voice] Surely I don't need to explain why ... I mean it's obvious, isn't it?' This level of explanation is unacceptable to reviewers and examiners and I sometimes think that no client should be prepared to accept it either.

First of all, if a psychologist does not know (or is unable to put into words) why they chose their particular intervention, then supervisors, assessors and lawyers would be well within their rights to start sharpening their proverbial knives. Second, if one makes a deliberate point of carefully choosing each support strategy and weighing up its strengths and weaknesses, then (at least) two coincidental benefits occur: (a) the psychologist gains a better understanding of how likely the strategy is to work, meaning the client's expectations can be managed accordingly; and (b) by doing a little bit of extra research (formal or informal), the psychologist may happen across hints and tips for making the strategy work as well as possible. Chapter 7 will explore this vital stage in detail, consider the consequences of paying it little or no attention and offer some exercises to help choose interventions and to evidence your process for the reviewers.

Step 5: Planning the intervention. This step could also be phrased planning the support strategy, but assuming a psychologist chooses to offer some kind of advice or input, then we could be viewed as 'intervening'. Here we hit upon another classic problem in sport psychologists' case notes: 'Client complained of lack of confidence. Questionnaire confirmed this. Recommended mental imagery. Summary and Conclusions ...' Again, this example is paraphrased, but you would be surprised how often this pattern is repeated in real-life reports. What it clearly overlooks is that, even if a good needs analysis and case formulation lead to one choosing a highly appropriate intervention, the client may still need support in performing it.

Children might need a simplified version of the intervention. Elite performers may need something tailored to fit around their busy, international schedules. Increasingly, athletes will have already heard of, and even tried interventions, and so they may be familiar with a version that doesn't work. This can particularly be the case for techniques promoted through word-of-mouth and the Internet/blogs. Almost certainly, each athlete is unique, and will have a different understanding of what is involved in an intervention, as well as how it applies to them. Suddenly, a case report that says only '... told athlete to try imagery' looks woefully irresponsible: as they may not know what you mean, or how, or when, or why to do the imagery.

A more positive way of viewing this step is that carefully conducting your intake, needs analysis, case formulation and intervention choices should all have generated a great deal of knowledge about your client: their inner workings, their current experiences of sport psychology, their schedule, etc. So it would be a real shame to recommend the right intervention, but then not give it the best possible chance of working. Fortunately, there are relatively clear guidelines for this step, so whether 'prescribing' an intervention or acting as a collaborator in the client's own planning, it is relatively easy to both classify the nature of the intervention (educational, acquisitional or using it in practice), as well as to ensure progression (such that the client may build from 'knowing about' a skill, for example, to being able to perform it effortlessly). Chapter 8 reviews the different ways that interventions (and support strategies) can fail, ways of supporting and planning interventions and emphasizes the 'gamble' one takes in failing to support (or even acknowledge) this process. Worksheets for reviewing one's 'intervention planning' are included to both support good practice and enhance your ability to record/evidence your process.

Step 6: Delivery and monitoring. Most clients will want to know that the advice they paid for has worked – remembering that sport is about getting *results*. Likewise, most responsible psychologists will want to check that their hard work and effort have actually helped (It is a very rare psychologist who can confidently claim: 'It was good advice. If it didn't help, it's not my fault'). Short of advice given in books or websites, where you may never meet the client or have any opportunity to follow up, any psychologist offering their services will encounter this step and either choose to ignore it (a choice which has its own risks and consequences) or to monitor for effectiveness, problems/issues and opportunities to 'tinker'.

Chapter 9 will argue that there is much more to this step than simply asking the client: 'Did it work? (In your opinion ...)'; or even 'Let me know if it doesn't work' – which in real life may happen more than we care to admit. A full range of options from the above 'laissez faire' approaches through to detailed methodologies are reviewed, from subjective judgements through to more objective measurements. In each case, the implications of such an approach and the opportunities to improve one's effectiveness are explored. The overlap of 'monitoring' with 'needs analysis' is explored, and the opportunities to weave strong, coherent needs analysis throughout one's service are considered. In addition, we explore the important difference between two approaches to evaluating success: 'any win' versus 'stickler win'. In the first instance, the psychologist will accept *any* improvement (perceived or measured) as evidence of having been a good psychologist, whereas in the latter, the psychologist focuses on the *exact* issues identified in the needs analysis, and only accepts a positive impact on those as 'success'. Likewise, as already described in the introduction, there can be a substantial difference between psychological benefits and performance improvements; so should we always look for improved performance, or should we accept that enhanced well-being, new skills or a different world-view could still indicate a job well done? Chapter 9 will explore all of the above, as well as offering worksheets to plan and evaluate your monitoring strategy so that you can be more familiar with the risks and/or benefits of your chosen approach.

Chapter 10: Learning and quality assurance processes. Sitting on top of the entire service delivery process are the quality assurance processes of reflective practice and supervision/mentoring. Ideally, these processes will record, evaluate and improve every aspect of the practitioner's approach and, at the very least, ensure the avoidance of poor practice.

Reflective practice. Assuming that nobody is born with the perfect skills to be a sport psychologist, the trainee sport psychologist must continually learn. In addition, almost all regulatory bodies (HCPC, BPS, APA, APS, AHPRA, etc.) require that sport psychologists must continue to learn even after they have qualified, by including continued professional development (CPD) as a requirement of registration. If one accepts these arguments, i.e., that constant learning is a necessary component of being a sport psychologist, then we have another (very strong) argument for recording and monitoring the six steps listed above. By keeping good notes, you are better able to extract the maximum possible learning from your practice experiences. Thus, before ever submitting your notes or portfolios to supervisors or assessors, you could analyse your practice and learn from your own 'mistakes' (or if you prefer, slight imperfections). Such a process is called 'reflective practice', and whilst most human beings do it anyway (i.e., that little review of the day before you go to sleep at night), it can also be applied more formally as a tool to analyse, improve and, once again, demonstrate your approach. Fundamentally, as the practising psychologist, you were deeply involved in the entire decision-making process, and so you are ideally suited to analyse what went well or badly. Reflection could, on the one hand, be a very individual and private venture, to guide and modify one's own practice. On the other hand, good reflective practice presents a tremendous opportunity to contribute meaningful lessons to others, to guide their practice or to generate new and interesting research projects. Such an accumulation and sharing of knowledge is, once again, characteristic of the 'science' that sport psychology aims to be. In addition, reflecting before, during and after supervisory meetings can also help to clarify emerging lessons and ensure that they enhance your practice sooner rather than later.

Thus, in Chapter 10, we will review what is meant by 'reflective practice', the ways it supports learning, the different types of reflection (ranging from simple 'mulling' to formal and structured diary entries). Worksheets are provided to help you identify the types of reflection you do, to help you get the most out of reflection and, importantly, to help you show reviewers and assessors how reflection has enhanced/supported your practice. Whilst the argument that reflection *automatically* improves your practice is queried, the chapter offers ways to *make sure* that reflection (a process you are probably doing anyway) is captured, maximized, refined and clearly demonstrated to others.

Supervision and mentoring. As a trainee sport psychologist, under any of the formal regulatory bodies, you will be (or were) required to find a supervisor. The supervisor's job is (or was) to train you, stimulate new ideas and thoughts, monitor your progress, evaluate your competency and ultimately stake their reputation on your readiness to act alone as an independent psychologist. In some cases, supervisors might also provide you with your clients at a time when you do not have the reputation or resource to gain your own. After this, many sport psychologists choose to continue some kind of mentoring relationship(s), either with the same supervisor or with a new colleague. As above, assuming that the regulatory bodies do this for a reason (and that constant learning is inherent in both trainees and qualified practitioners) then supervision and mentoring are key opportunities for a sport psychologist to develop and improve. On top of this, supervision also offers a degree of quality assurance; both to clients receiving help and to the profession as a whole when new practitioners are 'signed off'.

Thus, also within Chapter 10, we will review the various approaches to supervision in systems where sport psychology is regulated, and examine the benefits of a good supervisory relationship (as well as the risks of a bad one). Following this, different approaches to supervision) are discussed and reviewed, with a view to helping you to: (a) recognize what type of supervisor/mentor suits you best; and (b) to get the most out of your supervisory/mentoring relationship. Checklists for finding a good supervisor and for getting the most out of each exchange are offered, as well as a 'recording sheet' to help trainees evidence how supervision has improved their practice. Continuing the theme of demonstrating good practice, these worksheets are offered with a view to helping practitioners demonstrate how they accumulate and maintain good practices.

At this point, the reader should be armed with *both* the knowledge to both *be* a sport psychologist, *and* the tools to demonstrate it to anybody who needs to know.

1.5   Ella's story: Part 1

Ella is 18 years old and about to go to university, with good grades having worked hard at school. Her ambition is to become a sport psychologist and to work with elite athletes at the Olympics. Ella has played sport all her life and has represented her state in both field hockey and swimming. Ella's parents always tell her she is a good listener, and her friends often confide in her. She likes the idea of being a psychologist, but she also wants to maintain her passion for sport.

1. Thinking about the country that you live in, what are her options for pursuing her ambition of becoming a sport psychologist?
2. What type of course should she choose, and what is the 'pathway' to becoming a registered sport psychologist? If you do not know, how could Ella find this information?
3. If there is more than one degree required, what else should Ella plan for? A masters? Supervised practice?
4. What other activities could Ella undertake to help her on her journey towards becoming a sport psychologist?
5. If you could give Ella any advice before she embarks on this journey, what would it be?

Our journey will follow Ella as she develops into a practising psychologist. The situations she experiences are purely illustrative, and any resemblance to real-life events are purely coincidental.

1.6   Review and reflect

1. What are the current challenges faced by applied psychologists, delivering sport psychology? Consider those listed above, as well as any you can think of yourself.
2. What criteria would you currently look for when trying to find 'the world's best sport psychologist'? Which criteria are helpful, and which are potentially misleading? Which criteria should be removed, or added?
3. What models are you aware of to guide you through the sport psychology service delivery process? How useful are they? And how 'valid'? How were they generated, and by who?

4. If you had to convince a coach that it would be worth involving a sport psychologist in preparing her/his athletes, what arguments would you use? Do you focus on results, performance, well-being or something else? Do you focus on guaranteeing outcomes or following sound processes?
5. What does psychology have to offer the world of sport? How is this different from physiology, coaching, biomechanics or strength and conditioning?

Ethical Considerations: Protecting the Client, Yourself and Your Profession

2

2.1 Introduction and overview

This chapter highlights the importance of ethical considerations as the very foundation of a sport psychologist's practice, emphasizing that ethical issues permeate every aspect of the sport psychologist's role. Put simply, ethical considerations pertain to morals – and can be construed both as an outcome of practice and a process one undertakes (Hays, 2006; also called 'virtue' ethics by Aoyagi & Portenga, 2010). Definitions of ethics as an *outcome* include both codes of behaviour considered correct; or the moral fitness of a decision, or course of action. In contrast, ethics as a *process* can be defined as the philosophical study of the moral value of human conduct and of the rules and principles that ought to govern it. In the words of Pope and Vasquez (1998, p. xiii), ethics can also be 'a process through which we awaken, enhance, inform, expand and improve our ability to respond effectively to those who come to us for help'. Notably, if one has a strong ethical process, then the resultant ethical outcomes should be much more defensible.

In this chapter, we will review what various governing bodies' codes of conduct have to say on the matter – and notably that all codes of conduct focus on the avoidance of harm, not (necessarily) the effectiveness of one's advice. Real-life case studies that have been experienced first-hand are used to illustrate the prevalence and importance of ethical issues in sport psychology. Core concepts are drawn from the code of conduct, illustrated and explored, including the avoidance of harm, competence and confidentiality; managing multiple relationships, informed consent, personal conduct and integrity; keeping accurate records; avoiding conflicts of interest, termination of the relationship and others. Where absolute 'red lines' exist these are noted, and equally where there are no simple answers, the key issues are mapped out to help inform the sport psychologist's decision process.

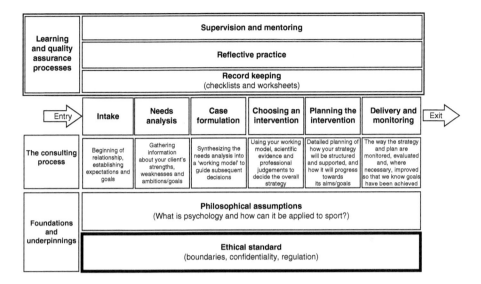

Figure 2.1   *The position of ethical standards as the foundations underpinning the sport psychologist's service delivery process.*

The chapter finishes by providing worksheets and sample forms, in order to assist the reader in understanding and managing their own ethical practices.

2.2   The importance of ethics in sport psychology

The following section overviews the argument that ethics permeate every aspect of a sport psychologist's role, and that the consideration of ethics is one of the most important yet oft-overlooked aspects of sport psychology practice. Whilst the subsequent sections involving case studies and real-life examples (combined with your own experiences of service delivery in the real world) may be much more persuasive regarding the importance of ethics, the diligent reader might return to this section in years to come and think: 'Ah, *now* I see'.

As a psychologist operating in sport, I was once told that there is 'no room for ethics': that sport is too complex, fluid and fast moving to ponder ethical dilemmas. Likewise, with sport focussing on performance rather than clinical disorders or highly sensitive personal issues, some feel there is less urgency about being ethical in sport. In contrast, authors such as Moore (2003); Stapleton, Hankes, Hayes, and Parham (2010); Haberl and Peterson (2006); and Aoyagi and Portenga (2010) argue that the opposite is true. The highly variable environment one experiences in sport – working with athletes, teams, coaches, physiotherapists and more, in locations ranging from a conventional consulting room to a team bus or pitch-/track-/poolside – poses substantial threats to a psychologist in sport, and make ethical awareness more, not less, important. There is rarely ever a receptionist, an office or a nice big desk to create clear boundaries, and yet there is often a very clear imperative to deliver results. In such a demanding and unpredictable environment, the sport psychologist (often viewed as disposable or having to 'prove their worth') is extremely vulnerable: facing many more potential ethical dilemmas than someone working in a controlled office/clinic. A psychologist in sport is arguably under more pressure to 'do what it takes' to deliver results (i.e., pressure to 'be flexible' on ethics). This chapter will demonstrate that ethical considerations are vital to a psychologist in sport (not least by placing it at the beginning of the book, and as the foundation of the service delivery model). An ethically aware sport psychologist protects: (a) the client from harm (first and foremost); (b) her/himself from harm and reputational damage; and ultimately, (c) the whole profession of sport psychology – from reputational damage and public cynicism.

Another common argument for being relaxed about ethics is when people feel that ethical issues are only really relevant to research, not applied work. This argument forgets that an applied psychologist collects, stores and analyses sensitive data, as well as offering 'interventions', just like researchers do. Whilst ethical considerations apply slightly differently in research and applied work, they apply nonetheless. For example, if a doctor offered a drug that changed the very way you think and feel, you would probably want to give informed consent before taking it – yet this is often the aim of psychological support. *Informed consent* meaning you are fully aware of the risks, benefits, effectiveness and possible side effects. This is especially important if the intervention proves ineffective or, even worse, harmful. Do you currently pause before each intervention to explain the likely effectiveness, possible side effects or even the alternative choices to a client? Do you currently seek informed consent *separately* for gathering and storing information about your client and then again before you start *each* intervention, or do you simply get 'blanket' consent at the start of relationship (i.e., before the client really knows what is going on)? Further, does each client you work with know exactly how the information they share with you will be stored, and who it might be shared with? Presumably, if an athlete knows you can pass information on to a coach or manager, they might wish to limit what they tell you. Or if an athlete knew you would use their future success and fame as advertising for yourself, they might think very differently about you. Each of the above examples would be strictly examined before a research project, yet there is no such board or panel to review how the applied practitioner behaves (or plans to behave).

So if nobody reviews a sport psychologist's ethical practices, and if athletes and coaches appear to be far more concerned with results and performance than strict ethical adherence, why devote an entire chapter to ethics? Three main reasons: first, almost every action the sport psychologist takes will have an ethical consideration attached, from the first phone call or email to the termination of a relationship. Second, even if there is no 'ethics application' process prior to each activity or intervention, the psychologist, and the wider profession, is ultimately judged by their ethical behaviours. In the long term, being ethical might even be more influential in shaping public opinions than claims of effectiveness. For example, it would take an incredible contribution to the athlete's success to compensate for a psychologist who divulged secrets to coaches, or used the athlete's fame to advertise her/himself. Third, there are moves afoot in many countries to pay closer attention to psychologists' ethical practices. For example, in Australia, the law dictates that psychologists must keep detailed and accurate records of every client interaction (Bradford & Stevens, 2013). It is possible, even (anecdotally) quite common, for these records to be subpoenaed in any court proceedings involving that client. Whilst the process may seem more likely for clinical clients, or perhaps those dealing with criminal proceedings, an increasing number of athletes find themselves requiring legal help in relation to drugs and doping, mismanaged injuries, contractual issues or claims made in the

---

Case examples: Marketing, advertising and confidentiality

Case example 2.1: After the lengthy process of qualifying as a sport psychologist, you need to advertise your business. You have been working as a sport psychologist for 5 years and have successfully helped many very famous athletes, players and teams. When you mentioned it to the clients, several suggested they would be happy to write testimonials for you. What are your options, in your own country, to help promote your business?

Case example 2.2: You meet a sport psychologist who has what he calls an 'open confidentiality policy' – where he tells all coaches and managers everything he speaks about and does with all the players who see him. This policy extends to advertising himself and persuading new clients of his effectiveness (e.g., 'this worked really well when I did it with Steve'). His reasoning is that he works in football where it is constantly necessary to 'prove your worth', and never more so than being a sport psychologist where people constantly question your value. It was not a requirement from the coaching staff, but they do not seem to have a problem with his decision.

The psychologist believes that it is ok to do this because he tells each player of the situation before he starts working with them.

(1) Has the psychologist broken any principles or rules?
(2) What are the risks and implications of adopting this approach?
(3) What harm could occur through adopting this approach – to clients, himself or the profession?

media. Suddenly, a psychologist's behaviour and procedures can be subjected to a level of scrutiny unheard of in the world of sport. Without knowing how common such a process really is, all I can say is: (a) I have met several people who have been through this process; (b) I would want to be fully prepared if it ever did happen; and (c) I would want any examination of my practices to reflect well on me. So what do regulatory bodies tend to say in their codes of conduct? What are ethical considerations, and where are the 'red lines'?

2.3   Ethics within codes of conduct

As a supervisor and assessor of sport psychologists, one key task is to compare a practitioner's reports and case studies to the regulatory code of conduct. Those who cannot demonstrate that they are practising ethically may be reprimanded, or even have their accreditation/registration delayed while this evidence is provided. Organizations in the United Kingdom, United States and Australia all offer slightly different codes of conduct, which immediately raises the question: 'Which one is right?' Whilst the answer depends on the laws within each country, the similarities and differences are reviewed in Table 2.1. A separate and more immediate question is: 'How should a code of conduct be used by the practitioner?' Some trainee psychologists believe it is sufficient to give the client a copy of the code of conduct (often in the full knowledge it will go straight in the trash). Others simply direct their client to the website with the code of conduct on. Still others keep a copy of the code of conduct to hand, and when questioned as to whether they have experienced any ethical issues, refer to it and (often very quickly) conclude: 'Well I haven't broken any of these rules' (focussing on the outcomes). However, if we read the text accompanying most codes of conduct, it is immediately apparent that this is not how they are supposed to be used. Rather, the code of conduct is (usually) intended as a set of guiding principles or considerations to be used in informing an ongoing ethical process – because it is impossible to anticipate all the unique and unusual situations a psychologist might experience, especially in sport. As such, most codes of conduct are necessarily vague: They do not specify a complete set of precise rules or procedures that must be followed. The American Psychological Association (2010), for example, clearly stated that: '... the general principles are not themselves enforceable rules, they should be considered by psychologists in arriving at an ethical course of action' (p. 2), and: 'Most of the Ethical Standards are written broadly, in order to apply to psychologists in varied roles ... The Ethical Standards are not exhaustive. The fact that a given conduct is not specifically addressed by an Ethical Standard does not mean that it is necessarily either ethical or unethical' (p. 2). This is a vital issue, and if a trainee psychologist is unable to use a code of conduct properly, then we probably should not expect their client to be able to use it either.

Table 2.1 *A review of the key ethical considerations covered in various codes of conduct and articles exploring ethics in applied sport psychology*

	Avoiding harm (beneficence and non-maleficence)	Competence	Confidentiality	Multiple relationships	Informed consent	Avoiding conflict of interest	Personal conduct	Evidence-based practice	Record keeping	Termination of role	Ethical advertising	Location of services	Time limitations
Codes of conduct													
Association for Applied Sport Psychology (AASP, 2010)	•	•	•	•	•	•	•		•	•			
American Psychological Association (APA, 2010)	•	•	•	•	•	•	•	•	•	•	•	•	
British Association of Sport and Exercise Sciences (BASES, 2006)	•	•	•		•			•			•		
British Psychological Society (2009)	•	•	•	•	•	•	•	•	•	•	•		
Australian Psychological Society (APS, 2007)	•	•	•	•	•	•	•	•	•	•	•	•	
Heath and Care Professions Council (2008)	•	•	•	•	•		•			•	•		
Papers (not intended to be comprehensive coverage of issues)													
Andersen (2005)	•	•	•	•	•						•		
Aoyagi and Portenga (2010)	•	•	•	•		•	•					•	•
Brown and Cogan (2006)	•	•	•	•		•		•	•				
Haberl and Peterson (2006)	•	•	•	•								•	•
Little and Harwood (2010)	•	•	•	•		•	•						
Moore (2003)	•	•	•	•	•	•		•	•	•		•	•
Stapleton et al. (2010)	•	•	•	•	•	•	•	•			•	•	•
Total	13	13	13	12	9	9	8	7	6	6	7	6	4

Source: Adapted from Rodgers, L. (2011). *Essay on ethics* (unpublished work) with kind permission from Luke Rodgers.

Table 2.1 summarizes and compares several codes of conduct from countries that currently regulate the profession of sport psychology, as well as some recent articles that have explored ethical issues specifically in sport psychology.

Table 2.1 illustrates 13 key areas of ethical consideration in sport psychology. The four most prominent principles are the avoidance of harm (also termed 'beneficence and non-maleficence'), competence, confidentiality and managing multiple relationships (these last two are often linked). In addition, other commonly discussed considerations include: gaining informed consent, personal conduct and integrity; keeping accurate records; avoiding conflicts of interest, termination of the relationship, evidence-based practice, ethical advertising, the locations where psychological services are provided and the time constraints faced by practitioners in sport.

Many of these considerations are general to all psychologists, whereas several are relatively unique to sport, where service delivery can take place on pitches, buses, in changing rooms and often under tremendous time constraints (e.g., international travel or bi-weekly matches). Likewise, many of these issues, whilst common, are more difficult to manage in sporting contexts, where teams and support staff often travel together in close groups, and where many 'locations' of practice are quite public and visible. Again, this pattern emphasizes the point that working as a psychologist in sport poses unique and often unpredictable problems.

2.4   Core ethical considerations

Avoiding harm – Beneficence and non-maleficence: Many of the ethical codes of conduct state that their very reason for existence is to avoid harm: to the client, the psychologist and the profession, to students, supervisees and client organizations (APA, 2010; APS, 2007; BPS, 2009). Of course, if psychologists only wished to avoid harm, we would simply do nothing, so the doctrine of 'beneficence and non-maleficence' clarifies that the psychologist should seek to help the client in a way that avoids harm. Notably, and this is often overlooked, the psychologist should not seek to help him/herself: only the client. This sacrificing of our own interests is what we are paid for, as well as our particular skills and knowledge, and the psychologist should not seek to benefit at the expense of the client. Examples might include using the client's fame to promote oneself (quite possibly breaching confidentiality), or asking the client to participate in a research study following the completion of support (which is arguably exploitation). Notably, the use of client testimonials for marketing/advertising was banned in Australia in July 2013. The codes of conduct specify that psychologists should actively seek to identify and resolve any way in which their actions might prove harmful, even if

Case example 2.3: Between a rock and a hard place

You have entered into a practice relationship with a 14-year-old female distance runner, organized by her father, but paid for by the National Governing Body (NGB). She has dropped out of her last three competitive races, mid-race, yet has been running competitive times in training. After three meetings you have been working on her race preparation and her thoughts during a race.

(1) After the third session, when your client has gone to the car, her dad seeks an update. What can you tell him?
(2) Upon submitting your invoice, the NGB requests to know what you've been working on, how should you respond?

You don't hear from your client for four weeks, then you discover that she has been forced to change clubs after becoming 'too familiar' with a boy at her previous club. Her parents catch you before the session and ask you to 'have a word' with their daughter about her behaviour, to try and get her to focus on running and not her new boyfriend.

(3) What should you do?

Case example 2.4: Avoiding harm, confidentiality and child protection

The parents of a 10-year-old female gymnast have asked you to help with her general mental approach, ranging from managing nerves to setting goals.

(1) Where and when should you meet with this athlete?
(2) What information should you share, and with whom, in order to:
    (a) help her (e.g., can you gather information from her coach or parents?) and
    (b) get paid (who can you tell about your sessions, their duration, content, etc.?)

She is generally a happy, friendly girl and has been very happy to sit and talk with you in the last few meetings. However, in the last two meetings she has been very quiet and unresponsive, unable to maintain eye contact and withdrawn. You also notice bruises on her upper arms which she tries to hide when she realizes they are exposed. You are aware that she is under pressure to make the step to the next level, developing much more demanding routines. You are also aware that she has had to move in with her father following her parents' separation.

(3) How should you proceed?

inadvertent or difficult to anticipate. Failure to do so may leave a client (or 'affected person') with a legitimate grievance.

Competence: All the codes of conduct reviewed above are very specific that a psychologist should not practice outside their area of training/experience, or attempt procedures that are beyond their current capability – in this case sport, exercise and performance enhancement. As Brown and Cogan (2006, p. 20) noted: 'Some individuals ... seem to believe competence in sport psychology can be established by having been a successful athlete, possessing strong interest in a particular sport, being well read on a particular sport topic, or joining professional organizations ... *These beliefs and practices do not establish competence'*. If a psychologist cannot evidence that their training or experience provided them with the skills and knowledge to perform a particular procedure, or work in a particular area, then the work should not be undertaken. Instead, the psychologists may seek to make a suitable referral (e.g., from a sport psychologist to a clinical psychologist), decline to take on the client/role, consider alternative procedures or (time permitting) seek training in the skills/knowledge required. This rule also applies to working in cultures, languages, age groups or special populations (e.g., disability) with which one has no experience. The main difficulty that competence requirements pose is during training and supervised practice: when a psychologist may not yet have experienced a situation, but will be expected to deal with it as part of their normal job role. To resolve this issue, the trainee should complete full due diligence in preparing for new situations, and may need to resist making diagnoses or undertaking interventions until they have competed their preparation. In addition, the supervisor or 'a senior psychologist' must be consulted, and should have sufficient experience to guide the trainee. As a final consideration, most codes of conduct specify that the psychologist should continue to seek professional development throughout their career, even after their core qualifications and registrations have been granted (e.g., BPS, 2009). This requirement for Continuing Professional Development (CPD) helps to ensure that the psychologist remains aware of recent developments, current best practice and, equally, does not forget/neglect any important considerations.

Confidentiality and data protection: Most of the codes of conduct specify that the psychologist should respect confidentiality and protect the client's privacy as a default; and any departure from this assumption requires specific justification. The APS (2010) guidelines, for example, specify that information obtained during the provision of psychological services can only be disclosed in specific circumstances: (a) with the consent of the client or their legal guardian (and not for advertising purposes); (b) where there is a legal obligation to do so (e.g., if the law has been broken, or if issued with a writ/subpoena); (c) if there is an immediate and specific risk of harm, to a specific person/group, that can be only be prevented by disclosing the information

Case example 2.5: The limits of competence

A female sport psychologist has recently given birth to her first child. She noticed that she used many techniques from sport psychology during the labour and birth: controlled breathing, relaxation strategies, positive self-talk and affirmations, positive and/or relaxing imagery, etc.

Following this experience, she sets up a business as a birthing partner offering mental and emotional support to women during labour. Birthing partners are an unregulated profession with no formal training or supervision. She believes that the core mental skills from sport psychology are highly applicable to the birthing process.

(1) Which ethical principles are highlighted by this case? Are any clearly breached or encroached?
(2) What are the risks to:
  (a) her clients
  (b) the psychologist
  (c) the profession as a whole
(3) Should she continue with this venture? And if she does, how could she protect her clients, herself and the profession of sport psychology?

Case example 2.6: 'Where's Kieran?'

You meet for the first time with a client who is complaining of anxiety before and during rugby matches. Your client performs several key roles in the team, calling all key moves, taking all kicks at goal and effectively being the 'pivot' for the whole team (i.e., like a quarterback). In order to manage this anxiety, your client has developed a number of routines which he must perform before each task. These routines now stretch back into his pre-match preparation, and even his daily life at home. He speaks of the demands of his sport taking a serious toll on him and reports feeling empty and burned out.

(1) Where do you start with this client?
(2) The client talks of 'needing some time off'. How could you proceed?

One day, 2 hours after a match, you enter the changing rooms to find your client still in his towel, shivering from the cold, yet folding his clothes, packing them and then tipping out and starting again. He is initially unresponsive when you try to speak to him, muttering 'don't stop me, I have to get this right; I have to get this right'. After you eventually point out that everybody is on the bus and the changing rooms will be locked soon, he stops what he is doing and breaks down in tears.

(3) What clinical disorder do his symptoms suggest?
(4) What should you do in these circumstances: (a) in the immediate situation, and (b) in the following days? Should you consider breaking confidentiality in any way (e.g., to make sure the coaches know to rest him?).

(i.e., not vague and not suspected); and (d) during supervision or mentoring, so long as the client's identity is hidden or the supervisor/mentor has explicitly agreed to protect the confidentiality of the client. Not only must strict confidentiality be followed, but the client should be made aware of the limits of confidentiality at the very outset of the professional relationship. Finally, and very importantly, the psychologist must make careful provisions for the protection of client's confidentiality in the collection, recording, accessing, storage, distribution and disposal of information. So computer records should be safe and secure, not simply on a loose memory drive, and computer files should only be viewed/accessed when one is sure nobody else can see the screen. Further, the psychologist must 'take reasonable steps to protect the confidentiality of information after they leave a specific work setting' (APS, 2010, p. 16) – and the client should be made aware (again, from the outset) about how their data will be stored, for how long and where.

These stringent, but highly necessary, requirements can be extremely challenging when working in sport. Whilst it may be relatively straightforward to store files securely and protect privacy in a confined office, a sport psychologist may find her/himself working whilst travelling with a team, with only a suitcase to store files and computers securely. Likewise, sport psychology can often be delivered in a very public arena (e.g., at pitch-side or track-side at big events, or even at a training ground). As such, it becomes extremely important for the sport psychologist to be highly aware of confidentiality issues, and proactive in managing them.

In addition, sport psychologists frequently find themselves working in team settings: reportable to a coach or director, yet working individually with athletes within the team. This raises the classic question: Who is the client? If the organization is paying your wage, yet the client believes s/he has the right to keep key information confidential, what happens if the coach requests an update on your work with the athlete? What if they refuse to pay your invoices without full reports on each meeting?

In reality, if this situation has been reached then the psychologist has failed in their ethical obligations. The solution to this problem (and many others) lies in managing expectations and roles from the outset, before any psychological support is provided. The APS (2010, pp. 20–21) guidelines are helpful in considering this 'third-party' situation (psychologist being the first party; providing services to a client, the second party; at the request of their team or parents, the third party): the psychologist must explain *from the outset*: (a) the nature of her/his relationship with each of them; (b) the psychologist's role and limitations/boundaries; (c) the probable uses of the information obtained; (d) the limits to confidentiality; and (e) the financial arrangements relating to the provision of the service. Fundamentally, no psychological services should be provided until all three parties understand and have agreed (freely) to the arrangements (i.e., informed consent, see below). Hence, it is possible to work for a team or organization and prepare reports on the athletes for managers or administrators or, under very different circumstances, it is possible to work for a team where the players/athletes are offered full confidentiality. Each approach will have notable advantages and disadvantages, and it is the responsibility of the psychologist to proactively manage the situation, minimize harms/risks and create a suitable environment for helping the clients. For example, players who know their data may be discussed with coaches or managers because of the third-party arrangement may choose to share less information and exclude important points, or they may simply refuse to seek support from that psychologist. However, some high-performance sport organizations believe that all coaches, managers and trainers need to know everything about their athletes in order to deliver them to international events 'podium ready'. To repeat, the *only* solution to this problem is to explicitly explain, clarify and agree the process before any psychological service is delivered. Thinking again about the nature of sport, this may even mean explaining an existing/agreed system to new players/athletes before they join the team, and certainly before they receive any psychological support.

If we think for a moment about how upset we would feel if a friend divulged information from a conversation that we considered private – without any reasonable expectation of confidentiality – then we begin to realize how damaging it can be for a psychologist to mismanage confidentiality issues. Confidentiality is central to the provision of psychological services, yet nowhere is it more challenging to maintain confidentiality than in sport. However, in speaking to a psychologist, any client can and should expect confidentiality, and would expect to be clearly instructed if this were not the case *beforehand*. Imagine a criminal confessing his sins to a psychologist and being told: 'Ah, confidentiality doesn't apply if a crime has been committed' ... he would have liked to know that *beforehand*. The final point emphasizes the importance of both managing confidentiality carefully, and explaining arrangements at (or before) the onset of support. In ethics, *prevention is always better than cure*.

Multiple relationships: A key consideration in providing sport psychology services is the high likelihood of being required to provide support to multiple athletes from the same team, or coaches/staff and athletes on the same team, or even athletes competing against each other. One interpretation of multiple relationships is this idea of working for multiple, related individuals and carefully managing expectations (e.g., about how much information can be shared with a coach – as described earlier) and making a concerted effort to reduce the risk of any harm, or any conflict of interests, occurring through forming these multiple relationships.

Second, it is possible to form different types of relationship with the same person. For example, a friend may ask for psychological help, or perhaps a psychologist might consider supervising their spouses training or teaching a student who is also a family member. In sport, where coaches can quite commonly be a spouse or parent, this cannot be the case for a psychologist. The potential for serious conflicts of interest and harm as a direct result of the dual relationships is too great, and should be avoided. For example, the BPS (2009, p. 22) clearly denotes that a psychologist should 'avoid forming relationships that may impair professional objectivity or otherwise lead to exploitation of conflicts of interest with a client'. These sentiments are explicitly expressed in four of the six codes of conduct reviewed, while the remaining two are clear about preventing any possibility of harm and acting in the client's best interest. In sport, where multiple relationships (particularly between athletes and coaches who are at least associated) seem unavoidable, two key strategies for managing this are relevant; prevention and resolution. Regarding *prevention*, the APS (2010, p. 21) is clear that: 'Psychologists who agree to provide psychological services to multiple clients: (a) explain to each client the limits to confidentiality in advance; (b) give clients an opportunity to consider the limitations of the situation; (c) obtain clients' explicit acceptance of these limitations; and (d) ensure as far as possible, that no client is coerced to accept these limitations'. Regarding *resolution*, AASP (2010, Standard 9(e) explains: 'If a [sport psychologist] finds that, due to unforeseen factors, a potentially harmful multiple relationship has arisen, the [sport psychologist] member attempts to resolve it with due regard for the best interests of the affected person and maximal compliance with the Ethics Code'. Once again, the responsibility falls to the sport psychologist to actively monitor these issues, notice any potential risks of harm and act to reduce/minimize them. As before, the point is reinforced that ethics is not a matter of waiting to get caught, and certainly not a matter of assuming not getting 'caught' (e.g., no complaint, investigation or prosecution) means no harm has occurred.

Informed consent: The ability to give fully informed consent is a central aspect of what it means to be human, and to override/undermine it is, arguably, inhuman. The issue is underscored if we consider the experiments that were performed using unwilling prisoners during World War II (described by Annas & Grodin, 1992). Prisoners were subjected to an array of cruel experiments, testing responses to poisons, extreme temperatures, different types of injuries or germs. In response, upon the cessation of war the Nuremberg Code was published in 1949 to try and prevent any such 'research' from ever taking place again. Notably, this is why many researchers insist on calling the people in their studies 'participants', as opposed to 'subjects': because they willingly and knowingly participate/collaborate, rather than being subjected to unknown or undesirable effects. As noted at the start of the chapter, if a drug or medical procedure changed the very way you think and feel, the chances are that you would want to know exactly how, and any risks involved, before agreeing to it: yet this is often the purpose of psychological strategies. As such, informed consent remains just as vital in sport psychology as in any other area where scientific knowledge is applied to humans.

All the codes of conduct reviewed specify that informed consent must be gained and recorded from clients receiving psychological support. Ideally, this consent should be in the full knowledge of many key issues: (a) confidentiality arrangements (and limits); (b) data protection procedures; (c) the psychologist's own expertise and limits of competence; (d) the effectiveness (or otherwise) of any procedures/strategies recommended; (e) any possible sources of conflicting interests (e.g., between coach and players, or other athletes on the team); (f) the process for completing or ending the relationship; and (g) the possible consequences of not consenting (e.g., remain the same, get worse, or possibly get better anyway!). Of course, the client may not be aware, at the start of the support, about the interventions that might be recommended. Hence, it may be necessary to gain new consent as one transitions from a needs analysis phase into an intervention phase – and the BPS (2009) guidelines actually do recommend this (p. 13). If a person is unable to give informed consent for any reason, for example children or vulnerable adults, consent must be gained from a suitable representative (usually a parent or guardian). In very rare circumstances, consent cannot be gained from the client or an authorized representative, and yet 'a pressing need for the provision of professional services is indicated' (BPS, 2009, p. 13). Here, the psychologist should consult (when feasible) with a person well placed to appreciate the potential reactions of clients (such as a family member, or current or recent provider of care or services), or with a senior psychologist. As such, it must be considered exceptionally rare to deliver psychological services without proper and recorded consent, particularly in sport where we are often seeking to promote performance enhancement, not manage serious clinical issues.

Avoiding conflict of interest. Within many of the ethical considerations presented here, avoiding a conflict of interest is a clear theme, yet many codes of conduct also specify it as an additional precaution. Fundamentally, in order to provide a proper caring/helping relationship, the psychologist must forego their own interests, and serve those of their client. Ideally, this is what the psychologist is paid for (in addition to skill and knowledge). But even in situations where no money changes hands, for example in work experience or supervision settings, the psychologist must not only avoid allowing their interests to conflict with those of the client, s/he must actively prevent such a possibility from ever occurring (APA, 2010; APS, 2010; BPS, 2009; HCPC, 2008). The most obvious example is that psychologists should avoid forming romantic or sexual relationships with clients, or anybody associated with a client, and avoid beginning any psychological support with such a person (APS, 2010, p. 22). Another good example, given excellent coverage by Andersen (2005), is the use of 'name dropping' and testimonials to advertise one's services. Andersen explores the issue that the psychologist will have gathered 'privileged' information, as well as (hopefully!) accumulating the respect and positive regards of the client: both of which could be viewed as 'leverage'. Andersen argues that even asking a client to sign a confidentiality release or write a testimonial carries the implicit threat: 'Look, I know some very personal information about you, and you owe me one, so sign the form'. Even if unintentional, such a sentiment must not be allowed to develop. Ostensibly, any situation where it could be argued that the psychologist's own interests have come into conflict with those of the client would be viewed as an ethical lapse/failure. Again, not only must a conflict of interests be prevented, but any situation where one might occur must be actively avoided (APA, 2010; APS, 2010; BPS, 2009; HCPC, 2008).

Personal conduct: During my PhD studies, I used to share a lift to the office with a colleague: a 30-minute journey often lengthened by traffic leading to in-depth and reflective conversations. Both of us were simultaneously studying for a PhD whilst completing our supervised practice in sport psychology. One day, reflecting on our applied experiences, my friend remarked: 'I'm finding that ... to become a psychologist, I also have to become a better person' – and this thought has stayed with me long after we both graduated and went our separate ways. On the one hand, the skills involved in becoming a good psychologist arguably do change you as a person; perhaps making you a better listener, less judgemental, more sympathetic and tolerant. On the other hand, and this is the main thrust of the 'personal conduct' consideration, there is no option to be a psychologist whilst also engaging in questionable or illegal activities in one's 'private life' (Not that my colleague in the above example ever did!). Five out of the six codes of conduct reviewed are clear that psychologists must alert their respective ethics committee of any criminal convictions, must not engage in any questionable or illegal activities and should not even tolerate such behaviour in other professionals. The APS (2010, p. 26) is very clear in explaining that: 'Psychologists recognise that their position of trust requires them to be honest and objective in their professional dealings. They are committed to the best interests of their clients, the profession and their colleagues'. Further, 'psychologists avoid engaging in disreputable conduct that reflects on their ability to practise as a psychologist ... [and/or] disreputable conduct that reflects negatively on the profession or discipline of psychology'. Whilst this seems glaringly obvious, personal conduct may also refer to apparently unimportant behaviours. Consider how a client would react if they saw your driving style, social media content (including photos) or perhaps saw you littering in the street. On a lighter note, do you also practice what you preach on the field/court, etc.? Likewise, how should a psychologist react upon noticing suspicious substances being passed between athletes, or even simply if an athlete cheats to win a competition? Would you want people to think you are 'ok' with those behaviours?

Evidence-based practice: The debates around what constitutes scientific evidence and how it should be used to inform applied practice are both addressed later on in this book. However, it is notable that several codes of conduct do specify that psychological support should be based on research evidence. For example, the BPS (2009, p. 9) states that in making ethical decisions, psychologists should ask: 'Is there research evidence that might be relevant?'. BASES (2006, p. 1) specify that a key aim of their code is: 'the encouragement of evidence-based practice in sport and exercise sciences'. Regarding needs analysis, the APA (2010, p. 12) guidelines are clear that 'psychologists [should] administer, adapt, score, interpret, or use assessment techniques ... in a manner and for purposes that are appropriate in light of the research on or evidence of the usefulness and proper application of the techniques'. At the very least, a sport psychologist may be required to demonstrate, through their record keeping, that research evidence has been used to inform their psychological services – both as a trainee and as a registered practitioner.

Record keeping: Five of the six codes of conduct reviewed in Table 2.1 specify that 'adequate' records must be kept, sufficient to satisfy the laws in each country. This vague definition is difficult to work with, as one often only discovers what is necessary by law when dealing with the law and legal issues (King, 2010). As a result, many psychologists report being confused about the amount and type of information required in clinical notes (Cameron & Turtle-Song, 2002; Fulero & Wilbert, 1988). However, good record keeping is vital to the supervision process and the assessment of competence prior to qualifying, where the onus is on trainees to provide evidence of their development. Post qualification, the reason a psychologist should keep records is to *prepare for the worst,* even if we hope it never happens (cf. Brown & Cogan, 2006). If one's practice or competence were ever called into question, detailed records would allow reviewers to access a record, made at the time, of the events in question. This concern was one of the main motivating factors for accurate record keeping in the psychologists interviewed by Bradford and Stevens (2013).

As for the content of practice records, the same study identified a range of information categories to include, any of which might be useful for both the psychologist or anyone reviewing his/her notes. These included (Bradford & Stevens, 2013):

(a) referral/intake information;
(b) signed consent form(s);
(c) signed fee agreement;

(d) client contact details;

(e) next of kin contact details;

(f) other treating practitioner details (i.e., general practitioner);

(g) evidence of a completed full assessment;

(h) family genogram;

(i) documented diagnosis;

(j) treatment plan;

(k) a summary log of the dates and types of services provided;

(l) case progress notes for every session;

(m) records of supervision or consultation;

(n) psychological test data;

(o) authorization for release of information; and

(p) the discharge summary or document of termination of treatment.

To be clear, any of these could be reasonably requested by anyone reviewing a trainee's progress, or reviewing a psychologist's practice in response to a complaint – so if you do not keep these records (organized and accessible but secure and confidential) then you probably should. We could add to this documented reflections on, and responses to, any ethical dilemmas, miscommunications, failed or ineffective interventions, etc. Finally, one should be aware that the client may legitimately seek access to these records, and has the right to request any inaccurate information be amended (e.g., APS, 2010, p. 20). Likewise, it is important for the psychologist to clearly separate their professional opinions from objective facts (Bradford & Stevens, 2013, p. 183).

Termination of role: The end of a professional relationship can be difficult for both parties, particularly if one of those involved wishes to continue it, or does not understand why it has ended. However, it would clearly be inappropriate to keep accepting payments from a client who was no longer benefitting from the psychologist's services, and there are many occasions when a referral is needed, or when a psychologist needs to take leave. As has been the case throughout this chapter, the solution lies in managing expectations from the outset. For example, both the BPS (2009) and APS (2010) specify that the psychologist should, from the outset, specify the circumstances under which the relationship will be terminated. In addition, both codes specify: that support should not continue once the client does not appear to be benefitting; that arrangements must be made if the psychologist changes job or takes leave; and that the psychologist must facilitate 'continuity of care' when making a referral. In all cases, the welfare of the client needs to be considered, as 'cutting loose' a client after you've agreed to help them could be viewed very dimly. On the one hand, in sport psychology we are often dealing with psychologically healthy individuals seeking a performance enhancement – so welfare may be less of a pressing consideration. On the other hand, another attribute of sport is the frequency with which staff and management can change in a team. Even if a psychologist were part of a support staff who were summarily removed after a bad season, s/he would still need to ensure each client was catered for, either by making a referral or agreeing that no further intervention is needed (Moore, 2003).

Ethical advertising: The BPS guidelines (2009, p. 21) specify that psychologists must: 'Be honest and accurate in advertising their professional services and products, in order to avoid encouraging unrealistic expectations or otherwise misleading the public'. This broad sentiment is echoed in the HCPC (2008) standards. However, both the APS (2010) and the APA (2010) go much further, in specifying that statements made by psychologists in advertising/marketing must not contain: (a) any statement which is false, fraudulent or even likely to mislead; (b) testimonials or endorsements from clients or any vulnerable persons (i.e., who might have been coerced in any way); (c) any statement claiming or implying superiority over any/all other psychologists; (d) any statement that might create unjustified expectations of favourable results; (e) any claim *unjustifiably* suggesting that the psychologist uses exclusive or superior techniques/equipment; and (f) any statement which might bring the psychologist or the profession into disrepute. If you review your answers to Case example 1 in light of these principles, how did you do? The online registers offered by the registration bodies provide minimal information, perhaps for the above reasons, but these should be the main way one receives clients. Any self-published website, brochures or pamphlets would need to be carefully vetted to comply with the above guidelines. At present, moves are afoot in most countries to better advertise the official registers of qualified psychologists, and to improve the level of reporting of materials that fail to comply with the above guidelines.

Location of services: Whilst many of the above considerations appear common across all of psychological practice, and may simply apply differently in sport, many of the papers reviewed noted unique challenges from working in sport. For example, Stapleton et al. (2010, p. 144) noted: 'The service of applied sport psychology can vary widely from that of traditional psychology practice ... Psychologists providing sport psychology services will find themselves facing ethical dilemmas unlike those in their clinical office practice'. Perhaps the most compelling example of this difference is the location(s) where sport psychology occurs. These might include: an office, a training facility, a changing room, pitch- or track-side, the team bus or coach, corridors and other transit situations, airport lounges and potentially even the breakfast or dinner table. Suddenly, without a private office and controlled physical boundaries, issues of confidentiality, personal conduct and conflict of interest abound.

Haberl and Peterson (2006) provide an excellent summary of the issues that 'location' generated for them, whilst working as embedded psychologists for Olympic teams before and during the event. One example included attending a dinner event where an athlete from the team who has not yet received (or requested) psychology services engages in a social conversation, but then begins to discuss her performance issues. At what point should confidentiality be explained, and how can it be enforced in such a location? On the one hand, there are clear benefits to being 'available' for athletes to speak to in this way, but who else can hear (or even see) the conversation? A second example, again very typical, is over dinner when the athletes are joking about someone's poor performance, and then say: 'I reckon you need to see the psychologist ... or perhaps you already are?' (perhaps all looking towards the psychologist at once). Very quickly, an innocuous conversation has become a serious risk of breaching confidentiality. The authors discuss how they have used humour and experience to navigate such situations, but equally Moore (2003) argued that such social situations should be avoided in the first place (as much as possible), so that such tensions cannot develop. None of the articles that addressed this point suggested that a sport psychologist should simply limit their practice to a closed office. Rather, the sport psychologist must actively and very carefully manage their behaviour at all times: never taking anything for granted, constantly self-aware and reflective.

Time limitations: Several of the articles reviewed also noted unique challenges of time constraints placed on sport psychologists. First of all, for many the job is not a full-time role, and sport psychologists often have 'day jobs', perhaps studying full time, or are academics at universities where they also offer sport-psychology services (Haberl & Peterson, 2006). This in itself poses a substantial problem to sport psychologists wishing to work normal office hours, or spend sustained periods with a sporting team or organization. Further, when we weigh the importance of spending time around teams and 'hanging out' (cf. Andersen, 2005), we run into the problem of what constitutes a billable hour, or 'contact time'. Second, whilst sport psychologists may spend a much greater proportion of their time in the physical presence of their athletes/clients (in the situations noted above under *location of services*), very little of this time is appropriate for offering psychological services to individual athletes. In fact, on a busy tour or training schedule, the sport psychologist can often be extremely limited in time available to meet individual athletes. This could force the psychologist into using evening slots, meal times or discreet meetings to offer one-to-one support – all of which blur professional boundaries (Little & Harwood, 2010). Such a relaxing of formal boundaries may represent a 'slippery slope' towards allowing situations that are (or could be viewed as) ethical violations (cf. Strasburger, Jorgenson, & Sutherland, 1992).

2.5   Summary and conclusions

The overall picture of 'ethical issues in sport psychology' might be summarized as follows: With a largely healthy population, and fewer clinical issues to deal with, the severity of ethical breaches might be slightly reduced in sport. However, the unique challenges of working as a psychologist in sport arguably generate many more ethical dilemmas, and issues that are much less predictable than other settings. As such, sport psychologists arguably need to be even more ethically aware and robust than other areas of practice. In day-to-day practice, individual 'ethically imperfect' decisions or behaviours may not generate serious consequences for the athlete or sport psychologist. However, the 'death by a thousand cuts' that occurs to the profession of sport psychology is too high a price to pay just because actively managing ethical considerations is considered time consuming, or cognitively demanding. Likewise, in the (hopefully) unusual event of being reported for a breach and found guilty, the consequences to a sport psychologist are just as severe as for any other domain of psychology. There does not appear to be any special dispensation allowing committees to reduce the penalties for sport psychologists, even if the demands listed above are unique and challenging.

2.6   Worksheets

With a view to assisting sport psychologists in monitoring their ethical practices – detecting, challenging, anticipating and, ideally, avoiding any potential conflicts – the following three worksheets are provided. The first allows you to capture and monitor your own ethical behaviours with each client: ironing out any potential problems and perhaps even developing a consistent approach for working with athletes. The second worksheet provides prompts for you to run through at (or even before) your first meeting with each client, thus assisting you in meeting your obligation to address each key issue at the outset of the relationship. The third worksheet will assist you in trying to turn an 'uncomfortable moment' into a valuable lesson, by encouraging you to capture, unpack, analyse and learn from any experiences you found ethically challenging.

2.7   Ella's story: Part 2 – From undergraduate to postgraduate training

Ella's undergraduate psychology degree contained very little reference to ethics in applied practice, focussing much more on research ethics. One of the first tasks in her postgraduate degree is to recruit an athlete, and work with her/him to generate an applied case study. There are 20 marks for ethical considerations out of 100 in total, which makes ethics an important aspect of the assignment. Ella is confused about how she might win those marks, and why so many marks are devoted to ethics.

1. How would you explain the ethics of applied practice to Ella? Why do you think so many marks are devoted to ethical considerations?
2. What opportunities will Ella have to demonstrate her competence with ethical considerations? Be as specific as possible.
3. What ethical dilemmas are immediately presented by being a trainee sport psychologist, seeking to work with a real athlete? How might these be managed?
4. Ella's client is a male rugby player, who admits he used to suffer from eating disorders and that these thoughts still happen sometimes. What should Ella do? What does she need to record, discuss and enact with this client?

2.8   Review and reflect

1. What are the main differences between viewing ethics as an outcome versus as a process?
2. How would you respond to the claim that there is no time for ethics when practising sport psychology, or that ethics 'get in the way'?
3. What core ethical considerations are specified in the country or jurisdiction where you live? How do they differ from other countries and regulatory bodies? If there are differences, how much do they matter?
4. In what way does sport generate additional or unusual threats to the maintenance of ethical standards as a sport psychologist?
5. What opportunities does the sport psychologist have to proactively manage ethical issues so that they may never become problems?
6. If an ethical dilemma or breach is suspected, what are the mechanisms for reporting and managing it in your country/jurisdiction?

Worksheet 2.1   Ethical self-awareness checklist for sport psychologists

Source: Moore, Z. E. (2003). Ethical dilemmas in sport psychology: Discussion and recommendations for practice. *Professional Psychology: Research and Practice, 34*(6), 601–610. Adapted with kind permission from Zella E. Moore.

Do I have the appropriate specialized education and training to offer and provide the psychological services that this client needs?

Yes / No / Not Applicable

Is my role(s) with the client/organization clearly defined and within defendable limits of competence as defined by my education and training?

Yes / No / Not Applicable

Did I describe/represent myself and my services honestly and accurately?

Yes / No / Not Applicable

Am I thoroughly aware of my relevant code-of-conduct and how it pertains to this client/organization?

Yes / No / Not Applicable

Did I (or will I) integrate new research findings and professional developments within my field, in order to provide up-to-date 'best practice'?

Yes / No / Not Applicable

Did I provide the client with written and verbal informed consent, recorded appropriately?

Yes / No / Not Applicable

Did I provide informed consent that was detailed, honest and appropriately described?

Myself (the practitioner)	**Yes / No / Not Applicable**
The services I provide	**Yes / No / Not Applicable**
Expectations of the services	**Yes / No / Not Applicable**
Limitations of the services	**Yes / No / Not Applicable**
Empirical support (or lack thereof) for the services	**Yes / No / Not Applicable**
Issues of confidentiality	**Yes / No / Not Applicable**
Fees	**Yes / No / Not Applicable**
Other intervention options	**Yes / No / Not Applicable**
The extent to which these interventions are likely to be effective	**Yes / No / Not Applicable**

Could I have exaggerated the likelihood of treatment success or promised the client an outcome that is unrealistic?

Yes / No / Not Applicable

Did I clearly define confidentiality, limits of confidentiality and how those limits are to be decided with the client, parents, coaches, organizational personnel, etc.?

Yes / No / Not Applicable

Am I receiving pressure from organizational staff to violate client confidentiality, blur boundaries or engage in unnecessary/inappropriate interventions?

Yes / No / Not Applicable

(continued)

- If so, have I discussed these dilemmas with the appropriate individuals within the organization, in an attempt to remediate the difficulties?

  Yes / No / Not Applicable
- Do I wish/need to discuss a client(s) and his/her relevant case material with other individuals, outside of a consultative role?

  Yes / No / Not Applicable
- If I wish/need to speak to other individuals about a client, have I obtained the necessary voluntary verbal and written consent from the client to do so?

  Yes / No / Not Applicable
- Have I kept detailed records of the client history, consent(s) and ANY other relevant materials?

  Yes / No / Not Applicable

Prior to obtaining consent from the client to speak to other individuals about the case, have I made the client aware of the possible consequences/outcomes of sharing/discussing case information, so that the client can make an informed decision?

  Yes / No / Not Applicable

- Have I recorded essential client information, evaluative information, progress notes, etc., in clients' records?

  Yes / No / Not Applicable
- Do I retain records and client data for the number of years mandatory in my country/state/jurisdiction?

  Yes / No / Not Applicable
- Are these records kept in a safe and secure place?

  Yes / No / Not Applicable
- Are legal reporting requirements clearly presented and understood (i.e., child abuse, potential self-harm, potential harm to others)?

  Yes / No / Not Applicable
- Do I have any non-consultative/therapeutic contacts with clients?

  Yes / No / Not Applicable
- If so, can I clearly defend the need for, or unavoidable nature of, these non-consultative/therapeutic contacts with clients?

  Yes / No / Not Applicable
- If/when I attend organizational events, do I remain superficial in my contact with athlete-clients and avoid excessive socializing in order to limit the potential for loss of objectivity or the development of unnecessary dual role relationships?

  Yes / No / Not Applicable
- Have I discussed with my client(s) the possibility of abrupt employment termination and thus made appropriate referrals ahead of time to provide continuity of care?

  Yes / No / Not Applicable
- Am I prolonging treatment past necessity and continuing to engage in a therapeutic relationship with a client(s), although my services are complete and intervention success has ensued?

  Yes / No / Not Applicable

- Have I developed an appropriate referral network so that issues out of my area of competence can be appropriately addressed/treated?

  Yes / No / Not Applicable
- Am I willing to refer clients to another professional if I can no longer be of assistance, or if personal objectivity is compromised, the therapeutic relationship becomes damaged, or if the client is not able to benefit from my services?

  Yes / No / Not Applicable
- Have I minimized the presence of more serious psychological concerns and thus denied the need for referral in order to continue working with this client(s)?

  Yes / No / Not Applicable
- If using psychological assessment instruments, do I have the necessary education and training to engage in these activities?

  Yes / No / Not Applicable
- Do I have professional liability insurance?

  Yes / No / Not Applicable

If and when an issue arises:

Am I thoroughly aware of relevant/applicable Code of Ethics regarding this situation or dilemma?

Yes / No / Not Applicable

- Have I read the relevant/applicable Ethical Standard directly regarding this issue?

  Yes / No / Not Applicable
- Have I contemplated how the issue at hand may impact my client(s)?

  Yes / No / Not Applicable
- Am I serving my needs and interests more than the needs and interests of my client(s)?

  Yes / No / Not Applicable
- Have I consulted with a colleague or another professional in the field?

  Yes / No / Not Applicable
- Have I contacted the relevant Ethics Board for suggestions and guidance?

  Yes / No / Not Applicable
- Have I read relevant literature within the field concerning similar issues and concerns?

  Yes / No / Not Applicable
- Am I comfortable and confident that I could defend my decision or intervention in front of an ethics board or court of law if necessary?

  Yes / No / Not Applicable
- If applicable, have I contacted my professional liability insurance provider?

  Yes / No / Not Applicable
- If applicable, have I contacted a lawyer regarding this issue?

  Yes / No / Not Applicable

Worksheet 2.2   'Outset' ethics checklist

To be completed before the provision of any psychological services, with each new client:

Outline qualifications, registrations or supervision status ☐

Outline areas of competence and limits of competence ☐

Outline services offered (specify what is not available) ☐

Check client understands the nature of your services and
limits of your competence ☐

Explain precise nature/context of relationship – including
multiple or 'third-party' arrangements ☐

Explain precise nature of confidentiality – limits in statute,
as well as limits resulting from third-party arrangements
or supervision (include in this how data will be stored, and
how long for) ☐

Explain theoretical approach, including use of scientific evidence ☐

Provide client with details of regulatory bodies and
complaints procedures ☐

Check client understanding of confidentiality arrangements ☐

Check client is content with your theoretical approach ☐

Obtain initial consent regarding data collection, confidentiality,
competency and theoretical approach ☐

Explain the precise nature of fees, payments or barters used
to secure psychological services (again, written consent preferable) ☐

Review for any unanticipated ethical issues
(age, vulnerability, culture, sport type, location of services,
time available) ☐

In your best judgement, are you competent and proficient to carry
out the services required? (seek advice of supervisor or senior
psychologist if necessary) ☐

Worksheet 2.3   Ethical issues reflective log

Source: Gibbs, G. (1998) *Learning by doing: A guide to teaching and learning methods.* Oxford: OCSLD. Adapted with kind permission from the Oxford Centre for Staff and Learning Development.

2) What aspects of what happened leave you feeling uncomfortable or unsure?

3) Can you specify any harm, risk of harm or conflict of interests? Real or anticipated?

1) Description of event or situation

4) Which specific ethical considerations are relevant to this situation? What does your relevant ethical code of conduct say about these issues?

6) What lessons can be drawn from these events for your future practice?

5) What action needs to be taken?

Preventative?

Remedial?

Report a breach?

Philosophical Assumptions: The Aims, the Substance and the Strategy

3

3.1 Introduction and overview

In the following chapter, we review a topic which receives insufficient attention in sport psychology yet which may hold the key to effective practice: the philosophical foundations of sport psychology practice. These can be divided into three broad categories including the *purpose of sport psychology* (aims could include resolving performance issues, promoting well-being, increasing participation, managing injuries and more), the *subject matter* of sport psychology (What is it, how can we measure/analyse it?) and the *practice style* one adopts when working with clients. Importantly, not only can we actually identify key themes in each category, we can also illustrate the consequences of adopting different assumptions, or sets of assumptions. Further still, we can uncover logical associations between different types of assumptions (aims, reality, style), and explore the impact of adopting consistent versus conflicting assumption sets. The problem for all sport psychologists is that all of the above assumptions are necessary, unavoidable parts of the service delivery process, but for many they will be implicit and undeclared. You may never be asked by an athlete or coach what your philosophical stance is, and many genuinely will not care, but knowing it will allow you to offer a more coherent, ethical and effective service – because you will actually be able to define what it means to be effective, and how best to go about being effective. This chapter builds the case that it is impossible to offer a coherent sport psychology service without knowing what you are trying to achieve, the type of materials you are working with and the best ways of working with those materials (this point is illustrated in the below case example). As such, this chapter aims to help all sport psychologists – from novice to experienced pro – to identify, explicate, evaluate and modify their underlying assumptions.

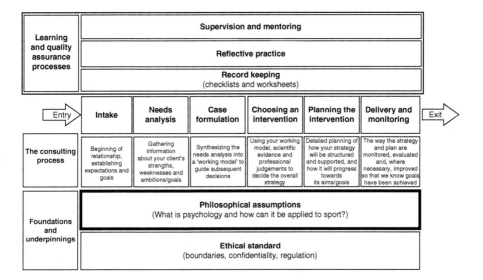

Figure 3.1   *The position of philosophical assumptions, underpinning the whole service delivery process, with only ethical standards being more foundational. Almost all key decisions made by a sport psychologist, as well as the recording, analysing and interpreting of events, are informed by philosophical assumptions.*

Case example 3.1: Negotiating a contract without knowing the law

I was debating the importance of philosophy with a colleague once, and he made what he felt was a compelling point:

> 'No athlete has *ever* wanted to talk about philosophy with me! Not Plato, not Aristotle, not Husserl … Heidegger, Sartre, Russell, Rousseau, none of them. No I tell a lie, I once discussed solipsism with a lonely elite athlete..! You just need to agree values and outcomes that you can both work towards..!'

Sounds compelling, however …

Unfortunately, this would be akin to a property lawyer saying that no client had ever asked him about the finer details of property law, and that this means there was no need to understand it. All he would have to do is deliver whatever the client wanted and he would get paid, regardless of whether the outcome was ethical, legal or sensible. Let's imagine how that conversation might go:

Lawyer: Hello, how can I help you?

Client: I'm moving house and I need a lawyer to act on my behalf.

Lawyer: Sure, what would you like me to do?

Client: Erm, what do you mean?

Lawyer: Well, my job is to agree some values and desirable outcomes with you, and then deliver those. That's what I get paid for.

(continued)

Case example 3.1: Negotiating a contract without knowing the law (*continued*)

Client: Well, I don't really know what's involved. I mean, I need some help selling my house and buying another one. Is that something you do?

Lawyer: Yes, absolutely, you've come to the right company.

Client: So, what happens now?

Lawyer: We just agree those outcomes, write it into a contract of service and sign it. Then you pay me for doing those things.

Client: No, I mean with the house move. What documents do you need, what signatures? What are the legal and ethical obligations on me to the buyer of my old house and the seller of my new one?

Lawyer: Oh, I find clients don't really care about that sort of stuff so long as we're working towards the agreed outcomes. I think it's really self-indulgent of lawyers to enforce such technical stuff on their clients.

Client: But I mean, you're the expert. I need to know what is going to be required of me. How exactly are we going to go about this process? What are the requirements and deadlines?

Lawyer: We'll work that out as we go along. For now, if we agree that you want to sell your old house and buy a new one, then I think we have a contract. Sign here. This is my fee.

Client: Do you actually know the laws for selling and buying houses?

Lawyer: We had a lecture on it, but I felt it was really unnecessary for *actually just getting on and doing the job.*

Client: Right. But you have no idea on the technical details?

Lawyer: No. That would really just get in the way.

Client: Goodbye.

*It should not be too difficult to substitute sport psychologist for 'lawyer', and sport psychology for 'buying/selling houses'.

3.2 What are philosophical assumptions?

As already noted, you cannot do sport psychology without making assumptions. As a practising sport psychologist, you need to find a way to: (a) examine, understand and influence someone's way of thinking/feeling/experiencing; in order to (b) achieve any number of aims (noted in the first paragraph) with (c) no clear guide on how best to achieve this. Such a task *requires* a broad range of assumptions to be made because you can never be sure you have a 'correct' answer to any of the above three issues. Rest assured, many millions of words have been devoted to trying to find answers to these issues, in psychology and also more broadly across all of science – from Plato to Popper.

Without ever being able to achieve certainty, how can one proceed to deliver sport psychology services? You must make assumptions, and your success will depend on how reliable, or trustworthy, these assumptions prove to be. Given the importance of these assumptions – your career could live or die depending on them – it seems the least we can do is to actually be aware of them and their consequences. In my 2014 paper (Keegan, 2014) on this topic, I used a 'map and territory' metaphor: comparing explorers who are fully trained in navigation and equipped with maps and compasses versus those who are not (and who most often end up calling mountain rescue!). A basic knowledge of philosophical assumptions might be considered a map, but reflective awareness and supervision might represent the compass to orient yourself. With practice, by repeatedly moving through this difficult terrain, a psychologist can accrue a range of practice experiences that will enable her/him to successfully 'navigate' a treacherous landscape.

Before we get to the core of this chapter, it is important to note one very important issue: we need to simplify the literature and make it 'comprehensible'. Over the history of psychology, and sport psychology, practitioners have identified a confusing array of ideas around philosophical assumptions. For example, in reviewing the literature in this area, Poczwardowski, Sherman and Ravizza (2004) identified numerous and varied attempts to capture 'professional philosophy'. Even after being organized and interpreted by the authors, the examples identified included (p. 448): '(a) *the consultant's role*: an educator, an observer and learner of a given team and sport, a mental coach, a facilitator and catalyst (e.g., Botterill, 1990; Boutcher & Rotella, 1987; Halliwell, 1989; Ravizza, 1990; Rotella, 1990; Salmela, 1989); (b) *areas of service*: performance enhancement, health and healthy lifestyle, personal growth/development, daily living, personal counselling, team effectiveness, organizational service (e.g., Boutcher & Rotella, 1987; Bull, 1995; Gipson, McKenzie, & Lowe, 1989; Gordon, 1990; Neff, 1990; Weiss, 1995); (c) *anticipated end-products*: client independence (e.g., Botterill, 1990), providing positive and productive training and competition environments (e.g., Gipson et al., 1989), meeting an athlete's every need (Orlick, 1989); (d) *understanding of the place of sport psychology* in the structure of the entire athletic preparation and how psychological skills are developed (e.g., Botterill, 1990; Gordon, 1990; Halliwell, 1990; Loehr, 1990; Rotella, 1990; Weiss, 1995); (e) *type of organization* in terms of group versus individual sessions (e.g., Botterill, 1990; Halliwell, 1989; Loehr, 1990; Murphy & Farrante, 1989); and (f) *general features of the intervention programme* and specific techniques used in developing identified psychological skills (e.g., Boutcher & Rotella, 1987; Gordin & Henschen, 1989; Halliwell, 1989; Murphy & Farrante, 1989; Rotella, 1990; Salmela, 1989) ... [as well as perspectives described as] educational,

educational/developmental, developmental, social-educational, clinical, humanistic, cognitive-behavioral, mental skills oriented and social psychological (Botterill, 1990; Brustad & Ritter-Taylor, 1997; Gill, 1995; Gordon, 1990; Halliwell, 1989, 1990; Jordansh, Petipas, & Hale, 1992; May & Brown, 1989; Nideffer, 1989; Ravizza, 1990; Yambor & Connelly, 1991)'.

The above passage is only a summary of writings in this area, and a chapter 'accurately' reflecting the disparate literature on 'professional philosophy' would only serve to confuse all but the most determined of readers. Instead, this chapter seeks to identify the core issues that could be considered philosophical assumptions – as opposed to specific 'schools' of psychological practice – and thus provide a scaffold for practitioners of all ages to structure their thinking. This is the reason behind the use of three core sets of philosophical assumptions described in this chapter.

Traditionally, the *overall purpose of sport psychology* has been viewed in two contrasting ways – although other options are available. First, there is the viewpoint that sport psychology is only about supporting athlete *performance*, particularly at the elite level. This perspective has been referred to as the 'Soviet model' (Stambulova, Wrisberg, & Ryba, 2006) but there are many practitioners across the globe who subscribe to the principal. In contrast, there is the viewpoint that sport psychology must balance the performance of athletes with the *welfare* of the athletes – on the assumption that mentally healthy athletes may both perform better and require less time a way from sport. This model appears to originate in North American and European approaches, but again, it is not exclusively 'owned' by these regions (Stambulova et al., 2006). In addition, one may simply be working to *educate* athletes, especially young athletes, about sport psychology skills and practices (again, largely viewed as originating in North America), or one could focus on encouraging participation in sport, for leisure and health purposes, thus moving away from a focus on performance. One's assumptions regarding the 'goals' of sport psychology are bound to influence what one counts as success or failure, and how one proceeds as a practitioner. These goals can also change depending on the circumstances, or type of client, and remaining aware of such a change may prevent incorrect assumptions from causing problems in the relationship.

Then we come to the *philosophy of science* in sport psychology. If we are content with the definition of sport psychology as 'the application of the scientific process to the mental processes of athletes and sport performers' (from Chapter 1) then we need to understand what the scientific process really is. Or rather, we need to understand the options, as there may not be one truly perfect scientific process (although there are definitely unscientific approaches!). The literature on philosophy of science is vast, and yet philosophy appears to be the 'elephant in the room' for sport psychology, with only a tiny proportion of research articles (and even fewer practitioners) identifying the approach that they take. Fundamentally, this issue concerns the nature of the 'reality' you believe you are dealing with (reliable physical objects or unique and complex social constructions), because this then determines how you can study and influence that reality. Remember that sport psychology spans from the study of neurons using electrodes to complex social interactions using interviews and observations. From a stormy history, four broad traditions can be identified in the philosophy of science, which can be loosely described as certaintism, construalism, fallibilism and pragmatism (see below).

Third, we will address the way we attempt to change or influence our client's psychological processes – one's practice style. Inevitably, this will depend upon what type of 'stuff' we think we are influencing, and our reasons for making such changes will depend on what we feel the 'aims' of sport psychology are – thus it is not surprising that there are broad trends between the three sets of assumptions. In the very broadest sense, I described this as varying from a 'practitioner-led' style ('I'm the expert, do as I say') to a 'client-led' style ('You're the most important person here, lead the way and I will assist' – Keegan, 2010). Each of these three assumption sets will now be 'unpacked' and examined.

Case example 3.2: 'Now I know why I messed up'

At the beginning of my career as a sport psychologist, in my first year of supervised practice, I was very lucky to work at a women's hockey academy where I was surrounded by elite players. By coincidence, I was approached by two players in quick succession who appeared to be experiencing identical problems. Both had recently made the transition to first-team hockey (and the academy), both appeared to lack confidence, especially following mistakes or when facing strong opposition, and both appeared to be deploying extremely negative self-talk and 'catastrophizing', wherein small mistakes are blown out of all proportion and the inferred negative judgements of coaches and teammates were being grossly exaggerated. When this happened, both players found themselves 'going to pieces', unable to perform tasks/skills they would normally find very easy because they were crippled by self-doubt and fear of further mistakes.

With Player 1, we focused on the negative thoughts, capturing them after and between matches in a diary and then immediately challenging them and reframing them into more helpful and adaptive thoughts. As well as being grounded in 'well-supported' theory and research (e.g., Gould, Finch, & Jackson, 1993), Player 1 reported really enjoying the intervention: immediately perceiving its relevance, the impact on her game and the benefits of building a new way of thinking. We also used physical cues and reminders (e.g., stickers placed on her watch and phone), to act as a reminder to practice being positive. The intervention worked wonderfully well, Player 1 re-entered the team she had been dropped from, and played well. Encouraged by this success, I recommended the same interventions with Player 2, who displayed all the same symptoms.

(continued)

Case example 3.2: 'Now I know why I messed up' (*continued*)

Player 2 never attempted her diary, never really gave the tasks a chance and never took the stickers out of the packet. For a while, she would come back and we would discuss alternative ways of building confidence, although after several further sessions she stopped attending and dropped out of the academy setup. Months later, I bumped into this athlete in the café where many of us ate lunch, and we spoke about what had 'gone wrong'.

It turned out that the things Player 1 had reported as a 'problems' that she desperately wanted to 'fix' were things that Player 2 did not want to 'fix'. Instead, she felt that she may be reaching the 'natural limit' of her ability in hockey and that it might be time to move on. Player 1 saw other people's negative judgements as *her problem*: and she had to improve to win back their approval. Player 2 saw other people's judgements as simply *their problem*. Player 1 saw her lack of confidence as something she must overcome in order to improve her game. Player 2 saw her confidence being unfairly attacked by other people; people who didn't understand her wants and dream. By failing to spot this, and by joining the list of people pushing Player 2 to 'get better', I had failed her.

If only I had stopped to listen more carefully, and allow her to tell her story more completely; if only I had not been buoyed by the incredible success I had with Player 1 only weeks previously. If only I had been more experienced and self-aware as a psychologist. At this point in my career, my assumptions were that: (a) sport psychology is about improving performance; (b) you can measure things like confidence using questionnaires and performance profiles; and (c) I had been studying this area for almost 5 years, so I must be the 'expert' who leads the process and 'prescribes' recommendations. For Player 1, these assumptions fit perfectly, but for Player 2 they were woefully inappropriate. Following these reflections, a key question for me became: *Shouldn't a **good** sport psychologist have been able to successfully support and help **both** of these athletes?*

3.3 The aims of the game

This is sport, so obviously the aim of a sport psychologist is to help create world champions, right? What if a player approaches you at an important stage of the season but they are burned out and emotionally exhausted? Do you help them forge through, stay positive and 'be a winner'? These are obviously leading questions, but the answer could easily be: 'No'. What if that athlete was suffering from depression/burnout, and you were the only person in their entire social network who they could speak to in privacy, and who might *not* push them to get back on the pitch? What if your attitude was what pushed them over the edge?

One solution would be to make it explicit to every single athlete, coach and team you work with (*before* undertaking any work) that you *only* deal with performance enhancement and talent development (so please take any other issues somewhere else). That would not only make your job much simpler and avoid the above scenario, but it would also render you less effective as a sport psychologist, because performance and personal issues frequently overlap and interlink in rich and complex ways. Attempting to separate them out may severely restrict the number of athletes you can actually help (or how much you can help them).

Another solution would be to accept and acknowledge, as early as possible in your development, that you may find yourself dealing with performance enhancement, talent development, psychological well-being, clinical and sub-clinical issues (i.e., recognize and refer), injury rehabilitation, life skills and character development and/or the management of career transitions (e.g., Henriksen, Stambulova, & Roessler, 2010; Stambulova et al., 2006; Wylleman, Alfermann, & Lavallee, 2004). This is not an exhaustive list at all. You may also find yourself working on relationship dynamics between players, coaches, parents, etc., and of course working on team cohesion and team cultures.

In order to develop as a practitioner, trainee psychologists should effortfully engage with the growing literatures in all these areas, and not just focus on mental skills. This may be easier said than done as the field of sport psychology has historically struggled to break free of the 'mental toolkit' approach: assuming that problems are caused by a deficiency in one of several key mental skills and so enhancing this skill will improve performance. Working under these implicit assumptions, a sport psychologist would merely need to look for a deficit in one or more areas (concentration, confidence, motivation, arousal control), and then reach into his/her toolkit and produce a suitable process/method which, when learned, would fill this deficit. Wonderfully simple, but also a wonderfully limited view of what a sport psychologist can offer – and an approach that has been rightly criticized from inside and outside of the realm of sport psychology.

Perhaps a more full and complete service would be offered by sport psychologists whose practice openly acknowledges the following: (a) psychological well-being is at least as important as performance (if not more) in a caring profession such as psychology; (b) psychological well-being may frequently come into conflict with sporting performance; and (c) career transitions, injuries and life-skill development are all inherent parts of sport, which clearly interact with performance and well-being. Sometimes, the issue does not pertain to performance but by being a politically neutral sounding board (i.e., offering confidentiality, understanding and not being involved in selection processes) a sport psychologist can help players feel supported and comfortable in often quite challenging environments. This support may even prevent a life event or interpersonal conflict from ever affecting performance in the first place, or it may help an athlete persist with tedious injury rehab and get playing sooner. I can even imagine that an athlete who feels supported by her/his club, in the form of a good psychologist, would be more loyal and less likely to be open to approaches from other teams. Finally, many athletes undergo key transitions during their careers, from a talented youngster to a development squad, and from there to the elite level. Many models exist to describe these transitions and the challenges they pose to athletes (e.g., Wylleman et al., 2004). Researching using this model suggests that there are many opportunities to support athletes through these transitions, and again, perhaps achieve higher retention rates, higher motivation for training, and so, happier more successful athletes/coaches/teams.

As noted earlier, focusing solely on performance may severely constrain the effectiveness of the sport psychologist. However, another danger would be to attempt any/all of these aims without stopping to *check that your aims match the client's aims*. So where this is not already happening, perhaps all sport psychologists, young and old, should attempt to explicitly classify the goals of their support with each client and, where possible, agree these goals with the client (discussed in Chapter 4).

Knowing what you do, and how to sell it (ethically)

As noted in the previous chapter, all ethical codes state that a sport psychologist must create accurate expectations in their clients regarding the nature and outcomes of their services. To do this with any certainty you need to know for sure whether you are offering 'guaranteed performance enhancement' or alternatively 'advocacy, support and critical questioning, with no guarantees for performance outcomes' (as an aside, if all the coaches and athletes you know only want the former, it might be a good time to educate them about the value of the latter too). That's philosophy.

Likewise, in several codes of conduct, there is clear specification that a professional psychologist must not make unsubstantiated claims of superiority over other service providers in attempting to promote or market their services. Again, philosophy helps with this. Remember, you want to 'promote' your services, but you cannot bad-mouth other psychologists or claim that your service is objectively better (a *very* difficult claim to prove = unsubstantiated). What you might be able to do, however, is accurately describe and compare the philosophies of different sport psychologists, and help potential clients to find the right one. 'Do you want to establish objective goals that your psychologist guarantees to help you achieve? Ok choose this guy. Do you want to explore the difficult experiences you've had since getting injured, with no pressure to return, and in a non-judgemental "safe" setting? Ok so talk to this guy instead'. If you can deliberately deliver different styles, then good: you have more 'products' to 'sell'.

However, at no point do you need to undermine, ridicule or criticize your fellow professionals – or indeed the whole discipline of sport psychology.

The idea is that any good sport psychologist should show their workings and explain the process when appropriate – but most ethical codes consider undermining or bad-mouthing other sport psychologists to be a clear breach of ethics. It damages the reputation of the entire discipline, purely to make a personal gain. The only way such a statement could go unpunished, once reported, would be if the speaker was *not a registered sport psychologist* and so not regulated by the codes of conduct that ban such behaviour.

So when you find yourself needing to promote your services, and separate yourself out from the crowd, knowing your approach in fine detail is vital, so that you can be accurate and avoid making unsubstantiated or inaccurate claims. For help with this, use the worksheets and tables available in this chapter to identify your current philosophical assumptions.

Perhaps you could also identify the assumptions you'd like to adopt, and compare how much these differ from your current approach. This would allow you to identify clear development goals for the future.

3.4   What is the psychological reality?

Here we hit upon the concepts of ontology and epistemology: two troublesome words for students and scientists the world over. *Ontology* captures our assumptions about how the (mental) world is made up and the nature of (mental) 'things', whereas *epistemology* attempts to describe our beliefs about how one might discover knowledge about the (mental) world. Having answers to these questions determines how we should go about changing/influencing someone's psychology. Answers to these questions frequently come in pairs (ontology:epistemology) – so if we assume a fixed and solid mental world then we set about measuring it reliably, but if we assume a world of ever changing and complex relationships, we might seek to simply describe and understand it in any way possible, or to participate in it and therefore understand it by being part of it. Spanning from the 'hard' and measurable (e.g., neuroscience and neurophysiology) to the soft and untenable (e.g., unique experiences and interpersonal relationships), sport psychology frequently struggles with these matters. However, there is a strong danger of 'getting it wrong' here, as coaches/directors frequently ask a psychologist to specify measurable outcomes that will determine if they are to be retained. However, if you promise to deliver something immeasurable, or in an area too complex to know with any certainty that your intervention will achieve its goals, you may find yourself out of a job and leaving a whole team/organization convinced that sport psychology is 'hokum'.

Consequently, what follows is a brief summary of the dominant positions within 'philosophy of science', in the form of simplified 'traditions' for ease of understanding. Armed with this knowledge, sport psychologists may be better able to understand their own service delivery process: its goals, measurement techniques, mechanisms and ways of intervening; and this knowledge may help to promote more coherent *and more successful* consulting practices. It must be noted, however, that these are simplifications of burgeoning and often contradictory literatures, riddled with debate and nuance – and these brief summaries cannot possibly do justice to that body of writing. As such, the interested reader is invited to follow-up and engage with texts such as Blaikie (1993) for further clarification.

3.4.1   Certaintism

Translation

Psychology is 'hard science' (also known as: empiricism, positivism).

Characterization

'If I can measure it objectively and accurately, then it is real. If I can't, it's not. Well-supported theories (applicable to all athletes) developed using accurate measurement tools allow me to make correct decisions with certainty'. See Table 3.1.

Based on the writings of

Bacon (1627, 1859); Carnap (1950); Feigl (1974); Locke (1690, 2009); Wittgenstein (1922/1961 – 'Tractatus') – and many others.

Review

To the *certaintist,* replicable observations in the form of accurate and repeatable measurements are absolutely key – because when observations of events co-occur or conjoin then we may begin to infer rules and laws (i.e., via inductive reasoning). Scientifically, these laws and rules become testable theories, which can be used to make predictions for future observations. If these predictions are confirmed the theory gains credibility, or certainty: it is proved right. The more consistently an idea/theory is supported, the better it is. The sport psychologist operating under these assumptions must deploy reliable and objective measurement techniques and well-supported theories: ideally backed by evidence that is both robust and voluminous (see Table 3.1).

Thinking critically, this approach does not accommodate what we might call 'catastrophic contradictions' – that is, clear and apparently incongruous exceptions to the law, yet these are relatively frequent in psychology (and this is exacerbated when considering unusual populations such as elite athletes or disabled performers). In the pure *certaintism* tradition, such exceptions might be dismissed as 'outliers' (either ignored or simply labelled 'wrong'). Second, this confirmatory approach allows many competing

Table 3.1 A summary of the relationships between traditions in the philosophy of science, and their implications for a practising sport psychologist. The four 'traditions' are described across the horizontal axis, with implications listed vertically below.

	Certaintism	Construalism	Pragmatism	Fallibilism
Compatible philosophies of science	Positivism, empiricism	Interpretivism, constructivism, subjectivism, phenomenology	Pragmatism, instrumentalism	Critical rationalism, critical realism
Compatible practising philosophies (cf. Keegan, 2010)	Practitioner-led, CBT, cognitive, behavioural, sophist and paternalistic	Client-led, humanistic, counselling and Socratic	Eclecticism (*likely* less critically self-aware, trial and error, experience based and heuristic)	Eclecticism (*likely* very critical and self-aware, cautious and deliberate/calculated)
Characterization	If I can measure it objectively and accurately, then it is real. If I can't, it's not. Well-supported theories (applicable to all athletes) developed using accurate measurement tools allow me to make correct decisions with certainty.	You can't measure something as unique as psychology; instead you must simply try to understand it and participate in its construction. Build a theory unique to your client and base decisions on that.	It doesn't matter what sort of reality you believe in, just do what works. Whatever you do, if it delivers results, go with it: that is the correct path.	Some aspects of psychology are measurable, some are not, and they interact in complex ways. Critically evaluate any evidence, theories and practical ideas that you use, as there is never any guarantee you will be correct.
Typical practitioner assumptions	• Practitioner knows best • Diagnose and prescribe • Practitioner drives questioning/agenda • Find and then solve a 'problem' • Practitioner determines intervention strategy	• Client knows best • Collaborative exploration • Agenda set by client's needs • There may not be a 'problem' per se • Ideally, client arrives at their own 'intervention strategy' through an improved understanding of their situation	• Sport psychology will have the answer • Deliver whatever the client wants/needs • Do whatever works to get the job done • Ambivalent towards theory and research – use them if they look useful, ignore them if they are not useful	• Critically question whether sport psychology is needed, and/or suitable for the client • Protect the interests of the client, the practitioner and the profession • Critical of theory and research but willing to use relevant and robust evidence to inform practice

(continued)

53

Table 3.1 A summary of the relationships between traditions in the philosophy of science, and their implications for a practising sport psychologist. The four 'traditions' are described across the horizontal axis, with implications listed vertically below (continued).

	Certaintism	Construalism	Pragmatism	Fallibilism
Practitioner's role	• Expert, Educator, instructor • Assessor, analyst	• Counsellor, supporter • Facilitator/catalyst • Collegial, but may challenge	• Highly flexible in approach • Enabler, helper, facilitator • Expert, networker • 'Get the job done'	• Highly flexible in approach • 'First, do no harm' • Cautious, deliberate approach • May be hesitant to intervene/make changes
Typical needs analysis methods	• Psychometric tests are generally viewed as useful and robust • Interviews are led by practitioner, informed by theory, and ideally follow a protocol to minimize practitioner bias • Quantitative and objective where possible	• Psychometric tests are generally viewed as inappropriate • Interviews are led by the client, with minimal formal theory and no requirement for protocol • Subjective account is central, quantitative measures generally avoided	• 'Anything goes' – preference given to techniques that will 'work' – i.e., assess the client's needs, provide evidence of intervention effectiveness or achieve the client's/practitioner's aims	• No preference for qualitative/quantitative • Critical evaluation of methods used, and data generated – including consideration of 'blind spots' (e.g., what was missed?) • Effectiveness and appropriacy of each method given explicit consideration – i.e., how sure can we be about this data?

54

How is data from needs analysis used?	• Theory informs practice and advice, much more so than the client's own interpretation/understanding • Data is understood in relation to theory, to the extent that theoretical measures may be deployed to confirm client's needs 'fit' • Well supported theories are considered 'true'	• Client's own experiences are given primacy and even where practitioner recognizes associations with a particular theory, this is generally prevented from guiding/influencing the course of the service delivery process	• No need to refer to scientific theory or evidence, but equally, no need to prioritize client's own experience/narrative • Likewise, if theory/evidence does offer help/insight, then use it • If a pattern emerges or a course of action 'works', then go with it	• Data is critically analysed for flaws and interpreted cautiously • Theories and evidence are critically analysed and carefully applied in light of any caveats or concerns • Theories are considered false/flawed even where evidence has been generally supportive
How are desired changes implemented?	• Prescription/recommendation of tasks in order to develop specific skills • Education as to the nature and utility of particular mental skills or ideas/concepts • Progress measures and targets are determined by practitioner	• Client is assisted in trying to understand their own experiences and responses to challenging situations – often a long process • If psychological techniques are deployed, the client would drive the process – finding their own ways of learning and applying the technique, and of evaluating its effectiveness	• Do *something* – the reasons don't really matter as long as it works (or feels like it might) • Prescribe, recommend, educate, negotiate – whichever approach gets results (or seems most promising) • Monitor results if you need to demonstrate effects, but all that matters is that the client thinks/feels it works	• Client is offered full informed consent, including a full awareness of the strengths/weaknesses of the analysis process, theories used and evidence supporting them • Individually tailored and fully agreed process • If in doubt, consider gathering more data rather than offering an intervention • Careful monitoring to assess effectiveness

theories (and systems/therapies) to exist simultaneously: for example, there are several 'well-supported' theories of motivation, confidence, concentration, etc. It is often very difficult to tell which theory is 'best' and so the *certaintist* practitioner must arbitrarily 'choose' a theory – perhaps either their personal favourite or one that seems to best accommodate the language or patterns the client provides.

A colleague of mine recently pointed out that there exists another version of 'certaintism', which he termed 'scientism'. In this approach, quantitative measurement is viewed as representing the ideal standard in science, and so any technique that generates a numerical value – even if it is not especially related to the thing it is intended to measure – is highly prized. Couple that with statistical analysis (usually culminating in a 'significant' *p*-value), and we have something science-like, but not actually science: *scientism*. This naïve and instrumental approach is argued to be a direct consequence of implicitly promoting certaintism, without ever stopping to reflect on what data really mean and how to interpret them. As such, scientism might represent quite a damaging (unintended) consequence of how certaintism and human–nature interact.

In practice, the certaintist tradition emphasizes using *reliable* assessment techniques in order to assess the athlete's needs, with typical examples including *validated* questionnaires, objective performance outcomes, neurophysiology (where available/practical) and established/repeatable interview 'protocols'. These needs are then fitted into a theoretical framework that should (if it is a good theory – See Chapter 6) point to a suitable intervention (or 'support strategy'). Practitioners adopting this approach should also ensure they use objective benchmarking and monitoring rather than relying on athletes' subjective perceptions of progress. *Certaintist* assumptions (and their cousin scientism) are widely adopted because validated measurement tools combined with well-supported theories give the practitioner a degree of assuredness and certainty. However, as noted above, many aspects of an athlete's psychology are inherently personal, complex, unique and difficult/impossible to reliably 'measure'. Strict *certaintism* would denote we should ignore those attributes and only focus on the objective/measurable, which may be both inappropriate and very costly if something that the client deems important is overlooked. However, in a business sense, practitioners (who are often competing for the clients that literally pay their wages) must 'sell' their own approach, track record and results – and the *certaintist* approach lends itself well to this practical reality. It is much easier to sell certainty to a client than it is to try and persuade them that wanting certainty (i.e., guaranteed results) might be inappropriate. This observation helps explain the prevalence and influence of the *certaintist* (positivist/empiricist) philosophy in the 'scientist practitioner' model of psychological practice (Corrie & Callahan, 2000; Roth & Fonagy, 1996 – discussed below).

3.4.2   Construalism

Translation

Psychology is 'soft science' (aka: interpretivism, constructivism).

Characterization

'You can't measure something as unique as a person's psychology when their personality, social context and world view are all completely unique. Build a theory unique to your client and base decisions on that. To do this, try to understand your client's unique experiences of the world as sympathetically as possible'. See Table 3.1.

Based on the writings of

Descartes (1954, 1970); Leibniz (1969); Weber (1949, 1962); Wittgenstein (1958 – i.e., post 'tratactus') – and many others.

Review

This tradition rejects the notion that: (a) anything about someone's psychology (intra or interpersonal) can be measured in a reliable or valid way; and (b) that such observations can be used to generate laws/theories that are applicable to all humans/athletes. Explicitly developed as a reaction against *certaintism* (cf. van Deurzen-Smith, 1990), there is a long history of *construalism* in psychology, beginning with Rogers (1961) and Maslow (1968). In *construalism*, psychological 'reality' is constructed by individuals and groups, as a function of their unique attributes and life experiences. A sport psychologist adopting *construalism* should seek to understand, as thoroughly and deeply as possible, the client's story and experiences: effectively building a unique and personal 'story' or 'theory' for that athlete. This task is performed with the primary emphasis being to help the athlete articulate and better understand their own situation (see Table 3.1). As such, one key difference between *certaintist* and *construalist* practitioners is the degree to which they use existing, accepted theories (i.e., from the literature). Strict *certaintism* would necessitate that the psychologist use scientific theory to frame the client's symptoms/needs *before* making a diagnosis and recommending interventions. In contrast, strict *construalism* would reject this approach, instead requiring the practitioner and client to work together in describing, organizing and analysing the client's experiences and interpretations of their world. In doing so, *construalist* theory would argue, the 'working alliance' of practitioner and client should either realize/discover appropriate solutions or reinterpret their reality in a way that solves the client's difficulty.

Thinking critically, however, how sensible is it to reject/ignore the theories generated by many years of scientific study? And in the 'results business' of sport, surely one needs to be able to objectively demonstrate measurable 'results' (noted above). As such, the *construalist* approach might deprive the practitioner of reliable needs analysis techniques, theoretical mechanisms and bodies of evidence (arguing that they are inappropriate/ineffective). Instead *construalism* relies on the psychologist being able to: (a) develop warm and caring relationships; (b) show genuine interest and care; (c) ask insightful (i.e., progressive but not leading) questions; and (d) have sufficient time to capture the client's full story. Thus, another criticism is that practitioners rarely have time to complete such a process in sporting contexts.

3.4.3   Pragmatism

Translation

Less thinking more doing (aka: instrumentalism, functionalism).

Characterization

'It doesn't matter what sort of reality you believe in, just do what works. Do not sit and analyse, get involved and benefit from trial and error. If it delivers results, that is the correct path'. See Table 3.1.

Based on the writings of

Dewey (1916, 1929; Dewey & Bentley, 1949); Kuhn (1962 – *normal science*); Peirce (1881, 1885) – and many others.

Review

The above characterization may initially sound like a parody or a 'straw man': set up only to be knocked down. However, authors such as those noted above have written very eloquently in attempting to extend 'construalism' into a new and novel ontology. Applying this ontology to the practice of psychology, the practitioner and the client form an interactive system, consisting of their different life experiences, assumptions, knowledge and attitudes. In such a world, idle theorizing is relatively useless, and established explanatory theories are irrelevant. The best (only) way to discover such a world, and/or make a difference to it, is to abandon theorizing and start interacting – that is, do something (see Table 3.1). *Pragmatism* argues that the psychologist (or researcher), once engaged, is too involved to be at all accurate or unbiased regarding observations and explanations. Instead, *pragmatism* emphasizes action: find what works either by trial and error, blind luck, professional judgement (Martindale & Collins, 2012) or similar. Crucially, if one accepts these arguments, then one's assumptions about reality are irrelevant, because 'truth' or reality is limited to the highly specific context of this unique practitioner–client pairing. Arguably, the *pragmatic* philosophy is apparent in psychological skills training (PST) approaches, if the teaching of skills and interventions is emphasized in an atheoretical manner – 'just do it, no need to ask why'.

Assessing *pragmatism's* implications for practice style is more difficult, because what 'works' might display observable attributes symptomatic of both certaintism and/or construalism. However, a *pragmatist* practitioner might be characterized as always *doing something,* with very little emphasis on theory or research evidence. As such, *pragmatism* may be much more reconcilable with the requirement for immediate/short-term impacts often required by the intense schedules of sport teams/athletes. Again, thinking critically, a *pragmatist* approach – *by definition* – discourages the practitioner from adopting any organizing constructs/principles or consistent systems in their approach. Such a practitioner could outwardly appear to be

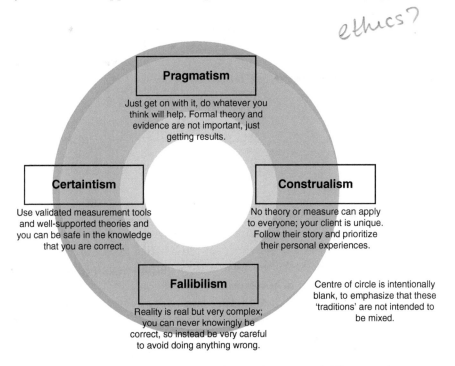

Figure 3.2 *A diagram to illustrate the similarities and differences between philosophical traditions in relation to psychology. Certaintism and construalism differ fundamentally in relation to their ontologies (fixed and generalizable versus totally unique and un-generalizable, respectively). In contrast, pragmatism and fallibilism differ in their epistemologies ('you know what you're doing, get on with it' versus 'we can never know what we're doing, be careful', respectively).*

disorganized or charlatanic, and an absence of theory/theorizing may also reduce the ability of practitioners to inform applied research (thus damaging the research–practice nexus wherein, in principal, researchers should be solving problems that actually need solving in the real world). Likewise, with no requirement to theorize or understand underlying mechanisms, if an intervention that appeared to work suddenly failed then the practitioner would be left with very little reliable knowledge of what went wrong or what to do about it.

3.4.4 Fallibilism

Translation

Primum non nocere (first do no harm). Be very careful because an athlete's psychology is complicated (aka: critical realism, critical rationalism).

Characterization

'Some aspects of psychology are measurable, some are not and these different phenomena interact in complex ways. Critically evaluate all the evidence, theories and interventions you use, because there is never any guarantee that they are right'. See Table 3.1.

Based on the writings of

Bhaskar (1975, 1979, 1989); Lakatos (1970); Kuhn (1962 – *extraordinary science*); Popper (1959, 1969, 1972).

Review

Whilst *certaintism* is based largely on confirming and supporting ideas about a true and objective psychological reality, both *construalism* and *pragmatism* reject that approach. In contrast, the tradition labelled *fallibilism* argues that while an objective truth may exist, it is too complex for us to ever assuredly reach a true/accurate understanding of it (i.e., correct theories, accurate measurements). Instead we should seek to avoid or reduce errors and, in terms of practice style, we must always be very careful because our theories and measurement techniques are flawed. So where *certaintism* emphasizes trying to be 'right', *fallibilism* emphasizes trying to be less and less wrong (as researchers), or wrong in a non-harmful way (as practitioners). As such, *fallibilism* permits a practitioner to use techniques and theories from the literature, but with a highly critical and self-aware attitude (described in Table 3.1). *Fallibilism* does ascribe an important role to theory, but only if deployed (very) critically – such that competing theories of confidence or motivation, for example, should be critically compared to establish the best one (even if they are all viewed as ultimately flawed, one must be 'least bad').

In practice terms, this means using theories (and measurement tools) carefully and judiciously: only if clearly appropriate and even then, looking out for potential pitfalls. The benefits of this approach are that the client, the practitioner and the reputation of the profession should all, in principle, be protected (*primum non nocere*) by making more realistic promises, fewer mistakes and producing a more thorough (more robust/defensible) audit trail. However, as Keegan (2014) noted, *fallibilism* places a substantial burden on the practitioner to be self-aware, critical and eclectically trained (familiar with the pros and cons of different techniques and styles), as well as ethically aware. The time and effort involved in these processes may render the *fallibilist* approach too impractical and cumbersome to be deployed in the cut-and-thrust results business of sport. Further, for a new or trainee practitioner (already racked by self-doubt in many cases), such considerations may be impractical.

As with all the assumption sets in this chapter, there is not a 'correct' or 'ideal' option to choose, and these four highly simplified 'traditions' only scratch the surface of the vast and highly nuanced literature on philosophy of science. However, knowing one's assumptions and being able to declare them can substantially strengthen one's practice-by stimulating consistency between assumptions, analysis techniques, conceptualization of needs and the way interventions are implemented. It must be emphasized that these four 'traditions' are not intended to be something one can 'mix and match' – especially not with an individual client. However, as discussed in Chapter 4, it may be possible to identify a client's own assumptions regarding their 'psychological reality' and match the way one practices to those, which could hold the potential to be an extremely powerful model of practice.

3.5   The scientist–practitioner model and sport psychology

Following its foundation at the Boulder Conference in 1949 (Benjamin & Baker, 2000; Raimy, 1950), the scientist–practitioner (SP) model has gained prominence in many other areas of psychology, and is currently receiving increased attention in sport and exercise psychology, following Weinberg's (1989) original paper. For example, consecutive conferences of the Association for Applied Sport Psychology (AASP) have emphasized a requirement for papers to support/facilitate an SP perspective, requiring: '... clarification of the integration and reciprocal relationships among theory, research and interventions/practice' (AASP Conference Speaker Guidelines, 2013).

In addition, as discussed in Chapter 2, the increased formal regulation of the sport psychology profession has meant that practitioners are increasingly held accountable for their practice, and there is an increasing demand for the integration of scientific principles into the practice of psychology (Chwalisz, 2003; Hayes, Strosahl, & Wilson, 1999). Consequently, science (and the deployment of the SP model) is of immediate relevance to practitioners – who may frequently be asked to either promote/sell or defend their processes and the quality of their decision-making (Acierno, Hersen, & Van Hasselt, 1995).

Whilst references to the SP model are relatively sparse in the formal sport psychology literature (Weinberg, 1989, p. 191 – being a notable exception), the concept itself is most succinctly explained by Shapiro (2002, p. 234), and adapted here for sport psychology, to include: (a) delivering psychological assessment/testing and psychological intervention procedures in accordance with scientifically based protocols; (b) accessing and integrating scientific findings to inform practice decisions; (c) framing and testing hypotheses that inform practice decisions; (d) building and maintaining effective teamwork with other relevant professionals that support the delivery of SP contributions (e.g., coaches, trainers, physiotherapists, other sport scientists, team managers, etc.); (e) providing research-based training and support to other relevant professionals in the delivery of sport psychology (examples as per (d)); and (f) contributing to practice-based research and development to improve the quality and effectiveness of sport psychology practice, that is, researching one's own practice and sharing the findings. Notably, those who are well versed in the philosophy of science will already have noticed that criteria a–c contain a number of assumptions about the nature of how science should be conducted, and this observation arguably captures the conflict at the heart of the SP model: a conflict which has previously been argued to have *undermined the proper implantation of the SP model* – its 'fatal flaw' (Albee, 2000, p. 247). Authors such as Eysenck (1949) and Shapiro (1955) argued that the SP model should only reflect positivist (certaintist) assumptions. However, many others have argued *both* that a positivist/certaintist philosophy underpins the SP model *and* that this is inappropriate: deepening the divide between researchers and practitioners, and suppressing other highly relevant, legitimate and useful philosophical stances (Breen & Darlston-Jones, 2008; Corrie & Callahan, 2000; Goedeke, 2007; Kanfer, 1990; O'Gorman, 2001; Page, 1996).

The primary goal of the SP model is to equip psychology practitioners with skills to apply basic scientific principles (APA Committee on Training in Clinical Psychology, 1947); basing professional activities on scientific foundations. The model aims to produce psychologists that are able to both provide successful services, and capable of contributing to the research literature during their professional career (Belar & Perry, 1992; Drabick & Goldfried, 2000; Milne & Paxton, 1998; Stoner & Green, 1992). The SP model was conceived to integrate science and practice, such that 'each must continually inform the other' (Belar & Perry, 1992, p. 72). However, so long as sport psychologists equate the SP model and 'being scientific' with ideas of certaintism (as described above), then there may remain significant resistance to the adoption of the SP model in sport psychology. Practitioners adopting different philosophical paradigms will simply reject the SP model, even if it means being thought of as 'unscientific' (Albee, 2000; Belar, 2000; Chwalisz, 2003; Drabick & Goldfried, 2000; Gaudiano & Statler, 2001; Stoltenberg et al., 2000; Stricker, 1997, 2000). The argument in this chapter is that each of the four 'traditions' presented in this chapter are, in fact, all legitimate ways of doing science and should be considered compatible with the SP model. As noted, however, an incomplete understanding of one's approach, or attempts to mix and match these carefully delineated traditions, begins to look more like pseudo-science or, on a bad day, not science at all.

3.6   Philosophy of practice – The practitioner's strategy and tactics

At this point in the chapter, we know what we are trying to achieve, and we know the lay of the land regarding what we are measuring/changing, but there remains the question of *how* to achieve this. To a large extent, the answers one adopts to the previous two issues will determine where one falls when it comes to 'philosophy of practice'. The literature describes a range of theoretical perspectives/philosophies, including: cognitive–behavioural therapy (CBT), a sophist approach, humanistic perspectives, a counselling approach, a Socratic approach, a task-oriented approach, a relationship-oriented approach, a psychodynamic approach or a gestalt theory approach (among others). As detailed earlier, Keegan (2010) set out to offer trainee sport psychologists a 'foothold' in this literature, by classifying these different philosophies into a single continuum, with paternalistic assumptions at one end and collegial/counselling assumptions at the other.

An extreme *practitioner-led* approach would involve the psychologist deciding what topics to cover, what questions to ask and how to define and measure success. As the 'expert' the practitioner would also be required to draw from existing theory and research in order to decide (unilaterally) which intervention(s) to prescribe and how. Reliable and objective measures of pre- and post-intervention levels would be prioritized over subjective judgements. In contrast, an extreme *client-led* approach would seek to 'follow' the client through their unique story and experiences, never leading and always asking open, non-directive questions. There may be no need to refer to known theories of confidence or motivation, etc., as their client's own beliefs take priority. The client would define the criteria for success, and the client would judge success and progress her/himself, with no requirement to use objective/valid measurement tools (Table 3.2).

Table 3.2 *A heuristic model of practice styles in sport psychology. The two central columns represent the broad differences between a 'practitioner-led' approach and a 'client-led' approach. Note that these are two ends of a proposed continuum and many practitioners will demonstrate characteristics from both columns, and eclectic practitioners may voluntarily choose to adopt different 'styles' depending on their client's needs, or the stage reached in the service delivery process.*

	Practitioner-led	Client-led
Compatible consulting philosophies	CBT, cognitive, behavioural, sophist and paternalistic	Humanistic, counselling and Socratic
Characterizing assumptions (informally worded)	• Practitioner knows best • Diagnose and prescribe • Practitioner drives questioning/agenda • Find and then solve a 'problem' • Practitioner determines intervention strategy	• Client knows best or soon will, with a little help • Collaborative exploration • Agenda/questions are set by client and their needs • There may not be a 'problem' per se • Ideally, client arrives at their own 'intervention strategy', perhaps with input from practitioner where appropriate
Consultant's role	• Educator/instructor • Assessor/analyst	• Facilitator/catalyst • Collegial, but may challenge or play 'devil's advocate'
Areas/aims of service (and approximate priority)	• Performance enhancement • Talent identification/development • Education	• Athlete welfare • Personal growth/development • Performance enhancement
Anticipated end-products	• Improvements in performance • Providing optimal training/competitive environments • Increased awareness of psychological factors in sporting performance (e.g., in athletes, coaches, etc.) • Possession of, and ability to use, appropriate mental skills. • Modifying thought patterns	• Client independence (e.g., 'you become your own psychologist') • Increased self-awareness and ability to 'navigate' through challenging experiences/situations

Who is the client?	Client may be: • the athlete him/herself • the coach, the parents • the athlete's employer/team • the athlete's governing body	In principle, every effort would be made to treat the athlete as the client and to represent their needs/desires, not those of other parties.
How are desired changes implemented?	• Prescription/recommendation of tasks in order to develop specific skills • Education as to the nature and utility of particular mental skills or ideas/concepts	• Client is assisted in trying to understand their own experiences and responses to challenging situations – either through probing open questioning, or perhaps the keeping of a diary • If psychological techniques are deployed, the client would drive the process – finding their own ways of learning and applying the technique, and of evaluating its effectiveness
Importance of scientific theory	Theory informs practice and advice, much more so than the client's own interpretation/understanding.	Client's own experiences are given primacy. Even where the practitioner recognizes associations with a particular theory, this is generally prevented from guiding/influencing the course of the consultancy process.
Importance of consultant–client relationship	Whilst a good (warm/friendly) relationship is not frowned upon, it is not thought of as vital in determining the success of the process.	A warm, trusting relationship with good rapport is believed to be vital in producing successful outcomes.
Approach to using psychometric testing	Psychometric tests are generally viewed as useful diagnostic tools, permitting a comparison to norms or between athletes or from pre- to post-intervention.	Psychometric tests are generally viewed as unhelpful and impersonal; as being unable to fully represent the client's worldview and experiences (which are inherently unique).

Source: Keegan, R. J. (2010). Teaching consulting philosophies to Neophyte Sport Psychologists: Does it help, and how can we do it?, Journal of Sport Psychology in Action, 1, 42–52. Adapted with kind permission from Taylor and Francis Ltd. www.tandfonline.com.

These 'styles' link with the other assumption sets discussed in this chapter. The certaintist tradition is likely to build confidence and offer guarantees, meaning that performance enhancement may well become the main aim of service delivery (whereas others may not feel brave enough to offer such a juicy prize). It may also lead the practitioner to feel like an 'expert' who can lead the session by directing questions (and topics), choosing analysis/ intervention techniques and deciding on realistic outcomes/goals for the sessions. In order to achieve this certainty, reliable and objective measures should be used aligned to well-supported theories and robust 'knowledge'. Hence, this set (performance enhancement and education → 'certaintism' → practitioner-led style) forms a fairly consistent pattern that might typically be displayed by a sport psychologist. In contrast, the 'construalist' tradition

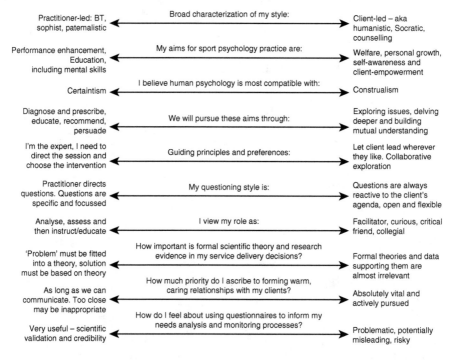

Figure 3.3   *A classification system for consulting philosophies in sport psychology (based on Keegan, 2010). Note that these are two ends of a proposed continuum and practitioners may display characteristics from either end, or mid-points. The main argument of this chapter is that practitioners should try to demonstrate a consistent approach with each client, but that it may be beneficial (as one develops) to adopt different 'styles' depending on the client's needs/preferences – i.e., mainly aligned dots/ crosses would be good, but widely differing or 'unsure' would be risky.* **You can use this classification system when conducting observations or following your own session to evaluate which consulting style is on display.**

would assume the client's experiences are unique and not subject to comparison with universal theories, or questionnaire measurements developed by averaging out the responses of thousands of participants. This approach may not feel confident offering assurances of performance enhancement, but may instead seek to enhance psychological well-being and offer emotional support through challenging transitions/injuries. In order to achieve this, a client-led, non-directive style, with open and responsive questions, seeking to build a mutual understanding of a situation (so that options for progress may become clearer), would be appropriate. In this case, a relatively consistent set is formed by assumptions of: well-being and support → 'construalism' → client-led style. The 'pragmatist' and 'fallibilist' approaches do not neatly align with the other assumptions described here to form a set – 'pragmatism', in its purest form, may not necessarily consider such things, whereas 'fallibilism' would not rule out any approach, but would likely pause to consider the pros, cons, implications and appropriacy of each assumption being made.

3.7   Summary and conclusions

Overall, this chapter might not have been the easiest reading in places – but we were trying to simplify some very complex literature to create an 'entry point' for sport psychologists from all levels to engage with issues of assumptions and philosophy. In many ways, this brief chapter is substantially more accessible than the likes of Heidegger and Husserl – and reading even a sufficient sample of philosophical writings took me a substantial portion of my PhD (Which also over-ran!). In a perfect world, practitioners will return to this chapter several times, and perhaps make use of the tables and templates to evaluate their own practice (or a colleague's!). It is important, however, to critically examine any argument that considering philosophy is 'too complicated'. Driving a car is a complicated skill which, through practice, becomes effortless. In the same way, navigating philosophical assumptions should be practised frequently and deliberately until it becomes second nature. Effortless excellence earned through practice, rather than effortless naivety.

Fundamentally, the assumptions outlined in this chapter are too important to overlook, as they inform and contextualize every single decision you make as a sport psychologist – whether you admit it or not. And given that everything you do as a psychologist reflects underlying assumptions, it seems best to uncover, examine and perfect these assumptions to make sure they work in your favour (and your client's).

It is ok for assumptions to change as we develop, this may even be an inevitable aspect of learning the job (Tod & Bond, 2010). Likewise, it is ok to adopt different assumptions with different clients, if their needs differ in such a way as to justify that. However, adopting an internally inconsistent philosophy with your clients is likely to generate any number of awkward moments, where claims mismatch evidence, or the client's reasonable expectations are overridden and ignored. In this respect, there is arguably a danger when sport psychologists adopt an 'eclectic' philosophy, or claim to be 'mixing' client- and practitioner-led assumptions, as each could easily be legitimizing an 'anything goes' approach: 'Wait, you started off all about me, but now you're trying to boss me around. What gives?', 'Ah, I am being eclectic'. In my experience to date, the strength of being an eclectic practitioner is that you are able to serve a wider range of clients successfully, without having to enforce a preferred style onto the process (perhaps against the client's wishes). But offering an inconsistent and variable service to a single client seems to open up a variety of risks and unknowns that a diligent sport psychologist should probably seek to avoid. Worse still, if you are working as a sport psychologist without knowing your own philosophical assumptions, and without any knowledge of what they might look like, you really are 'flying blind' – and exposed to all sorts of risks and unknown conflicts. On reflection, the early part of one's career may even be characterized by getting into, and somehow out of, these tricky moments. Imagine however, having the knowledge and tools to reflect more effectively, learn faster and make fewer mistakes … That was a key aim of this chapter.

With the underpinning foundations of ethics and philosophy explained, we can move on to consider the service delivery process itself, beginning with the moment the client makes first contact: the intake. Each subsequent chapter will signpost where ethical and philosophical considerations inform each stage of the process, through intake, needs analysis, case formulation, choosing and then planning interventions and monitoring progress. It is hoped that by starting the book with ethics and philosophy, the very way you read and understand the following sections will be enhanced. More meaningful, more useful and more enjoyable.

3.8 Ella's story: Part 3 – Beginning supervised practice

As she neared the end of her postgraduate training course, Ella was advised to find a supervisor and so she could begin supervised practice. She found someone willing to train her, but unable to supply clients. Instead, Ella must market/sell her own services, generate clients, work with them and learn the job in this manner. Her regulatory body requires her to accrue over 700 hours of face-to-face contact over the next 2 years, not including preparation and record keeping. In addition, by the end of this process she will need to be able to demonstrate competence across a range of criteria – both in documented evidence and a face-to-face verbal examination.

1. How can Ella describe her service to new clients? What are the options she can focus on regarding: (i) aims; (ii) ontology; and (iii) style. How would you describe your own approach against these three criteria?
2. Ella notices that some clients appear to 'get it' and 'buy in' almost immediately, and these clients benefit more from her service. She is worried by a number of clients who just want to talk and do not complete their homework tasks, or mental training. These clients often simply stop seeing her, and do not seem to benefit from the support. One client, Bonnie, does not adhere to her mental skills training or diaries, but does return. Bonnie is a highly talented Judo player, recovering from spinal surgery following repeated stress fractures. She reports that thinking positively, or 'differently', doesn't feel right, and is not interested in hearing about the evidence to support Ella's recommendations. Bonnie keeps returning to the raw emotions, and fears she holds that she may never return to elite competition. Ella realizes this is a key opportunity to modify her approach, but what is she changing from, and to? And why?
3. Over time, it becomes clear that Bonnie will not recover to a level where she can compete again. Ella does not know what to suggest, as she cannot find a sufficiently evidence-based technique for managing the situation. She notices, however, that Bonnie does not want a 'technique', and she keeps coming back each week just to talk through her emotions. What appear to be the aims, ontology and style that would best suit Bonnie?
4. After working with Bonnie over several months, Ella feels there is value in both the practitioner-led work for some clients and the client-led style that worked with Bonnie. However, Ella is worried that she does not know how to tell what a client wants/needs, and it may even be too late by the time she works it out. What advice would you give Ella to help manage this issue? Should she stick to one style or find ways of adapting to each client? If she adapts, how might she be able to know what style to adopt?

3.9   Review and reflect

1. Why does philosophy matter – in terms of having clear aims, sound ontology/epistemology and a clear style? How do these considerations impact on the practice of a sport psychologist?
2. How would you respond to the claim that philosophical considerations do not matter, and we should just 'get on with the job'?

3. What combination of aims, ontology/epistemology and practice style do you naturally gravitate towards, and why?
4. What might be the pros and cons of being able to pursue different aims, using different assumptions, adopting different styles?
5. Can you think of an example from your own experience where considering 'philosophical assumptions' might help explain the events you observed?

The Intake Process: Establishing a Relationship, Aims, Expectations and Boundaries

4

4.1 Introduction and overview

Continuing the theme of identifying and then critically examining key tasks that every sport psychologist undeniably performs, we have the *intake* process. Technically, without performing some type of 'intake', the sport psychologist could not have any clients and would be reduced to simply writing for an unknown audience (i.e., blogs, books, etc.) or perhaps just theorizing in private. Intake really is an unavoidable, and therefore very important, component of the sport psychology process. In order to establish a helping relationship with a client (individual or team), there must be a phase in which a relationship is formed and formal/informal rules are agreed.

As such, in this intake phase, expectations are established (or managed), goals and aims are expressed and a decision is made as to whether the relationship should proceed – and both the sport psychologist and the client participate in these decisions. For example, either the client or the psychologist could decide not to proceed, and both parties contribute to the establishment of goals and expectations. It is also worth remembering that the solutions to many of the ethical dilemmas described in Chapter 2 lie in establishing or agreeing a principle *'from the outset of the relationship'*. The intake process is, by definition, the outset of the relationship, and so this is where important tasks are performed that cannot be ignored or assumed.

There is more to the intake process than simply 'getting the client in the door' – literally or proverbially. There are specific goals for the intake process which, ideally, precede and inform the subsequent needs analysis. It is important to note, therefore, that in the model being used in this book, the intake and the needs analysis are separate, or at least separable, processes. Intake is where the relationship is formed, expectations and ethics are agreed, the client history/context is established and a decision is made

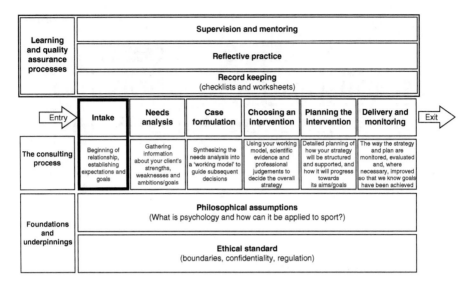

Figure 4.1   *The position of the intake process at the beginning of the consulting process, closely related to needs analysis, as well as being highly dependent upon philosophical assumptions and ethical considerations.*

about whether, and how, to proceed. Subsequently, needs analysis is where various techniques are used to assess, measure or understand the client's current psychological skills and needs. Of course, there are aspects of needs analysis that may inform the intake, and needs analysis tends to occur near the beginning of the process, but that does not make these two important processes functionally equivalent. This chapter aims to illustrate the key elements of the intake process, and critically evaluate the implications of different choices/approaches (including attempting to skip over it or rush it). By establishing the relevance and importance of the intake process, its position in the sport psychology service delivery model is clearly illustrated. Likewise, the reader (i.e., the practitioner) will be able to make informed decisions about how to conduct their intakes in future such that they will be both more effective, optimized to the client and context, and equally important, able to write coherently about this stage of their work for case studies, assessments and record keeping.

4.2   The importance of the intake process in sport psychology

Fundamentally, if we define the intake as the beginning of the relationship, then no intake means no clients. But more pragmatically, a poor or incomplete intake opens up wide range of risks and threats that really cannot be tolerated by any serious sport psychologist. Fail to notice a clinical disorder and recommend actions that exacerbate it: trouble. Fail to agree key issues around confidentiality or consent and then get into a conflict with the client: trouble. Fail to establish open and effective channels of communication: trouble. Fail to understand the client's expectations, goals or reasons for seeking help: serious trouble. As in, 'why are you doing this job?' trouble. All of these issues can be avoided with a good intake process, notwithstanding the fact that a good intake process can (and sometimes should) lead to a referral (to a more appropriate individual), or even the decision not to continue. So for example, if you do notice a clear clinical issue, that is often good reason to refer to a clinical psychologist. And if it was clear that your client wanted a style/brand of psychology that you simply do not offer – either through lack of training/experience or a fundamental difference of opinion – then it would be wrong to accept this client. A client-led/counselling psychologist (as described in Chapter 3) would not be well advised to accept a client seeking instant and 'guaranteed' results, but likewise a strongly practitioner-led psychologist would frustrate a client seeking to gain personal insight and autonomy. But the intake is possibly the only/last opportunity to decline the work and say 'I am not the right person to help'. Be it a meeting, phone calls or emails – the initial intake is the only chance to manage which clients you take on, and thereby manage one's 'track record' or 'score card' of satisfied versus dissatisfied clients.

What sort of sport psychologist would actually reject a client? Well, perhaps one who wants to actually help clients and not simply 'take their money' – unthinkable in some spheres of sport psychology, but in the long term discretion really can be the better part of valour. With the gift of hindsight I can think of several clients I should never have taken on at that stage of my development. A trail of dissatisfied or failed clients can be poisonous to a sport psychologist's career (and the wider profession), and even undermine one's effectiveness if current clients cross path with 'failed' clients. Likewise, the whole profession can suffer if sport psychologists continually attempt to support athletes using inappropriate assumptions, strategies or goals because, realistically, people talk. In contrast, the best referrals you will ever receive will be from happy clients telling their friends how good you are: new clients will arrive 'primed' and ready to accept almost anything you say!

If these arguments are accepted, and experience will probably be the main arbiter as there are very few published articles on this, then we need to ask what a good intake process delivers. Establishing the relationship: yes. Establishing ethical principles/standards: yes. Understanding the client's goals/expectations: absolutely. Introducing yourself and your styles/preferences: if possible, yes. Recording a solid client history: well that sounds very responsible, so yes. Agreeing fees? Seems sensible. Making a good first impression: of course. One of my mentors once admitted to giving very serious thought to what to wear with each new client group: academics or managers might prefer a suit, some sports might require you to wear the right sporting apparel, yet other situations might require the psychologist to clearly distinguish her/himself from the team's management by wearing 'neutral' clothes. Such considerations might seem superfluous, but one of the key determinants of success in psychology is the relationship itself (Assay & Lambert, 1999; Wampold, 2001), and first impressions are formed extremely fast (Bernieri & Petty, 2011; Etcoff, Stock, Haley, Vickery, & House, 2011; Guadagno & Cialdini, 2007; Naumann et al., 2009; Raki, Steffens, & Mummendey, 2011; Uleman, Saribay, & Gonzalez, 2008). Further still, should you offer your client a drink when they arrive? Most athletes carry their own drinks everywhere now. How should you arrange the seats? Facing each other square-on or perhaps a slightly oblique angle? Or perhaps around a table to create a shared workspace? And if you get it wrong in the first session, how easily could you switch things in the next session, once expectations are established? Each of these decisions affects the nature of the relationship, and the implicit assumptions of the interaction. It follows that these apparently meaningless decisions therefore influence the amount and quality of the information shared, the quality of the resulting decisions, the client's adherence to any changes or interventions and even the way the client appraises the effectiveness of the relationship. Suddenly the intake process looks to be an extremely important consideration in determining one's effectiveness, ethical practice and reputation. Importantly, and frustratingly for some readers, this chapter will not offer a 'correct' interpretation of how to conduct the intake. Rather we will review the key tasks of the intake, the options for approaching them and the implications of the choices you make. Ultimately, the sport psychologist will metaphorically live or die by these decisions, and so the individual practitioner needs to be comfortable with each and every one of them.

4.3   Core considerations

Now that we have established the importance of the intake process, each of the core outcomes it achieves (or should achieve) can be illustrated, complete with the likely options and their consequences. At a minimum, the intake process should achieve the following five outcomes: (1) establish the relationship or working alliance; (2) establish/agree ethical boundaries, expectations and fees; (3) clarify the psychologist's approach and check that this fits with the client's needs; (4) generate a comprehensive client history, including reasons for seeking help and desired outcomes; and (5) appraise the psychologist's own suitability for working with that client (individual or team/group). Obviously, this may take more than one session and it is absolutely possible to return to these assumptions and review them if necessary. However, only once these basic considerations have been achieved can the substantive tasks of assessing the client's needs and attempting to actually help the client be competently and assuredly attempted. As is the case throughout this book, it is worth pausing to consider: 'Do I currently do all these things in my intake? And do I do them deliberately, to the highest possible standard?' In team and organizational settings, there is the additional consideration of assessing whether you are able to fit in and provide effective support. This may involve the application of 'contextual intelligence' (Sternberg, 1985, 1997), wherein one either *adapts* oneself to the environment, *shapes* the environment to suit oneself or simply *selects* optimal environments in the first place. We will pause to consider this aspect of the intake process as well. The following sections will address each of these core tasks in turn.

Before considering the following task, the following quote from Andersen (2000, p. 3) may be illustrative: "By clinical, and most counselling psychology standards, the initiation of helping relationships in sport psychology, and the delivery of service is admittedly loose. And so it should be... Seeing, meeting and engaging athletes and coaches in such a wide variety of situations... actually means that we might have to pay even greater attention to our roles and our boundaries than a psychologist working in a managed health-care clinic from 9-to-5 would". How many different channels can you think of through which an athlete can first approach the sport psychologist, and in how many different settings? There is no clear receptionist, or private office. Perhaps attempt to think of some really unusual situations, because the chances are they have happened already, many times over.

Making contact

Consider the different ways a sport psychology client can first make contact with a sport psychologist.

Nature of first contact

- Email. Phone. Website enquiry. Face-to-face. Online video call.
- Chance meeting in the corridor, clubroom or treatment room
- At pitch-side (or track-side or poolside) or in training
- Formal appointment made in office hours, through a secretary
- In a lift/elevator, on a team bus
- At a team dinner/breakfast, in front of others
- Totally away from sport (e.g., "Oh you're a sport psych, I need to talk to you!")

(continued)

Making contact (*continued*)

Reasons for seeking help

- Independent decision/independent research (e.g., "I found you on the internet")
- Recommended by a friend
- Compulsory appointment (e.g., "Everyone has to meet the psych at the start of the season")
- Referral – from coach or physiotherapist (and is the athlete happy with this?)
- Referral from a parent (and what is the parent's role, does the parent have a vested interest?)
- Actively recruited by practitioner ("I noticed you struggled to cope with that mistake, would you like to talk?")
- Following on from group workshops (e.g., "That session really made me think, can I book an appointment?")

Questions for consideration

(1) How might these differences influence how you act? Or how the interaction proceeds?
(2) To what extent can you start to address the five main intake considerations (establishing the relationship, agreeing ethical boundaries, clarifying your approach/philosophy, taking a client history and assessing suitability), depending on the nature of the contact?
(3) If it is not possible to complete these tasks due to the nature of the first contact, when can you complete them? And when can/should you record all this information in your practice records?

4.3.1   Establishing the relationship (or working alliance)

The quality of the relationship between the psychologist and their client has been consistently shown to be one of the most influential factors in determining successful outcomes (Bedi, Davis, & Arvay, 2005; Beutler, 2009; Beutler & Malik, 2002a, 2002b; Hill, 2001; Malik & Beutler, 2002; Norcross, 2011; Wampold, 2001). That's over and above practice style, years of experience, scientific evidence for interventions, fame/celebrity, etc. Forming a close, collaborative and trusting relationship is the biggest predictor of whether or not the client will deem your support 'effective'.

Forming a good relationship is difficult to 'fake'. If you really don't like someone, or they really don't like you, it is difficult to put on a brave face on and forge. However, if we examine the factors that tend to generate trusting, collaborative and productive relationships, three key factors tend to emerge: warmth, empathy and unconditional positive regard (cf. Katz & Hemmings, 2009). These factors are not independent, but highly interdependent. *Warmth* might be defined as a caring and interesting attitude towards the client, which involves genuinely wanting to help and demonstrating a non-judgemental attitude. *Empathy* represents the skill of following, grasping and understanding as fully as possible the client's subjective experience from his/her point of view. Also within empathy, the psychologist must be able to demonstrate that they are experientially alongside the client: sensitively striving to understand what s/he is feeling or trying to articulate. This is different from simply offering sympathy (Watson, 2002). Finally, *unconditional positive regard* revolves around acceptance of the client without reservation, and is characterized by a consistently non-judgemental attitude which allows the client to relax, trust and disclose. This can be difficult when one disagrees with a client's actions or attitudes, and so Feltham and Dryden (1993) helpfully denote that it should involve acceptance of the person, but not necessarily all the persons' behaviour. Each of these attributes can be deliberately worked on and developed by the sport psychologist. They are learnable but notably only a privileged few are simply born with these relationship skills (they may even be developed in response to certain family situations, such as having many siblings).

The challenge for the sport psychologist is establishing these conditions/ attitudes as early as possible, in order to facilitate a strong working alliance. But how can this be achieved on a team bus, or in a short break between events at a competition? By way of reassurance, there may not be a correct answer, but the practitioner must actively seek to manage each intake situation such that the relationship is given the best start in life. The advice of Lukas (1993) is helpful in this respect: The practitioner's job is to convey to the client that they will be *listened to*, and that the psychologist her/himself is *working to understand*. Another useful rule of thumb, in order to avoid being seen as prying or too intense, is to avoid 'why' questions in the first meeting, sticking to 'who, what, when, where and how' (Lukas, 1993, p. 8). 'Why' questions are often quite difficult for the client to answer at the beginning, and can cause awkward moments when the relationship is still in its infancy. In the absence of clean-cut recommendations for how to form good relationships, the main solution becomes to learn from your experiences – through reflective practice. Individual practitioners will generate different solutions to this problem, such that a physically fit practitioner of the same age and gender as the client might find it easier to establish shared interests than would an older, physically inactive, suit-wearing practitioner. However, donning a tracksuit wouldn't help the older practitioner in this example, so what would?

Remembering the message throughout this book that every key step listed is one undertaken by a psychologist, whether they admit it or not, every helping relationship formed between a client and a sport psychologist goes through an intake process. During this intake, a relationship is formed and nurtured, and all subsequent communications are transmitted (and interpreted) through that relationship. It may happen differently each time – perhaps try to recall a client with who you had 'instant chemistry' versus one where you had to work hard to win their trust – but failing to establish a relationship means, by definition, failing to help the athlete. Likewise, evidence shows that the stronger/better the relationship (in the client's eyes), the better the likelihood of positive outcomes. So imagine the risks, and the sheer negligence one could be accused of, if a sport psychologist failed to actively manage this vital aspect of their role. Unlike the forming of friendships, to be a successful sport psychologist, one cannot work to the assumption that relationships are uncontrollable or natural, and that 'I'll get on with some people but not others'. You are doing it all the time anyway, so you have to be on top of it. Reflect a lot, in the moment and between sessions, alone and with supervisors, about how you tend to act in these situations, and how it affects the relationship. Likewise, identify your 'blind spots' – ranging from a lack of eye contact to a bright distracting wrist band – and deliberately work on them in order to support your relationship forming. A recent example is (was) my own tendency to dismiss certain types of alternative medicines: scientifically sound perhaps, but not a great way of making a good impression on the athlete who 'swears by it' …! Just as we would implore our clients to 'control the controllables', so must we become students of our own interactions and relationships. If it helps, you can (should) switch off this tendency when you're not being a psychologist …!

First questions

You would be amazed how much thought and effort goes into a psychologist's first question. Questions such as "How can I help you?" or "What brings you here to see me?" can emphasize the role of the psychologist too much, and immediately start to stamp some sort of control or authority on proceedings. In contrast, "What would you like to talk about?" or "What brings you here today?" are less likely to produce this feeling.

Then there is the difference between styles and philosophies (as discussed in Chapter 3). As Anderson (2000, p. 4) points out: 'the rational-emotive-trained therapist will be interested in stories primarily as a source of information about adaptive and maladaptive thinking processes...; client-centred therapists will listen... with an ear for detecting discrepancies between where the athletes are and where they would like to be... [whereas] behaviourists might listen to stories for what they say about athlete associations, classical or operant conditioning, and current contingencies of reinforcement'. Suffice to say: 'Where would you like to start this journey?' and 'Tell me about your relationship with your father' are two very different openings, sending clear signals about the practitioner's preferences/styles.

Another issue for sport psychologists is that we don't always get the chance to use our carefully refined, 'never-fail' opening. Imagine how you might respond to an athlete who grabs you in the corridor, seething about a bad refereeing decision, or an athlete slumped on a bench after a poor performance. None of the above would really cut it.

Like many of the key issues in sport psychology, most practitioners will trial a number of different versions, before perhaps choosing something fairly neutral to start out the conversation. Much more importantly, the psychologist should then listen carefully to the client's responses, and react in a manner consistent with one's own philosophy and preferred style – ideally reflecting in the moment as well as afterwards on how the interaction is going, and how to counter, or manage and slightly awkward moments (as they will happen!).

What openings do you currently use?

What impressions might your openings give the client, and is that what you intended?

How compatible is your opening with your overall philosophical approach (Chapter 3)?

How might you react if your 'opening' was nullified by an athlete who speaks to you at a crowded breakfast table, or as you are walking back from training together?

4.3.2   Establish ethical boundaries, expectations and fees

Chapter 2 argued that ethical considerations are both paid too little attention in applied practice (relative to their incredible importance), and that the best/only time we get to establish many ethical issues is 'at the outset of the relationship'. Establishing confidentiality has to be done before a coach or parent asks how it went, and a client should not be asked to give information without knowing it could be subpoenaed by a court. Getting informed consent, at least for data collection and storage, can only technically happen before data has been collected. The client must know what you can and can't realistically deliver from the outset. And technically, the client should know, from the outset, the conditions under which the relationship will be terminated (i.e., 'I am no longer helping you, you got this'). Given that the intake process is the only chance one gets to address these issues, it really ought to be done meticulously, and with a smile – *you're doing something right!* I remember feeling real reservations about 'undermining' the relationship forming process by talking about ethics in the first email, phone call, or meeting, but in reality, I have never met a client who reacted badly. As my supervisor correctly predicted, my experience has been that most see it as a sign of professionalism, and so it increases trust (the rest just want to get on with it, but they still need to know).

If a sport psychologist – working in a profession noted for the ethically challenging and frequently unpredictable situations it creates – failed to address ethical considerations during the intake then the consequences can be quite serious. Many of the 'worst case' scenarios presented in Chapter 2 can only be prevented by establishing the ground rules from the beginning. And if they were to become issues after that – it is already too late and an ethical breach has occurred. As already discussed, ethical breaches can incur penalties including fines, bans and the loss of your practice licence. So, why wouldn't a sport psychologist take the only *bona fide* opportunity s/he has to address ethical issues safely? A separate issue is how a psychologist might deal with ad hoc intakes in corridors, on buses and at mealtime. Realistic approaches might include an information sheet/card given to all athletes pre-season, and the careful management of such interactions (again, this won't feel 'natural' but it is responsible), such that once it becomes clear an athlete is seeking help, ethics are covered as soon as is pragmatically possible.

4.3.3   Establish and clarify the psychologist's approach/philosophy

Following from the discussions in Chapter 3, it is clear that a sport psychologist can choose to adopt a single philosophy or practice style, or attempt to be eclectic. However, it is vital to (re)emphasize that repeatedly switching styles when working with a client will probably lead to a disjointed and potentially dissatisfying experience for the client (Robinson, 2009; Strong & Claiborn, 1982; Van Audenhove & Vertommen, 2000; Vertommen & Van Audenhove, 2000). Perhaps the best opportunity that an 'eclectic' practitioner might have to switch styles is during the intake process, when expectations have not been fixed. In fact, it may be a very worthwhile strategy to be able to detect and then adopt the client's preferred (or rather, optimal) practice style. For example, the way the client talks about their situation and how it came about, the types of answers provided (and sought), their goals for the relationship/support and even non-verbal responses to some lines of questioning can all indicate a client's preferences, or expectations. However, this is arguably an extremely high-level skill: only available to sport psychologists capable of adopting multiple styles/assumptions, as well as inferring them in others. Experience and reflection must, by necessity, play a vital role in developing such a capacity.

Another way to develop the skill of always ensuring your assumptions and practice style match the expectations of the client is to simply ask them. Of course, most people are unfamiliar with the terminology around the philosophy of science and different 'ways of being' in a relationship, but that does not preclude a collaborative negotiation process (Van Audenhove & Vertommen, 2000). By attempting to identify, articulate and evaluate the client's expectations, the chances of simply 'missing the mark' are vastly reduced. The process may even help the client to understand how their own assumptions or world view have contributed to the current need for psychological support (Duncan, Miller, & Sparkes, 2004).

Alternatively, if a sport psychologist follows one style exclusively, then this should be very clear from the outset; perhaps it should even be on their business card! Certainly, during the intake process, the assumptions and implications of adopting one approach exclusively should be clearly conveyed to the client. For example, a 'pure' client-led (counselling) practitioner should probably make it clear that 'I'm not going to give you any answers; the answers have to come from you'. In contrast, a 'pure' practitioner-led approach (perhaps CBT) might benefit from clearly stating: 'In these sessions, I am the expert and you have sought my help. I will make a diagnosis and plan the intervention, and you will need to accept what I say for this to work' (or words to that effect).

In both the above cases ('detect and evaluate' versus 'announce/declare'), the option remains to simply not enter the relationship – for both parties. If a psychologist detects that the client's expectations are incompatible, unrealistic or unhealthy, s/he can choose not to become involved (and perhaps make a referral). If the client does not like what s/he hears from the psychologist, then the session/relationship can end there and then with no hard feelings. Perhaps the only reasonable excuse for not being able to manage this process effectively – aside from chance meetings in the corridor, within competitions or over meals – is if the psychologist is too new to accurately understand their philosophy yet (Although after Chapter 3, let's hope that is not the case!). For those neophyte practitioners, neither 'detect and evaluate' or 'announce/declare' would appear to be the ideal option, but during the early part of one's career, the psychologist should already be explaining very clearly: 'I am a trainee, I have a supervisor to oversee me, this may lead to occasional delays while I consult with my supervisor ... etc. Within that, there is still scope to try and identify preferred, or more versus less effective approaches.

Notably then, none of the first three options discussed were: 'ignore it and forge on'. The dangers of having unidentified differences in assumptions with the client, inappropriate assumptions relative to the client's needs or simply inconsistent and unpredictable assumptions were all explained in Chapter 3. As such, naivety – whether genuine or deliberate (i.e., 'no time, it's inconvenient, ignorance is bliss') – is just too risky. There are too many ways for the relationship to break down, and for the client to be 'let down', if the assumptions and strategies of the support are not agreed from the outset. Only a small amount of research has examined the idea that addressing assumptions is helpful (summarized in Van Audenhove & Vertommen, 2000). You can instead reflect on the logic of the above arguments and your own practice experiences and make an informed decision about whether and how you want to manage the process of negotiating/agreeing the approach to support. In my own practice: (a) it has never caused any harm; (b) it often puts the client's mind at rest; and, (c) as noted above, it often opens up avenues towards self-awareness and/or the reframing of problems that would not have been available if we had simply 'glossed over' it.

As a final note in this section, it should be possible to complete the same process with a team or group as a client – although perhaps not as straightforwardly. More people in the system may mean more different sets of assumptions, and more chance of 'irreconcilable differences' between factions. However, it may be possible to at least negotiate one's style/approach with the coaches and management in establishing expectations and boundaries (as most ethical guidelines specify that we should – see Chapter 2). For example, one could not only specify 'I won't be involved in team selection' (a fairly common request from sport psychologists), but also 'my approach is to encourage personal growth and self-awareness, not to give out magic bullets'. Anecdotally, I have heard excellent examples of this from psychologists such as Corinne Reid and Keith Henschen – and whenever I enter a team setting I try to do the same. My own reflection would be to make sure that this point has been heard *and understood*, as even after emphasizing it I have occasionally been surprised to find a coach or manager expecting me to step outside the agreed approach/expectations. Likewise, if you are very lucky (or organized) you could run a session or workshop (flip charts, board pens, sticky dots, etc.) where the team/squad are given the opportunity to specify the sorts of things they want from their sport psychologist. Reflecting on my own experience again, this process usually generates a pleasingly coherent and sophisticated 'job description', perhaps with a little 'management' along the way. Better still though, because the athletes themselves generated the ideas, there is much less likelihood of disagreement or 'amnesia' further down the track.

In guiding the process of agreeing your philosophy with teams and groups, the idea of 'contextual intelligence' (Sternberg, 1985, 1997) may be very useful. It can be defined as: 'the ability to quickly and intuitively recognize and diagnose the dynamic contextual variables inherent in an event or circumstance and results in intentional adjustment of behaviour in order to exert appropriate influence in that context' (Kutz, 2008, p. 23). The task box below offers an insight into the types of variables and heuristics one might use to develop contextual intelligence as a sport psychologist – although notably this area has not been well studied to date. In each case, you may wish to reflect on how the ideas listed might influence your own approach, style or philosophy in working with such a client group.

Contextual intelligence

We are aware of different sport cultures (e.g., "football culture" versus "cricket culture") and how they might affect how we practice. However, how can we get a handle on these differences and their implications? Below are two models that can inform 'contextual intelligence'.

1) Cultural symbols – What to look for (Trice & Beyer, 1984)

One useful way of appraising culture is the examination of cultural symbols, which can be 'high profile' – such as mission statements and mottos, or 'low profile', which are less obvious and tend to be observed at the more pragmatic level. Low-level symbols are argued to be much more informative than the carefully managed public and media messages, and may include:

(a) Practices (e.g., what time does everyone actually get in each morning, and leave? When's a good time to suggest an idea, and who to?)
(b) Communications (e.g., the stories and legends that are popular and reflect the way people like to think about their club/team)
(c) Physical forms (e.g., standards of dress, layout of dressing rooms, posters on walls)
(d) Jargon (shared language that reflects real attitudes to work and people – e.g., nicknames and running jokes/slang) (Trice & Beyer, 1984).

These lower profile symbols often give a much better indication of a sport organization's culture than the higher profile symbols such as the motto under the crest or the blurb on the website. Recording and reflecting on these cultural symbols may be a useful way of informing your intake process, and the decision as to whether to proceed.

2) The importance of results to the organization – What's at stake and how often? (Deal & Kennedy, 1982)

Another approach that can be applied before you even meet your new team is to consider both the degree of risk associated with their activities (amounts of money involved, financial stability, league situation, media attention/judgements) along with the speed that results become apparent (fast/frequently or slow/infrequently) (cf. Deal & Kennedy, 1982). With both of these considerations, the practitioner can make an educated guess before arriving, and this may help in formulating one's initial approach. The framework is summarized in Figure 4.2.

The sport of football (sometimes called soccer) can help us to consider all these types of culture. For example, in high level competitive football results are everything, and they come thick and fast, so you'll probably find yourself in a 'tough guy' culture, needing to deliver fast (and very evidently) or be gone. At the same time, many of the players in high-level football are extremely financially secure and may feel less exposed to risk. This may lead to a 'work-hard-play-hard' culture where results are still fast, but it's not the end of the world if you make a mistake. Hence, highly secure players might be likely to ask, "Why do we need

(continued)

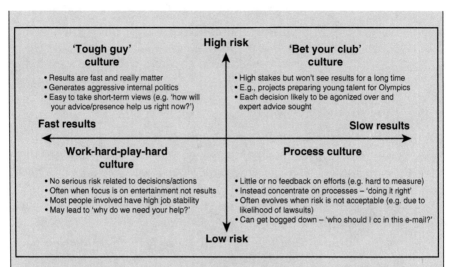

Figure 4.2   *The four types of organizational culture in relation to 'degree of risk' and 'frequency of feedback', as described by Deal and Kennedy (1982).*

Source: Keegan, R., & Killilea, J. (2006). Entering sport cultures as a supervised practitioner: What am I getting myself into? *The Sport and Exercise Scientist, 1*(7), 22–23. Reprinted with kind permission from The British Association of Sport and Exercise Sciences.

your help?" In contrast, small clubs, facing financial difficulties may present a 'bet your club' culture, where the result of appointing a new manager or sport psychologist may not be seen for a while, but it could still decide if the club goes bust or not. Hence, your advice may be actively sought but still be treated cautiously. Finally, development centres and academies, whilst playing regular matches, are largely judged by their 'output'. In this respect, they often see slow feedback from their efforts (e.g., annual progression or release of players) with relatively low risk ("as long as we show some results we'll keep getting funds"). Here the emphasis is likely to be on processes: doing the job right. In this situation practitioners may also struggle to be heard and will need to carefully justify each proposal in order to see it implemented (possibly by 'filling in the right form'), but at least the risk isn't as serious in this setting as in others.

4.3.4   Client History

When you go to a doctor (at hospital at least), physiotherapist or any other caring professional (even social workers, etc.), the first moments will be spent taking a detailed history. Sometimes the entire first session can be devoted to this. And notwithstanding the fact that sport psychology relationships can begin in a wide variety of contexts – as already noted – before the 'intake' can be considered complete, the sport psychologist should have recorded an accurate client history (e.g., Chapter 2, Record Keeping). On the one hand, avoiding the negatives, we really need to be thorough as the idea of 'missing something' is (or should be) quite terrifying. For example, on one occasion, a client chose not to tell me that he had previously been treated for obsessive compulsive disorder (OCD) until our third session. Obviously, this information would have changed much of my questioning and reasoning if I had known it earlier! On the other hand, supporting the positives, establishing a broad based and complete client history puts much of the information you subsequently gather into context: adding meaning to statements that might otherwise seem meaningless or confusing. So for example, the above OCD client's extremely negative (and irrational/unfair) self-talk suddenly made a lot more sense. Likewise, when we established that it was affecting his life outside of sport, the decision to refer back to his clinical psychologist was a 'no brainer' rather than a sensitive judgement call. Rather neatly, many of the things that are recommended/expected as part of good 'record keeping' (Chapter 2; see also Bradford & Stevens, 2013) are encompassed within the client history process. Taylor and Schneider (1992) developed the Sport-Clinical Intake Protocol (SCIP – see below worksheet), which is extremely thorough, and may act as a good checklist of ideas to cover before the intake can be considered 'complete'. As for whether the sport psychologist actively asks about each issue and plans a whole session around it, or simply allows the client to cover this ground in their own time: that depends on the preferred practice style (e.g., Chapter 3). Without doubt, it could easily take more than one session to cover all these issues, even in the (rare!) relationships that do take place in the controlled surroundings of a comfortable office and last for a 'psychologist's hour' (typically 50 minutes). Generally speaking, wherever possible, it is beneficial to have covered the below issues before completing the needs analysis (Chapter 5) and case formulation (Chapter 6), and before attempting to identify and plan interventions (Chapters 7 and 8). Acknowledging that sport often requires immediate intervention and 'fixes', the practitioner who finds her/himself in this situation should almost definitely be thinking: 'When can I get all the background information and history?' Realistically, without a strong history (and intake process), any help given must by definition have been a guess (although it is often surprising how experienced sport psychologists develop a knack of making good guesses in such difficult, time-pressured moments). In reviewing the SCIP (below), it is worth considering which of these questions you regularly seek to answer, which you may wish to consider in future and which you might never ask (e.g., too intrusive, not relevant), *and why*. The SCIP is provided in this case as a suggestion for what to include in your client histories, and not as a prescription. The prescriptive advice is that, wherever possible, a sport psychologist should seek to generate and record a client history that can: (a) inform the needs analysis and intervention processes; (b) demonstrate due diligence to any supervisors or auditing bodies; and (c) allow an informed choice to be made about whether, and how, to proceed with the psychological support.

Worksheet 4.1   Sport-Clinical Intake Protocol

Source: Appendix, pp. 324–325, from Taylor, J. and Schneider, B.A. (1992). The Sport-Clinical Intake Protocol: A comprehensive interviewing instrument for applied sport psychology, *Professional Psychology: Research and Practice,* 23(4), 318-325. Copyright © 1992 by the American Psychological Association. Reproduced with kind permission. No further reproduction or distribution is permitted without written permission from the American Psychological Association.

Cursory Description of Presenting Problem

A. Describe the presenting problem.
   1. What is it?
   2. How often does it occur?
   3. When did it begin?
   4. How long has it lasted?
   5. Where does it occur?
   6. What do you think is causing it?

Description of Athletic History

B. Describe athletic development.
   1. How did you get involved in your sport?
   2. How did you get to the level you are at now?
   3. What were some of the high points of your career?
   4. What were some of the low points of your career?
   5. Who have been the most significant people in your sports participation?
   6. What role did these people play in your development?
   7. What were your goals when you began your sport?
   8. What are your present goals?

Family and Social Support

C. Family.
   1. Parents: married or divorced, ages, quality of their relationship, educational background, current occupations, your relationship with them.
   2. Siblings: same questions as above.
   3. Your educational background.
   4. Previous psychiatric history of client and family (experience with and perceptions of psychology).
   5. Family involvement in sports participation.
      a. Parents' previous athletic participation.
      b. Parents' current participation in sports.
      c. Parents' involvement in your sports participation.
      d. Siblings' participation in sports.
D. Support system.
   1. Number and quality of friendships within sport.
   2. Number and quality of friendships outside of sport.
   3. What is your relationship with your coach?
   4. What is your relationship with your teammates?

5. What are other sources of support you have?
6. How satisfied are you with the support you receive from your family, friends, coaches, teammates and others?

E. Health status.
   1. How is your health at present?
   2. Injuries.
      a. What injuries have you had in the past and when?
      b. Do you have any injuries at present?
      c. If present, how do these injuries affect your training and competitive performances?
   3. Sleep.
      a. How are you sleeping lately?
      b. Are you tired often?
      c. Has your sleeping changed recently?
      d. Do you have difficulties getting to sleep?
      e. Prior to falling asleep, what thoughts are going through your mind?
      f. Are you waking up during the night?
      g. If so, what thoughts are going through your mind?
      h. Have you been having any dreams lately?
      i. What was in your dreams?
      j. If sleep difficulties are present, how do they affect your training and competitive performances?
   4. Eating.
      a. Describe your eating habits.
      b. Have you had any recent changes in your body weight?
      c. How has your appetite been?
      d. Have your eating habits changed?
      e. Has your eating influenced your training and competitive performances?
   5. Alcohol and drug use.
      a. Do you drink alcohol?
      b. How much and how often?
      c. Do you take drugs of any kind?
      d. What kind and how often?
      e. If alcohol and/or drug use are present, how have they influenced your training and competitive performances?
   6. When was your most recent physical examination?
      a. Were there any physical problems?

F. Important life events.
   1. What do you recall as the most important events in your athletic career, for example, events that influenced you a great deal?
   2. What do you recall as the most important events in your general life?
   3. Has anything important happened to you recently in your athletic life?
   4. Has anything important happened to you recently in your general life?

(continued)

Changes Prior to Onset of Presenting Problem

G. Athletic changes.
   1. Physical.
      a. Quality and quantity of training.
      b. Technique.
      c. Physical conditioning.
      d. Health: injury, illness, fatigue.
   2. Mental.
      a. Self-confidence.
      b. Anxiety.
      c. Concentration.
      d. Motivation.
      e. Precompetitive mental preparation.
      f. Precompetitive and competitive thoughts and feelings.
   3. Competitive.
      a. Competitive level, for example, regional, national.
      b. Stage of competitive season.
      c. Current performance level, for example, winning record, competitive statistics.
   4. Equipment.
      a. New equipment.
      b. Deterioration of old equipment.
H. Social/environmental.
   1. Changes in relationships: family, friends, school, work?
   2. Teammates or coaches.
   3. New relationships?
   4. Training and competitive sites.
I. Changes in cognition-affect-behaviour.
   1. Changes in cognition: negative, obsessional?
   2. Changes in affect: sadness, anger, joy?
   3. Changes in behaviour: routines, habits?

Details of Presenting Problem

J. Detailed description.
   1. Indicate typical situation: what was going on at the time?
      a. Competitive setting.
      b. Competitive scenario.
K. Personal influences.
   1. Describe thoughts.
   2. Describe feelings.
   3. Describe behaviour.
L. Social influences.
   1. What other people were around you?
   2. What were they doing?
M. Consequences.
   1. What happened after the problem occurred?
   2. How did significant others react?

3. What kinds of thoughts and feelings did you have?
4. Your attributions of problem.
N. Greater exploration.
1. Has this happened in the past: when and why?
2. When does it occur: practice, particular competitions?
3. Is there a consistent pattern of occurrence?
4. What sorts of things are going on when the problem is worst?
5. What sorts of things are going on when the problem gets better?
6. What do you think is causing it?
7. What do you think you can do to get over it?
8. What do you want to accomplish by being here?

4.3.5 Can this relationship work?

Van Audenhove and Vertommen (2000) argued strongly for the importance of this question; explaining that during their investigation they 'became more and more convinced of the importance of the intake-process phase *preceding* the start of psychotherapy' (p. 296 – italics added). This may even inform a tighter definition of the intake process as something that occurs *before* the helping relationship begins in earnest: before needs analysis and before intervention. In real life, and especially in sport, these processes are likely to overlap (sometimes substantially), but the value of the intake as a separate process that informs the subsequent steps is emphasized in this definition. As already noted, the most important influence on the effectiveness of psychological support, and therefore the most likely reason for failures and problems, is the quality of the relationship itself. As such, the *only* cast iron opportunity a sport psychologist has to avoid failures and conflicts and, thus, to *avoid harm*, is to avoid entering into relationships where it is clear that important considerations are not aligned. For example, irreconcilably different assumptions and expectations (e.g., 'Just tell me the answer!' leading to 'Erm, that's not how I work'), conflicts of interest or issues outside of the psychologist's competence. Perhaps the best opportunity a sport psychologist has to 'quality assure' their work, and ensure a track record of satisfied customers, is to manage which clients one takes on in the first place. On personal reflection: with the gift of hindsight, are there some clients I shouldn't have taken on at that stage of my development? Absolutely. On the very few occasions when I have declined to enter a relationship (usually making a referral), how has the client reacted? All the clients I have met again after such a decision were grateful that I did not 'waste their time', even if they were initially a little taken aback, or unsure what it meant. One rugby player described it as: 'very professional, the right thing to do' – which is good because that's how I felt too.

Overall, what exactly are we saying here? You don't have to take on every client that knocks on your door. Use the intake process to ensure that the client is fully aware of the likely process you will follow, and that you both have enough information to make an informed choice about whether or not to proceed. In this way, the client, the practitioner and the wider profession are all protected from the damage caused by ethical issues, ineffective support and any possible dissatisfaction that may occur from unidentified conflicts or inappropriate support measures.

4.4   Conclusion

In summary, this chapter has argued for several key ideas. First, that the intake process is separate, or separable, from the needs analysis process. Second, the intake process is something that every sport psychologist must do with every key client, and whilst the option is there to rush through it, there are also options to be extremely careful and deliberate. Third, by definition, the intake process represents the all-important outset of the relationship. As such, it serves an important ethical cause in offering an opportunity to establish key ethical principles, or decisions, which are very difficult to renegotiate or establish after this 'outset' phase. Unknown (and un-guessable) risks/harm can therefore be prevented by using the intake process intelligently to manage ethics. Fourth, a strong intake also allows for the collection of information that will inform subsequent decisions around needs analysis, intervention choices and planning/monitoring, as well as reducing the likelihood of key issues being 'missed'. Fifth, and very important, the intake process is where the relationship, norms and expectations, and ways of being are all established: all of which are very difficult to change thereafter. Finally, the intake process is perhaps the best/only opportunity to decide, with relative impunity, that the relationship should not go ahead. Retaining the 'power' of this decision, rather than simply waiving it, empowers both the psychologist and client to significantly reduce the possible risks from mismatched assumptions, expectations or competencies. On balance, this chapter aimed to convince the reader that the intake process is important, and that sport psychologists (in particular) should devote serious consideration and reflection to their intake process.

4.5   Ella's story: Part 4 – Intakes, hanging out and missed opportunities

Ella successfully negotiates a role for herself to perform a work placement with a top-level men's professional football team (i.e., soccer in the United States). She hopes the placement will be the springboard for her to provide some psychological service, still under supervision, if it goes well. The team does not currently have a sport psychologist, and despite paying many staff well, they insist that they will not be able to fund any psychological services. She is not provided with any kit to wear or travel expenses. The players arrive slowly each morning, with training only really beginning at 10 am, and as soon as training ends, most players leave immediately. By midday, the car park is mostly empty. The players wear inconsistent kit, with some still using last year's training jerseys, and some instances of generic sports clothing. Only injured players appear to stay longer, making use of the weights room and physiotherapist and/or masseuse. Historically, the team has not played in the top league often, and their presence there this season is viewed as unusual. However, the team is safe from relegation this season, but also appears to underperform in some matches, only showing glimpses of their real potential.

1. What high- and low-level signs are available for Ella to consider, and what might they be telling us about the culture of this team?
2. During the placement phase, Ella stands with the club's sport scientist during a training session. The live heart rate data shows that the players are not working hard enough, and so will be getting no cardiovascular benefits from the session. In her enthusiasm, Ella suggests he should tell the coach to adapt the game by making the teams smaller or have more goals between rests. The sport scientist replies: 'What? In front of the players? I can't do that, the gaffer would *kill* me! We'll just have to call this a wasted session'. What might this episode tell us about the culture and leadership at the club?
3. Ella notices that the players prefer to see the young female masseuse, and not the male physio – queuing up outside her door. The physiotherapist believes some may even have undiagnosed injuries requiring time out of competition, but they do not seek his help and only want to see Melanie for massages. Ella is confused when several players ask her if she is going to be helping Melanie and providing massages before and after training. What might these observations suggest, and how could Ella best deal with them?
4. The coach asks Ella to speak to one player about his confidence, as a 'trial'. She asks if there is a private space, but is told to try and catch him after training (when she knows the players are keen to leave straight away). After two failed attempts, the coach insists they speak, and they have a productive conversation in a corner of the canteen. Ella feels sure the player would benefit from psychological support. Immediately after the meeting, the coach asks what was said, and even when he can expect the player to be 'on song' again. She is worried this might involve breaching ethics. What can Ella do to manage this situation? What could she have done beforehand to avoid such a potential conflict.
5. In your opinion, should Ella agree to become the team's sport psychologist? Explain your reasoning. If she could specify conditions, what might be good criteria to have agreed up front?

4.6   Review and reflect

1. What is the role of the intake process, and why is this important?
2. In what ways are intakes separate from the needs analysis process? And in what ways are they similar?
3. What criteria would you look for in order to qualify as an excellent sport psychology intake? And what might a particularly bad intake look like?
4. What tools, cues and prompts could you use to try and ensure that your own intakes were as strong as possible?
5. What options are available to you if an intake process suggests the client's needs may not suit your approach, or sport psychology in general?
6. Can you think of an example from your own experience where a stronger intake might have produced a better outcome, or expedited a client's progress?

Worksheet 4.2   Intake checklist

To be completed during the intake process and 'signed off' once you are happy to enter into formal service provision (perhaps agreed with the client too).

First contact – how was first contact made and what key issues were covered?

Transition into formal intake process – when was it clear that your services were being sought? Did this necessitate a change in the conversation/setting? If so, how did you manage this?

When and how did you cover ethical considerations? And what was agreed for this specific relationship? For guidance, see Chapter 2, Worksheet 2.2.

How did you go about establishing or agreeing the approach (philosophy, style, assumptions) that should be taken? What was the final decision on this issue? For guidance, see Chapter 3.

[ ]

Have you generated a comprehensive client history, including reasons for seeking help and desired outcomes? Are there any other issues that you may need to consider that you have not covered (see SCIP, earlier, for possible suggestions). If you are missing information, how satisfied are you that you will not need it in the future?

[ ]

How would you characterize this relationship or working alliance? Is there a teacher and pupil, or two people collaborating (i.e., power differential)? Do you feel able to demonstrate (appropriate) warmth, empathy and unconditional positive regard with this client? If not, why not?

[ ]

Contextual intelligence: In what context is this psychological support being provided? Is there any information you can glean from cultural symbols or broader contextual influences that should inform your thinking? If so, what are they, and how do they change things?

[ ]

Should formal psychological support services go ahead? Is it in the best interests of the client, the psychologist and the broader profession to enter into this relationship? What issues might be, or become, problematic?

[ ]

Are there any remaining issues that have not been clarified?

[ ]

Worksheet 4.3   Intake Reflections

Source: Gibbs, G (1998). *Learning by doing: A guide to teaching and learning methods.* Oxford: OCSLD. Adapted with kind permission from the Oxford Centre for Staff and Learning Development

1) Description of intake issue/process

2) How do you feel about the way this specific issue/decision was handled?

3) What are the specific positive or negative outcomes (including risks) of the way this aspect of the process was handled?

4) How or why were these outcomes generated? How much of this was under your own control?

5) What action needs to be taken?

With this client?

With future clients?

6) What lessons can be drawn from these events regarding your own development, style or assumptions?

5 Needs Analysis – Establishing Needs, Skills, Demands and Goals

5.1 Introduction and overview

A needs analysis involves using various techniques to assess, measure and ultimately understand the client's current psychological needs: usually with a view to working out how best to help the client. The needs analysis process can include attempts to: (a) classify or diagnose the client's issues/concerns; (b) identify the aetiology (causal chain) producing the client's issues/concerns; (c) assess the impact/consequences of the current behaviours, issues, conflicts, etc.; and (d) to offer a 'prognosis' or prediction of what changes are needed, and how they might generate an impact (e.g., Gardner & Moore, 2006, p. 43). This chapter will also suggest other uses, such as monitoring progress and informing the termination process. As noted in Chapter 4, aspects of needs analysis may be deployed during the intake process and, likewise, needs analysis should ideally continue throughout the relationship in order to evaluate the effects of advice or responses to recent events. The needs analysis process incorporates various techniques, both objective and subjective (often in combination), and the choice of techniques will depend on the philosophy and approach adopted by the psychologist. For example, a certaintist approach (as described in Chapter 3) would favour a consistent process, largely based on reliable and validated quantitative measures, whereas a construalist needs analysis would proceed uniquely each time, responding to the client's story telling and very likely favouring qualitative information. The primary, or most common, aim of the needs analysis process is to facilitate an informed appraisal of the client's needs in relation to the demands being placed on them – by their sport, ambitions or life situation. However, the needs analysis can also inform the intake process, or contribute to the monitoring of intervention effects and changes made. In the counselling approach – closely linked to a construalist philosophy as described in this book – the needs analysis approach is also intended to generate increased self-awareness in the client, and so becomes an intervention as well as a way of generating information.

There are many techniques and methods available for gaining data from a client – interviews (structured, semi-structured or unstructured), informal chats, observations, questionnaires, performance profiling, stakeholder analysis (e.g., speaking to coaches or teammates), analysis of the sport itself (often overlooked) and performance statistics. Within this, some of the techniques (e.g., interviews) can be approached very differently, and will vary substantially depending on the philosophical approach adopted. Further, relying exclusively on a single technique, or a limited range of techniques, can create 'blind spots' that the practitioner (and client) should at least be aware of. Being aware of the strengths and weaknesses of each needs analysis technique, including how they might work in combination, is a key difference between blindly 'doing what you think you ought to do' and working in an informed, measured and accountable manner.

In this chapter, the importance of the needs analysis process in relation to the broader service delivery is considered, including the way it informs case conceptualization (Chapter 6), intervention design (Chapters 7 and 8) and ongoing monitoring (Chapter 9). The different techniques/methods are each explained in relation to applied practice (notably not in relation to their use in research, which is a common mistake), and the pros and cons of each technique are highlighted. From here we move on to a more detailed consideration of the exact aims of a needs analysis, and the ways that different techniques can be combined into a coherent assessment strategy

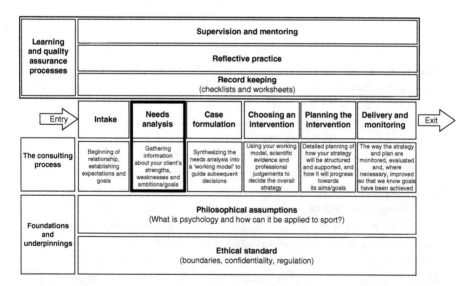

Figure 5.1   *The position of the needs analysis process at the heart of the service delivery process, closely related to intake and case formulation, as well as being highly dependent upon philosophical assumptions.*

which achieves these aims. We also consider the idea of ensuring that a needs analysis is consistent – such that if one prioritizes the client's unique personal story, what place is there for treating everyone the same, or using population-level questionnaires? Likewise, adopting a needs analysis consistent with one's philosophy is also considered, as well as how one might mitigate when one is forced to deploy an incomplete needs analysis (e.g., within time constraints, or if important information is withheld). The argument is emphasized that a strong needs analysis produces a stronger case conceptualization and a stronger intervention plan – once again enhancing both the effectiveness of one's practice as well as the quality of one's write-ups for assessment. A checklist is included for use with each individual client that allows the practitioner to detail which techniques were used, where 'gaps' may remain and so promoting a critical awareness of the quality of one's 'data'.

5.2   The importance of needs analysis in sport psychology

The needs analysis process, like all the other processes described in this book, is an unavoidable component of the applied sport psychologist's process. So to be clear, we are making the argument that it is not possible to deliver applied sport psychology without some kind of needs analysis taking place. As an extreme example, even a psychologist who leaps straight into offering advice and recommendations without collecting any information has effectively already completed their needs analysis *in advance*: they have made some appraisal – perhaps based on age, sport or past experiences – that the athlete will benefit from the advice being given. Alternatively, the practitioner may have assumed that the advice they are offering is new and special, and applicable to all athletes regardless of age, sport or other more personal considerations. In these instances, a needs analysis has arguably taken place; it was just a very quick (and ostensibly ill-informed) needs analysis. Realistically, such an approach should only be practised when one is asked to deliver generic group workshops with minimal information about the audience, but situations of extreme time pressure can also mean that a 'rushed' needs analysis becomes necessary. However, by considering such an extreme example, we can begin to understand the importance and relevance of a good needs analysis. Put simply, the better and more thorough the needs analysis, the more 'tailor-made' and well informed the intervention/advice can be, the more likely it is to work. In fact, going to the other extreme from the 'rushed' example above, a very thorough needs analysis can often render the way forwards extremely obvious, such that both practitioner and client can easily agree a course of action, goals monitoring measures, and even alternatives if 'Plan A' fails. However, in all applied instances of sport psychology practice, some sort of needs analysis has taken place: rushed or thorough, generic or personalized, precise or imprecise, correct or incorrect. And in all instances, the effectiveness of the support offered can depend very heavily on the quality of the needs analysis process. Put differently, if your sport psychology provision to a client 'fails' having passed the all-important intake stage, a key candidate for critical examination is likely to be the needs analysis process. Incomplete understanding, inappropriate or ineffective advice, incompatible assumptions and more can all be traced to an ineffective needs analysis.

5.3   Core considerations

Now that we have established the importance of the needs analysis process, and the core outcomes it achieves, we need to examine how these outcomes can be achieved. Needs analysis techniques can include any combination of the following, and this list is probably not exhaustive: (1) interviews (structured, semi-structured or unstructured); (2) informal chats; (3) observations (e.g., of performances or training); (4) questionnaires; (5) performance profiling; (6) stakeholder analysis (e.g., speaking to coaches or teammates); (7) analysis of the sport itself (often overlooked); and (8) performance statistics. Each of these shall be briefly explored here, with key issues signposted for consideration. From the outset, it should be clear that there is no perfect needs analysis technique, nor is there any perfect combination. Likewise, whilst certain techniques, may be more compatible with particular philosophies or practice styles, again, there is no clear way of aligning particular techniques to particular approaches. It should also be noted that each of the following techniques will manifest very differently in applied settings, as opposed to research settings, serving different uses and taking different criteria for validity/reliability. A common mistake, for example, is to assume that a well-validated questionnaire used widely in research settings will also give meaningful and relevant information about a client in an applied setting. Athletes, especially elite athletes, often differ substantially from the 'normal' population upon which the questionnaire is based – the motivation and high standards they exhibit are, by definition, way above normal – so sometimes a particularly high or low score can be misleading. More realistically, many clients do not want to be compared to the average of the broader population, but rather to understand their own unique and personal experiences. For now, however, all we need to know is that whilst data-gathering techniques often overlap between research and applied practice, the meaning and relevance of the data they generate varies substantially between the two contexts. The present chapter focuses on needs analysis techniques for use with individual clients, and whilst many of the techniques would be appropriate for working with teams (e.g., observation, performance statistics), there are often additional considerations available to psychologists working at the team level.

5.3.1 Interviews

Perhaps the most obvious technique for a sport psychologist to gather information about their client is to talk to them. An interview can be defined as a formal meeting or conversation in which the psychologist elicits facts or statements from the client. Conventionally, this can take place sitting down in a comfortable office or meeting room, but as we have already discussed, such settings are not always available to the sport psychologist. I have heard of psychologists conducting their interviews walking along riverbanks, in cafeterias during training camps, even in a small, cold referee's changing room. Likewise, it is becoming increasingly common to conduct interviews using telephone and video calls, especially with elite athletes whose busy travel schedules often prevent face-to-face meetings. Interviews can be *structured* to ensure that key questions or themes are addressed (e.g., the Sport-Clinical Intake Protocol, as introduced in Chapter 4); *unstructured* in a manner that allows the psychologist to follow the client's lead and make ad hoc decisions about which areas to explore further; or *semi-structured* – wherein certain key topics need to be covered but not in any particular order, and with scope to follow-up/probe any interesting responses. Broadly speaking, structured interviews would be more closely aligned with certaintist (positivist) and 'practitioner-led' approaches, whereas unstructured interviews would be more consistent with construalist (interpretivist) and 'client-led' approaches (cf. Chapter 3).

Perhaps more than any other needs analysis technique, the type of interview conducted is extremely dependent on the philosophy and style of the practitioner (see Chapter 3 for coverage of these issues) – which is yet another argument for ensuring that issues around philosophy are well understood by the practitioner (and client!). This is important because key claims for validity or relevance/meaning can only be correct or incorrect within the particular philosophical paradigm used by the practitioner. For example, Gardner and Moore (2006) argued that unstructured interviews are extremely unreliable, citing a meta-analysis study by Grove, Zald, Lebow, Snitz, and Nelson (2000; see also Groth-Marnat, 2000). Grove et al. collated 136 papers, all of which compared 'mechanical' diagnoses/predictions (based on mathematical modelling of questionnaire data) with psychologists' professional judgements of the same data (often with added interview data). In nearly all 136 papers, mechanical prediction was more accurate. Such an argument seems very compelling until we realize that the existence of a 'correct answer' – which depends heavily on human psychology being sufficiently uniform and predictable that we can have any certainty about 'correctness' – only exists within the *certaintist* philosophy of science. *Construalism* would deny such consistency exists because each person's psychology is completely unique, whereas *pragmatism* would define correctness as whatever produces a desired result (meaning an 'accurate' diagnosis is pretty irrelevant, unless perhaps it motivates behaviour change). Finally, *fallibilism* would posit that a 'correct' diagnosis may well exist, but that within the complexity of human psychology – perception, cognition and sociology – we can never knowingly achieve a 'correct' answer and so we must remain tentative and qualify our claims. As such, there are arguably very many ways of conducting interviews, and so the emphasis shifts to adopting approaches that are effective within the specific context they are used. So long as one's approach remains internally consistent, so as to create a coherent and meaningful experience (questioning style, ideas developed, formulation/synthesis, no conflicting assumptions), the only way a psychologist's interview data could be labelled 'wrong' would be if the criticism originated from someone committed to a completely different set of philosophical assumptions.

Whilst it is not possible to offer precise/prescriptive guidance for how practitioners adopting different assumptions might deploy the interview technique, there is space here to offer some hints and tips for those wishing to use interviews in their sport psychology practice – which presumably is all sport psychologists. Chapter 3 and the above discussion have offered some insights into how different assumption-sets will precipitate different interviewing styles. However, in order to be able to fully enact a particular style, a trainee psychologist will need to: practice different styles; observe the effects/outcomes of different questioning styles (as well as how it feels to adopt different approaches); reflect on these outcomes; and discuss their experiences with a supervisor or mentor. This learning experience can be informed by theoretical knowledge of practice principles, and by careful planning and preparation, such as planning questions to ask and topics to cover. Learning will be facilitated in this manner, because when real-world applied practice does generate learning experiences, the feedback gained is more relevant and meaningful when you 'knew what you were doing'. In contrast, the experiences and feedback gained from conducting an interview where you were simply 'flying blind' will be much more difficult to understand, classify and process: reducing the likelihood of learning occurring. As such, being fully conversant with the principles of applied practice and fully prepared before each interview are the first two 'tips' to be offered.

Further to the above, a very useful way of developing one's interview technique is to experiment with different approaches, from highly prescriptive to highly fluid and flexible. My own supervisor was very clear that she never wanted to create a 'mini-me' (or rather, 'mini-her'), by training me to simply replicate her preferred practice style. To achieve this, we role-played various approaches, particularly when working as a supervisory group, and we also recorded mocked up interviews attempting to enact different styles of interview (mocked up because we weren't happy using real clients to produce videos to share with others). The opportunities to try, and sometimes fail, in 'safe' circumstances from extensive reflection and feedback (and with both a supervisor and other trainees) were extremely valuable learning experiences. The videos, in particular, allowed us to identify tiny behavioural quirks that I had been unaware of previously. For example, I once used to offer athletes a drink upon entering the waiting room and session, but I never seemed to develop any way of drinking my own glass that didn't interrupt the flow of the session – it was just too awkward! So additional 'tips' include: try multiple styles and don't just become a disciple of your supervisor; use role-plays with any willing colleagues or peers to 'play' with different styles of interviewing; and where possible, try recording 'mocked up' sessions with willing volunteers (i.e., not real clients – confidentiality issues abound!) to generate material for sharing, reflection and fine-grained analysis – you cannot pause and rewind a live observation or role-play, but whilst video presents some ethical issues, it can also be extremely valuable to the developing practitioner.

Reflection, or reflective practice (RP – discussed in Chapter 10) can also be very useful in developing one's interview style. Whilst it remains unproven as to whether training in RP might automatically improve the performance of psychologists, reflecting is undoubtedly an excellent opportunity to improve one's interview style. Whether structured and formal or spontaneous and natural, we all review and replay meaningful events in our minds, and this behaviour allows us to notice both the positives and negatives of our session, with a view to constantly improving our style. Be it the overall session, a particular segment or phase, an individual question or even tiny fragments of body language: reviewing and reflecting on how we performed is key. Of course, reflection requires applied experiences to 'fuel' it, so getting out there and generating experiences from early on is arguably very important. Likewise, many regulatory bodies recommend a minimum number of contact hours required to qualify, which also emphasizes this point. Experience from early in one's training, generating a large number of hours across a wide range of contexts (ages, sports, etc.), becomes the sixth tip for developing one's interview style, and the seventh is to reflect on these frequently and deliberately.

Finally, we can consider the good habits and tools of a strong interview, which arguably include developing a good set of 'stock questions', summarizing and paraphrasing skills and using silence as a tool. Briefly, developing your own set of 'go to' questions allows you to both start good interviews, as well as maintaining good momentum and preventing 'stalling'. In counselling training, it is often a cliché to ask 'How did that make you feel?', yet this is an excellent example of a 'stock' question/response to keep the client talking and giving valuable information. Others might include: 'What goes through your head in those moments?'; 'How does that compare to your best/worst performance (or when you're playing well/badly)'; 'What have you tried so far to deal with this?'; 'Was there anything different about that game/day/shot/moment to produce that experience?' or even 'That sounds interesting, tell me more about it'. There are *many* of these, but having them in your armoury, available for immediate and automatic use at the appropriate moment helps you to effortlessly maintain a good and informative interview. The same goes for strong paraphrasing/summarizing skills, where you pause to check that you have heard the client correctly. Paraphrasing would generally involve using the client's own words/ideas and little more, whereas summarizing might involve attempts to relate themes to each other, or link disparate ideas into a coherent picture – that is, to synthesize and add value. Whilst these contributions are rarely phrased as a question, they often encourage the client to continue talking, as well as demonstrating that you have heard the client and that you are making an effort to understand their situation/experiences. Cutting against all of the above, there are moments where staying quiet, and allowing the client to speak can become a really useful tool. Effectively, if you stop taking your 'turn' in the conversation, the other person generally continues talking to avoid the awkward silences – often volunteering useful information that you might have missed if you jumped in with your next questions. Alternatively, replacing your 'turn' with brief 'sub-verbal reinforcers' ('Mmm-hmm, aha, ok, yeah') or even non-verbal reinforcement (nodding, eye contact, etc.) can encourage more information into the shared 'space'.

In all the above cases, the 'tips' provided will not allow you to claim a more reliable or valid interview technique, not when different philosophies and traditions are considered. However, good interviewing skills form the core of the sport psychologist's role, and these tips should assist the psychologist in being able to be more effective – things many experienced psychologists wish somebody had told them when they were starting out. There is no ideal time for an interview to last, but many people expect an hour, or the so-called psychologists' hour (50 minutes). Sport psychologists must often make the most of very brief exchanges, or likewise get maximum benefit from a rare 2-hour slot between training sessions. If you are able to find a relatively private space and talk in a controlled one-to-one manner, we could reasonably call it an interview. However, very brief and opportunist 'informal chats' are also an option for gaining (or giving) important information in a less controlled, formal setting.

5.3.2   Informal chats

Informal chats could easily be grouped in with interviews as a needs analysis technique, including as they do qualitative, verbal information exchanged between two people. However, as noted above there is a subtle difference between informal chats and structured interviews. Informal chats can occur in the transitions between training sessions, on the team coach, in the food hall or even in corridors and when walking around grounds or training centres. Characteristically, they are less controlled, relatively brief and can end at any moment as there is no office, door or time expectation. It might be tempting to consider such exchanges as meaningless, or simply the precursor to a proper interview at a later date. However, it is possible – particularly in sport – for these informal chats to form the entirety of a supportive relationship. I can definitely recall one player who was part of the team I was working with, and who dealt with me exclusively in informal chats. In retrospect, it took me a while to realize he was seeking help at all. On the occasions that I did try to bring the relationship into the 'safer' confines of a formal meeting, he resisted and shied away: declining formal interviews yet still seeking advice when it suited him. Should I have made my advice/ support conditional on him entering a formal relationship in a controlled consulting room, or helped him in a suitable way in the fleeting moments where he did approach me?

If the ethical issues described in Chapter 3 can be resolved (in this case, by having a team-level ethics agreement outlined in a workshop before the season), then informal chats can be an excellent way of delivering sport psychology services *in situ*. Benefits may include being closer to playing or training sites, being less of an inconvenience to busy athletes, being more comfortable for the athletes (i.e., able to initiate or terminate the conversation as desired), and perhaps many more too. Risks and problems might include the potential lack of privacy, and the loss of control over the flow of the conversation. Likewise, if this becomes the main method a client allows you to use for gathering information, it can place quite a demand on your own memory and record keeping if you are to keep up to speed and 'pick up where you left off' each time. As such, the technique of informal chats may be less amenable to those adopting a 'certaintist' philosophy, whereas construalist and pragmatist practitioners may use it quite deliberately, and fallibilist may choose to use it with caution (as with all other techniques).

5.3.3   Behavioural observation

Behavioural observation involves the direct observation of your client, be they an individual, dyad, group or team, and can occur across a variety of contexts. The psychologist can observe performance behaviours, body languages, communication style and content, responses to mistakes (and successes) and much more. All of these observations can provide either confirmation of reports from the client, additional insights beyond existing data or even suggest inaccuracies or an incomplete needs analysis. Whilst performances and training sessions are often favoured sources of observation data, the cultural and procedural aspects of a team/group (e.g., Chapter 4) can also be ascertained by observing weights rooms, analysis sessions, media events, meals and social gatherings, etc. One thing that is worth noting from the above is that observation is often most useful when supplementing previous data. Attempting to analyse a client's psychological skills or needs simply by watching is arguably little better than attempting to analyse athletes' psychology from their performances on television. Observations are generally much more useful when informed by some sort of prior knowledge: that is, knowing what to look for, rather than looking for 'anything'.

One important distinction to make when observing athletes is the difference between objective and subjective observations. A good tip is to have different columns in your observation sheet for the objectively observable behaviour (something that could be recorded on video and agreed by the vast majority of observers with minimal interpretation/ knowledge), versus the subjectively interpreted meanings of behaviours (guesses as to the meaning of objective observations, informed by knowledge/theory and even by previous conversations with the client, that might not be agreed between different observers from different backgrounds). For example, 'crinkled nose after mistake' might be viewed as an objective observation. Subjective interpretations of this behaviour might vary from 'suppressed anger after mistake' to 'quickly shrugged off mistake'. However, ethical guidelines also require psychologists to separate out subjective opinions from objective observations, so this is an important consideration. By effectively placing the practitioner in a position of 'judge' or 'expert', behavioural observation is often favoured by certaintist and 'practitioner-led' psychologists, and frowned upon by construalist and 'client-led' ones.

It is important to note that the very presence of you, as the psychologist, may affect the way your athlete performs – so you may wish to choose which events you observe very carefully, or even attempt to prevent the client from knowing which exact event you will attend (e.g., events with crowds, and by saying 'I will attend one of your matches this month but I can't commit to which one yet'). There is also a decision to be made about whether you speak to the client immediately after the observation, or decide to have a cool down period where you can analyse, reflect and consider the most effective ways of introducing any information to the analysis (i.e., keep it private versus discuss it all with the client, versus only share selected issues, when and where to do this, etc.). Various authors identify the relative objectivity of observations as a good way of identifying potential discrepancies – for example, between the client's reported and actual behaviours, or between training and performance contexts (Watson & Shannon, 2010).

Observations of performance can be used to track progress over the course of the relationship, again either for the individual or at a team level observing communication, leadership structures or responses to challenges. Likewise, if you are aware of specific issues to consider in the athlete's relationships (with a coach or other athlete) then this might also be worthwhile observing. Overall, observation can vary from 'extremely useful and worthwhile' right through to 'damaging and misleading' if used inappropriately, with 'ineffective and unhelpful' somewhere in between. Borrowing from the fallibilist philosophy, if performance observation is deployed judiciously and interpreted carefully, then it can become an excellent part of the sport psychologist's armoury for needs analysis.

5.3.4   Questionnaires and psychometric assessments

Paper or electronic questionnaires can include quantitative or qualitative data, and can be administered either face-to-face by the psychologist, or by the client on their own (perhaps before a session, but more likely after a file or link is sent by email/post). In the vast majority of cases, sport psychologists favour the validated quantitative instruments developed by researchers in the field, with unvalidated or qualitative types being much less commonly deployed in sport psychology. In both cases, the convenience of completing a questionnaire anywhere in the world, in the athlete's own time, and providing a permanent (often numerical) record is not to be underestimated. However, the following few lines will also illustrate some of the core considerations and risks for sport psychologists using questionnaires in their practice.

Typically, psychometric tests require the client to respond to a series of specific questions or statements on a numerical scale, called a Likert scale (cf. Likert, 1932). These scales will often vary from 'strongly disagree' to 'strongly agree', on either five or seven points. Occasionally, questionnaires ask clients to choose between two statements that they feel best describes them. The number of questions, or 'items', can vary from very few (e.g., 5–6) to very many (e.g., 60), and are usually grouped to form 'subscales'. As such, within a questionnaire containing 30 items, we might find 3–4 'subscales'. For example, the Competitive State Anxiety Inventory-2 (Martens, Vealey, & Burton, 1990) contains 3 subscales: cognitive anxiety, somatic anxiety and self-confidence. This neatly illustrates a key point, which is that a high 'total' score can often be irrelevant, because anxiety and confidence are quite different and adding the scores for them would be meaningless (They would probably 'cancel out'!). The client should not notice this at all, as the questions are usually presented in a random order, but when it comes to scoring the questionnaire you, as a psychologist, will need to be very clear on which questions relate to which subscale (and what each subscale means). In addition, many questionnaires contain 'reverse-scored' items. On a 1–7 scale, this would mean that whereas a score of 1 would usually mean 'strongly disagree' and 7 would mean 'strongly agree', the inverse becomes the case, *just for that item*. So 7 would mean 'strongly disagree' and 1 would mean 'strongly agree'. In your 'key' or scoring sheet, these items are usually represented by a '*' or 'R' in the margin. Students in my course used to frequently get confused by reverse-scored items, so it is worth being clear on which questions they are, and how you will process them – which is actually very simple (e.g., a score of 1 becomes 7; 2 becomes 6; 3 becomes 5, etc.). As a final consideration, 'high' and 'low' scores on each subscale *on their own* are often totally meaningless. If the possible scores range from 4 to 28, for example, four questions scored from 1 to 7, and someone scores 24, that is not necessarily a 'high' score, even though it is far above the mid-point. The reason is it depends on the mean score that everyone else gets. If 50% of people completing the questionnaire score 24 or over, then 24 is not a high score at all, compared to the normal (or target) population. This issue also trips students up surprisingly often. All validated questionnaires have been designed and tested on large samples – and the original 'validation' paper should contain all this information. Indeed, some questionnaires have even been tested on different populations – for example, the Test of Performance Strategies (TOPS – Thomas, Murphy, & Hardy, 1999) comes complete with mean scores for athletes across all the levels, from high school and recreational level up to national and international athletes. As such, you can compare your athlete's scores to the norm for their current level, as well as their desired level. You must compare your athlete's scores to the mean, and not assume that a high or low number is necessarily good/bad.

Further to consider means within scoring considerations, you really need to consider 'standard deviation' (SD) that is reported alongside the mean in the validation study. Without going into unnecessary detail, the SD is a measure of the spread or variability around the mean, and 68% of the population who first filled in the questionnaire fell with one SD above or below the mean. For example, if the mean is 24 and the SD is 2, then this means it is really *very typical* for people to score between 22 and 26, and only those above or below these values are at all noteworthy. If someone is more than two SDs above or below, that puts them in the top or bottom 2.5% of scores, and that would be quite a notable result, although elite athletes are often quite unique and so they do produce scores that differ from the 'norm'. This leads to one final consideration, when it comes to questionnaires, it is often better to use questionnaires and normative data from sporting populations rather than the wider population or clinical patients. The comparisons will be more relevant and meaningful, although unfortunately this is often not possible, which leaves you as the psychologist to interpret the results with caution. For example, scoring much lower on anxiety than a clinical population (i.e., diagnosed and perhaps even hospitalized patients) does not mean that the athlete is free from anxiety, or that anxiety is not affecting their performance.

Sticking with the technical considerations for just a little longer, we need to also be aware of 'reliability' and 'validity'. Reliability refers to the consistency of a questionnaire's scoring (Gardner & Moore, 2006; Kazdin, 1998, Marchant, 2010), and tends to come in two forms: internal and 'test retest'. Put simply, internal reliability (represented by the letter alpha – α) describes the degree to which questions within a subscale are linked/correlated, and the convention is that it needs to be above 0.7 for a subscale to be reliable. You won't need to measure this, but if you can find it, reassure yourself the questionnaire is reliable and even report it in your case studies, you are doing well. Test-retest reliability refers to the degree of consistency when a person fills in the questionnaire on two separate occasions, and again, 0.7 is a good level of correlation – but again this should have been addressed when the questionnaire was first designed. It does raise the issue, however, that we wouldn't expect certain psychological constructs to remain consistent over time. Mood, affect, emotion, attitudes, etc. should change, almost by definition, whereas stable attributes such as personality would be expected to remain fairly constant. An unreliable measure is unhelpful (or even dangerous) in the same way that trying to measure distances with an elastic band, rather than a tape measure, would lead to a very uneven set of shelves!

Validity, in contrast, refers to whether our measure actually captures the 'thing' it is supposed to, and comes in many forms (Gardner & Moore, 2006; Kazdin, 1998, Marchant, 2010). When we look at how many questionnaires are designed, there is often a stage where 'experts' from around the world are invited to comment on whether the proposed questions/items are appropriate. This stage is where 'face validity' and 'content validity' are established (Anatasi & Urbina, 1997). Face validity refers to whether the items 'fit' and 'feel' appropriate, and in relation to theory or dictionary definitions – and tens or hundreds of sample questions are often rejected at this stage when designing questionnaires. Content validity is a little different in that the items are then viewed together and judged as to whether they fit together, as a coherent group, and reflect the desired subscale/concept. Again, many sample questions never make it past this stage. Following this, we then hit upon 'construct validity', where relatively complex maths (for most of us mere mortals, eigenvectors qualify as 'difficult'!) is used to establish whether and how the items can be combined, and whether they do in fact sit comfortably together. That is, does the same person tend to score similarly on items that are intended to measure the same thing? Questions that do not appear to fit with the others in their subscale, or ones that appear to link with more than one subscale, are usually deleted and never make it into the final 'validated' version. Finally, there is predictive validity, wherein most validation studies will check that each subscale actually links to something meaningful – so, for example, another similar questionnaire or a theoretical construct. If we consider self-esteem for a moment, we could test whether a newly designed questionnaire correlates with confidence (a similar concept) and that it predicts enjoyment or satisfaction (which it should, in theory). As above, knowing and reporting these properties in your write-ups is arguably 'best practice' for those that do decide to use questionnaires within their psychological support. It also allows you to choose between similar questionnaires as new ones become available.

Now, all of the above technical content is fine and well, but you must also consider the 'diagnostic utility' of each questionnaire – does it tell you something useful? If you measure something with all the technical precision in the world but it does not relate to your athlete's particular issue (performance, well-being, etc.) then we've wasted everybody's time. And adding in a reflective point, athletes tend not to enjoy filling in questionnaires, so the applied sport psychologist really needs to be careful as to which, and how many, questionnaires are used with each athlete.

Regarding pros and cons: on the plus side, questionnaires often do provide a degree of scientific validity to proceedings, as well as allowing you to quantify issues that are famously difficult to capture and evaluate. This then allows comparisons to the 'norm' (as noted above) as well as the comparison of pre- to post data, to see if the athlete has improved over time. Questionnaires are also relatively cheap to administer, and can be completed at a distance with minimal supervision from the psychologist. This has made them particularly popular in research (which is arguably their primary purpose), where large samples can be gained through a mail-shot or online survey. Psychometric testing also reduces the importance of soft skills such as listening and rapport building, as well as reducing the scope for (mis) interpretation by the psychologist. Some of the cons of psychometric testing have already been alluded to above, but to summarize: (1) questionnaires only measure very narrow and specific constructs, which often may not be what is needed within your needs analysis (i.e., with this particular client); (2) this narrow focus means you can easily miss key ideas, and/or miss key interactions and complexities in how the client's issues actually 'play out'; (3) the vast majority of the time the questionnaires must be completed outside of the sporting moment, which creates a level of separation between the immediate/real experience and the actual measurement of it. Consider, for example, the difficulty of measuring 'flow' – an inherently 'involved' and all-consuming experience – by requiring the athlete to stop what they're doing and fill in a questionnaire; (4) historically, questionnaires have been designed in university settings, and primarily for research purposes (cf. Marchant, 2010). In fact, when we look closely, many questionnaire validations are completed using university and college participants, sometimes in return for course credit (e.g., perhaps the lecturer simply asked students to complete the questions before a lecture). This property of questionnaires again limits their applicability to athletes in real-world settings; (5) the mathematics of questionnaire design forces them to simplify by generating 'parsimonious' solutions. Likewise, 'cross-loadings' where questions seem to relate to two subscales are deleted. As a result, the subtle complexities of the client's experience are, by definition, ironed out and ignored and it falls to the psychologist to ensure that these are addressed some other way (e.g., interviews, etc.); (6) great care is required when scoring and interpreting questionnaires, some aspects of which have been noted above, but there are additional issues such as whether a score of four reflects something double a score of two: what do the scores really mean?; (7) there is a recognized tendency for anyone filling in a questionnaire to make themselves look good in some way, perhaps by exaggerating positives and minimizing negatives. It is called 'social desirability bias' (Crowne & Marlow, 1960). Some questionnaires instruct people to 'give your first response, as quickly as possible' to try and reduce this bias, but it is a genuine issue nonetheless; (8) very inconveniently, athletes often score themselves higher on questionnaires before a training programme, and then after realizing how hard the skill actually is, their scores go down – which can make it look like the intervention actually failed; (9) To a client who is very concerned about being understood as a unique individual, or a psychologist who wishes to recognize this viewpoint (e.g., a construalist philosophy), the objective and standardized approach of questionnaires may be highly counter-productive. Said client could easily become disillusioned by being dehumanized (as they might see it) in this way, whereas said psychologist would effectively be gathering meaningless data in relation to their beliefs about the nature of the mind.

Overall, questionnaires remain a relatively controversial and divisive topic amongst practising sport psychologists. This passage set out to present a balanced account of their usage, pros and cons and, in doing so, suggest there is no 'right and wrong' when it comes to questionnaires. Instead, the appropriacy of using questionnaires depends on your philosophy, your client's needs, what you are trying to achieve by using them and what claims you make based on the data from them.

5.3.5   Performance profiling

In response to what was perceived as an over-reliance on objective measurement – which construalists and client-led practitioners might perceive as inappropriate – Butler and Hardy (1992) proposed the performance profiling process of needs analysis. The process was derived from Kelly's (1955) Personal Construct Theory, in which a premium is placed on the way that individuals uniquely construe the world – that is, their personal constructs. In an attempt to remedy the apparent legitimacy that comes with numerical data, Butler and Hardy proposed a mechanism for quantifying uniquely personal viewpoints – thus potentially opening up the benefits of comparing the relative importance of ideas and progress over the course of training. In this respect, performance profiling is quite explicitly conceived from a construalist tradition – as described in this book – but realistically practitioners from all backgrounds often use the technique, as the quantitative element also appears superficially compatible with certaintist assumptions. Indeed, Doyle and Parfitt (1996) went as far as testing the validity of performance profiles, which is an approach that would appear to be based on highly certaintist (i.e., positivist) assumptions.

There are several processes proposed for completing a performance profile: from the highly simplistic 'dartboard' model to the extremely complex approach proposed by Gucciardi and Gordon (2009), which might even be too complex for some neophyte practitioners to use without practice. In effect, however, we need to capture and record the attributes (or 'constructs') that the individual athlete perceives to be important to performance, and then gain some sort of self-rating (usually out of 10, but 100 has also been suggested). The skills and attributes should be physical, mental, social, technical and tactical, but it is worth reminding the athlete that a psychologist can only help with the mental and social aspects, and experts in other areas should be sought if improvements are required in technical skill or physical conditioning. A list of skills and attributes (all unique to the individual athlete), with each attribute rated numerically, would probably be the most basic form of performance profile, perhaps applicable to young children or an athlete with almost no time at all to participate in sport psychology. Ideally, whilst the ratings must be the athlete's own personal judgement, it is preferable to 'anchor' them – for example, 10 = world champion, 1 = beginner; or 10 = selection standard for Olympics, 1 = selection standard for club. The next level of complexity would involve asking the athlete to identify their 'desired' level/score, as well as their 'actual' score. The difference between desired and actual can quickly suggest the areas in most urgent need of improvement *according to the athlete's own judgement*. Some psychologists (or athletes) prefer to assume that 10/10 is the preferred score by default, but allowing the athlete to choose a target level increases their autonomy and facilitates the separation of which skills are more influential/important. Both the above versions of performance profiling can be done using the 'dartboard' or 'wagon-wheel' approach, and both are probably quite suitable for children and adolescents.

In order to add more sensitivity to the process – that is, to be able to distinguish between multiple attributes with the same 'discrepancy' score – it is possible to add an 'importance' rating. So for example, if an athlete rates herself at 5/10 on confidence, and 6/10 on concentration, but her desired levels are 8/10 and 9/10, respectively, we get a 'discrepancy' of 3 for both. So which should we prioritize? If our performance profile also asked the athlete to rate the importance (out of 10), and our athlete scored confidence as 9/10 but concentration as only 8/10 – in terms of actually generating results in competition – then we might lean towards confidence. A nice trick is to include a spreadsheet which calculates [desired − actual] × [importance]. You could ask the athlete to do the sums, but many report disliking this part! However, using this little progression of the technique, bigger discrepancies in important skills/attributes will return higher scores, immediately pointing to those skills as requiring attention. Again, everything that has been included in the process, including the numbers/outcomes it generates are *according to the athlete's own judgement* – and this is why the process is more consistent with construalist traditions than certaintism. Pragmatists and falliblists may both use the technique for different reasons – the former purely because it appears to 'work' in some meaningful way, and the latter with extreme caution and consideration (see Chapter 3 for explanations).

In support of the original reasons for developing performance profiles, recent research suggests that athletes and psychologists do, as intended, perceive the following benefits: (1) they provide basis for goal setting (which goals to set, and what numbers to aim for); (2) they clearly identify strengths and weaknesses; (3) they raise the athlete's self-awareness; (4) they facilitate the evaluation and ongoing monitoring of performance; (5) they encourage athletes to take responsibility for their performance and development; (6) they are believed to enhance athlete's intrinsic motivation to make any improvements identified; and (7) they facilitate discussion, communication and interaction – in fact, some psychologists pay more attention to the conversation and interaction than to the raw numbers it generates (Weston, Greenlees, & Thelwell, 2010; 2011a, b; 2013). These benefits, however, do need to be balanced against the possible drawbacks, not least of which is that there are many possible ways of conducting a poor performance profile, or misinterpreting the results. First, to anybody adopting or holding certaintist/positivist philosophical assumptions, the highly subjective nature of performance profiling will be uncomfortable, or even inappropriate. Exploring more pragmatic considerations, athletes will frequently produce lists of attributes that are highly idiosyncratic – using language that we might understand very differently having been trained in the technical terminology – but it is important to try and retain the athlete's own 'constructs'. Further, athletes frequently produce lists containing very similar concepts – such as 'commitment', 'motivation' and 'determination' all alongside each other, or 'self-belief', 'confidence' and 'positivity'. With a view to obtaining benefit number seven in the above list, these should be viewed as opportunities to discuss and clarify exactly what is meant.

You may either wish to choose one label that suits best, or to clearly delineate between the labels that have been used. As an example, when I once asked an athlete to discriminate between 'concentration' and 'focus', he described how the former meant 'getting and staying focussed', and the latter meant 'regaining focus after it's been broken'. That helped us both, and we kept this distinction in. Another common mistake is failing to 'anchor' the ratings by defining what is meant by zero versus ten, and what is really the difference between a six and a seven. It can feel fussy and pedantic, but the benefits are much more likely to be realized this way. Likewise, 'settling' for too few attributes is something we commonly see in students' case reports, when the process is really intended to generate a very thorough and detailed understanding – even if this involves forcing the athlete to become a little more self-aware and reflective.

As a final consideration, performance profiling is a great example of the 'garbage-in-garbage-out' (GIGO) principle, because what you, as the psychologist, ask for inherently determines the quality of the process and the outcomes it generates. As such, it is a very good idea to practice delivering performance profiles with a range of clients (ages, sports, experience levels, etc.) to gain some understanding of what works with each group, and how best to present and manage the process. Overall, performance profiling can be an excellent tool for generating personally meaningful quantitative data, boosting the athlete's self-awareness and generating numerous 'entry points' where further questions can be asked, or progress made. Further, performance profiles can act as a useful 'baseline' for subsequent comparisons when monitoring progress although, like questionnaires, athletes often modify their 'frame of reference' as they come to understand the skill/attribute more deeply. Performance profiling is also an extremely flexible needs analysis technique: it can be used by an entire team (either by keeping it personal or by generating attributes that the whole team agrees on); it can be used to compare coaches' and athletes' perceptions (within agreed confidentiality limits); and it can even vary in the depth and thoroughness sought (from speedy and simplistic to lengthy but thorough). To conclude this section, it is also worth remembering that the numerical outcomes are only one aspect of the performance profiling process, and athlete self-awareness, shared qualitative/interview data, increased athlete autonomy and motivation and potentially a stronger working relationship are all outcomes that can be realistically pursued using this technique.

5.3.6 Stakeholder analysis

Stakeholder analysis simply involves seeking information from other people, whose interests are related to the athlete's success or well-being. It is therefore extremely important to clarify the athlete's preferences regarding confidentiality before embarking on such a process. With the appropriate permission, you may wish to approach coaches, teammates, parents or friends/colleagues with a view to perhaps gaining additional information, or perhaps checking and verifying information gained from the athlete. It may involve formal or informal contact (e.g., interviews, phone calls, emails), or (as noted above) you may wish to see if the athlete's self-ratings on a performance profile are compatible with the coach's appraisal. Such an approach would generally involve giving less weight or esteem to the athlete's own narrative – in fact, some athletes may even see it as undermining their own story-telling efforts. As such – by assuming, a more 'objective' reality can be accessed by involving other people – stakeholder analysis is arguably more aligned with a certaintist philosophy and practitioner-led style. A strictly construalist and client-led approach would prioritize the athlete's own experiences and narrative above all else; only referring to other people in terms of what the athlete perceives they may think or believe. A key assumption of this approach is that the 'stakeholders' have the same aims and goals for the client as the client – discrepancies here could lead to anything from losses in clarity of information to deliberate disinformation (say from a competing teammate). Likewise, the thoughts and experiences of any stakeholder are just as susceptible to imprecisions and personal bias as anyone else, so there is always a necessity to pause and critically examine any discrepancies between the athlete's data and stakeholder input. One very useful aspect of involving 'stakeholders', however, is that they may wish to help support the athlete's attempts to make changes in their lives. For example, coaches, parents or peers may be much better placed to reinforce key messages *in situ*, or to challenge undesirable thoughts/behaviours, many of which do not occur when the psychologist is there to observe! Overall, like many of the techniques described in this section, when deployed carefully stakeholder analysis can be an excellent addition to a needs analysis – but used inappropriately it could also cause substantial harm to the relationship and data gathered.

5.3.7 Analysis of the sport

According to Taylor (1995), any psychological intervention should take into account three factors: (1) the physical, technical and logistical demands of the sport; (2) the psychological demands of the sport; and (3) the specific needs of the athlete(s). This passage refers to (1) and (2) in Taylor's list. Fundamentally, as defined earlier, a sport psychology needs analysis seeks to establish the athlete's current skills, attributes, attitudes, etc., *in relation to* the demands of the sport they are playing, and their goals/aims for that sport. As an additional consideration, being familiar with the sport can be incredibly helpful in understanding particular terminology and jargon used by the athlete (e.g., Patrick & Hrycaiko, 1998; Terry, Mayer, & Howe, 1998). Thus – while it arguably shouldn't matter if a psychologist occasionally pauses to ask 'what do you mean by that?' – the conversation will flow a lot more smoothly if you don't need to, and some athletes will want their psychologist to understand the finer points of their sport in order to fully trust your judgement (Fifer, Henschen, Gould, & Ravizza, 2008; Ravizza, 1988, 1990, 2001). In Taylor's (1995) view, sports can vary in terms of: (1) whether they are individual versus team sports; (2) continuous and 'open' versus momentary and 'closed'; (3) seasonal – in which case, how long is the season? When is off season? When is the 'finale', etc.?; (4) the frequency of competition – weekly, monthly, etc.; (5) the type(s) of fitness required – anaerobic, aerobic, strength, etc.; (6) the duration of competition – seconds, minutes, hours, days; and (g) the social context of the sport – the geographical and socioeconomic determinants – for example, Australian Rules football is only really played in an Australian context, and is often considered a 'working' man's game, whereas Rugby Union is played across all continents, but in both Australia and the United Kingdom it is often considered a game for the upper middle classes (e.g., it is taught in private schools more than public schools). This list is not exhaustive and other considerations may also be in play, such as the availability of funding and the publicity of performances (i.e., crowds, TV audiences, etc.). Likewise, the same argument can be made for understanding the classification systems in disabled and Paralympic sports, especially as these classifications often play a vital and very contentious role in determining performance outcomes. I once heard of a blind cricket team spending substantial time and effort having a bowler classified as 'B1' (totally blind) in order to improve their chances. Similarly, an athlete I once worked with was effectively dropped when a more able-bodied athlete was controversially classified as having the same level of disability. Such pragmatic considerations can have a huge effect on your service delivery, and can greatly influence the goals you set with the athlete. Overall, analysis of the sport can play an integral role in one's sport psychology needs analysis, and is almost always worth a few lines in any case study. Preferably, however, this step should be completed before you meet the athlete, in order to optimize the interactions and ensure all the information you gain can be immediately placed in context and understood properly.

5.3.8   Performance statistics

As a final, and often overlooked, consideration, performance statistics can often prove to be a useful needs analysis tool. Example might include examining 'slumps' in form over a season, or perhaps a golfer's reaction to one poor shot (if the next two or three holes are also affected, for example). The nature of the performance statistics you can obtain will vary substantially between sports, levels and clubs, but examples might include: results; performances (e.g., times, distances, heights, goals scored – in training versus competition etc.); and mistakes (e.g., 'unforced errors in tennis, handling errors in rugby). Also note that performance statistics are much easier to obtain in some sports than others (e.g., golf, tennis). The emergence of performance analysis tools such as video and ProZone have helped to generate more indices of performance – although care is always required in interpreting some data. For example, having a high 'pass accuracy' statistic may simply mean a soccer player has only attempted short, simple passes and none of them were ever likely to create scoring opportunities. Whilst it would be almost impossible to base a full psychological needs analysis on performance statistics (!), they can be used to usefully supplement the process, in the same way that performance observations and stakeholder analysis can be additional sources of information beyond the athlete her/himself.

5.4   Combining techniques and synthesizing findings

The preceding section detailed eight needs analysis techniques, and it is worth noting that there may be other techniques available or other variations of those described. However, being aware of, and proficient in, such techniques is only part of the equation. If, for example, a psychologist simply rolled an eight-sided dice in deciding which technique to follow, and put all their faith in the outcome of the technique selected by the dice, the result would be an unreliable/inconsistent approach. This approach would pose a risk to the quality of both the needs analysis and the ensuing support package – as the success of the support package depends very heavily on the quality of the needs analysis. The point, here, is that the psychologist must also carefully and judiciously combine needs analysis techniques in order to 'stitch together' a coherent overall picture of the client's current psychological processes: attributes, requirements, causes, mechanisms and effects. Chapter 6, which follows, details the 'case formulation' stage, wherein a coherent working model of the client's psychological make-up is created, which can then be compared to the situational challenges and goals of the client. However, there remain a few points that are worth noting within the needs analysis section.

One of the most common mistakes made by students and trainees in a needs analysis is to carry out a piecemeal, or 'scattergun' needs analysis. In this approach, multiple techniques are deployed, but with no obvious logic joining them, and often no attempt to synthesize the information from them. Related to this is what we often call a 'formulaic' or 'colour-by-numbers' needs analysis, where the student has heard of (or seen) an approach that appeared to work (or gain a good mark), and they simply replicate it – again uncritically and without any attempt to synthesize or 'build' a coherent overall picture. A typical needs analysis, conducted without time constraints, would typically build from broad exploratory techniques towards developing and testing specific ideas. So, for example, an intake might include an initial interview touching upon almost all aspects of the athlete's sporting life, and a second interview might then explore the specific nature of the problem, issue or area that the athlete wishes to work on. Perhaps in between times (or even before the intake) the psychologist might have conducted an analysis of the sport. From this broad, wide-ranging beginning, specific areas for exploration might be identified that you may wish to focus on, perhaps using questionnaires or observations. Alternatively, if, for example, the psychologist still wanted to explore at a broad level, then a performance profile could be used to help tease out which areas would be best to prioritize. This step, in itself, would help to identify which areas to focus on, which can often be a difficult decision for the psychologist (or client–psychologist team) to make. Upon identifying clear areas to focus on, the client might agree (or even ask) to be observed to check that the particular issue is relevant – for example, affecting their performances. Likewise, some psychologists might wish to deploy questionnaires at this point to specifically test whether the client scores above or below the levels that are typical of the wider population (or preferably, a sporting population of the level required!). As the emerging picture of the client's needs and goals becomes clearer, it might be agreed to check certain aspects of your thinking with a coach or parent in a stakeholder analysis, before a clear 'working model' is finally agreed – either by the psychologist alone (= highly practitioner-led – cf. Keegan, 2010); by the client and psychologist together (= client-led), or perhaps even at the agreement of all interested parties/stakeholders.

As detailed in the following chapter, a good 'working model' should include situations, causes, mechanisms and effects/consequences, meaning that it clearly identifies where to make changes, and what results to expect when these changes are made. We need to pause and note two things here as well. First, there are many ways to construct a coherent needs analysis, with no 'correct' or 'ideal' approach. For example, some psychologists may open with a wide-ranging 'battery' of questionnaires, and use this to help focus their subsequent interviews. The options are numerous. Second, time constraints and other limitations (such as physical separation) are common in elite sport, and where this leads to an 'incomplete' needs analysis, the psychologist is forced to make an educated guess (or 'professional judgement', cf. Martindale & Collins, 2013) as to how best to proceed. Obviously, this constrained/limited needs analysis contains more risks – of being incorrect, or perhaps wasting time on making changes with little/no impact – and the quality of the professional judgement arguably depends on the experience and astuteness of the psychologist. It cannot be emphasized enough that a high-quality needs analysis should lead to a high-quality support package, but as a follow-up point – as detailed in this section – a high-quality needs analysis should 'build': from exploration towards refinement and prioritization of needs. Further still, a strong needs analysis arguably needs to acknowledge and ameliorate its own 'blind spots' (See Table 5.1). So for example, a needs analysis based purely on questionnaires, whilst unlikely, would be heavily reliant on the 'simplifying' tendency of questionnaires and thus very likely to overlook the personal nuances and unique aspects of the individual client. In contrast, a needs analysis that is 100% dependent on the client's own interview data might be quite susceptible to personal biases and deliberate omissions, particularly if the psychologist were hesitant about probing unclear areas, or challenging tensions and inconsistencies. A strong needs analysis should carefully and deliberately seek to ensure that any potential blind spots are acknowledged and corrected wherever possible. Hence, whilst situational considerations can easily restrict or limit the needs analysis process, being *deliberate* and logical, *building* towards a coherent synthesis or 'working model', and *ameliorating* any potential blind spots are all key considerations. This chapter builds the case that being able to demonstrate these considerations in your records and case studies will greatly assist both your prospects (i.e., for qualification) and, over time, the quality of your practice.

5.5   Conclusion

In summary, this chapter has detailed both the overall aims and goals of the needs analysis process, as well as detailing the core techniques that are used within it – including their strengths and weaknesses in different contexts. We have clearly positioned the needs analysis process within our models of sport psychology practice: sitting predominantly between 'intake' and 'case formulation', but equally informing intakes, and the ongoing monitoring of progress. We have attempted to outline how the quality of key decisions in the psychological support package is heavily dependent on the quality of the needs analysis process, and we have highlighted several key properties of a 'strong' needs analysis, to serve as a guide for planning and evaluating practice. And just as needs analysis informs other phases of the service delivery process, needs analysis is, itself, informed by one's philosophical standpoint, ethical assumptions and information from the intake phase. In fact, needs analysis is a good example of how all the steps/phases in our model are separable, but inextricably linked and interdependent. Overall, whilst a good needs analysis can 'make' your support package and a poor one can 'break' it, in real life we often observe needs analyses that could be better: that could require less guess work or compromise, and offer more certainty in the path chosen, as well as more motivation for the client.

Table 5.1 An overview of the core needs analysis techniques used by a sport psychologist. By considering how much you have relied on each technique with your client, you may be able to identify your own blind spots and act to ameliorate them.

Needs analysis considerations	Variations and considerations	Most compatible philosophical standpoints (Only certaintist and construalist are listed, others are more flexible)	Most compatible 'practice style' (See Chapter 3)	Strengths	'Blind spots'	Usage with this client (Use either Y/N or a percentage reliance on each technique)
Interviews	Structured	Certaintist	Practitioner-led	Allows direct focus on specific topics/areas.	Can be alienating for client. Can overlook areas where real issue may lie. Client may choose to omit certain information for any number of reasons.	
	Semi-structured			Facilitates a good blend of planned questioning and responding to new information.	Depends heavily on the ability of the psychologist to balance directive and responsive questioning.	
	Unstructured	Construalist	Client-led	Places client's perceptions and experiences at the centre of the process, which can often be beneficial to motivation and self-awareness.	Practitioner forsakes ability to 'steer' to conversation, and important issues might either be overlooked or under-explored as client sets agenda.	
Informal chats				Can take place in comfortable environments or in moments closer to actual performance/training.	Can be a risk to confidentiality. 'Unofficial' tone reduced ability of psychologist to 'steer' towards certain topics/issues.	

118

(continued)

Behavioural observations	Competition vs. Training	Certaintist	Practitioner-led	Allows exploration of events occurring in the real-life context – which is a relative rarity in psychological practice.	Can easily be over-interpreted. Can be distracting for the client. Ideally needs to be informed by previous information, or else anything could appear meaningful.
Questionnaires	'Battery' or specific? Validated or tailor-made? Face-to-face, by email? Results discussed or kept private?	Certaintist	Practitioner-led	Usually well validated with comparison to normative data. Quick and easy to complete. Numerical and scientific approach can be more persuasive with some clients.	Usually very focussed on one specific issue, often even specific to a particular theory of that issue. As such, you stand no chance of finding things you do not look for in the first place. By nature, questionnaires must simplify complex issues. Combined with comparisons to norms this can leave client feeling a little alienated.
Performance profiles	(1) Simple desired vs. actual, (2) 'anchored' to levels/goals and (3) importance added and score calculated	Construalist	Client-led	Explicitly sets out to create a quantified representation of a highly subjective and personal world view. Thought to be very suitable for prioritizing areas to focus on, setting goals and supporting client autonomy/ motivation. Excellent for generating new discussion points.	Lots of scope for misinterpretation, replication and wasted effort: garbage-in-garbage-out principle. If not presented well or not supported and followed up appropriately can create a messy/unhelpful result. Clients' scores often change with experience.
Stakeholder analysis	Who to approach and for what purpose?	Certaintist	Practitioner-led	Allows for an external comparison of client's reports to others perceptions. Potentially more objective.	Presents a risk to confidentiality. May risk alienating client or appearing to 'doubt' their story.

Table 5.1 An overview of the core needs analysis techniques used by a sport psychologist. By considering how much you have relied on each technique with your client, you may be able to identify your own blind spots and act to ameliorate them. (continued)

Needs analysis considerations	Variations and considerations	Most compatible philosophical standpoints	Most compatible 'practice style'	Strengths	'Blind spots'	Usage with this client
		Only certaintist and construalist are listed, others are more flexible	See Chapter 3			Use either Y/N or a percentage reliance on each technique
Analysis of the sport		N/A	N/A	Provides and important context for interpreting client's concerns. Facilitates easier interaction without pauses to clarify rules/terminology.	Tells us very little about the specific client, only provides context.	
Performance statistics	Which ones to use and what do they mean?	Certaintist	Practitioner-led	Allows for detection of objective changes in performance, often using publically available data.	Linkage between changes made with a psychologist and objective performance are often quite unclear and unreliable. May need to supplement this information with consideration of the specific skills/attributes being worked on, i.e., skill has improved, results will follow.	

As such, what we really see is sport psychologists constantly striving to improve their needs analysis – both with individual clients and with each new client – and this chapter has been written with a view to supporting that ongoing process of self-improvement. The hard work of constantly reflecting, and positioning all the above ideas in relation to one's own practice will fall to the individual sport psychologist. However, the tools and basic considerations to inform that process of constant improvement are included here, with as much nuance and context as can practicably be offered.

5.6   Ella's story: Part 5 – How much is enough?

Ella has reached the point in her development where she has become acutely aware of the different approaches to being a sport psychologist. In particular, she is concerned about the differences between 'practitioner-led' versus 'client-led' styles. As such, the following questions make reference back to Chapter 3. Ella is contacted by a female tennis player, 21 years old, who has been experiencing difficulties with confidence and concentration in 'big' matches. The player has never received psychological support and shows no indications of clinical issues. The player believes this season may be her last opportunity to 'make it', having spent several years playing at national and international level, but never quite becoming established as a tour player.

1. What needs analysis techniques would a predominantly 'practitioner-led' needs analysis incorporate? And what might be the 'blind spots' of this approach?
2. What needs analysis techniques would a predominantly 'client-led' needs analysis incorporate? And what might be the 'blind spots' of this approach?
3. What might be the constraints on Ella's needs analysis due to the client travelling often, including different time zones, and having very little spare time? What might be the most suitable needs analysis techniques given these constraints?
4. Ella is still looking to accrue sufficient client hours to complete her supervision, and is pleased when a colleague informs her that he is leaving the area, and would like to refer all his clients to Ella. When the case files arrive, each client has completed the same needs analysis process: a clinical screening questionnaire, a mental toughness questionnaire and a test of which mental skills they currently use. The clients' progress ranges from just beginning support through to almost completing their psychological support. What are the implications of inheriting this needs analysis approach? What actions might Ella decide to take if she is not

content with this needs analysis information alone? What philosophical assumptions underpin this type of needs analysis?

5.7   Review and reflect

1. What is the role of the needs analysis process when providing psychological support? When does needs analysis begin, and end? What aspects of being a sport psychologist depend on the needs analysis process?
2. What criteria would you look for, in order to qualify as an excellent psychological needs analysis? And what constitute a bad needs analysis?
3. Can you think of any circumstances where the same suite of needs analysis techniques might become insufficient, having been fine with another client? Consider differences in the client's needs, preferences, circumstances, etc.
4. What tools, cues and prompts could you use to try and ensure that your own needs analyses processes are as strong as possible?
5. Which needs analysis techniques best lend themselves to ongoing monitoring of a client's progress?

6 Case Formulation – Creating a Working Model

6.1 Introduction and overview

While sport and exercise psychologists frequently carry out core tasks of needs analysis (Chapter 5) and delivering interventions (Chapters 8 and 9), there is very little consensus regarding the ways that these key roles are related, with the one informing the other. This chapter (as well as Chapter 7) seeks to help practising psychologists to structure, record, evaluate and reflect upon their decision-making processes. As is the case throughout this book, the core task of case formulation is presented as being carried out by a psychologist *whether explicit or not*. Even if it has never crossed one's mind to perform a case formulation, a practising psychologist is doing it anyway. It might be that the psychologist develops unique, detailed and fully operational working models for each client they encounter. Alternatively, it might be that s/he has 'settled' (consciously or unconsciously) for one model that explains how all people's minds work, and so simply slots each client into this model. Indeed, some sport psychologists have been criticized for behaving as though 'all these techniques work, regardless of which model one uses' – which in itself is effectively a case formulation decision, just one that chooses to overlook or ignore the underlying mechanisms. In this chapter, the different options for case formulation are detailed, explored and critiqued, developing pros and cons of each and allowing the reader to make informed decisions about how to conduct their practice.

A case formulation simply involves creating a working model of the core issue – be it a problem of some sort, or a desire for increased performance. This working model should include the causes, context, mechanisms, explanations and consequences – that is, the what, who/where/when, how, why and so what? This model can be drawn from the needs analysis, existing theoretical knowledge, research evidence in the literature and even personal experiences – in fact by defining case formulation as a separate and subsequent activity, we must be extending beyond

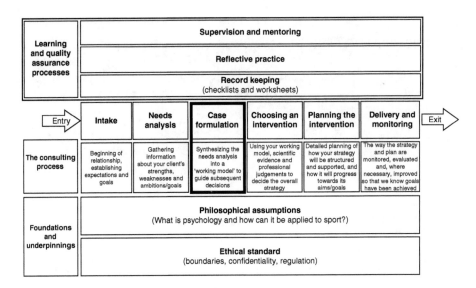

Figure 6.1 *The position of the case formulation process at the heart of the service delivery process, closely related to needs analysis and intervention choices, as well as being highly dependent upon philosophical assumptions, and supporting/feeding into reflective practice and supervision.*

the client's basic data/story and include some level of inference/theorizing. Underlying mechanisms can be biological, psychological, social or developmental, but will both adequately explain the current situation as well as offering logical/sensible options for progress or improvement. This chapter will argue that deliberately and forensically detailing both the formulation (working model) and its sources/basis (data, theory, evidence or experience) offer both the practitioner and the supervisor/assessor a better understanding of both their client's needs and the quality/reliability of their 'working model'. Worksheets are included to support readers in designing and recording their case formulations as well as for evaluating the quality of their 'working model' – in terms of the quality of the data, theory, research and experiences that prop it up.

6.2 The importance of case formulation in sport psychology

Case formulation is perhaps one of the least understood (or least written about) concepts in sport psychology, with only rare attempts to address the idea directly (e.g., Gardner & Moore, 2006). However, case formulation is extremely important, as outlined in the following quote: '[When] we fail to identify an organizing state of affairs at the centre of the client's problems [or needs/desires], the danger becomes that of needlessly pursuing change in a piecemeal fashion ... ... taking his [or her] list of complaints, prioritizing them, and pursuing them one at a time' (Bergner, 1998, p. 291). No meaningful case formulation means no understanding of the underlying issues, and no clear starting (or ending) point. Fortunately, case formulation receives a little more attention in clinical psychology (e.g., Eells, Kendjelic, & Lucas, 1998; Page, Stritzke, & McLean, 2008), which, while still sparse (cf. Eells et al., 1998), is sufficient to fuel our discussions in this chapter. As a result, it is worth noting that much of the 'case formulation' literature available is derived from a clinical perspective, which quite often adopts the specific assumptions of 'certaintism' and 'practitioner-led' practice, as described in Chapter 3. Bergner's quote above neatly summarizes the importance of case formulation – effectively arguing that we should attempt to treat the root cause, and not simply the symptoms – by carefully employing a working model of the client's situation, needs and challenges. One aim of this chapter is to demonstrate how all approaches to sport psychology will include a case formulation stage, and that – as with all the other chapters – this process is an unavoidable part of delivering sport psychology support.

Paraphrasing from Nezu, Nezu, and Lombardo (2004), case formulation can be defined as a process of hypothesizing the causes, mechanisms and outcomes/consequences behind the client's presenting issue or problem: and it is generally framed by a particular theoretical or philosophical approach. Case formulation is a description of the client's 'complaints and symptoms' (or rather, goals and barriers/challenges), *as well as* an organizing mechanism to help the psychologist understand how the client's situation came to be. As such, the likely consequences of any advice, interventions and/or non-intervention can be reasonably anticipated and evaluated. Those italics are important, as the research of Eells et al. (1998) reviewed practitioners' case notes and found that only 46.5% even attempted to include a mechanism (42.9% psychological mechanisms, 1.8% biological and 1.8% sociocultural), with only 5.4% of those being rated 'adequate' and none being rated as 'strong' (i.e., 'good'). This chapter will argue that, more than simply (re) describing data from the needs analysis, case formulations must attempt to extend these basics and offer a working model of the client's experiences – be it derived directly from published theories or uniquely constructed in collaboration with the client.

Likewise, if we paraphrase Kuyken, Fothergill, Musa, and Chadwick (2005, p. 1188 – paraphrased due to a strong emphasis on cognitive behavioural approaches in the original): case formulation aims to describe a person's presenting concerns and uses a theory or working model to make explanatory inferences about causes and maintaining factors that can inform interventions. First, there is a top-down process wherein the theory/model provides useful descriptive frameworks that adequately encompass and capture the presenting concerns. Second, the formulation enables practitioners and clients to make explanatory inferences about what caused and maintains the presenting concerns. Third, case formulation explicitly and centrally informs any actions taken. As such, case formulation is a cornerstone of psychological practice. For any particular case, formulation is the bridge between practice, theory and research. It is the crucible where the individual particularities of a given case, relevant theory and research are synthesized into an understanding of the person's presenting issues in order to inform any actions taken.

From the above definitions – reducible to 'an estimation of causes, mechanisms and outcomes' – it should be clear that the case formulations possess three properties that separate them out from other steps in our model: (1) case formulations make inferences beyond the raw data provided by a client, and preferably should include an indication of how 'sound' these inferences are; (2) as such, case formulations may contain a large component of professional judgement, reflecting the 'working model' that emerges from the client's story and data; and (3) the 'working models' generated can exist at the 'micro' level of specific issues, as well as fitting together to form a 'macro' level – the overall system including interactions of separate mechanisms or issues (cf. Eells et al., 1998). The same authors also note that the contents of a case formulation are highly dependent upon the guiding philosophy or theory adopted by the practitioner; such that the same data viewed by psychologists from different traditions can often be formed into 'widely divergent' (p. 146) working models. This issue once again highlights that there is rarely ever such a thing as a 'correct' answer in psychology, but rather the tradition (philosophy and style) from which the case formulation is attempted determines the strength and 'validity' of the inferences being made (more on validity shortly). Perhaps most difficult of all is that different case formulations, generated by practitioners in different traditions, and resulting in different advice/interventions, *can still generate positive, meaningful progress for the client* (Crits-Christoph, Cooper & Luborsky, 1988; Silberschatz & Curtis, 1993). In such circumstances, transparency, accountability, reflection and ongoing development are really all that will separate out the good practitioners from the rest – in the long term at least. Interestingly, research has shown that where practitioners do adhere to a coherent case formulation process, even when different practitioners use different underlying models, the results still tend to be better for the client (Crits-Christoph et al., 1993). Kendjelic and Eells (2007) showed that even the most basic training can improve the quality of the case formulation process. Their training covered only: symptoms and problems; precipitating stressors; predisposing events/conditions; and inferred explanatory mechanisms – that is, no coverage of underlying philosophy or preferred models – yet the outcomes were improved for those receiving the training.

In light of the above arguments and evidence, there is a strong case to be made that deliberately and explicitly performing a clear and recorded case formulation is preferable to being unclear, laissez-faire or allowing undeclared, implicit and potentially damaging assumptions to play a key role in one's practice. Whilst this phrasing might appear dramatic, it reflects the real risk that one takes if case formulation is not given adequate attention: a risk that may not always eventuate, but a risk nonetheless. In a world of increasing accountability, increasingly stringent qualification processes and increasingly informed clients/coaches, being relaxed about case formulation may become a very serious risk: as the risk becomes both more likely and more consequential.

6.3   Core considerations

Now that we have established the importance of the case formulation process, and the core outcomes it achieves, we need to examine key considerations that will inform the way we perform case formulation. Amongst these key issues, we need to consider: (1) what actually constitutes the theories or working models at the centre of the formulation process? (2) the reliability and validity of such models; (3) the ways that these models might vary – in terms of their sources and usage – in different traditions or philosophical approaches. Finally, (4) we will consider how using case formulation in one's practice actually allows us to write better case studies, be more accountable, increase adherence and even contribute to the scientific discourse in our field: something which many practitioners may consider unlikely or impossible if they are not doing 'proper' research. While considering what is written below, it is also useful to consider the following. Bergner (1998) proposed that a good case formulation should ideally identify opportunities to change the current state of affairs, rather than simply identifying a relevant but ultimately unchangeable factor – such as an aspect of childhood, or a deeply engrained personality trait. A case formulation that identifies fixed entities as causal and integral is effectively dooming the client to suffer the same situation forever: it can render the client as a powerless 'victim'. Instead, Bergner argued that we should focus on the specific aspects of the client's thoughts, behaviours or feelings that are causing, maintaining or exacerbating the current difficulty, and attempt to develop a case formulation that suggests genuine opportunities for progress. In short, 'There is [or rather, there *should be*] nothing so practical as a good theory' (Lewin, 1951, p. 20). Importantly, this means that even if a framework is labelled a theory – even if it has the word 'theory' in its name – if it does not meet certain conditions, such as offering useful suggestions for progress, it may not be a theory at all. This observation leads us to the following section asking: 'What constitutes a good theory or working model?'

6.3.1   What constitutes a 'good' theory or working model?

So far, this chapter has placed a high tariff on the use of theories or working models to form the centre of the case formulation process. As such, it is important to be as precise as possible in defining exactly what is meant by these terms. A popular and well-argued explanation was given by Stephen Hawking in his book *A Brief History of Time* (1988, p. 11 – emphasis added): 'In order to talk about the nature of the universe [or the mind]... *you have to be clear about what a scientific theory is*. I shall take the simpleminded view that a theory is just a model ... and a set of rules that relate quantities in the model to observations that we make. *It exists only in our mind and does not have any other reality*. A theory is a good theory if it satisfies *two requirements*: (1) It must accurately describe a large class of observations on the basis of a model that contains only a few arbitrary elements; and (2) it must make definite predictions about the result of future observations. For example, Aristotle's theory that everything was made out of four elements, earth, air, fire and water, was simple enough ... *but it did not make any definite predictions*. On the other hand, Newton's theory of gravity was based on an even simpler model, in which bodies attracted each other with a force that was proportional to a quantity called their mass and inversely proportional to the square of the distance between them. Yet it predicts the motions of the sun, the moon, and the planets to a high degree of accuracy'. Two conditions: it must explain the existing observations (e.g., needs analysis) and it must make testable predictions about future events. The 'it' that we are talking about is a set of prepositions or rules – but without meeting these two conditions they could just as well be the rules of a game or a sport. Hawking went a little bit further to say that the theory should ideally be as simple as practically possible – and I would add that, if it is to serve our purposes, the theory must be communicable such that someone other than the 'holder' can understand it too. But that's it.

We can go on to consider what makes a good theory, as opposed to a bad one, but the 'working model' at the heart of our case formulation process is both incredibly simple, and yet (as already discussed) incredibly misunderstood and often totally overlooked. As a final point here, even though much of the literature on case formulation originates in the clinical domain, this chapter argues that such theories and working models are just as important and useful in the certaintist, construalist and fallibilist traditions (as described in Chapter 3), with pragmatism adopting a slightly different approach (see Section 6.4, below).

Hawking's definition is consistent with that of Karl Popper, a philosopher of science who, despite frequent attempts to criticize his viewpoint, has fundamentally influenced the way science is done. For example, the statistical assumption that the null hypothesis is true until it can be discarded is very closely aligned to Popper's viewpoint that a theory or hypothesis should be considered wrong by default. In his attempts to delineate scientific theories from either non-scientific or pseudo-scientific theories, Popper offered a range of criteria for a 'good' theory. First, a good theory should be 'bold' in that it should rule out, or prohibit, a range of events or possibilities. One key criticism of many theories, discussed shortly, is that they often permit numerous and even contradictory possibilities. The following passage illustrates the problem as Popper saw it, in relation to psychotherapy (1969, p. 368 – emphasis added): "I may illustrate this by two very different examples of human behaviour: that of a man who pushes a child into the water with the intention of drowning it; and that of a man who sacrifices his life in an attempt to save the child. Each of these two cases can be explained with equal ease in Freudian and in Adlerian terms. According to Freud, the first man suffered from repression (say, of some component of his Oedipus complex), while the second man had achieved sublimation. According to Adler, the first man suffered from feelings of inferiority (producing perhaps the need to prove to himself that he dared to commit some crime), and so did the second man (whose need was to prove to himself that he dared to rescue the child). *I could not think of any human behaviour which could not be interpreted in terms of either theory*. It was precisely this fact – that they always fitted, that they were always *confirmed* – which in the eyes of their admirers constituted the strongest argument in favour of these theories. *It began to dawn on me that this apparent strength was in fact their weakness*."

So by prohibiting certain eventualities, a theory exposes itself to being false, and Popper viewed this as a strength. As such, practitioners should not be swayed by theories that appear unfalsifiable, or perhaps able to explain any and all circumstances. This may even mean the theory/model is not scientific in any formal sense – because there is no way to ever test it and falsify it. The more possibilities a theory rules out, the better. Pragmatically, this is actually very useful, as we need our working model to identify specific courses of action and preferably not to permit/allow a wide range of interventions/'treatments'.

Further to the above, if a theory rules out possibilities that we might ordinarily expect (or makes unusual/unexpected predictions), and these predictions are then tested but remain unfalsified, then the theory is a good one. Successfully predicting things that other theories do not is clearly a strength, especially if it can be done with as few rules and qualifiers as possible. This latter idea of simplicity originates from the trend that many existing and popular theories tend to 'sprout' additional qualifiers (I sometimes call them 'Yeah buts and what ifs') when faced with problematic observations – the so-called Duhem-Quine principle (Gillies, 1998).

So, a couple of paragraphs of slightly heavy-going there, but a couple of vital principles to keep in mind when choosing (or developing) working models to use in our case formulation process. First, we should choose or develop theories that make predictions we can test against experience – either our own or those of the client. These predictions should be bold and clear such that, if incorrect, the theory itself would be wrong or at least damaged. Second, the theory or model we choose should exclude as many options as possible, leaving us with a clear way forwards. If, when we 'plug in' the client's current situation and needs, a theory allows us to simply pick from a wide range of options then it really may as well not exist. Third, and perhaps most counter intuitive, better theories distinguish themselves by predicting things that other theories do not. This rule may, realistically, operate over a longer time span and with the benefit of experience. However, if several theories all predict the same possibilities (perhaps even for different reasons), but one makes quite different predictions, it may hold promise. The deviant theory should be investigated and tested, not ignored because it is different. In terms of progressing science over the long term, if the 'deviant' predictions of our theory, *crying out* for falsification, cannot be falsified then the 'deviant' theory should become our central theory.

6.3.2   The reliability and validity of case formulations

Both reliability and validity are tricky concepts, particularly in psychology where our subject matter is difficult to define and often changing/developing, in response to experience. In general terms, reliability refers to the consistency of measurement ('Is this metre really a metre? Will it still be a metre tomorrow?'). Regarding case formulation, this would mean that different psychologists reach the same formulations when presented with the same client details. Likewise, in the broadest sense validity refers to whether we're actually measuring what we intend to ('Is this metre really a unit of distance?'). In applied psychological support, validity can most usefully be judged in terms of 'predictive validity' – does our model accurately predict future events, or the outcomes of future actions? Methodologists will note that other types of validity do exist, but those are arguably best applied to measurement issues, such as questionnaire design, and not the applied sport psychology support process. As such, reliability would be indicated through agreement between different psychologists viewing the same client details, whereas validity might best be judged by examining the outcomes when case formulation models are used to predict/guide desirable outcomes.

The discussion of these issues by Kuyken et al. (2005) is illuminating and worth re-presenting here. They begin by noting that establishing the reliability of case formulations is often very difficult, because ensuring that each practitioner has the same information means using written summaries and case notes. This means that, perhaps by necessity, studies in this area have so far failed to use the data available to 'real-world' practitioners: such as a comprehensive intake interview, standardized assessment instruments, the clients' body language, tone of voice and emotional shifts in session – amongst other things (see Chapter 5). The authors begin to explore whether developing more systematic and objective case formulation systems would lead the profession to be less at risk of bias and improve the rates of agreement between practitioners. Nevertheless, if practitioners can agree about the content of a case formulation, *this does not mean that they are necessarily producing good formulations*. That is, a reliable formulation does not guarantee: that the formulation is coherently structured; that it adequately explains the array of presenting concerns and issues; or whether the formulation provides useful (testable) predictions as to what course of action will prove beneficial. As such, establishing a way of ensuring that practitioners reliably formulate the same case into the same working model or theory may be of limited value if the formulation is incoherent and/or unhelpful. What we see in real life is that two different formulations of the same case may have few elements in common (and therefore be *unreliable*), but both may enable focussed and high-impact recommendations or interventions (Crits-Christoph et al., 1988). In short, on the available evidence, it may be more important for a formulation to be a coherent and defensible account of a person's presenting concerns than to be replicable (or agreed/approved) by another psychologist.

To some extent, the finding that the reliability of case formulations does not matter is a little uncomfortable to contemplate. However, to ease this discomfort, it is helpful to review the role of theories and models in the case formulation process. The theory or model should encompass the data from the needs analysis and make concrete predictions about what will be helpful. As such, the theory is a *tool* to be used for the benefit of the client: it is expendable. Drawing from Popper (1959) again, theories can be sacrificed and discarded, but we (and more importantly, the client) live to fight another day. At the beginning of a career, and with the current literature to hand, a sport psychologist's set of known theories might be compared to a cheap set of tools: adequate but fragile and likely to break after a few uses. An alternative approach would be to 'custom-build' the tools (i.e., theories) for each job (i.e., client), which would be labour intensive but would guarantee the right tools for each job. The second option is intended as a metaphor for more 'client-centred' approaches as described in Chapter 3. As a realistic compromise, many professionals will have their 'favourite' tools – both builders and psychologists alike – that they use as often as possible just for the comfort they offer. However, while a successful or rich builder is able to purchase high-quality tools that will last a lifetime and be suitable for many jobs, the same is arguably not yet true in sport psychology: We have very few high quality theories that are suitable across many situations without breaking (see above for the criteria concerning a good versus bad theory). Within this metaphor, different psychologists might use different tools for the same job and still get positive outcomes. Some may use an old favourite and some may custom-build their tools, but it is almost impossible to guarantee 'the right tool for the job' at this time. Personally, I like to think that we may gradually improve the quality of the tools/theories/models available to sport psychologists, but in the meantime we should be clear that they are expendable, and quite likely flawed, but we can still do our job if we're careful.

6.3.3   Case formulation in the four 'traditions'

If we pause for a moment to consider how the four traditions described in Chapter 3 would incorporate case formulation, we uncover some interesting differences and similarities. The four traditions outlined were: certaintism (confirmed theories are universally true); construalism (theories are unique to each individual/group); fallibilism (theories are useful tools, but wrong in ways that we don't yet know, so be careful!); and pragmatism (If what we do appears to work it doesn't matter what theory we use – also outlined in Keegan, 2014). In the below passages, each of these characterizations of how psychological practice can be approached are linked to the case formulation process.

Certaintism

First, a strictly 'certaintist' tradition – derived from positivism and empiricism – would seek to fit the client's data in with existing theory and/or research. Remembering that questionnaires are often directly and deliberately compatible with a 'parent' theory (as noted in Chapter 5), this can minimize the necessity of *inferences* (sometimes viewed as 'guesswork') in attempting a case formulation. Instead of making inferences, a practitioner holding certaintist assumptions would place their trust in the veracity of the relevant theory (i.e., research has given us increased certainty in the theory), and use the theory to derive ideas for interventions. For example, Bandura's (1977) theory of self-efficacy – often equated with confidence – proposes that there are four key sources of self-efficacy: performance accomplishments, vicarious experiences, social persuasion and physiological factors (i.e., arousal, butterflies in the tummy, sweating, nausea, etc.). Thus an athlete who reports lacking confidence might be supported through: using the setting and monitoring of goals to build awareness of performance accomplishments; seeing videos or examples of similar athletes performing well (i.e., modelling or vicarious experience); positive feedback from the coach, parents, peers or the self (i.e., positive self-talk) to constitute social persuasion, or an intervention to either control or reframe feelings of arousal and anxiety that accompany performance. Notably in this case, a relatively simple theoretical model offers up a very wide range or potential intervention strategies, and this is not unusual in sport psychology. This issue could be viewed as useful (e.g., 'It lets me do any intervention I like!') or quite useless (e.g., 'It doesn't get me any closer to knowing what the best intervention is!'). Notably, the issue is rarely addressed in case studies and assessment submissions. Even in the research literature we can often find very popular/prominent theories generating what might be called 'kitchen sink' interventions: where many changes are implemented leaving the researchers unable to conclude which bit (or bits) actually generated the effects observed (also discussed in Keegan, Harwood, Spray, & Lavallee, 2010). Realistically, this can often mean the psychologist still needs to work with the client in selecting the one or two most promising or most practical changes: as offering numerous ideas can be overwhelming and possibly detrimental. A highly informed practitioner, who follows the research literature very closely, might be able to cite recent research supporting the effectiveness of one intervention over the others (preferably in delivering the specific aims of the client, and not just a general improvement). [Such clarity would assist] in deciding which approach to choose (as discussed in Chapter 7). However, a review by Gardner and Moore (2006) concluded that at the time of writing there was not sufficient evidence to *conclusively demonstrate* that any of the most popular interventions in sport psychology actually improved athletic performance (i.e., goal setting, imagery, self-talk and arousal control – although note that the 'causal chain' between a skill such as these and performance is quite long and uncontrollable). Their recommendation was that sport psychology researchers should conduct the kind of randomized control trials (RCTs) that are used to evaluate the effects of new medicines in order to allow applied practitioners to be more certain in their recommendations. However, in the 8 years since the publication of their book their advice has either been ignored, or even attacked in some cases as impracticable (e.g., Hardy, 2012).

The problem with this state of affairs, which will be discussed further in Chapter 7, is that to be 'certain' that our theories and interventions are making important differences – and not other factors such as regression to the mean, maturation or normal athletic training – we do, technically, need RCT evidence (even acknowledging the many criticisms of adopting RCTs as the 'gold standard': to be at all certain requires very strong evidence not just a large volume of weak evidence plus 'belief'). In the absence of such evidence within sport psychology, a certaintist (positivist/empiricist) psychologist must either look at other fields of psychology (e.g., clinical) or make informed guesses after all. Overall, while a psychologist who wishes to pursue 'certaintist' aims/traditions has a clear 'recipe' to follow, in reality the current literature struggles to provide the necessary 'ingredients' that would offer sufficient certainty: even if the 'recipe' were followed to the letter.

Construalism

Second, we can consider the 'construalist' characterization of psychological practice, which is based on the philosophies of interpretivism and constructivism, and which arguably gave rise to 'client-centred' approaches such as counselling (as discussed in Chapter 3). Returning to the builder/carpentry metaphor used above, a construalist psychologist should look to custombuild the tool (theory/model) for each job (client). As already discussed, this approach would likely be very labour intensive. However, by developing the perfect 'tool' (i.e., model) for each client, the ways forward should be clearer and the outcome should be more assured than when using a one-size-fits-all theory/model. Importantly, however, there remains a working model at the core of the construalist approach, so a good case formulation is still eminently possible and should be included in any record keeping or case studies, etc.

In this approach, the construalist practitioner abandons any notion that one client's unique model can be used with another client, or that there is a readymade model that can be used 'off the shelf' with a wide range of clients. Likewise, questionnaires and measures that have been validated with a large population would be inappropriate for use with the unique and individual client in front of you. This situation can cause a lot of difficulty and self-doubt for a psychologist adopting the construalist tradition, as there is no ability to claim that one is drawing upon a reliable or validated theory or model with 'proven' results. Instead, the method or approach of developing a tailor-made working model for each client is, in itself, the strength of this approach. By always developing the perfect tool for the job, you stand a much better chance of being successful. Ideally, the model developed for case formulation should be so personalized and detailed that it quickly identifies a very small number of very promising strategies – to *both* the practitioner and client. The 'answer' should be obvious to both parties. However, that utility does come at the cost of reliability (other people might not have picked the same tool) and validity (a brand new tool will have no proven track record of solving that type of problem – instead the judgement will be whether it works *going forwards*). Researchers and practitioners adopting construalist assumptions should not look for reliable and valid theories/models in the formal certaintist sense, but often become a little conflicted and insecure when these issues are raised. Instead, however, it is possible to replace reliability and validity with transparency and credibility. For transparency, how clear and well evidenced are all the key aspects of the model (between the psychologist and client ... not necessarily anyone else!). Is there good agreement and does the model developed sit comfortably with the existing story/events? For credibility, how thorough has the construction process been? How much 'data' has gone into developing it and how good are the 'checks and measures' along the way to ensure a solid, dependable model was built? Further, where there are any doubts or weaknesses, what would you look for to be able to change these aspects of the model you're using for case formulation? Returning to the Kuyken et al. (2005) study (above), we can also recall that the validity of a case formulation is more important in terms of whether it actually generates meaningful progress, and this remains compatible with the construalist viewpoint.

Overall, the tension between certaintism and construalism in regard to case formulation can be boiled down to the following. Does the psychologist put her/his trust in the method of always developing tailor-made bespoke models, or in existing theories and models that claim a degree of reliability and validity? There is no correct answer to this question, as the answer depends on what set of philosophical assumptions one is adopting. It is interesting to reflect on Tod, Andersen, and Marchant's (2009, 2011) studies following trainee and post-qualification psychologists as they developed. They noted a tendency to move from certaintist case formulations (and overall approaches) towards construalist ones as practitioners gain experience. Perhaps the practitioners they interviewed found the validated theories covered at university unsatisfactory for use with individual clients. Perhaps the existing theories and models, being developed through formal research, lend themselves better to large-scale research using questionnaires, than to the task of case formulation with individual clients? Either way, such a developmental trajectory or transition *should* be accompanied by a fundamental change in the way that one case formulates. One approach looks to use existing models/theories 'off the shelf', and apply them to the client's situation, the other looks to meticulously develop a highly personalized working model for that specific client. One depends on the reliability of the *theories and models* available to be chosen, the other depends on the effectiveness of the *method* of developing custom-made working models, and the ability of the practitioner to do so. These two types of case formulation should look completely different, and practitioners adopting either of these two approaches arguably should not try to 'look like' they are addressing aspects of the other (or both..!). In my experience of reviewing case studies, confusion, contradictions, poor writing, anxiety and even frustration/anger (especially in response to assessors' feedback!) tend to follow when practitioners are unaware of the type of case formulation they are developing.

Fallibilism

Third, we can consider the fallibilist tradition in the philosophy of science (described in Chapter 3) and how it might apply to case formulation. In its purest form, a fallibilist practitioner would attempt to 'depend' on neither the quality of the off-the-shelf models, nor the quality of the process followed by the practitioner in developing a model. Instead, a purely fallibilist sport psychologist would place their trust in no part of the process – neither the theories nor the methods – and continually question every aspect of the case formulation (as well as the needs analysis, practice style, etc.). A fallibilist case formulation could draw from existing theories, tailor-made working models or combinations of the two, but it would be constantly very aware/cautious of the weaknesses and compromises in doing so. If the theoretical framework, the research supporting it or the applicability of the theory were questionable (as they always are under fallibilism), then a fallibilist case formulation would note this and attempt to manage the risks. If there is any chance that the practitioner's ability to develop a working model with the client is even slightly imperfect (again, as it always is under fallibilism), then a fallibilist case formulation should capture this, identify weak spots and attempt to react accordingly. And if the working model being used to case formulate shows any signs of slipping – failing to reconcile with recent events or making predictions that prove unsuccessful – then a fallibilist practitioner would arguably be the most likely to amend or replace the working model. As such, in a fallibilist case formulation, everything is tentative and 'under review', but not only that, there should also be clear criteria defined for whether the model in use is proving valuable, and contingencies in place to manage any threats or problems. These additional details arguably separate out a fallibilist case formulation from the certaintist and construalist approaches, because superficially the working models themselves could look like established theories, tailor-made models or hybrids. The faith/trust placed in either the model or the method might mean that certaintist and construalist case formulations, respectively, contain much less emphasis on managing risk and ameliorating problems. However, whilst the working model may change and evolve quite rapidly, and be continually viewed as tentative and imperfect, there does remain a working model at the heart of a fallibilist case formulation. In this respect, certaintism, construalism and fallibilism all make very clear and explicit use of case formulations in their practice and case reports. Pragmatism, on the other hand, does something a little different.

Pragmatism

Going back to our characterization of the pragmatist tradition from Chapter 3, we might describe it as 'what works is right'. Given that the goal posts often move during the provision of psychological support, we might need to replace 'worked' with 'generated positive change for the client'. As noted earlier, it is easy to criticize this apparently superficial and instrumentalist viewpoint, but philosophers such as Dewey (1916) argued that you find a solution/strategy (by any means other than pure luck) and that strategy appears to work, then you must, *on some level*, have known something about the underlying mechanisms and structures (if luck is the reason, the psychologist probably wasn't right after all). Alternatively, it could be reasoned that the very fact a strategy appeared to work tells us something very important about the underlying mechanisms and structures – even if they were not acknowledged when the strategy was proposed. In this respect, there is still a place for models and case formulation in a pragmatist philosophy. However, it might need to be repositioned from the very heart of the service delivery process to become, instead, an important element of the monitoring, evaluation and reflection. In pure pragmatism, a working model may not explicitly inform the interpretation of past or current data (circumstances, stories, etc.), nor is it deliberately deployed for the selection of strategies and interventions. Rather, the success or failure of these interventions tells us something important about a model or theory that we held (and used) whether we recognize it or not.

To explain this reasoning, we need to explore what would happen if we simply did not have or use an explanatory model/theory. It would be the same as if our builder did not have any tools. Either nothing would get done or it would be a hit-and-hope 'bodge job'. In psychological practice, this might appear as either no action, as noted, or more likely a fairly random and inexplicable pattern of suggesting interventions that are often quite incongruent with the client's situation/needs. As far as we can make out to date, humans are incapable of truly random behaviour (Nickerson, 2004, 2005), always producing patterns and assumptions even when the person involved is convinced they behaved randomly. More substantively, philosophers, ranging from Sextus Empricus (AD 160–210) to David Hume (1738) and beyond, have comprehensively shown that no human decision can be made in a vacuum – that is, there is always some assumption, theory, heuristic or presumption guiding human decisions. So if you, or you and the client together, happen to have chosen a strategy to generate positive change for the client, you will have undoubtedly used some kind of working model, and therefore, a case formulation.

As such, rather than explicitly and deliberately guiding the decision process, as case formulations do (or should) in the other three traditions, a pragmatist case formulation should at least attempt to capture the model you used implicitly, or unconsciously. If your actions/strategies didn't 'work', then the model you implicitly used to inform your decisions is flawed, and may need to be exposed, examined and refined (i.e., through reflection).

If your actions/strategies did appear to 'work', then according to pragmatist philosophy, there was something 'right' (or valuable or meaningful) in the underlying models/ideas you used. In this respect, there is still valuable work to be done in identifying the model(s) used, clearly expressing them and attempting to uncover the right/valuable/meaningful parts – preferably using the definitions of a good theory from earlier (i.e., 'What constitutes a 'good' theory or working model?'). Such an exercise is not a waste of time at all, as it may prove valuable to: you, the practitioner; or the client (e.g., if it was the client's model that was used to inform key decisions); or to science more broadly (especially if you've accidentally happened upon a new and successful model that can be tested or used by others). It can also, of course, inform supervisory and mentoring processes. Overall, however, even if you could absolutely swear you did not use a working model or theory to inform key decisions in your psychological practice: (1) that's impossible, so; (2) you did, just implicitly; (3) you were almost definitely working under a pragmatist approach (e.g., if you were under time pressure or in a new and unfamiliar environment); (4) you still need to try and record it in your notes and/or case studies; and (5) there are still important lessons to be learned – whether it 'worked' or not. The following section on the benefits of case formulation will add to this argument.

To summarize this section of the chapter, case formulation is applicable to all four historical 'traditions' in sport psychology – with traditions referring to common pairings of ontological and epistemological assumptions. In each tradition, the way that case formulation is deployed differs, sometimes quite substantially, but underneath those differences the core tasks of explaining current/past situations and predicting future changes remains constant. The important role case formulation plays in all four traditions is a strong argument that we should recognize the process, include it in our case notes and case studies and 'make the most' of analysing, reflecting on and improving our case formulation processes.

6.3.4   Additional benefits of case formulation

As noted at the beginning of the chapter, case formulation may be a missing link in the many trainees' case studies, sitting at the important juncture between needs analysis and interventions. Sitting as an examiner of applicants seeking to gain recognition as a sport and exercise psychologist, I was overwhelmed by the continued lack of this important component in the case studies that were submitted. There is no doubt in my mind that, in terms of the all-important demonstration of competence, case formulations play an important role. However, there are additional benefits to explicitly and deliberately recording our case formulations, which largely arise from the important role they play in the service delivery process. These additional benefits can be briefly summarized below, although research supporting these claims is lacking – so any interested researchers have an 'open goal' to examine whether these benefits really do arise from doing good case formulation:

1) *Case formulation allows us to be more accountable.* Assessors, supervisors, peers, clients, researchers and the public may all have legitimate reasons to examine the models that drive psychological support. Further, the case formulation process is extremely important, and anything that might constitute a good case formulation is therefore very valuable. As such, rather than working behind closed doors, where both mistakes and successes might go unnoticed, the broader field of sport psychology (and people's confidence in it) may well be enhanced by sharing what works, what doesn't and exploring why. If you make a bad mistake but you have a good case formulation recorded, you can fix it. No case formulation, no ability to improve. Unlike magicians, if we cannot legitimately answer the question 'How did you do that?', people could, and should, become suspicious. I often refer to case formulation with students as 'showing your workings', in an analogy to solving maths problems. If a student consistently gets the right answer but without showing their workings, they're either a maths genius or cheating. Worse, if they did go wrong you cannot tell where/why. Indeed, some maths exams give more marks for showing your workings than for getting the right answer. The same should be the case for psychology.

2) *Shared case formulations can increase adherence.* A core assumption of counselling and the 'construalist' tradition is that when the case formulation comes from the client and is couched in their terms/language, motivation and adherence are stronger (Rogers, 1957, 1961). This therefore means the interventions/support are much more likely to work (e.g., Bouvy et al., 2003; Faulkner, Wadibia, Lucas, & Hilleman, 2000; Friedman et al., 1996; Ogedegbe et al., 2008). The same can be applied to the other approaches too though, such that if the practitioner has a working model in mind that leads to a strategy for generating the desired changes, they may wish to share it with the client. As noted above, psychological support based on guessing is fragile at best, and our clients don't want to feel that we're guessing when it comes to their performance/health/well-being. Likewise, research has shown that providing a rationale, even when decisions are made autocratically by a leader/coach, still boosts athlete motivation compared to simply 'declaring' a course of action (e.g., Reeve, Jang, Hardre, & Omura, 2002). Involving the client in the decision process, and clearly demonstrating where advice is originating from is a good way of enhancing motivation and adherence, which is a strong predictor of positive outcomes in the long run (Reeve et al., 2002).

3) *Good case formulations can contribute to the scientific discourse in our field.* As noted earlier, theories exist to be practical, useful guides in determining actions. If theories from research do not prove useful in guiding practice, then the people doing the research need to know. Likewise, if theories are generated as part of applied practice, they might also become good candidates for testing through formal research and development/ distribution. In this respect, practitioners who might ordinarily feel like the customers or recipients of scientific research can actually contribute very meaningfully to the ongoing discourse. In fact, given that some approaches involve developing a unique working model for every client, recording and sharing (anonymously) case formulations might even become an endless source of potentially interesting and meaningful theories worthy of further investigation. Commonalities between small groups or types of client could be identified and developed into formal research questions, even if each individual model/formulation was completely unique to the specific client. At the moment, this appears to be a very rare occurrence in sport psychology, yet the position of practitioners 'at the coalface' of sport psychology suggests they may be encountering important questions and solutions, every day, that the research community could fruitfully help with (and learn from).

4) *Guiding ongoing data collection and interpretation.* One criticism that is sometimes made of researchers adopting a 'guiding theory', especially when researching a new and unknown topic, is that the theory tells you what to look for and how to measure it (e.g., Keegan et al., 2010). Thus, if we only look for what the theory tells us to look for, we could miss something important in our research. However, once you've taken the time to develop or select a model or theory that is highly appropriate to your client, and that sits well with their previous/current experiences, it's no longer a 'pre-emptive guess'. Suddenly, the property of theories whereby they tell you what data to look for, and how to measure or interpret it, becomes quite useful. Let's take risk taking as an example. If our client's case formulation demonstrates someone lacking in self-esteem, trapped in a pattern of powerlessness and self-handicapping, we might view reports of risk taking behaviour as positive. If this client confronts someone for queue jumping: that's probably a good thing. However, what if our client's case formulation involves a rugby player who has been forced to retire from the game? Deprived of any suitable outlet for his aggressive impulses, and still dealing with feelings of resentment and anger about the forced retirement, then the same behaviour would be viewed very differently. If we were a bystander in this situation without any access to the client's backstory, we might not infer either of these histories, and instead just assume the argument started because he was in a rush, or a real believer in manners and etiquette. Theories,

which is how we are defining case formulations, *lend meaning* to the observed behaviour. Theories tell us what to look for, how to measure it and how to interpret it. As such, a good case formulation should tell you not only what the best options are for your client, but also how to implement, monitor and evaluate those actions/strategies. Once clear and agreed/established, a good case formulation tells you which data to focus on and include, as well as which data to ignore or simply 'store' for later. Choices of questions, topics, questionnaires and more can all be informed by having a good case formulation. Likewise, the interpretation of answers.

5) *Check and revise if necessary.* As already noted above, theories are completely expendable, but relationships and clients' outcomes are not. So if there is anything amiss in a psychological support package, the case formulation is a good place to look. It will not complain if it is updated, modified or replaced – but disappoint a client and they may well complain. Likewise, it does not need to give informed consent to be changed. However, research examining confirmation bias (Darley & Paget, 1983 Nickerson, 1998; Plous, 1993) suggests that human beings are extremely reluctant to update our theories, even in the face of compelling evidence that we are wrong. Further, as a caveat to Point 4, above, we tend to only collect information that supports our theories and totally ignore or reject information that contradicts them (Baron, 2000; Lord, Ross, & Lepper, 1979). However, the case formulation is by far the most changeable, malleable aspect of the process and if there are any signs that our support is missing the mark, perhaps we should look first at the model we are using. It is certainly much easier to conclude: 'We're looking at this a little wrong' than 'I am an ineffective psychologist' or 'this client is resistant to change and refusing to implement the strategies'. Both of those 'sources of the problem' come with pretty serious consequences. In addition, we can ask 'What is even more useful than a good theory?' to which the answer is: 'An even better one'. So even if a case formulation is working adequately, there is no reason not to keep updating and improving it as new information emerges, and as the effects of suggested changes begin to show through. In reality, we should even expect certain aspects of the case formulation to change as we implement changes, perhaps adding new skills and options, or removing certain influences. Imagine referring back to an old case formulation with a client who has substantially changed in between times. It could both suggest inappropriate courses of action, as well as potentially causing offence! And finally, if you modify a case formulation slightly, but the changes turn out to be incorrect or unhelpful, you can always change it back. However, it can be very difficult to take back poor advice, or an implication of non-adherence.

6) *Case formulations allow reflection and improvement.* Considering the very central role that case formulation is given in our model of the service delivery process, it becomes clear that recording, analysing and improving our case formulations can become a powerful source of improvement for the sport psychologist. Are there models you tend to gravitate towards, and are they the most effective ones available? If you tend to custom-build models for each client, how skilful are you at this, and how accurate/effective are they? To what extent do you check that your case formulations fit with the client's previous and current experiences before adopting them? How clear and explicit are your case formulations: can you write them down or sketch them out, or do they remain quite implicit and undeclared? Do you share and check your case formulations with the client? Do you monitor and update your case formulations as necessary? Do you discuss case formulations with your supervisor or mentor, and does this lead to changes in the way you conduct the process? If we accept case formulation as the core of the service delivery process, and if we agree that the benefits described in this chapter are facilitated through good formulation, then improving the way we do case formulation improves the quality of our practice.

6.4 Conclusion

In summary, this chapter has detailed both the overall aims and goals of the case formulation process, as well as detailing the core considerations within it. We have clearly positioned case formulation within the sport psychology service delivery process, sitting predominantly between 'needs analysis' and 'intervention choice', but equally informing many other aspects of the support process. We have attempted to outline how the quality of key decisions in the psychological support package are heavily dependent on the quality of the case formulation, and we have highlighted several key properties of a 'strong' case formulation, to serve as a guide for planning and evaluating practice. It should go without saying that just as case formulation informs other phases of the service delivery process, it is, in itself, informed by other stages. Philosophical standpoint, ethical assumptions and information from the intake phase and needs analysis all feed into the case formulation, whereas the effects of interventions, the monitoring progress, client feedback, reflection or supervision can all modify or change a case formulation. Case formulation may even be the perfect example of how all the steps/phases in our model are separable, but inextricably linked and interdependent. Overall, the most notable finding regarding case formulation is that it is frequently only implicit in psychologists' practice: commonly missing from practice records and case studies. As such, in order to improve our practice we need to explicate, record and analyse our case formulations, and this chapter has been written with a view to supporting that ongoing process of self-improvement. As is often the case, the hard work of constantly reflecting, and positioning all the above ideas in relation to one's own practice will fall to the individual sport psychologist.

6.5   Ella's story: Part 6 – The moment of doubt

Ella is working with a promising young (15 years old) cricketer who has recently 'hit a slump' – getting out cheaply in a string of innings, and becoming visibly nervous at the batting crease. He walks around between deliveries, performing several ritualistic movements and extensively 'gardening' (tapping down perceived lumps in the pitch). Having been a star player for his club for many years, he is now struggling after being selected to play in the development squad for his local elite team. He describes how several of his recent failures involved 'not seeing' the ball, yet his vision remains unchanged and he does not need glasses.

Ella consults the literature for theories of confidence and concentration, both her old textbooks and the latest research articles. She finds several theories that appear to incorporate the symptoms described by Lachlan. She also finds that the theories are relatively unhelpful when it comes to offering specific recommendations and interventions. Ella feels unhappy with this situation when case formulating for Lachlan, but unsure of what to do.

1. If Ella chose to stick with the existing theories form literature, what criteria could she use to discriminate between them? What would constitute a good theory for case formulating, versus a bad one?
2. If Ella remains unhappy with the existing theories and models, what options does she have for generating a new one? What sources of information should she use when generating this new case formulation model, and how will she know whether it is adequate?
3. Ella's supervisor asks why she has not used a 'validated' model with Lachlan, what could she say in response?
4. Ella remains a little unsure about the case formation she has used with Lachlan, as she herself lacks the confidence to 'tailor-make' her approach to an individual client. How could Ella evaluate the strength of her case formulation, and the strategies she has derived from it to assist Lachlan?

6.6   Review and reflect

1. What is the role of the case formulation process when providing psychological support? When does needs analysis begin, and end? What aspects of being a sport psychologist depend on the case formulation process?
2. What criteria would you look for in order to qualify as an excellent psychological case formulation? And what might constitute a weak case formulation?
3. Can you think of any circumstances where a thorough case formulation might not be necessary? What might be the risks of rushing or neglecting the case formulation phase? If constrained by time or lack of information, how could a rushed case formulation be mitigated?
4. What tools, cues and prompts could you use to try and ensure that your own case formulations processes are as strong as possible?

Worksheet 6.1   Case formulation scoring criteria

Source: Page, A. C., Stritzke, W. G. K. and Mclean, N. J. (2008). Toward science-informed supervision of clinical case formulation: A training model and supervision method, *Australian Psychologist*, 43(2), 88–95. Reprinted with kind permission from John Wiley and Sons.

Mark/note the level you achieved

Problem list

All relevant problems noted; clearly distinguishing between primary and secondary issues.

Most relevant problems noted; but no evidence of distinguishing between primary and secondary issues.

Some relevant problems noted; but also some irrelevant issues noted AND at least one primary problem missed.

N/A

Predisposing factors

Predisposing variables noted; and clearly linked to specific problems in problem list.

Predisposing variables noted; but these are not clearly linked to specific problems in the problem list.

No evidence of considering predisposing variables.

N/A

Precipitating factors

Precipitating event(s) noted; and clearly linked to specific problems in the problem list.

Precipitating event(s) noted; but not clearly linked to specific problems in the problem list.

No evidence of considering precipitating factors.

N/A

Perpetuating factors

Perpetuating factors noted (e.g., core beliefs, contingencies of reinforcement, etc.); and clearly linked to specific problems in problem list.

Perpetuating factors noted; but these are not clearly linked to specific problems in the problem list.

No evidence of considering perpetuating factors.

N/A

Provisional conceptualization

Well-integrated hypothesis that links the relevant problems with predisposing, precipitating and perpetuating factors, and provides a good explanation of the patient's presenting problem(s).

A hypothesis that provides a plausible but incomplete explanation of the patient's presenting problem(s).

A poorly integrated explanation of the client's presenting problem(s).

N/A

Problems potentially hindering treatment and strengths and assets

Potential problem(s) and strength(s) or asset(s) noted; and clearly linked to specific problems in problem list OR specific aspects of treatment plan.

Potential problems and strength(s) or asset(s) noted; but not clearly linked to specific problems in problem list OR specific aspects of treatment plan.

No evidence of considering potential problems and strength(s) or asset(s).

N/A

Choosing a Support Strategy – Case Formulations, Evidence and Professional Judgement

7

7.1 Introduction and overview

Choosing the best course of action for our clients is a metaphorical 'black box' that needs to be opened up. As noted in previous chapters, whilst sport psychologists frequently conduct needs analyses and recommend interventions, the intervening steps of case conceptualization and choosing the support strategy are often very unclear – yet exploring and strengthening these processes arguably leads to more effective outcomes and better case reports. There is also a particular issue in sport psychology where different interventions (imagery, self-talk, relaxing/psyching-up, goal setting) are used to achieve many different outcomes (performance enhance, confidence, motivation, arousal/emotional control, concentration, etc.). There is little or no pattern, at this time, regarding which techniques are used to achieve which aims or why. In this chapter, we explore how this apparently haphazard approach can be damaging to clients (in unmet goals), practitioners (in lost clients and poor case reports) and the profession as a whole ('If they can't explain it properly, it's all hokum!!").

By way of solution, an approach is outlined where practitioners draw intelligently from their: (a) case conceptualization; (b) the existing evidence base; and (c) hard-won professional judgements. Likewise, a terminology is sketched out for describing and analysing the decision-making process within sport psychology practice. These sections will help sport psychologists to not only pick the most suitable support strategy, but to be able to explain to a client, colleague, supervisor or assessor why it was chosen. Readers will be encouraged (and assisted) to construct a comprehensive and critical/nuanced understanding of the quality of their decisions and the way they are combined to inform their decisions regarding a support strategy. These support strategies, or 'interventions', may range from 'none' to a single technique, to prolonged counselling to a 'kitchen sink' approach (i.e., 'throw everything at it!') – but in each case, being able to explain **why** is vital for the client, for your own development and awareness, and to be able to explain to assessors and supervisors.

7.2   What is meant by 'choosing a support strategy'?

There is a subtle but important distinction to be made between choosing a support strategy (this chapter) and Case Formulation (Chapter 6). It is possible to argue that case formulation only exists to inform intervention choice, and that the two are so inextricably linked as to be viewed as one stage. However, case formulations are largely theoretical: dealing with abstract concepts and mechanisms. In contrast, support strategies seek to achieve a real world, meaningful change for the client. Likewise, it is logically possible to 'end' the psychological services between case formulation and intervention – for example, if the client strongly disagrees with the psychologist, or if all that was sought was an investigation, but not an intervention. Further, an intervention effectively tests the validity of the case formulation, so they cannot therefore be one and the same. This chapter conceptualizes choosing a support strategy as a separate (or rather 'separable') process from the Case Formulation (Chapter 6) and Needs Analysis (Chapter 5) that precede it, as well as from the Planning (Chapter 8) and Monitoring (Chapter 9) that follow. All these tasks are interrelated and interdependent, but conceptually separable.

Working definition. For the purposes of this book, and the model it presents, we can define choosing a support strategy as *the process wherein one course of action (or intervention or treatment) is selected from many possible alternatives*. The process can be distinguished from Needs Analysis, Case Formulation, Intervention Planning and Monitoring. However, intervention choice is inextricably linked to these other processes, as well as heavily dependent on ethical decisions and philosophical assumptions. Without doubt, aspects of the intervention choice can, and regularly do, appear alongside these other processes. For example, needs analysis can be informed by trialling an intervention, and monitoring can directly feed back that we need to adopt a new approach. However, conceptually the process is separable and important enough to warrant individual attention. The act of choosing an intervention is a defining feature of the helping professions, and a key feature on which our work is judged. If our support strategies are demonstrably effective, theoretically appropriate and transparent/logical, our profession will arguably be judged more favourably. What's more, it will be *science*.

Stepping in to 'intervene' in someone's life is a relatively big decision, and the one that is most likely to require explanation. Yet strangely, while doctors are quite frequently required to explain decisions over the choice of drugs or surgery prescribed, sport psychologists have – to date – tended to operate under less scrutiny. However, if you were offered a drug that might fundamentally change the way you think and feel (in sport or exercise, but also elsewhere), chances are you would want to know the mechanism, the evidence and the practitioner's own experiences of it. 'How does it work?' 'Has it been tested?' and 'Would you do it with yourself … or your own kids?' These fundamental questions can be translated to case formulation, evidence base and professional judgement. Choosing a support strategy is both the most consequential stage in our process, and the stage most likely to be subject to scrutiny. As such, we should do it well, and transparently, and constantly seek to improve the way we do it. In this light, it is surprising that there is very little literature available on how to select interventions (or 'treatments' in medicine) and how to evidence this process. While case formulation and intervention planning have both received attention, the specific moment where one intervention – or support strategy – is chosen has neither a definitive name nor an identifiable supporting literature. By proposing appropriate terminology and bringing in related literature, this chapter is necessarily speculative in places. We can certainly borrow from research into decision-making such as Tversky and Kahneman (e.g., 1983). However, the specific deployment of such theories in psychological practice, and where risks and consequences cannot be known in advance, is relatively under explored at this time.

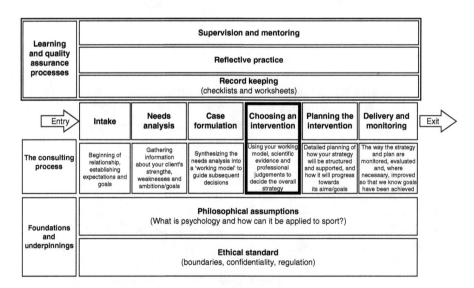

Figure 7.1   *The position of choosing an intervention, closely related to the case formulation process at the heart of the service delivery process. Highly dependent upon ethical considerations and philosophical assumptions, as well as supporting/feeding into reflective practice and supervision.*

7.3   The importance of intervention choice in sport psychology practice

Effectively, there are only two points to make here. First, the quality of applied sport psychology will almost inevitably be judged on the quality of the outcomes generated for clients. Yes, people can think the psychologist is a nice person (and luckily, that does boost adherence and effectiveness), but actually it is the outcomes we generate – and how they are perceived – that will determine the success or failure of sport psychology support (the individual and the entire field). Second, left unexamined, human decision-making can be extremely fragile and flawed. By way of illustration, we will review several classic and well-known decision-making errors and apply them to sport psychology.

7.3.1   A pivotal process (and outcome)

As outlined in the preface and introduction, the quality of our 'intervention choices' as applied sport psychologists will ultimately define the success or otherwise of our profession. Preferably, our applied practice should generate the exact meaningful changes our clients desire. However, even where we occasionally fall short of this lofty ambition, our field will remain professional and scientific if our decisions are transparent, logical, defensible and recorded for reporting/review purposes. Put simply, it would be indefensible and/or unsustainable to have a field of applied practice that fails to deliver the outcomes it promises and does not permit the continued pursuit of this aim through clear reporting, analysis and reflection. All we would be left with is an unscientific and unethical marketing exercise: selling the proverbial 'snake oil'. To prevent such an outcome, we first need to have a vocabulary to define, categorize and discuss the decisions we make. As already noted, there is a good literature on the frailties of human decision-making in general, but very little on the specific choice of 'support strategies' in psychological practice (it is generally blended into the case formulation literature). Second, we need to define the core sources of information that psychologists may draw from in choosing their support strategies: the evidence base, the case formulation and professional judgement. Where a practitioner is unable to explain the choice of support strategy in relation to these sources, we might justifiably enquire: Well what did you base your decision on? The issues of vocabulary and information sources are addressed in 'core considerations', shortly. For now though, we've established that the process of choosing a support strategy is very important, but surely, we do this every day: it's our 'bread and butter'. We *must* be good at it, right?

7.3.2   The fallibility of human decision-making

Readers who have previously studied psychology may be quite familiar with the following research. However, it is important to make the point here – and in support of the whole book – that humans are not naturally good decision-makers (and all sport psychologists are human!). The following section describes how cognitive research has identified (at least) two types of thinking, or decision-making: heuristic (fast and risky) versus elaborate (slow and deliberate – Kahneman & Tversky, 1979). One system that we might call 'gut' or 'instinctive', requiring very little thought or effort, and one that requires careful, deliberate and effortful analysis (Kahneman, 2011). In general, research shows that we tend to favour the faster heuristic system for everyday tasks, only resorting to the more sophisticated system when we realize we have a difficult problem to solve (often because our 'normal' approach failed – Reyna, 2008; Marewski & Gigerenzer, 2012). It is an important evolutionary adaptation that helps us save time and resources (Kenrick et al., 2009), and it is reinforced by our affective system which often registers a diminished mood after we are forced to solve more difficult cognitive tasks (Carver & Scheier, 1998; ; 2002; Carver, 2003). We're programmed not to enjoy thinking hard, especially if it involves pressure and self-evaluation. As such, the mental shortcuts we take are often deeply ingrained, and we don't enjoy being forced to challenge them. Just as visual illusions are perceptual errors that persist despite explanation, heuristics can produce decision-making illusions that are almost impossible to avoid (Kahneman, 2011).

To illustrate the conviction we feel regarding certain key decisions, let's consider the famous *Monty Hall* problem (Krauss, Stefan, & Wang, 2003; Selvin 1975a, 1975b; vos Savant, 1990a). It goes as follows: *Suppose you're on a game show, and you're given the choice of prizes hidden behind one of three doors. Behind one door is a car – the star prize. Behind the other two doors are wooden spoons. You pick a door, say No. 1, and the host, who knows what's behind the doors, opens another door, No. 3, to reveal a wooden spoon. He then asks you: 'Do you want to change your mind and pick door No. 2?' Is it to your advantage to switch your choice?*

Almost nobody changes their mind, but statistically, you should. When you first chose a door, you had a 1-in-3 chance of being correct. Most people feel that when a wrong choice is removed, their odds increase to 1-in-2, but that is not correct. Only a new player joining at the halfway stage would have a truly 1-in-2 chance. You chose from three and the odds remain the same as they were at the start of the game: 1-in-3. The host, however, knowing where the car was hidden, was choosing from 2-in-3. As a consequence of him knowing where the spoons were, if you change your mind you effectively steal that (better) 2-in-3 chance of winning the car. The presenter had to avoid the car when he chose a door to open, a 2-in-3 choice so weirdly, the one remaining door that you didn't choose now has a 2-in-3 chance of being correct. To this day, it still hurts my brain and over 10,000 readers (including 1000 with PhDs) wrote to *Parade* magazine (where it was also published) to complain. However, numerous mathematical proofs have shown that changing your mind is the right thing to do (Gardner, 1959b; Vazsonyi, 1999; vos Savant, 1996). *Not only do we get it wrong, but even after having it explained to us, we still insist it can't possibly be true.* Humans really can be bad decision-makers.

While not immediately applicable to sport psychology, the Monty Hall problem illustrates the strong argument that we make guesses all the time, and we should perhaps be more open to changing our minds. The Monty Hall problem is a clear example of the persistence and pervasiveness of certain heuristics. However, there are many more examples of how our reasoning can be flawed. Asch's (1951) *conformity* experiments showed how susceptible we are to social pressure. With the participant sitting at a table of secret actors (presented as other participants), the experimenter announces that this is a study about visual judgements. She places two cards before the group. The card on the left contains a vertical line, whereas the card on the right displays three lines of varying length. One at a time, group members had to choose which of the three lines on the right matched the line on the left. The task was repeated several times. Every so often, the other 'participants' (i.e., actors) unanimously chose the wrong line. Despite the correct answer being very obvious, one-third (32%) of the participants conformed with the incorrect answer. *They knowingly gave the wrong answer.* Out of 12 critical trials about 75% of participants conformed at least once, whereas only 25% of participants never conformed. In the control group, with no pressure to conform to confederates (secretly written answers), less than 1% of participants gave the wrong answer. As above, our decision-making process suddenly looks very vulnerable, and that is just with relatively easy clean-cut decisions regarding line length. How many decisions in applied sport psychology are this straightforward? How many ideas in sport psychology survive using social consensus and popularity? And how many key ideas depend on the fame and influence of their proponents and supporters, instead of their merits alone? We may never know the answer to those questions, but the issue of social conformity is worth bearing in mind when choosing a support strategy for an athlete. Some interventions do appear very popular, especially among particular groups or subcultures, when we should really be basing such decisions on the case formulation, evidence and clearly documented professional judgement/reasoning.

In a similar vein, we have the *availability heuristic*, where people make decisions based on what information comes freely to mind – perhaps as a result of recent exposure, familiarity or habit (Kahneman & Tversky, 1974). So for example, people who see a lot of news stories about violent crime will believe that they are much more likely to be attacked, even if every objective measure shows that the area is crime free and violent crime has reduced over time. What intervention techniques do you hear about most frequently, and from which sources? Does your information come from unbiased, objective and critically informed sources (examining theory, evidence and application)?

Then we have the *confirmation bias*, defined as: the tendency for decision-makers to seek, and attach more weight to, information that is consistent with their initial beliefs or preferences. The idea is reminiscent of the joke: 'My mind is made up; don't confuse me with the facts!'. As an example, Lord, Ross, and Lepper (1979) recruited participants who declared themselves either in favour of, or completely against, the death penalty. Participants were asked to read studies about the effectiveness of the death penalty that were both fabricated and balanced for evidence levels. An unbiased observer should conclude that the evidence is equivocal or contradictory. However, participants: (a) did not change their minds; and (b) evaluated the studies that matched their preference as more robust, and those that were contradictory as methodologically weak. Functional magnetic resonance imaging (fMRI) studies suggest this bias avoids the discomfort ('cognitive dissonance') of having one's beliefs questioned (Westen, Blagov, Harenski, Kilts, & Hamann, 2006). Further the effect seems to be just as strong regardless of intelligence or level of education (Stanovich, West, & Toplak, 2013) – nobody is immune!

Without wanting to list these issues exhaustively it is clear that human decision-making can be deeply flawed and illogical. As a final note, there is a persistent overconfidence bias, wherein over 90% of people rate themselves as 'above average' on a task (e.g., driving – Svenson, 1981), which is mathematically impossible. It is worthwhile to at least reflect on the question: could this be the case in sport psychology, or in your own practice? Such a situation would pose a substantial risk in the field of psychological support, where the quality of such decisions determines the quality of the client's outcomes. Further, in a profession where it is increasingly necessary to demonstrate due care and diligence – in case notes and supervisory reports – we cannot afford to be making decisions that are flawed or illogical. Even in the best-case scenario, the case reporting of a flawed heuristic decision becomes about trying to justify an intervention, or support strategy, *retrospectively* rather than a faithful reporting of events as they took place. To be clear though, one's heuristics don't need to be fallible, or flawed. The coverage of 'professional judgements' (below) explores ways of explicating, analysing and even training these heuristics to be more robust.

So there we have it: the effectiveness of your practice arguably depends very heavily on the quality of your decisions. However, humans are demonstrably quite poor decision-makers. So what can you do about it? The below section details some core considerations that may guide our thinking in this area, and help to develop our practice.

7.4   Core considerations

Now that we have established the importance of recording, analysing and improving the way we choose support strategies, we need to examine key considerations and terminology of this area too. Amongst these key issues, we need to consider: (a) A clear terminology and nomenclature for recording this specific type of decision; (b) the central issues of how we use evidence, case formulations and professional judgement; and (c) the ways that different philosophical traditions might approach both the decisions regarding support strategies and their recording/reporting.

7.4.1   Mapping the conceptual 'space' and offering a terminology

Imagine reading a practitioner's case notes with the following passage, regarding a decision to write 'be positive' on a rugby player's wrist tape at half time. Between the team talk and the second half, the player complained of being overly self-critical and 'tearing himself to pieces' after every pass. He was very concerned than this new habit was undermining his performance:

> My decision to offer a simplified self-talk (cuing) intervention was made under great *uncertainty* but relatively *low risk* (i.e., low expectation). There was less than a minute between presentation of the issue and the *decision threshold* (beginning of the second half). As such, the *'collapsed'* decision was truly *ad hoc*, and *prescriptive*. To manage the risks posed by this type of decision, we agreed to meet immediately after the match and review his experiences of the intervention. I also reflected on the quality of the *heuristics* that I used in making this decision.

In the first instance, it might seem incredibly jargonistic and self-indulgent. However, after reading the following section, come back and read it again. It's a test of whether this section is serving its purpose, not of you! If it begins to look like those terms convey a large amount of important information in a very small number of words – that's great. The terminology offered here should also allow practitioners to record, report/discuss, reflect on and improve their practice more efficiently. If it remains impenetrable and confusing, and especially if it fails to save words when reporting/recording practice, perhaps this section missed its purpose. I want to be clear that: I am creating this set of names and labels afresh in this text;

I have never read a case study with these terms in; but if I did, this sort of awareness would facilitate extremely clear and specific reporting of sport psychology practice. Such reporting would therefore share, inform and promote high-quality practices, and help to push new boundaries in the way we support clients and share our work.

7.4.2   A new terminology for the process of choosing a support strategy

Certainty and risk

First, we must clearly delineate the specific variety of decision-making we are referring to. A core distinction can be made in terms of probability/certainty (high or low) and risk (anticipated gain or loss). The most famous example is 'Pascal's wager' in which one weighs the unknown/unknowable existence of God versus the infinite gains won from this belief being correct (eternity in Heaven, etc.). His conclusion was that everyone should believe and live as though God existed. Pascal's wager is an extreme example – maximal uncertainty of an infinite gain – but it neatly illustrates the differences between certainty and risk. In most cases, the choice regarding support strategies is made under conditions of *uncertainty* – there is no guarantee a specific intervention will achieve the desired aims for a specific client. Building on this, we must consider risk, and the *level of risk* can vary substantially between clients, practitioners and situations. Notably, decisions made under *both* high uncertainty *and* high risk can be very stressful, and are highly susceptible to errors. However, high uncertainty combined with low risk is often a situation we deliberately aim to create during learning situations (e.g., simulations, role-plays). In contrast, deliberately accepting high levels of risk, with a high probability – such as when gambling in a casino or trialling a new and extreme medical treatment when everything else has failed – would largely be viewed as undesirable in psychological practice.

Thresholds and horizons

Second, we hit upon two variations of decision-making that might be viewed as sitting at two ends of a continuum. Where multiple possible courses of action exist, and we are somehow forced to choose one over the others (e.g., a decision *threshold*), the decision might be viewed as 'collapsing' the possibilities from many down to the one chosen. Admittedly, a whole array of choices is immediately encountered *in light of* the decision to choose Option A: stop, continue, modify, etc. But the other original options B, C and D are all no longer available. The idea of 'collapsing' decisions can be analogized to the famous 'Schrödinger's cat' example. In this thought experiment, a cat, a flask of poison and an unpredictable radioactive source are placed in a sealed box. If a sensor detects the random radioactive decay, the flask is shattered the poison kills the cat (painlessly, we hope!). Until some-body actually looks inside the box, the cat is theoretically both dead and alive at once. Only by choosing to 'collapse' the possibilities (by looking) do we resolve the uncertainty. Similarly, when we're not sure which course of action might help a client, when we choose one, we are 'collapsing' the options. Sometimes, there are distinct advantages to delaying a decision (see below), but sometimes it can be beneficial (or necessary) to make a decision and then deal with the consequences.

In contrast, there is a specific term in military parlance for the conceptual 'distance' between a plan (or the person making the plans) and the place where plans interact with reality (or the enemy, in military terms). There is proposed to be a strategic advantage by increasing the 'distance' between the planners and the place where the plans hit reality: because it allows the planner to consider and maintain multiple options, observe which approaches appear to be working best and to adapt and respond accord-ingly. This second approach, which we could call 'extending the event hori-zon', allows the planners to partially implement multiple options. As such, the planners may benefit by continuing to gather information about their effects in the real world. However, the cost of this approach is that the dis-comfort of uncertainty is prolonged, and it can require substantially more resources or effort to contemplate many changes at once. These limitations can undermine the strategy by either forcing an early 'collapse' or by tak-ing resources away from the one approach that might have worked – that is, you'll never find out as you never tried it properly.

A priori, *ad hoc* and *post hoc*

Decisions regarding a course of action can clearly occur prior to the deci-sion threshold ('a priori'), or at the decision threshold ('ad hoc'). A sport psychologist who has spent time between meetings reflecting and plan-ning may decide before the meeting which course of action to follow. This might largely ignore any new information that may have come about in between times. A very pure *a priori* approach might go so far as to prede-termine the correct course of action before ever meeting the client: for example, 'All athletes are deficient in this mental skill so I will teach it to all of them'. In contrast, a more responsive approach might be to create several options when planning, and choose one in response to additional information gathered at the next meeting. Where no information is avail-able and no decisions have been made beforehand, decisions can be made *ad hoc* – in the moment. So a situation where the event horizon is short, and information gathering, planning and implanting are all taking place close together, then decisions might be referred to as *ad hoc*. When it comes to the term *post hoc*, clearly a decision cannot be made after it was made, so to speak. However, when reading case reviews and applied portfolios (and research reports for that matter), there is a detectable pattern wherein practitioners appear to be 'retrofitting' an explanation to whatever they did. It reads as follows: 'We didn't really think it through at the time but we need to reference this and make it sound proper'. In terms of facilitating (or glorifying) practice that was poorly thought out and therefore potentially unscientific and unethical, *post hoc* decision-'making' appears to be the most problematic approach. It might better be termed decision justification, or even (more cruelly) pseudo-scientific behavioural reporting ('I did what I did, here is a reference that is loosely related to the thing I did'). As you can tell, when assessing case studies I, personally, find this latter approach very problematic. That said, there is absolutely an opportunity for capturing implicit ad hoc decision processes, analysing them and reflecting on them in order to improve them in future (see Chapter 10, Reflective Practice). Likewise, *a priori* decisions and *ad hoc* decisions have clear risks and weaknesses too, alluded to above. For now, all we are doing is offering a terminology that might allow practitioners to better understand the types of decisions they made regarding support strategies. The argument throughout this section is that knowing the type of decision we made, and having a head start in understanding the consequences of that type of decision, will help us to improve our practice.

Prescriptive, negotiated or regulatory decisions

Another important consideration is the source of the decision: the practitioner alone, the client alone or in collaboration. Notably, regardless of the source, the psychologist remains responsible for the quality of the decision regarding a support strategy – in terms of reporting, ethics and more. As such, the decisions we make regarding support strategies can be characterized in the three following ways: A *prescriptive* decision process is followed exclusively by the psychologist, and the decision is recommended to the client. This process mirrors the way we might be prescribed a drug by our doctor. In direct contrast, a *regulatory* decision process is one where the client creates or chooses their course of action, but – because the psychologist remains responsible – s/he must check the quality of that decision. Could it be harmful? Is there evidence directly contradicting this course of action? Does the decision fit with the case formulation?

If a client disagrees with a prescriptive decision, they may choose to end the relationship. Likewise, if a psychologist disagrees with a decision they have been asked to regulate for their client, s/he may also choose to end the relationship – that is, 'Not in my name'. As a third path, the psychologist and client may be able to consider the options together, in a collaborative manner: a *negotiated* decision. This approach should minimize the likelihood of the above described 'stand-offs' if either practitioner or client are not content. As above though, while the client is 'responsible' in terms of having to live with the consequences of the negotiated decision, the practitioner is responsible in terms of recording, monitoring, reporting, etc.

Heuristic versus systematic decision-making

Covered briefly earlier, heuristics are simple and efficient rules used to make decisions. Deployed when either time or cognitive resources are limited (but perhaps even as a default setting), heuristics are mental 'shortcuts' that involve focusing on one aspect of the decision and ignoring others. Due to their superficial logic, and tendency to generalize across many situations (e.g., 'this always works'), heuristic decision-making can lead to quite glaring and inexplicable errors. Notably, however, they often do work – delivering a successful outcome rapidly with very little cognitive effort or time expended in the process. In fact, because heuristics arguably exist to preserve cognitive effort/capacity, heuristics are usually automatic and intuitive judgments, with little conscious regulation. Ironically, the way to improve our decision-making heuristics may be to expose ourselves to a wide array of situations, and ensure that we do deliberately analyse and reason through decisions. This way, if and when we are forced to 'take a shortcut', it will be based on a good sample (i.e., large, heterogeneous and well understood).

In contrast, a systematic decision-making processing involves comprehensive and analytic, cognitive processing of judgment-relevant information (Chen, Duckworth, & Chaiken, 1999). A systematic decision process relies heavily on in-depth treatment of judgment-relevant information: actively seeking as much information as possible and then analysing from as many angles as possible. Also in a clear contrast against heuristic processes, systematic decisions require considerable cognitive effort and time, because the conscious and logical thinking system is slow (e.g., very limited bandwidth) and deliberate (e.g., it can be quite counter-intuitive to override the heuristic processes, as they deliver results quicker). Notably, however, because the decisions were elaborated and considered, the outcomes and contents (i.e., the 'audit trail') are more memorable. In contrast, the contents and outcomes of heuristic decision-making processes were not deeply processed and are therefore not as memorable at all. Characteristically, when we ask people why they made a decision, but the decision was heuristic, their response will be 'I don't know'. On the plus side, the above-described categorization system (or vocabulary/nomenclature) may at least allow us to go back and forensically analyse such a decision – with a view to understanding and improving how we practice.

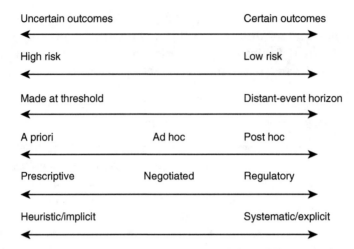

Figure 7.2   *A system for classifying your own intervention decisions using the terminology outlined in this section. By classifying decisions in this manner, our analysis of their impact and effectiveness becomes more contextualized and, ultimately, useful.*

7.4.3   Information sources to inform the process of choosing a support strategies

So far, this chapter has alluded to three key sources of information when choosing a support strategy: the case formulation (Chapter 6); the evidence base (described below); and professional judgements (also described below). In terms of explicating, communicating, challenging and improving our decision-making, these three considerations are positioned as vital. While the different traditions/approaches (Chapter 3) to sport psychology will favour each source to different degrees, these sources are potentially the most valid.

Case formulation

Described in detail in Chapter 6, this process involves clearly identifying a suitable 'working model' of your client's current needs, abilities, situation and goals. The model could be taken 'off the shelf' by using a textbook example, or it could be 'tailor-made' by working closely with the athlete to build a unique model for their specific situation. In either case, a good working model should detail the causes, mechanisms and outcomes that are currently experienced by the client – and as such it should clearly identify a small number of possible interventions. A case formulation that suggests a wide variety of interventions may work arguably need to be improved and refined, as it is not serving its purpose. A model taken from published research should have been researched and tested, so its 'validity' will depend on the quality and findings of this research. In contrast, a model that was tailor-made for the client won't have been researched, but it can be 'tested' by working through the athlete's experiences and seeing if the pattern 'fits', as well as by seeking full and informed client 'buy-in'. Finally, if a 'tailor-made' model is sufficiently good, the best courses of action often become obvious, in a kind of 'Eureka' moment for the client. In this respect, practitioners adopting 'construalist' assumptions (e.g., Chapter 3) will arguably rely more on case formulation as a source than those adopting a 'certaintist' approach, who should also be examining the research evidence.

Evidence-based practice

This approach can be defined as: 'conscientious, explicit and judicious use of current best evidence in making decisions about the care of individual patients' (Sackett et al., 1996, pp. 71–72). A more recent definition might be that: 'Evidence-Based Practice (EBP) requires that decisions about [health care] are based on the best available, current, valid and relevant evidence. These decisions should be made by those receiving care, informed by the tacit and explicit knowledge of those providing care, within the context of available resources' (Dawes et al., 2005, p. 1). The EBP approach has been strongly advocated by Gardner and Moore (2006) in response to increasing concerns that sport psychology was being built on a weak foundation of correlational studies (p. 66). For example, sport psychology researchers have often conducted correlational studies linking the use of 'mental skills' with more advanced performance levels (Gould, Eklund, & Jackson, 1992; Orlick & Partington, 1988). The argument from such correlations can be satirized as follows: 'In Michael Jordan's book he described how he used imagery throughout his career, and he ended up being the best basketball player in history, so this shows that imagery must work!' Initially that sounds quite persuasive, but what if we replace performing mental imagery with wearing purple socks? 'In Michael Jordan's book he described how he wore purple socks throughout his career, and he ended up being the best basketball player in history, so this shows that wearing purple socks must work' (cf. Gardner & Moore, 2006, p. 70). To push a bit further: (a) we have no control group, so it may be that being a talented basketball player causes people to use imagery (e.g., maybe all coaches insist on it regardless of whether it works); (b) it is completely possible that imagery has no effect and Michael would have been the best player in the world anyway; (c) even if it did somehow 'work' for Michael, it might not work for everyone else; (d) we have no idea if/how/when the imagery was used so we don't know whether it contributed in any way to a performance improvement; and (e) without controlled administration, a comparison to a control group (or normative data), and a decent sample size (at least!) we cannot say that the imagery is a causal factor in determining the level of performance. The key here is that if we want to say a particular intervention or strategy 'works' – in the sense of improving performance – then we really do need the evidence to support that claim. Gardner and Moore (2006) detailed how that evidence was missing (see below). Two simple conclusions followed – first, if we want to make such claims, we – as an entire discipline – should go out and generate the necessary evidence. Second, in the meantime, to stay ethical, all we need to do is reign in the claims that we make regarding such interventions. So for example, in Burton's (2008) chapter on goal setting, a story is presented where a practitioner 'guarantees' his performers a 70% improvement in performance by using goal setting – yet when viewing Gardner and Moore's (2006) analysis, there is insufficient evidence to sufficiently support such a bold claim.

Note, however, that the consideration of EBP is highly compatible with the 'certaintist' tradition described in Chapter 3. Whereas the 'construalist' tradition may be much less affected by these arguments: relying instead on the integrity of the method/process, not the interventions themselves. There are also some valid counter-arguments worth noting. First, elite athletes are, by definition, a very special group at the top of their respective fields. This introduces 'ceiling' effects where they often cannot get much better, and the effects of our interventions may be hidden. Second, there are some pretty serious ethical concerns when (potentially) interfering with the performance levels of elite athletes – particularly the use of 'control groups' who may be severely disadvantaged by not receiving the support (Anderson, Miles, Mahoney, & Robinson, 2002). Likewise, however, using relatively untested intervention strategies in such a setting might also be difficult to get through an ethics committee, as large sums of money are at stake. However, is it more or less ethical than withholding treatment from particular patient groups in trials of new medical drugs, when the findings are incredibly valuable and will benefit many more in the long run (Nathan & Gorman, 2002). A viable alternative, however, is to establish some strong, valid data from randomized control trials and then use carefully designed and robust single case studies to compare to those 'benchmarks'. So for example, if we did clearly establish that an intervention achieves a certain effect, and a new intervention was able to consistently match or outperform the original, then the new intervention would also be considered 'well established'.

To expand, Gardner and Moore (2006) proposed several levels of evidential support: 'well established', 'probably efficacious' and 'experimental'. To be classified as 'well established' an intervention must demonstrate efficacy in at least two good between group experiments, in at least two of the following ways: (a) superiority to a placebo (i.e., not just 'no-intervention' controls); (b) equivalence to an already well-established treatment with adequate sample sizes; or (c) a large series of single case design experiments demonstrating effectiveness with both good experimental design and a valid comparison of intervention to another treatment. In addition: (d) experiments must be conducted with treatment manuals (so that other scientists can clearly see what was done and replicate it); (e) characteristics of the client samples must be clearly specified (to avoid over-generalizing); and (f) the effects must have been demonstrated by at least two different investigators or investigating teams (to avoid bias – list from Chambless et al., 1998; Chambless & Ollendick, 2001). This is a very demanding set of conditions, to which we might also add: (g) the desired outcomes – for example, performance, motivation, confidence, enjoyment – are specified *in advance* of testing (to avoid the 'cherry picking' of positive findings and to ensure consistency between the evidence and the claims made). 'Probably efficacious' interventions tick one criteria from (a), or (b), or (c) above, but still d–g, and 'experimental' interventions have not yet been tested using the above criteria. For completeness, we might also add a category of 'discounted/discredited' interventions that have been tested and have never reliably demonstrated efficacy. There is also an issue of equivocal and contradictory findings, even when one may appear to have achieved the above criteria. In this situation, rather than accepting an intervention as 'well established', an EBP-focussed sport psychologist should begin to examine the methodologies, delivery manuals and analyses of the studies to ascertain why such contradictory findings have emerged.

Before we move on, it is worth noting that as a profession, we appear to really want our interventions to work; to demonstrate efficacy. Consider the following examples of unfavourable findings being 'explained away' and so the treasured theory/idea can survive to fight another day. 'The non-significant main effect for goal groups was attributed to the spontaneous goal setting behaviour of the control group' (Boyce & Bingham, 1997, p. 312), and 'The imagery condition was not as successful as anticipated perhaps because the participants stated they simply thought too much about the actual movements they made when shooting the free throws' (Lerner, Ostrow, Yura, & Etzel, 1996, p. 392). Such issues with the interpretation of findings are quite common, and reflect an underlying desire for sport psychology to demonstrate efficacy and legitimacy. However, these behaviours arguably have the opposite effect. For now, it is certainly worth reflecting as we read papers in sport psychology: 'How much might the authors really *want* their intervention to work? And how much do I really want it to work? Could these desires be influencing their reporting, or my interpretation of the data?'

As a final consideration, systematic reviews and meta-analysis, which quantitatively sum up the findings of a whole literature on a particular topic, are often used to resolve equivocal findings and strengthen our resolve towards certain theories and support strategies. In principle, these are excellent, but the findings of such a summary can only be as strong as the studies sampled (Gardner & Moore, 2006; Harwood, Keegan, Smith, & Raine, 2015). So if the quantitative summary is of a literature heavily dependent on correlations, then it gets us no closer to establishing a causal link. Correlation is always present where causation is clear, but it can also appear in (numerous) non-causal associations: causation is necessary but not sufficient to infer causality (Aldrich, 1995; also noted in Harwood et al., 2015). In contrast, narrative reviews can be heavily influenced by the preferences of the author, in terms of sampling, analysing and interpreting the data. As such, Burton's (2008) narrative review of goal setting for performance enhancement in sport is very positive, whereas Meyer et al. (1996) and Moore (2003) used the more robust and objective meta-analytic methodology and concluded that 'the predicted impact of goal-setting on performance has not been verified' (Meyer et al., 1996, p. 142). Moore (2003) – also reported in Gardner and Moore (2006) – applied the above strict criteria for well-established interventions. Of the two studies that met these criteria (out of 27 that examined goal setting and performance), neither demonstrated a clear advantage for goal setting over a placebo control group. The same pattern was observed for imagery (30 studies, six met criteria, none demonstrated advantage over placebo); self-talk (12 studies, four met criteria, none demonstrated advantage over placebo); and arousal control – for example, relaxation, breathing, centring, etc. (13 studies, four met criteria, none demonstrated advantage over placebo). Hence in 2006 (and very little has changed since), we had two options: (a) go out and perform the exact experiments that would allow us to claim our interventions improve athletic performance; or (b) reign in our claims for efficacy when talking about classic sport psychology techniques (i.e., 'mental skills'). The only other solution to the problem outlined here is to closely examine one's philosophical assumptions and ensure that one's claims, methods and support strategies are clearly 'philosophically aligned'. Realistically, just like 'reigning in our claims', such alignment would also necessitate a significant change in language and claims.

Professional judgement

Members of a profession such as sport psychology are, by definition, permitted a degree of discretion or autonomy in their decision-making (Evetts, 2002). For example, as already discussed, there are numerous situations where a case formulation may suggest several equally viable courses of action, and the evidence linking specific interventions with specific outcomes is frequently inadequate. This forces practitioners to either do nothing, or to exercise a degree of 'professional judgement'. As noted by

Martindale and Collins (2005), this therefore places an onus on the practitioners to record, communicate, analyse and improve such decisions – as do the regulatory frameworks in most countries (e.g., record keeping, case studies, reflective practice, etc.). Perhaps the only way to proceed when both case formulation and the evidence base offer insufficient information is to use personal experience and/or 'best guess' judgements. As such, in the specific context of this book – and the model proposed within it – we might define professional judgement in one of two ways. Either: (a) the soul reliance on personal experience and judgements in choosing support strategies; or (b) the supplementation of information from case formulations and/or the existing research with personal experience and judgements. Ostensibly, (b) seems more defensible than (a), but some approaches do appear to reject theory and evidence altogether in the 'craft' of applied practice (e.g., Martens, 1987).

In practice, professional judgement involves the combination of information from various sources – theorizing, recent readings, personal experience and drawing inferences – and can be implicit or explicit. It can occur between active sessions (reflection on action) or 'live' within the provision of support (reflection in action – cf. Schön, 1991). Martindale and Collins (2012) provide a good example of professional judgement informing support work with an injured elite judo player. Likewise, Collins, Evans-Jones, and O'Connor (2013) also provided good examples of how this process can be recorded and used to explicitly develop one's practice. In support of this deployment of professional judgement, Martindale and Collins (2007) argued that recording and analysing professional judgements should become an integral part of the way we evaluate our effectiveness in applied sport psychology. So with a working definition and a clear argument in favour of the importance of professional judgement, the question becomes: 'How can we do it well?' or perhaps 'How can we become better at professional judgement?'

While not entirely made up of heuristic, implicit decision-making processes, professional judgement is perhaps the most likely aspect of choosing support strategies to be processed implicitly, or unconsciously. Drawing from cognitive psychology (Evans, 2006; Kahneman, 2011; Kahneman & Klein, 2009) – and in sport psychology Martindale and Collins (2013) – there is a strong argument that our intuitive decision-making can be 'trained' and refined. Specifically, where a heuristic decision process is viewed to have failed or been inadequate, the more systematic and elaborate system can be activated to describe, evaluate, analyse and improve the way intuitive decisions are subsequently made. In this way, we can turn 'haphazard intuition' into 'skilled intuition'. Simon (1992) provided a good definition, which helps to reduce the perception of intuition as intangible or irrational: 'The situation has provided a cue: This cue has given the expert access to information stored in memory, and the information provides the answer. Intuition is nothing more and nothing less than recognition' (p. 155).

Summarizing the findings of Kahneman and Klein (2009), Klein (1998), Shanteau (1992) and Martindale and Collins (2012) – to abridge some of the finer details and growing pains – there are two core ways of improving one's professional judgement from 'uncritical intuition' to 'skilled intuition'. First, one must practise as much as possible across as wide a variety of contexts as possible. For example, various regulatory bodies prescribe a minimum number of contact hours – 500 hours for BASES, 400 hours for AASP in the United States, 1114 hours for AHPRA in Australia) and these really should be considered a minimum. The more exposure one gets, across the widest variety of contexts (sports, ages, levels, special populations), the more opportunities one has to refine one's professional judgements. Second, we must consistently and deliberately explicate our professional judgements. Record them, analyse them, discuss with supervisors, perhaps publish them in applied journals (all the while protecting confidentiality, of course). Whilst recognizing that it may always be frustratingly difficult to know whether one's judgements are becoming objectively 'better', Yates and Tschirhart (2006) described three perspectives on evaluating the quality of decision-making: (a) satisfying results (whether the result is satisfying; e.g., whether the athlete is satisfied with the intervention employed); (b) coherence (the procedures employed are logically coherent; e.g., goodness of fit between the athlete needs and the support strategy adopted); and (c) process decomposition (the successful execution of specific elements within the overall process; e.g., successful implementation of mental skills training within a performance enhancement programme). All of these processes are consistent with, and supported by, the model outlined in this book. Subjectively, you may also experience a pattern of variable and awkward performances becoming more consistent and smooth. As such, one-off acts of individual judgment are gradually integrated into coherent and explicit strategies. This represents a shift from focusing on isolated variables towards perceiving of complex patterns; and towards an increased self-reliance, including the ability to form new strategies as needed (Glaser, 1996). For a fuller exploration of how to train professional judgement, Martindale and Collins (2013) provide a very detailed history of the arguments in this area.

In summarizing this section, it is clear that there are three main sources of information that can inform the decision regarding which course of action to follow: the case formulation, the evidence base and one's own professional judgement. Each may be deployed to different degrees within any single decision process, and different philosophical approaches will favour different combinations. As such, all that remains is to briefly sketch out how

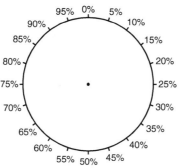

Evidence-based practice
What type of evidence was available for the **specific** outcome(s) you are hoping to achieve? None, correlational, longitudinal, controlled trials? Did you use only selective studies, a wide search or systematic and meta-analyses? What might be the issues with the evidence you have drawn from?

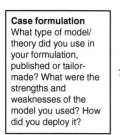

Case formulation
What type of model/theory did you use in your formulation, published or tailor-made? What were the strengths and weaknesses of the model you used? How did you deploy it?

Professional judgement
Were the judgements you made implicit or explicit? Heuristic or systematic? Were they based on personal experience, popularity, trends or new ideas? Did you have to create a new and novel approach? If so, how did you reach that conclusion? Would you act the same in future, or differently, and why?

Figure 7.3   *A template for evaluating the sources of key information when choosing a support strategy. Use the above pie chart template to ascribe an approximate percentage to the degree you relied on each source of information in making your decision. Once you've done that, use a separate document to record the details of the way you deployed each source.*

the different traditions described in Chapter 3 might approach the various aspects of choosing a support strategy.

7.4.4   Different traditions' approaches to deciding on a course of action

The following paragraphs briefly sketch out the ways that each philosophical tradition – certaintism, construalism, fallibilism or pragmatism (see Chapter 3 for details) – aligns to the key decision-making considerations outlined in this chapter.

Certainty and risk

On the face of it, a certaintist tradition should prioritize certainty – seeking objective and valid 'factual' observations and using well-supported theories and evidence to justify any intervention. In this light, risk may appear to be minimized, or well managed. In contrast, a fallibilist approach would hold very little hope of achieving certainty, and instead would focus on minimizing the risks involved in any intervention choice – to the client, the practitioner or the profession. Both construalism and pragmatism might be less easily aligned with considerations of risk and certainty. However, characteristically grounded in counselling psychology, construalist approaches might also seek to minimize risk, and draw certainty from the level of personalization achieved through the client-centred counselling approach. Pragmatism may seek a level of certainty because this is known to boost athletes' confidence in (and adherence to) intervention, but this philosophy would appear relatively ambivalent towards risk.

Thresholds versus horizons

Superficially, a certaintist practitioner might look to perform 'clean' decisions, with precise thresholds, whereas construalists and fallibilists may wish to keep pushing the 'event horizon' further away by continuing to collect data and using 'trial and error' to test ideas and improve understanding. Again, pragmatism may appear relatively ambivalent and simply follow the moniker: 'What works goes'.

A priori, post hoc and ad hoc

Drawing more heavily from published theories and research, a certaintist approach may display more *a priori* decision-making, whereas the constant refinement and reflection required by construalism and fallibilism may force their decision processes to be more *ad hoc*. Of the available options, pragmatism seems to most likely candidate for *post hoc* decision processes – wherein a practitioner may follow their gut in choosing an intervention but then be required to retrospectively consult the literature to support the decision with theories and evidence.

Prescriptive, negotiated and regulatory decision styles

The position of the practitioner as the 'expert' in a certaintist approach (i.e., practitioner-led) means that a prescriptive decision style seems most likely. 'I'm the expert, do as I say'. Likewise, this view point may be most consistent with the pragmatist approach, as realistically most athletes and coaches presume the sport psychologist should act as an 'expert', so it fits most of the time. Construalism should be more aligned with regulatory decisions – 'That's your choice and, given I'm not aware of any reasons to avoid it, I support you in it'. Given its assumption that certainty cannot be achieved in sport psychology, a fallibilist approach may prefer to avoid acting as an expert, and instead pursue intervention decisions using negotiating or regulatory styles.

Heuristic versus systematic decisions

Perhaps the approach most likely to 'follow your gut' is pragmatism, so that appears the main candidate for a heuristic style. However, the importance of putting key decisions in the athlete's hands (i.e., client-led) may also render key aspects of the construalist process quite heuristic – as we cannot expect the client to always draw on extensive knowledge of the literature when choosing a course of action. While certaintism appears to offer quite a clear recipe for systematic decision-making, it is also quite easy to become dependent on the apparent reliability and validity of certain theories and interventions, thus becoming uncritical and heuristic again. Of all the traditions, fallibilism would appear to shun any and all temptations towards being heuristic, and should characteristically favour systematic approaches to choosing a course of action.

Case formulation

Certaintist case formulation, drawn from existing literature, will play an important part in the choice of support strategy, but the theory and specific combination of intervention and goal should ideally have been tested robustly as well. In contrast, a construalist approach may depend almost entirely on the case formulation, and reject validated theories from the literature in favour of a highly personalized formulation, specific to that athlete. A fallibilist approach would almost definitely include a good case formulation, but use it carefully and judiciously. Whereas a pragmatist approach may be happy to use anything from a minimalist 'one-size-fits-all' formulation, through to a highly personalized approach, so long as it appears to 'work'.

Evidence-based practice

As above, a certaintist approach grounded in positivism and empiricism should prize valid and robust research evidence and draw on it heavily in reaching decisions regarding the choice of support strategy. The problem, as things stand, is that the available evidence may not be sufficient to support the claims made, or to offer the necessary certainty. With a view to being objective and valid, a certaintist approach would look to favour robust studies and objective syntheses (e.g., meta-analyses). In contrast, a construalist approach would only be concerned with evidence in relation to the 'regulation' of the athlete's choices – is there any evidence that this is a bad idea, or potentially harmful? A fallibilist tradition may treat the available evidence with extreme caution – mindful of the methodological weaknesses and equivocal findings – and so the way research evidence is deployed may depend very heavily on the quality of the available studies. Finally, a pragmatist approach would appear to be relatively ambivalent towards the evidence – flawed as it often is – except when using it might appear to 'work'. This might, for example, mean selectively presenting supportive studies in recommending an intervention, but overlooking methodological weaknesses or conflicting findings.

Professional judgement

Arguably, all four traditions should draw heavily on professional judgement in order to maximize the benefits of experience. The precise way that it is used may vary between traditions – perhaps spotting potential pitfalls in fallibilism versus finding more persuasive ways of presenting ideas in pragmatism. However, as a precursor to reflective practice, which is positioned as a key process in sport psychology practice (Chapter 10), professional judgement is unavoidable, and very important in all four traditions.

7.5   Conclusions

In summary, this chapter has delineated and defined a specific stage of the sport psychology service delivery process devoted exclusively to choosing the most appropriate course of action (or 'intervention'). While a separate, or separable, stage is identified, it is clear that choosing a support strategy can be closely interwoven with needs analysis, case formulation, planning and delivering/monitoring. Likewise, decisions regarding a support strategy may be heavily dependent upon one's underlying philosophy or assumptions. After detailing the critical importance of this stage in determining one's overall success, we also outlined the reasons that 'decision-making' is just as (potentially) fallible and flawed as all human cognition. With a view to ensuring that decisions regarding support strategy are well documented, well understood and well analysed, a framework for classifying these decisions was sketched out. Further, the core sources of information to inform this decision are clearly identified as the case formulation, the available evidence, and one's professional judgement. Overall, this chapter argues that by recording, evaluating and analysing our processes when choosing support strategies, we can continually improve this important process. In this way, we both advantage ourselves by becoming a more effective psychologist, and we are better able to meet the reporting obligations of our regulators and accrediting bodies. Further, we are better able to share our practice with others, benefitting the field as a whole and helping to inform the public about what might constitute 'good' sport psychology support.

7.6   Ella's story: Part 7 – 'All things being equal...'

Ella has completed a thorough intake and needs analysis with an international female football/soccer referee who is visiting from the United States. Genevieve has refereed international women's fixtures and national-level men's fixtures. However, following a career break to have children, she now lacks confidence in many key areas. In particular, Genevieve has become 'hung up' on the new fitness requirements for referees, and seems to under-perform, inexplicably, every time she takes the test. She is injury free and believes that she is fit enough to pass the test – rather she seems to 'choke' when the test begins. Genevieve describes significant increases in cog-nitive and somatic anxiety around the time of the tests, which she feels undermines her performance. However, she will not be permitted to referee international fixtures again without passing the new fitness tests. Ella's case formulation focuses on the simple issue of low confidence, leading to anxi-ety, over-arousal and under-performance. However, this case formulation offers many possible intervention pathways (i.e., to regain or build confi-dence). Further, the research literature appears to offer a wide variety of 'well-evidenced' interventions for building confidence. While she remains under supervision, Ella is uncertain of her 'professional judgement' and seems unwilling to use it. When it is time to 'choose' a support strategy, Ella doesn't know how to proceed.

1. What additional information might Ella seek to help her decision? How could she strengthen her case formulation and evidence base?
2. If Ella were to consider using her professional judgement, what sort of experiences should she draw from? How could she evidence and demon-strate her professional judgements to her supervisor or assessors?
3. In relation to practising philosophy, what sort of decision process would Ella follow if she was using a 'certaintist' tradition, and a 'practitioner-led' style?
4. In contrast, what considerations would Ella refer to if she was using a 'construalist' tradition, and a 'client-led' practice style?
5. What support strategy (or intervention) would you recommend to Genevieve, and why? Try to detail the sources of information you have used in making this decision and justify it as clearly as possible (i.e., for an assessor or supervisor).

7.7   Review and reflect

1. How would you describe the process of 'choosing a support strategy' in less than 10 seconds, to a friend or family member? How can you quickly and effectively convey the core issues and importance of this process?
2. What information is used when deciding on a support strategy in sport psychology? What are the risks involved if this information is lacking (i.e., either too little, or unsubstantiated).

3. What criteria would you look for to qualify as an excellent 'decision process' regarding support strategy? And what might constitute a weak 'decision process'?

4. Can you think of any circumstances where a thorough decision process might not be necessary in choosing a support strategy? What might be the risks of rushing or neglecting this process? If constrained by time or lack of information, how could a rushed decision regarding support strategy be mitigated?

5. What tools, cues and prompts could you use to try and ensure that your own choices of support strategy are as strong as possible?

8 Planning the Support Programme

8.1 Introduction and overview

If only we could stop once we have identified a good 'answer' for our clients' questions – 'just do this!' – life might be so much easier. However, sport psychologists not only need to identify a promising course of action (or 'intervention' – i.e., Chapter 7), we also need to help ensure it actually happens. This takes the form of both planning (this chapter) and monitoring (Chapter 9) the support programme. There can be an enormous difference between knowing an appropriate strategy and meticulously implementing the desired actions every day. Many psychologists can recall the frustration of meeting an athlete and asking: 'How did it go?' only to be told: 'I didn't do what we talked about'. Likewise, as a reader and assessor of case studies, it is notable how many simply recommend a broad strategy (e.g., imagery, pre-shot routines, cognitive reframing, etc.) without any further explanation. Perhaps by consequence, it is unsurprising when case studies conclude that the support package might have worked (or worked better) if the athlete had carried out the intervention as intended. Bearing in mind that case studies are most commonly submitted by practitioners at the end of their formal training – about to become independent and registered practitioners – then we, as a profession, 'could do better'. By offering a carefully designed, personalized, realistic and practical plan for athletes to implement the desired changes (this chapter), and then monitoring the implementation/outcomes (Chapter 9), we give ourselves a much better likelihood of success.

As is argued throughout this book, planning is a step which we experience *whether we admit it or not*. For example, a sport psychologist who concludes a relationship by simply prescribing goal setting, for example, has effectively planned to 'let the client work it out for her/himself'. Now with a highly educated, motivated and self-aware client, this could still be effective. But for a client who is inexperienced in goal setting and lacking awareness of the intended processes and outcomes, it would almost guarantee failure. In contrast, some psychologists may wish to meticulously plan every aspect of a client's progress, setting targets and deadlines for each milestone and contingency plans for any anticipated problems. It is perfectly possible, however, that such an approach could still fail to anticipate certain unexpected challenges. Likewise, it may disempower the client to the extent that they simply choose not to comply with the strict schedule of work. Other approaches, such as client-led counselling, deliberately plan to continue meeting the client and supporting progress, by considering each new challenge and barrier as it is experienced. As always, this book argues that we should not leave such important decision to chance or, rather, to implicit and heuristic decision-making (as explained in Chapter 7).

Scouring the literature for definitions around planning a support programme (treatment plans, intervention planning), we hit upon several related but slightly imperfect passages. Mosby's Medical Dictionary (2009) offers the definition: 'A tentative plan that may be modified or continued upon re-evaluation' and 'the intended sequence of procedures for the treatment'. Perkinson's (2007, p. 75) book on chemical dependency counselling offers a thorough overview drawn from a clinical perspective: 'The treatment plan is the road map that a patient will follow on his or her journey through treatment. The best plans will follow the patient for the next 5 years where the relapse rates drop to around zero (Vaillant, 2003). No two road maps will be the same; everyone's journey is different ... Treatment planning is a never-ending stream of therapeutic plans and interventions. It is always moving and changing.' Five years may be inappropriate for sport psychology, longer than some athlete's careers, although the above definition is referring to alcohol addiction. However, road map, individualization and adaptability are key features we can transfer into sport. A neat definition for our purposes might be as follows: *A sport psychology intervention plan is a road map containing desired end-goals, milestones, the broad strategies and specific activities for the pursuit of the client's agreed outcomes.* Contingency plans might also be a worthwhile inclusion. Once defined, we can clarify that these plans can vary in terms of their individualization (very specific versus one size fits all), and flexibility (fixed programme versus constant monitoring/refinement).

The fine-grained examination of the service delivery process outlined in our model (Figure 8.1) means that the specific type of 'intervention planning' we refer to here has not received significant attention in the literature. In fact, once again, the closest we get is in the clinical psychology literature, where standardized treatment plans are quite common – although notably over 50% of the template for such plans concerns the needs analysis, case formulation and monitoring/evaluation of outcomes. It might also be described as a record-keeping template. Realistically, it may be very difficult to offer a universal template for planning interventions, especially considering the different traditions and approaches in sport psychology. As such, this chapter draws appropriately from existing publications, without necessarily 'subscribing' to any particular approach. By recognizing the legitimacy of the different traditions in sport psychology – certaintism, construalism, pragmatism and

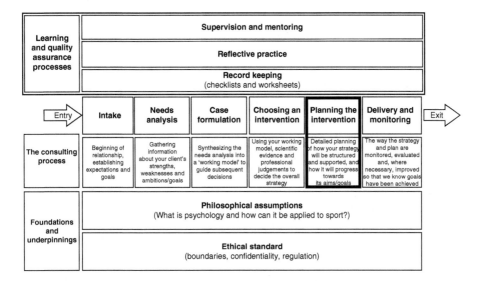

Figure 8.1   *An illustration of the position of the planning process – closely related to intervention choices and delivery/monitoring, as well as being highly dependent upon philosophical assumptions, and supporting/feeding into reflective practice and supervision.*

fallibilism outlined on Chapter 3 – this chapter aims to provide readers with the vocabulary and critical awareness to approach the planning of support programmes independently, and to continue improving throughout their career.

After illustrating the importance of a strong planning process, this chapter overviews some key considerations that sport psychologists may wish to make when planning their client's development: progression, differentiation, individualization and more. While we make plans every day, from careers to coffee, planning a psychological support programme is quite different, containing important considerations that can affect the effectiveness of the process. The awareness facilitated by these considerations should support both personal reflection and improved supervision, leading to more directed and effective ongoing development. To support record keeping, reflection and supervision/mentoring, worksheets are also included to help practitioners describe and analyse their planning processes.

8.2   The importance of planning psychological support

Now that we have introduced and defined the idea of planning a support programme, it is worth pausing to consider why this step is so important. We have already illustrated how the model used in this book positions planning as an unavoidable process, even if the plan is simply to let the client work it out for her/himself, or 'get back to me if you have any problems'. In such situations, the planning phase is still present, but perhaps given insufficient consideration (depending on one's philosophy of practice and practice style). As the famous quote by Winston Churchill goes: 'He who fails to plan is planning to fail'. Focussing specifically on the provision of sport psychology support, we are referring to planning *once a decision has been made* regarding the best course of action[1]. Why, for example, don't all athletes simply know what imagery is, and how best to use it? Or similarly, why aren't there universal guidelines so that once we establish a suitable course of action we can simply refer athletes to those? Both situations might mean we didn't have to plan our support programme quite so meticulously. Unfortunately, while we might expect athletes and coaches to have heard of some of the techniques used in sport psychology, there are numerous and often conflicting recommendations on how to approach them. Often, the most effective approaches have only recently been published, and often behind 'pay walls' that prevent many people from accessing them. Even in the era of open access, however, where the latest evidence testing strategies may be publically available, it can easily be 'drowned out' by competing ideas. A core element of the sport psychologist's job is to cut through this 'noise', and ensure that the specific approach adopted holds the most promise for this specific client, with these specific needs. This then relates to the reason why there are not generalized guidelines for implementing different 'recognized' psychological strategies: personalization. Unlike some medicines, which chemically affect the same cell receptors in almost every human being, psychological techniques require particular tailoring to be appropriate for the individual client. This, too, is a core role of the sport psychologist.

If we accept that identifying specific activities (not just overall strategies) and tailoring them to the client are both central aspects of being a sport psychologist, then we need to establish terminologies and frameworks for this planning process. Once we are aware of the available options in planning the support package – their advantages and disadvantages – and able to record the ways we use these options, then we can reflect on their effectiveness. In this way, (1) the continual improvement of practice is facilitated and supported. Further still, (2) we are better able to meet our reporting obligations with regulatory bodies, (3) we can also make better referrals (where required). Best of all: (4) we can share best practice with the public (through published case studies, word of mouth, sales and marketing, etc.)

---

[1]Realistically, however, it is also likely that these two processes – intervention choice and planning – may inform each other. For example, if something is difficult to plan appropriately, perhaps it is not a good course of action after all.

and ultimately inform both our profession (4a) and our clients (4b) about what constitutes best practice. This way, next time a coach or athlete is presented with a 'miracle' one-size-fits-all programme, delivered in a one-off half-day course, they might be able to weigh the pros and cons for themselves. They might even conclude: 'Ok that does sound impressive, but this other psychologist is prepared to develop a highly personalized plan for me and then support me as I try to implement it'. At the very least, it might create a different expectation: 'That half-day workshop was a nice taster, but I need to work out whether the ideas in it are applicable to me personally and, if so, how I might apply them in my particular day-to-day life'. Unfortunately, I can clearly remember coaches in the past declining psychology services having attended such courses: courses that often undermined other approaches to sport psychology and conveyed the idea that 'this will be all you need'. Unfortunately, I was too young and inexperienced to know how to argue my cause. Consequently, the following chapter should help psychologists – novice and experienced – to (5) better 'sell' their services (i.e., more accurately, more ethically and hopefully with more success!).

Specifically, if you can understand how different approaches to planning support generate different outcomes (and pros/cons) then you can make potential clients aware of these. Likewise, you can create more accurate expectations of your services so that clients walk away knowing that they 'got exactly what they paid for'. Importantly, meeting or exceeding expectations is one of the strongest determinants of customer/client/student satisfaction in several studies (Boyer et al., 2003; Elliott & Shin, 2002; Thomas & Galambos, 2004; Wiers-Jenssen, Stensaker, & Grogaard, 2002). In fact, in one of these studies, expectation was a bigger influence than objectively rated quality of care (Boyer et al., 2003). So it would appear that both establishing appropriate expectations ('selling') and then delivering a good service are both very important – in planning support as well as throughout the service delivery process. A psychologist 'selling' her/his services should be able to manage the client's expectations about how their work together will play out – in terms of planning and delivery.

Before moving onto the next section, perhaps just pause to consider the extent to which you consider planning important. In the above text, we have argued that planning is an unavoidable step in the delivery of sport psychology support. Further, we have outlined how explicitly and deliberately planning our support packages benefits our professional development, reporting obligations referrals, the sharing of best practice and the marketing of our services. If we accept those points, then we need some vocabulary, concepts and frameworks with which we can analyse the way we plan our support.

8.3 Core considerations

If we are happy to accept that planning is a vital step in sport psychology support, then we need to examine key considerations that will inform the way we approach such planning. Despite the common conception, 'plans' don't have to be rigid and inflexible (in fact that can often be counter-productive). However, plans do have to sketch out both the direction of progress and the manner in which that progress will be achieved. Finding a balance between a dependable plan and the required flexibility is perhaps one of the best reasons to continue meeting with clients long after the identification of appropriate ways forwards. One reason this often does not materialize, however, is the experience that one is no longer doing 'psychology', but rather simply solving pragmatic problems. For example, Client: 'I know I need to practice my imagery like we discussed, but I keep forgetting to do it'. Practitioner: 'Would it be helpful to set a reminder in your phone to go off at a certain time each day, or perhaps to use an app that will remind you until you've completed it?'. This is not so much specialist psychological knowledge as a simple practical solution that a friend or colleague might offer. However, as the psychologist who helped choose the course of action, it is arguably your responsibility to help see it through.

Ensuring our support is effective is where including progression, structure and contingencies into the support programme can be beneficial. *Progression* can be approached by considering the client's starting point, end goal and the milestones along this journey. In this instance, we will use the EAP acronym – education, acquisition and practice – to guide the progression element (cf. Boutcher & Rotella, 1987; Martens, 1987). *Structure* can be achieved by considering the 'skeleton' (i.e., key dependable concepts) that your support can be attached to, or built around. Physical, psychological and social cues are good ways of reinforcing a support package, and periodization is also relevant here. *Contingencies* involve having a 'back-up' plan, in case the first option proves to be inappropriate. This may vary from simply recommending a different technique to perhaps even adopting a different style with the client. Finally, we will briefly consider the ways that each of the different core philosophical traditions will tend to approach planning considerations.

8.3.1 Progression in the support programme

It is important to ensure that the support package progresses during its course, so that the client does not feel s/he is 'going round in circles'. Experiencing progress, as a client, is also very beneficial for generating self-efficacy and, of course, positive feelings towards the psychologist (and wider profession). Without careful consideration, 'progression' can often be misconstrued as several things: (a) more 'stuff'; (b) different 'stuff'; (c) more difficult (or more complex) 'stuff'; or (d) more up-to-date 'stuff'. For example, an intervention might be proposed which 'progresses' by adding in additional mental skills (first imagery, then goal-setting, etc.): both (a) and (b) would fit this pattern. Likewise, I have seen proposed support programmes that simply progress a client's understanding through the textbook – for example, from 'inverted-U' arousal (Yerkes & Dodson, 1908) towards an understanding of multidimensional anxiety (somatic and cognitive; cf. Martens et al., 1990). In neither case are the client's specific goals being pursued in a structured, coherent manner.

Perhaps the most helpful way of approaching planning is to consider the stage the client is at, and match the support/advice to the client's current level of development. A very popular stage model in psychology is the Trans-Theoretical Model (TTM – Prochaska & DiClemente, 1983), which develops through 'pre-contemplation' (not interested in changing behaviour), through 'contemplation' (thinking about it), 'preparation', (preparing to change), 'action' (taking appropriate action) and maintenance (effective action lasting over 6 months). A 'relapse' stage is included to capture moments where clients fall back into old ways. One problem with this model of progression is that it is chiefly applied to problematic or undesirable behaviours (smoking, drug taking and sedentary lifestyles). When considering athletes who are pursuing positive changes and achievements – perhaps the vast majority of clients in sport psychology – then the first two to three stages are a given. Likewise, 'relapse' is less clearly defined when the existing behaviour is neither unhealthy nor inherently wrong, but rather it appears not to work for that specific athlete in pursuit of their specific goals. A useful model for application in sport is the Education-Acquisition-Practice model, outlined by Boutcher and Rotella (1987) and expanded here. As with the TTM, the idea would be to accurately specify the client's current stage and plan activities according to that stage.

Education

The *education* phase seeks to: (a) introduce any new ideas to the client; (b) illustrate their relevance and potential impact (to them personally); (c) highlight key concepts and helpful rules; and even (d) identify key moments/opportunities where the intervention is needed/helpful. So for example, in the early stages when a client may be unsure of the benefits of a particular strategy or idea, you might ask them to keep a diary of when they used it, why and what happened. You might go a step earlier and look to record the moments when they appear to perform below their desired level, and describe those in more detail. This would be a clear example of extending the needs analysis stage in order to improve the case formulation, reinforce intervention choice and then assist with planning. Once the relevance and meaning of the concept is grasped, an athlete may need assistance in applying it appropriately. Worksheets containing the latest recommendations on how to enact an intervention can be useful in educating a client how best to approach the task (e.g., SMARTER goals and process-performance-outcome goals – e.g., Weinberg, 2010 – and the PETTLEP acronym for imagery – cf. Holmes & Collins, 2010). Note that the constructivist tradition characterized in counselling and client-led approaches would not seek to 'prescribe' what to do and how to do it; as described in the above examples. Once a client has grasped the basic concepts, relevance and guidelines regarding the support package, you can move on to acquiring the new skills, behaviours, attitudes, etc. that will assist the client.

Acquisition

The *acquisition* phase involves learning the desired skill, through repetition and practice – often through quite deliberate tasks and sometimes away from the sporting setting. Notice that this stage could also be considered practice to gain the skill, whereas the next stage concerns putting the new ideas/skills into practice. Effectively, where skills or knowledge are missing, they may need to be deliberately developed through setting specific tasks, activities and challenges. In contrast, if the client already possesses the skills or knowledge but simply does not use them at the right time, it may be possible to move directly to the next stage. There is an argument for developing some skills and knowledge away from the environment where they are needed, so that any difficulties or failures (inherent parts of learning) do not impact on the target outcomes. For example, if learning to use a mental skill such as self-talk in golf actually caused a client to become distracted and perform worse, *purely because they were still learning to use their new skill*, they may abandon the idea before it really had a chance to help. In addition, if a client lacks a certain skill or has developed bad habits, this phase may take some time, but in other circumstances it may be possible to progress through this stage quite fast. As another example, when time is short I often advise against learning a totally new skill, but rather adapting an existing capability. For example, a client struggling to learn new tactics (and losing confidence as a result) once told me he was unable to do mental imagery but constantly 'narrated' his life. At the time, being unable to use one's mind's eye was foreign to me, as I had always been very good at it and I assumed everyone else must be too. It would have taken months, however, to learn how to do good imagery (to practice the moves and skills), so with time of the essence we chose to 'hijack' the existing capability and use it to his advantage (in the form of cuing – associating key moments with desired team moves/calls). One key goal of the acquisition phase, as with motor learning processes, is to achieve a level of 'automation', where the athlete no longer has to deploy cognitive effort to perform a particular task or skill. Automation is when a skill becomes effortless and can occur unconsciously, like the way most of us are able to drive and talk, plan, navigate, etc. -when initially this skill overwhelmed our cognitive system. Generally, psychological skills – in the conventional 'mental skills' sense – only reliably benefit performance when the client can use them effortlessly (cf. Thomas, Murphy, & Hardy, 1999). The end of the acquisition phase is signalled when the client is ready to be putting the strategy into everyday practice.

Practice

The *practice* phase involves putting the (new) skill into practice. As such, extensive practice was used during acquisition, but now the skill is deployed in real life – it is 'put into practice'. At this stage, the skills, knowledge, attitudes, etc. are fully established and ready/able to contribute towards the client's goals. To assist this application, the times/moments where it is necessary to deploy the skill are identified and the client is encouraged to use their skills/ideas at the appropriate moment through various means. It may become necessary to recognize important moments and opportunities to use the skill – as already considered during the education phase – and use these as cues to deploy the skill. Ironically, it is perfectly possible for an athlete to spend time acquiring a new skill or concept, only to 'forget' to use it at the appropriate time. Likewise, once the new ideas have been put into practice, monitoring their effects (next chapter) also becomes important.

8.3.2 Structuring the support programme

Another useful consideration in planning an intervention, or course of action, is the way it will be supported through structure. Self-evidently, planning progression into your support, as above, should already provide some structure. For example, the use of diaries, structured drills and practice tasks, etc. However, psychological support also often requires additional reinforcement, in terms of the way it is built into/around the client's day-to-day life. Physical, psychological and social cues are good ways of 'scaffolding' a support package, while periodization is a key consideration in managing these issues.

Physical cues

Physical cues include any non-human environmental stimuli that can be used to stimulate, organize or drive any changes the client is pursuing. As noted earlier in this chapter, many athletes can agree with the reasoning

---

Pavlov revisited

We often skip over the work of Pavlov in our pursuit of performance excellence. It was, after all, Psychology 101. However, when it comes to structuring our psychological support, using different types of cuing, his work is highly relevant (Pavlov, 1927; Douglas, Medin, Ross & Arthur, 2009).

During his research on digestion, Pavlov noticed that the dogs in the experiment began to salivate in the presence of the technician who normally fed them, rather than simply salivating in the presence of food.

This led to the hypothesis that some external stimulus could become associated with food and cause salivation on its own, *if* that stimulus was present when the dog was given food.

To investigate, Pavlov rang a bell and then gave the dog food; after a few repetitions, the dogs started to salivate in response to the bell even when no food was present. Pavlov called the bell the conditioned (or conditional) stimulus (CS) because its effects depend on its association with food. He called the food the unconditioned stimulus (US) because its effects did not depend on previous experience. Likewise, the response to the CS was the conditioned response (CR) and that to the US was the unconditioned response (UR).

When working with athletes, it is often useful to consider the current unconditioned responses displayed in and around day-to-day training, competition and home life: the effectively unconditioned stimuli.

Our planning can benefit from identifying key aspects of this day-to-day environment and turning them into conditional stimuli, which can then be used to cue the desired changes: a conditioned response.

Further still, we can introduce new conditional stimuli (phone alarms, diaries, stickers, wristbands, etc.) to try and help reinforce the desired changes.

Such considerations return us to the consideration of informed consent, from Chapter 3. Clients should ideally understand the risks, costs, aims and benefits of such an approach prior to using techniques that might be viewed as quite intrusive and, at times, annoying!

---

behind a support programme, and even think it is a fantastic idea, but simply 'forget' to carry out the activities. Put simply, humans can be creatures of habit – both behaviourally and psychologically. Indeed, some approaches to psychology are based on the assumption that our thought patterns and typical responses are simply habits (Ellis, 1994, 2004; Rachman, 1997). Some of the most persistent habits – nail biting, smoking, etc. – require pretty intrusive physical cues to help change them. Typically, nail biting can be remedied by applying a foul-tasting liquid to the nails, so that the person receives a nasty shock each time they bite! In sport psychology, we may not need to go so far, but the following story may illustrate the point.

One of my favourite examples of physical cuing is 'borrowed' form an Irish rugby coach I once knew, who required his players to stick small orange dots in locations throughout their daily lives. Phone screen, computer screen, bathroom mirror, TV screen, car steering wheel, protein powder container, etc. Every time they noticed a sticker (i.e., a lot!), they had to perform which-ever mental task they were working on at the time. Not only did I 'steal' this idea (with good results), but once under tremendous time pressure, I went a step further and attached a cat-bell to a player's wristband. Every time he noticed the bell he had to listen to his inner monologue, challenge nega-tive thoughts and produce positive ones. One week later, getting back on the team bus (with the national trophy!), he waved at me, showed me he was still wearing it and gave a big thumbs-up. I say this because most play-ers' reactions have been (jokingly): 'I now hate you, but it definitely helped!' In the same ilk, clinical psychologists often require clients to pass paper clips or coins from one pocket to another each time they notice a negative thought, with a view to slowing and stopping the flow. *Physical cuing* is just one way of supporting change that should be an important part of the sport psychologist's planning.

Psychological cuing

Psychological cuing involves attempting to associate particular thoughts, emotions and moods to the changes involved in your support programme. For example, 'next time you feel that red mist descending, try to take a deep breath and count to 10'. Perhaps rather obviously, this is one of the more challenging types of cuing to use when structuring an intervention. Someone who is feeling very angry after being sent from the playing field (e.g., fouled out, red/yellow carded, etc.), or very anxious having made a costly error for their team, may believe their thoughts and feelings are com-pletely natural, appropriate and uncontrollable. Telling someone to 'calm down' or 'cheer up' in these moments is not likely to make you very popular. Worse still, asking someone to remember to act differently ahead of time, and then perhaps chastising them for not doing so. Such approaches seem doomed to fail and to generate the response 'you can't tell me how to feel' – which might be viewed as pretty damning for a psychologist.

More optimal approaches might include: (a) an awareness-raising exercise, whereby a client records and reflects on critical incidents in a diary (causes, thoughts and feelings, consequences); or (b) an anticipatory/proactive approach of identifying situations where problems have occurred and plan-ning the desired response. The latter option can be highly effective as it allows the athlete to both plan and rehearse the desired responses – and ongoing research into mental imagery suggests that such rehearsal makes the desired responses much more likely (Wakefield & Smith, 2012; Wakefield, Smith, Moran & Holmes, 2013). Likewise, while it may be a 'slow burner', option (a) carries the added benefit of letting the client record, evaluate and respond her/himself, rather than being 'told how to feel'. Ultimately, while physical cues are external and non-human, and social cues are external and human, psychological cues perform the same role but draw on intrapersonal stimuli psychological cues. On personal reflection, using psychological cuing can be more challenging, but equally more empowering to the client, and highly effective in the long term.

Social cues

Social cues can be operationally defined as human contextual factors that can be used to stimulate, reinforce or even monitor the changes the client is pursuing. So long as confidentiality considerations can be appropriately managed, it may be possible to request assistance from coaches, teammates, parents, partners or support staff. For example, with younger athletes, parents are often very useful for providing timely reminders about 'homework' developed alongside the psychologist. Likewise, physiotherapists are often excellent at providing reminders to reset rehab goals and the like. There is also a growing belief that sport psychology can be at least reinforced and maintained by coaches, who see players much more frequently than the psychologist. As such, working with coaches is one way of providing strong and consistent social cues for athletes to develop and receive psychological support. The utility of social cuing is one good reason for considering the athlete's social network during the intake and needs analysis stages. Knowing the athlete's social support structures allows us to consider the available options for supporting any changes the athlete chooses to pursue.

Beyond simple cuing, there are several mature schools of psychological practice that emphasize the importance of families and social networks in psychological health: systems therapy (e.g., Meadows, 2008); family and group therapy (e.g., Skynner, 1984); and network therapy (e.g., Speck & Attneave, 1972), for example. In these approaches, social support is vital for change, but also a central factor in establishing, reinforcing and propagating behaviours – both healthy and unhealthy. In this respect, it is important to consider that the athlete's social network may be one of the causes of the athlete's difficulty, and the pattern of interactions may be quite engrained. As such, the athlete's social network holds potential to either significantly impede or enhance the support package. This is why it is important to include the consideration of social support structures in the intake and needs analysis.

A note on periodization

In light of the above coverage of 'stages' it is worth considering which times of an athlete's season lend themselves to wrestling with new ideas, learning new skills and putting new strategies into practice. Generally speaking, learning new skills and concepts is best reserved for out-of-season and pre-season, so as not to interfere with competitive performances. Unfortunately, however, it is competition that often exposes weaknesses and shortfalls in the client's psychological approach, and waiting till the off season would mean writing off the rest of the season. As noted above, there are approaches that involve adapting and hijacking existing skills in order to support progress. Likewise, if sufficient separation can be created where the skill can be grown or developed, then it may be possible to 'grow' the skill alongside competitive performances and introduce it once it is ready. Equally, putting a skill into practice meaningfully – both in training and competition – is much more difficult in the off season. As a final note on periodization, we need to consider the assessment and review process. Asking an athlete in the peak of their competitive season to perform a 'root-and-branch' review of their psychological approach would arguably do more harm than good, so it may be best left for the off season. During the season, small and reactive changes would appear most suitable, whereas the off season facilitates larger changes and proactive planning.

Over the longer term, at the career level, there are increasing calls to consider the way we develop the psychological capabilities of young athletes, to prepare them for competition at higher levels. Clive Woodward, head coach of the 2003 World Cup winning England side, quoted a conversation with Steve Redgrave, where the five times Olympic gold medallist said: 'As soon as you need a sports psychologist telling you how to win you might as well pack it in' (ESPN, 2013). However, in his 2004 autobiography, Redgrave also talks about extensive psychological preparations that went in before the big events. For example, 'Athletes train their body to incredible levels, everything is put into the physical training, yet very little is done mentally. Most of the time the limiting factor is the mind and not the body... In the Olympic final, there's very little difference between the athletes in percentage terms. What is the factor that makes someone better than their nearest rival? Most of the time it is their mind' (Redgrave, 2004, p. 136). Overall, his narrative suggests that if you *still* need a psychologist's help when you stand (or sit) on the start line, then that's a problem. The psychological preparations need to take place well in advance. If we accept this view, then we need to consider not only the time of season, but the time of career when working with athletes. Career-level periodization will vary by sport, with gymnastics and soccer requiring athletes to reach the elite level much earlier than sports such as archery or eventing. In general terms, if an athlete has plenty of time to learn, embed and engrain a totally new psychological approach before they reach elite level, then such a large-scale overhaul might be a good option. However, if an athlete is already at the peak of their career and looking to overcome one issue so they can have 'one big push' before retiring, then a total overhaul of their psychological approach seems inappropriate. It might simply take too long. Overall, periodization, at the level of season or career, can affect a number of key planning decisions, from the way a support programme is structured to the type of cues that might be available for supporting the programme.

8.3.3 Contingencies

Planning contingencies simply involves having a 'backup' plan, in case the first option proves to be inappropriate. This may vary from simply recommending a different technique to perhaps even adopting a different style with the client. Perhaps the original plan for progression was misjudged, or some of the cues used to support progress become unreliable. In many cases, remember, the core of the support package may be highly appropriate, but difficulties come from simply putting the ideas into practice in daily life. Case studies submitted by sport psychologists very rarely discuss contingencies, although many appear to 'switch' between ideas without explanation, which is frustrating for a reader (or assessor). Such switches may simply reflect the notion that the original plan was not working, but they do not convey whether the change in approach was planned or performed 'reactively' – on the fly, so to speak. In terms of 'best practice', planning contingencies into a support programme may appear redundant, or 'planning for failure', but consider the following. If we want to demonstrate competence to our client, and reassure athletes, supervisors, assessors and the broader public that we 'know what we are doing', planning contingencies is arguably more persuasive. One alternative, switching, can often appear to an outsider as lacking consistency, rigour and transparency. The other obvious alternative, 'sticking to your guns', can quickly lead to a degeneration of the working alliance with the athlete, especially if they perceive the barriers experienced to be genuine and fair/reasonable. Overall, if we want to have the luxury of adapting when our 'best laid plans' are exposed to reality, while also being able to demonstrate that we know what we're doing, planning contingencies is important.

Unfortunately, not even psychologists can predict the future regarding how effective or useful our support will be. It is unrealistic to try and anticipate every possible barrier and impediment to a psychological support package. An excellent resolution, perhaps most closely aligned with the counselling and 'client-led' approaches (cf. Keegan, 2010), is to plan to monitor, re-evaluate and even reset goals; deliberately and in collaboration with the athlete. Rather than an approach built around a clear and prescriptive 'Plan A, then Plan B', client-led approaches might be described as 'tinkering'. Try a little change, notice differences (or lack of), try it again, notice again, try something different, etc. If a psychologist is prepared to deliberately and explicitly cede ownership of this planning process to the client – that is, client-led – then it should be acceptable to convey such a decision in one's case records, case report, supervisory meetings, etc. Contextually, it would make sense within a counselling or 'construalist' philosophy, as described in Chapter 3. However, from a certaintist philosophical perspective, it might seem quite incongruous: 'I know all about this problem, as I am the expert in psychology ... but work it out for yourself'. The inevitable return to discussion of philosophical standpoints reinforces the point that, as per our model, philosophy underpins almost all aspects of the service delivery process. It also segues nicely into our final section, considering how different philosophies and styles might approach planning.

8.3.4 Different traditions' approaches to planning psychological support

The following paragraphs briefly sketch out the ways that each philosophical tradition – certaintism, construalism, fallibilism or pragmatism (see Chapter 3 for details) – aligns to the planning considerations outlined in this chapter.

Certaintism

As discussed previously, a philosophy that might be characterized in the 'certaintist' tradition is based on the notion that the psychologist's theories and processes are correct, or at least the most certain/assured ones available. Likewise, certaintism assumes that there are core commonalities amongst all human psychology, so that two athletes with the same issue could realistically expect to receive very similar support packages. Such a philosophy might lead to the development of 'tried and tested' workbooks and materials, and perhaps branded or 'badged' resources that are offered to any athlete facing a certain situation. Returning to the idea of 'selling' our services, from earlier, it is certainly easier to have such a 'marketable product' on the shelf, ready to go. Regarding core considerations, purely certaintist assumptions would necessitate the setting of clear and objective goals regarding progression – what is the exact aim of this particular step in our work together, and how will we know when we have achieved it? Such goals may benefit from being reconciled with the EAP model discussed here, in order to be constructive and coherent. Regarding structure, as already noted, structured materials such as workbooks would be the most obvious solution as they permit relatively consistent 'matching' of solutions (course of action and specific activities) to problems (i.e., the goals and barriers identified in the needs analysis). While there will also be an argument for 'personalizing' plans from a certaintist practitioner, the degree of tailoring or flexibility would need to be relatively low in order to fit with pure certaintist assumptions. It seems likely that a purely certaintist assumption set would be more likely to use physical and psychological cues to support change. Using social cues would require more dependence on the 'social construction' of the athlete's psychological reality, which is really the realm of 'construalism'. Likewise, certaintist assumptions arguably underpin calls for stronger forms of periodization, because we might reliably expect the same contextual demands at different stages of the season (or career), regardless of individual differences between athletes. Regarding contingency planning, the purest form of certaintism would be more likely to adopt a 'stick to your guns' approach, because theories supported by extensive evidence prove that 'this is the right way to go'. Where contingencies were to be acceptable, an expert-led and prescriptive 'Plan A-Plan B' approach would be more likely than a 'tinkering' approach.

Construalism

The various approaches contained within the construalist tradition hold that psychological reality is not objective and generalizable, but constructed uniquely for each person. In light of this core assumption, the planning of support work from a construalist tradition would need to be highly tailored and personalized. There can be no one-size-fits-all resource pack when people – and the support networks they are enmeshed in – are so different and complex. As such, rather than setting an 'end-point' goal, a construalist approach might identify a 'direction of travel' with the expectation that barriers, hold-ups and deviations are inevitable. While many of the core considerations remain similar at the superficial level, the way they are approached will be different under construalism. The client will be empowered to progress at their own pace, spending longer at certain stages or stepping back a stage, as s/he deems necessary. Likewise, the client may wish to explore their own use of cues and support structures, rather than being encouraged (or asked) to by the practitioner. The overall approach becomes one of: (a) sensitizing the client to the likely steps s/he will experience and how to identify progress; (b) signposting the likely barriers or how to identify barriers; and (c) considering how to identify tools and resources that will help along the way. Relinquishing the authority and responsibility for progress in this way may be quite an uncomfortable experience for the psychologist. However, construalist approaches argue that this strategy leads to long lasting, sustainable changes and decreases any dependence on the psychologist. Regarding contingencies, a construalist practitioner might simply plan to share the journey with the client, listening with interest to the way s/he identifies and overcomes challenges on their route.

Pragmatism

The pragmatist tradition, as described in this book, uses the logic that 'whatever works must be true'. In some respects, this approach performs the process described in this book in reverse. Pragmatism involves finding any course of action that appears to deliver results for the client and then retrospectively infers that the mechanisms or processes used were appropriate. As such, planning may be difficult to reconcile with such an approach. However, the necessity for progression towards the clients' goals remains, and the framework described in this chapter, education-acquisition practice, might still be used to infer which actions are 'working' versus those that aren't. It may even help to clarify what is defined as working versus enjoyable. Likewise, the options for structuring a support programme remain the same, but the way they are engaged might look quite different: perhaps more opportunistic and less planned. The idea of contingencies is heavily entwined in the pragmatist tradition, as it is imperative to keep going until an approach is discovered that 'works'. As such, Plans A, B and C, etc., are all readily tried and when one appears to work then success can be claimed. As noted previously, there are threats that using such an approach can appear disorganized and opportunistic. However, most of the problem occurs when the reflection and retrospective analysis are missing. Assuming the final approach adopted by a pragmatist practitioner really did work, then it is important to go back and analyse the various choices and decisions that led to this successful outcome. These would include the planning decisions. In principle, failure is not an option as the pragmatist practitioner must continue working until their support works. As such, one must always attempt to learn from these successes. In reality, it seems just as possible to fail – alienate a client, miss important information, etc. – in a pragmatist tradition as any other.

Fallibilism

The fallibilist tradition, drawing from the work of Popper (1969), Munz (1985) and Bhaskar (1975), proposes that there is indeed a 'real' reality (like certaintism in some respects). However, fallibilists argue that psychological 'reality' is too complex and unknowable to make firm claims about. One common criticism of such an approach is that we would never get out of bed in the morning if we could not be 100% certain that the floor would be there for our foot to land on. However, rather than saying, 'Do not do anything, as you can never be certain', fallibilism really tries to guide practitioners towards recognizing the fallibility of their processes, learning and decisions. Not so much 'don't do it' as 'proceed very carefully'. Any parent will tell you of the dangers of leaping out of bed in the morning without checking the floor for discarded toys first. But a quick check, and the decision becomes less of a risk. In light of these foundations (described in detail in Chapter 3), a fallibilist practitioner would arguably both plan, and plan for failures. What is Plan A? What are reasonable responses if Plan A fails, or Plan B, etc.? And what would be sufficient to make us completely revise our approach and start over? No theory would ever be regarded as sufficient, alone, to drive the planning process, nor would existing evidence override the requirement to personalize and tailor the plans accordingly (i.e., there are always exceptions even when a particular approach seems very well supported). Regarding core considerations, a fallibilist practitioner would both set clear goals regarding progression (while reflecting on whether the goals themselves were appropriate), as well as considering the contingencies from the outset. The goals may be aligned with the EAP model discussed here, but there would also be a reflection on whether the level of progression had been correctly identified. Likewise, one would need to consider whether we might be asking too much (or too little) of the client? Regarding structure, while materials such as workbooks would definitely be an option, they would not be used in a 'matching' paradigm wherein a particular set of symptoms (or characteristics) was invariably paired with a particular plan of activities. Physical, psychological and social cuing would all be options but every instance of using such structure would need to be carefully considered on its own merits. Is that coach/parent likely to help or hinder? Does the client like them enough to accept their input/help? Is this physical cue frequent enough, or perhaps too frequent (i.e., annoying!). Will the cues achieve the aims and sufficiently support the goals? Likewise, any periodization included in a fallibilist plan would likely need to be carefully judged and personalized in order to try and minimize the likelihood of proving fallible. There would also be a strong tendency towards incorporating checks and balances to detect the effects of any advice or new strategy, assess its costs/benefits and either change or replace it as required. Overall, a fallibilist approach to planning would involve both planning for the best case (i.e., 'Plan A works') as well as expecting and planning for other eventualities. There would be no room for blind optimism or 'faith in the method' under a fallibilist approach.

8.4 Conclusion

In summary, this chapter has detailed both the overall aims and goals of the support planning process, as well as detailing the core considerations within it. We have clearly positioned support planning within the sport psychology service delivery process, sitting between 'intervention choice' and 'monitoring progress'. Likewise, planning can be informed by considerations of ethics, philosophy and ideas from the intake, needs analysis and case formulation. Planning can feel very presumptive and preemptive, meaning that one wrong assumption might mean it's time wasted. However, this chapter has outlined the benefits of planning, the ways that plans can vary and adapt and the ways that different styles of practice might approach planning. Overall, this chapter has argued that we, as sport psychologists, must engage with the planning process whether we admit it or not. This engagement can range from 'delegating' the implementation phase to the client, right through to carefully trying to predict all possible future eventualities and plan for those. Realistically, we can also 'plan to adapt': considering how we will measure progress and development; evaluating whether we are on track or falling behind; and anticipating likely actions that might help. It is worth noting that, even if one client only follows one path (meaning a large portion of planning may feel wasted), the deliberation and reflection can benefit future clients, and improve future services too.

8.5 Ella's story: Part 8 – Playing with planning

Ella is approached by a 15-year-old male trampolinist who, in his very first session, says he wants to learn imagery. He has been experiencing difficulties executing his routine in competitions, although it is often perfect in practice. After exploring the areas of confidence and anxiety, Ella and Mitch agree that his difficulty appears to be generated by arousal and somatic responses. Physiological arousal generated by the presence of a crowd and judges was a good fit for Mitch's story. Given his strong preference to use imagery to address the issue, Ella was content to assist him learning this new technique 'from scratch' (in his words).

1. Describe the progression that would need to be planned to provide Mitch with sufficient 'imagery skills' to manage his physiological arousal in competition. What activities would you plan under (i) education, (ii) acquisition and (iii) practice?
2. What physical, psychological and social cues might be available for a 15-year-old trampolinist, to help prompt and support his support programme?
3. What checks and measures should they plan in, to evaluate whether the chosen intervention is 'working'? And what should they do if, for some reason, imagery is not the best approach for Mitch?

Ella receives a call from a local, government funded 'academy'. The academy identifies young athletes 'with potential' from a wide range of sport and offers scholarships including specialist support from all areas of sport science (as well as media training and academic support). Ella is excited to be asked if she could design a 'programme' of workshops to offer over the course of the year. However, when she sits down to write it, she feels uncertain. She calls her supervisor who asks her to design two separate programmes: one full of 'off-the-shelf' prescriptive sessions, that would be very similar with each group; and another that incorporates the specific needs and feedback from each group, delivering tailor-made services.

4. What sort of content would you plan into the 'off-the-shelf' programme? In what order would you deliver the sessions, and why? What are the pros and cons of this approach?
5. What sort of content would you plan into the 'tailor-made programme? As above, in what order would you deliver the sessions, and why? What are the pros and cons of this approach?
6. After reviewing these two options, what 'package' would you suggest to the academy, and how would you justify it?

8.6   Review and reflect

1. Why is it important to plan your psychological support with athletes? What are the pros and cons of planning support?
2. What core considerations are used when planning psychological support in sport psychology? What are the risks involved if the plan is rushed, or given insufficient attention?
3. What criteria would you look for to qualify as an excellent 'planning process' for psychological support? And what might constitute a weak plan?
4. What tools, cues and prompts could you use to try and ensure that the way you plan psychological support is as strong as possible?

9 Delivery and Monitoring (… and Knowing When You're Finished)

9.1 Introduction and overview

Following on from the previous chapters, sport psychologists can choose to actively monitor an intervention (set and monitor goals, compare to benchmarks, pre to post) or they can choose to be much more passive, assuming their advice has worked perfectly unless they hear otherwise. This chapter will explore the various options for the delivery and monitoring of an intervention. The available options and their advantages and disadvantages are reviewed and analysed. The consequences of failing to monitor, or monitoring inappropriately are considered in relation to the impacts on the client, the practitioner and the discipline as a whole. In addition, the preceding chapters set a clear precedent for 'asking the right question'. Rather than simply asking 'does it work?', practitioners are encouraged to ask specific questions in relation to their core assumptions, the aims of the service delivery process, the client's aims and the aims of the specific intervention. If you were seeking to enhance motivation and enjoyment, then why look for a performance improvement? If you were looking for improved communications and working relationships, how exactly should this be 'measured' – what would constitute acceptable evidence that the practitioner has been effective?

Why is this important? Because this is exactly the sort of evidence that clients, coaching staff, governing bodies, supervisors, teachers and assessors/reviewers will want to see – and if they (or you) are asking 'Is he playing better?' when actually you only set out to support your client through a difficult life transition, then you might experience some real problems.

9.1.1   What are delivery and monitoring in sport psychology?

> **deliver** - *verb* - \di-'li-vər, dē-\ - *To do what you say you will do or what people expect you to do: to produce the promised, wanted, or expected results...*
>
> Reprinted with kind permission from Merriam-Webster's Collegiate® Dictionary, 11th Edition ©2015 by Merriam-Webster, Inc. (www.Merriam-Webster.com).

'So remember that client who was having problems with confidence? Well I sent him away to work on his self-talk. Gave him a self-talk diary to keep. He came back this week. Still lacking confidence. One mistake can ruin his game. Turns out he hasn't been doing the diary I gave him. For 2 months! So that's it really, I mean, how stupid is that? I told him to do the damn diary and come back in 2 weeks'. In this (completely fake) example, is the psychologist truly delivering a good service? He made an evidence-based recommendation, supported it with the diary, monitored the consequences. But yet, something isn't working. The client isn't benefitting and isn't carrying out the activities intended to create a benefit. Is the client likely to be happy with the service he received in this story? Somewhere, there is a significant disparity between the service being delivered and the expectations of the client. Even if the advice and diary were completely appropriate – evidence based, clearly indicated in the case formulation, aligned to a clear philosophical foundation, etc. – would the support in this example ever be rated as 'excellent' by the client, or his coach, or teammates? More basically, has the client actually been helped?

On first impressions, 'delivering' may appear to simply mean 'getting on and doing the job' (at last!). In the above example, that might simply mean giving advice and a plan, and considering the job completed. In light of the preceding chapters, what exactly is there left to do? We have analysed the client's needs, performed a case formulation, chosen a support programme (or intervention) and planned it carefully. *Just do it... Surely?* And 'monitoring'? *That must just mean measuring the results, right?*

In actuality, 'delivery' takes place in a complex environment of expectations: from the client, the practitioner and many others too. Some of these expectations can be managed by the psychologist (e.g., the client's expectations) but others remain justifiably fixed and inflexible (e.g., the regulatory body). Thus, in order to deliver, one is constantly both performing work, and making sure that the work is aligned to these expectations. If we consider the 'moveable goalposts' that psychology offers (detailed in Chapter 3) we must constantly work to make sure that the service being delivered is aligned to all stakeholders' expectations: whether that be by modifying the service or the expectations. As such, as well as monitoring the service delivery, we should also be monitoring the expectations. Constantly. Failing to maintain a close alignment between the service being delivered and the expectations of the service is, to all intents and purposes, failing.

Delivering to expectations: After reflecting on wildly divergent feedback comments from students in their class surveys, many university teaching staff can be quite puzzled. How can two students in the same class respond 'Best professor ever, promote this guy!!' and 'Worst professor ever, no point learning this subject', respectively? Many of us believe that consistently delivering a high-quality service will, on average, lead to more 'satisfied customers'. But what about the others, and what if that 'dissatisfied minority' were to grow? When investigating this problem, research shows that in many cases, meeting the client's (or student's) expectations proves more important in 'satisfaction' than any objective measurements of the actual service delivered (see discussion on p. 175). In fact, in many studies the degree to which clients'/customers'/students' expectations were met was the *only* significant predictor of satisfaction: that is, the 'match up' of expectation and delivery. Coincidentally, this pattern also persists for PhD supervision, and the supervision of applied psychological practice (Chapter 10). If we accept that expectations are important, remembering that even the dictionary definition says they are, the 'delivery and monitoring' stage of our model' takes on a new meaning. While we may be delivering and monitoring progress against our own favoured model/framework, it may be more important to monitor the client's expectations and ensuring a match-up between those and what is delivered.

In fact, if we stick with the professor and students for a moment, there can often be quite a severe disconnect between the expectations of each (i.e., 'Teach them new/different facts' versus 'Teach them how to think'), and this leads to an additional key consideration: Who actually gets to judge whether a service has been effectively delivered? In the case of the university, the students have a set of expectations regarding what 'teaching' means, as do the professors. Further, the university itself may also have a policy. Sitting above all of this will be a regulatory body that defines what teaching should achieve at university level (as opposed to at school). Sometimes, the students and professor will disagree, in which case the professor may have to explain 'poor feedback' to the university. Likewise, every few years the regulator will visit to check the university's practices. What we see, effectively, is a situation in which the service being delivered is judged by several 'masters': this situation is called *multiple accountability* (cf. Braithwaite, 1999; Scott, 2000). Not only that, but it is extremely difficult to identify a truly objective measure of the quality of delivery (in teaching, as well as in psychological services). Instead, we tend to quantify subjective judgements of the various stakeholders, for example with questionnaires, and use that as a measure. Remember, we are dealing with issues here that are not easily measured objectively (as noted in Chapter 3). Numerically, or quantitatively, yes: but those numbers reflect subjective judgments regarding service quality, not true objectivity (e.g., questionnaires). And the biggest determinant of what scores are given is the expectations held by the rater. If a student expected that they were required to memorize facts and then simply write them on the exam paper, *but* the professor tried to inspire the student to question the world: 'Worst professor ever...'

Likewise, the sport psychologist is accountable to the 'client' (e.g., athlete, parent, coach(es), director(s) and, if different, the service recipients) as well as her/himself, the regulatory body and, potentially, the organization employing the psychologist too. So for example, a registered/regulated sport psychologist operating on behalf of *World's Best Brain Consulting Ltd*[1], to deliver a programme to the athletes, paid for by the national governing body, and overseen by the coaches ... serves many masters indeed! This can pose significant difficulties in judging (i.e., monitoring) whether a service is being successfully delivered.

Who can we afford to 'let down' in such a situation – by which we might rephrase: from whose expectations can we afford to digress? If the psychological service fails to meet regulatory requirements, one's licence will be lost: no more livelihood. However, if the clients' expectations remain significantly different from the service being delivered, we quickly run out of clients: no more livelihood. And what about if we practice in a way that we know, in our heart, to be ineffective, but the clients seem to like it and the regulator permits it, is that a sustainable life choice?

In light of the above discussion, we reach quite a unique definition of 'delivering and monitoring' service delivery in sport psychology. We: (a) perform, instigate or support the activities of the support programme, as planned (i.e., in Chapter 8); (b) monitor any effects or progress; (c) monitor the expectations of the client and any other stakeholders; and (d) constantly attempt to ensure the best possible overlap between stakeholder expectations and service delivery. This chapter argues that all four of these activities are inextricably linked, and none is more important than the others. By consequence, if we reach a point where the client no longer expects/needs support and the psychologist is not carrying out any psychological support activity; this defines the ideal opportunity to 'terminate' the service.

The following sections emphasize the importance of getting this process right; detail key considerations to be made in delivering and monitoring (and terminating service); and explore how the four archetypal philosophical

---

[1] To my knowledge, this is a fake name.

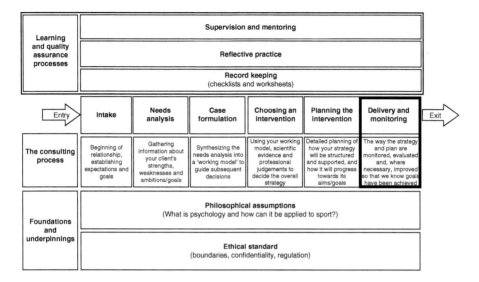

Figure 9.1   *The position of the delivery and monitoring processes within the service delivery process means that this may be the final part of our work with a client. Of course, if the monitoring of delivery notes raises a number of problems, we may have to return to the planning stage, choose a new intervention or even query the case formulation or needs analysis.*

traditions might approach these processes. Real-life examples are provided, and the reader is encouraged to reflect on examples from their own practice, or life. Finally, a checklist for recording and monitoring one's 'delivery' is included to support practitioners' decisions in relation to each client.

9.2   The importance of delivery and monitoring

Now that we have introduced and defined delivery and monitoring, it is worth pausing to consider why these processes are so important. This book argues that maintaining close alignment between the service being delivered and the expectations of all relevant 'judges' effectively defines a 'good' service. To achieve this, as well as providing the support that has been agreed and planned, the psychologist should monitor both the progress towards goals and the expectations of those who have a vested interest in the outcomes. The next section will discuss different approaches to ensuring such alignment, but first this section will quickly explore the consequences of getting the alignment process right or wrong.

Let's imagine a practitioner who insists his only purpose as a sport psychologist is to deliver gold medals, at (almost) any cost. 'Athlete welfare be damned, you have to push yourself hard. Confidentiality be damned,

I will tell the coach or physio whatever they need to know. Athletes know what they signed up for, and it's brutal out there'. To some extent, the approach seems to work: it delivers new business and existing clients generally seem content. The psychologist only works in elite sport, and the current zeitgeist in elite sport mirrors this attitude (largely because current funding arrangements in many countries only award money to the sports that deliver medals). But now imagine deploying such an attitude in children's sport, where participation and enjoyment are key, or even in a 'talented youth' programme. How would it work at a training centre for referees? Is it an approach we should recommend to new trainee psychologists, who undoubtedly will do most of their training outside elite sport. And as a member of a helping profession, who else can the athletes go to for emotional support if not the psychologist? Nonetheless, so long as there is good alignment between the psychologist's approach, the governing body and coaches' expectations, and sufficient athletes 'sign up', then the psychologist has a business to run. The psychologist in this example can be considered to be 'delivering' successfully.

If we look at this from the other perspective, what would happen if the same organization was using a psychologist who prioritized athlete welfare and operated by offering strict confidentiality to the athletes – regardless of who was paying the bill? Even if the psychologist could sleep safe in that knowledge that he was being very ethical and morally defensible, would the 'medals at any cost' organization care? Would they rate this service as 'excellent' and want to retain him when budgeting time comes around? In this instance, the psychologist is 'delivering' a service different to the one that is expected and, as such, the coaches, athletes, governing body may all justifiably be (or become) unhappy with the service.

This example also leads to the importance of monitoring. Assuming the service was 'sold' as a complete package of welfare, performance and education, whose fault it is if the client(s) subsequently realizes they actually only care about performance? Does assigning fault even matter, when such discontent can ultimately lead to the premature termination of services – complete with negative connotations for the psychologist (e.g., financial, reputation), athletes (support removed, relationships lost) and wider profession (reputation)? In such an example, the psychologist is trying to be ethical and holistic yet he may perhaps be considered 'substandard' by the organization employing him. By consequence, many of the core reasons ethical considerations exist (no harm, protecting reputation of profession, etc.) can all be undermined by trying to be ethical in an environment that doesn't value such an approach. Hence, even if a psychologist did market and sell the service appropriately, the divergence of expectations can be very damaging. It should, therefore, be clear that monitoring both the progress *and* the expectations of service is vital. Delivering what you think is a good service to a client who doesn't appreciate it can be heart-breaking (just ask the professors in the above example!).

When faced with a diverging set of expectation, the psychologist has several choices. It may be possible to revise the 'intervention choice' (e.g., Chapter 7), or 'treatment plan' (e.g., Chapter 8). It might be necessary to revise the goals of the service, by reconsidering the client's very needs (Chapter 5) or the case formulation you developed (Chapter 6). Alternatively, of course, the psychologist might wish to change, or correct, the client's expectations of the service, such that the 'divergence' of expectations is reduced. What you do not want to do though is deliver perfectly to where the goalposts used to be.

For examples of how expectations can change as a result of service delivery, we need only consider how clients' self-ratings change in questionnaire responses or performance profiles (as noted in Chapter 4). 'At the beginning of the programme of support I rated myself as 7/10 for concentration, but now I realize how hard it is, I'm actually a 6, even though I've definitely improved from before'. Another example I've heard is as follows: 'My scores on the screening questionnaire indicated I might be suffering from clinical anxiety, but I don't think I am at all, so we reduced the scores'. Finally, in a more positive example, I have occasionally (and very cautiously) permitted athletes to 'think the unthinkable' and consider whether they wish to continue their involvement with a team or programme in the face of frustrations over selection or injury. Managing the transition out of competitive sport can be an important aspect of the sport psychologist's role. However, by beginning to consider such a change, many athletes realize that they do not want to 'quit' at all. In these instances, the goal of support quickly moves from dealing with frustration to a renewed focus on improvement and performance. The 'goalposts' moved, but very much on purpose!

Fundamentally, it should be clear by now that it is important to both be sure that you are delivering on your original goals, but that these remain aligned with the client's expectations. However, after spending a few moments focussing on delivering *to expectations*, it is also important here to emphasize the importance of being sure that we are, in fact, generating progress. If we only deliver to expectations, and the expectations are permitted to change arbitrarily week to week, we become a passive pawn in somebody else's game. It would be neither scientific, nor pursuing any sensible goal except 'appeasement'. During training and supervision, each psychologist will evaluate her/his service; often by using some sort of before versus after comparison. Likewise, when working on a specific contract or for a large organization it often becomes necessary to demonstrate progress as objectively as possible (although as noted above, people often happily substitute numerical for objective). The value of being able to demonstrate such improvements should be self-evident. If a trainee can document effective work, then her chances of successfully qualifying are greatly enhanced. If a psychologist can provide evidence of effective practice or the achievement of contracted goals, then he will be in a strong position to pick up more work with that client (and of course, any word-of-mouth recommendations that might follow). So in these examples we see the most obvious argument for why monitoring our services is important. In the world of psychology, where change is very difficult to measure and opinions can often differ, we need to be able to show that we did produce 'results' – both as trainees and fully qualified practitioners. However, the way that we approach such monitoring will change depending on both our approach and the context, such that some psychologists might only need to convince each individual client (i.e., one at a time), and so the focus can be on simply monitoring whatever that client sees as progress. However, there are very many situations where the athlete you support may be overjoyed with the service, yet the person paying the bill (as above – coach, parent, governing body, etc.) may not agree. In these instances, careful consideration needs to be given to what is monitored, how and who needs to agree with the definition of 'success'. It is an extremely important decision, because what you agree to deliver and monitor can completely change the way you approach the service delivery, right down to requiring different ethical stances or philosophical assumptions.

There is, however, one additional and very valuable benefit to delivering with high fidelity and then monitoring the effects. It gives practitioners the opportunity to feed back into the research process and more broadly contribute to the development of the field. Remember, for sport psychology as a field to advance and add value, it has to offer genuine benefits to the 'end users': the athletes, coaches, other sport scientists and sporting organizations. In this respect, practising sport psychologists should not be cast simply as recipients or customers in the research process, but rather, active participants. If a technique or concept is being developed in theory and research, practitioners are best placed to inform researchers whether it holds value in practice. Some of the most popular and oft-cited theories[2] in sport psychology are barely mentioned when it comes to real-world applied practice – so are they really ecologically valid? The recent trend towards single-case research designs appears to be one very good opportunity for practitioners to generate published papers that inform scientific progress (e.g., Barker, McCarthy, Jones, & Moran, 2011; Barker, Mellalieu, McCarthy, Jones, & Moran, 2013).

Some ideas that appear promising to practitioners need to be properly tested and refined in order to both inform theory development and to

---

[2] Best not to cite any as this is a personal observation shared over drinks at conferences, and there may be people outside my social circles using these theories in their practice.

accrue a suitable evidence base. An applied concept which is both inconsistent with existing theory/knowledge and lacking in reliable evidence may only really qualify as an 'experimental' approach – and that's a polite way of putting it in some circles. When people talk about the conflict between science versus 'craft' or art in applied practice, that is not to say that science and art must remain separate, or conflicted. If an applied practitioner uses experience and 'craft' to generate a new idea or create a new approach, there are numerous benefits to sharing it with the research community. Hence, if practitioners accurately record what they did, and why, what changes it appeared to create, etc., then we gradually describe a new model, system or technique. In the right hands, the newly created ideas can be examined, compared to other theories and ideas, and ultimately, we can test to see whether it really does what it claims to. If the idea is genuinely good and survives such a process, outperforming existing approaches, then the field is demonstrably stronger than before.

At present, the 'reinvestment' from applied practice into the research process is highly under-utilized in sport psychology, and countless opportunities to advance the field are very probably being missed. The only reason not to share ideas in this way is if one believes that a new idea/approach is a valuable commodity, intellectual property, to be protected and costed out accordingly. *Why share when there is profit to be made?* I would argue that this approach only really holds sway in the *certaintist* (i.e., positivist) tradition, where one-size-fits-all generalizability is theoretically possible. However, many psychologists will be the first to admit that there is no such panacea, and if there were then we would all be out of a job once that solution was uncovered and shared. Even within the certaintist approach, protecting a new idea in this way is effectively claiming to know more than the collective wisdom of all the other scientists and researchers in your area: 'My new idea is better than everything else that exists in the world, I haven't tested it but I'm pretty sure'.

In science – and remembering that we have defined sport psychology as a scientific discipline from the start of the book – theories, models and evidence are not generally thought of as copyrightable. Admittedly, I would be slightly irritated to see a diagram I drew or a paragraph I wrote being used by someone else without crediting it properly. But actually if my theories or research papers are being adopted elsewhere, that equates to success in science. Likewise, practitioners may wish to protect their logos, branding, etc., but if they generate a theory, intervention or strategy that holds promise, it ought to be 'reinvested'. If the channels do not exist for this, we should create them. But to assist the process of 'reinvestment', careful delivery with monitoring of effects and consequences will enable a much better transition from practice to research. Remember, the core purpose of the method section in any research paper is to permit transparency, not to say: 'We did a special secret thing but we aren't telling you what it is'...! As such, the practitioner should effectively be asking: 'Here is exactly what I did, and why, can you test to see if it was a one off or if it really does work?' Practitioners are scientists, and scientists need to share their ideas, or else their hard work dies with them[3].

There is one final consideration regarding the importance of monitoring delivery – how else will we know when to finish? If we end our support services early, any benefits may be lost or incomplete. If we carry on too long, we eventually begin to look like we are just taking the client's money without actually helping them anymore. I can still clearly remember one client who really wanted to come back every week long after our aims had been clearly met, and even though we could not identify any additional areas in need of support. In the end, I had to start asking the client what the goals were of any new sessions at the point of making the booking, and if it looked like we were going to end up just 'having a chat' then we should defer the meeting. After a few weeks, the client realized she really was self-sufficient and no longer needed any psychological service. So while it was nice to chat and we had a great relationship, we agreed it was time to end the formal provision of services, and only meet again if a new need was identified. At the point where the client's goals have been clearly met, and any new goals have also been demonstrably achieved, that is probably a defensible time to terminate the relationship. Of course, there are many occasions where we must finish before that moment: for example, if finance, travel or relocation prevent the continuation of work. Even so, at least the careful monitoring may allow an informed evaluation of whether the client is ok to go it alone. It may even be possible to empower the client to self-monitor. But if we do not terminate at the right time, or if we do not carefully appraise the termination process, then all the dangers and ethical issues around failing to benefit the client (and avoid harming the client) become distinct possibilities.

So to summarize this section, the importance of delivering and monitoring can be distilled into the following four points: Carefully delivering your service and monitoring the effects: (a) ensures a happy client, or clients, as their expectations will closely match the actual results being generated; (b) facilitates the demonstration of effectiveness for the purposes of qualification, supervision and reporting (to regulators and governing bodies); (c) protects the psychologist and the wider profession from accusations of ineffectiveness; (d) facilitates the advancement of the field of sport psychology, by both field testing the outputs of research and by generating new ideas to feed into the research and theorizing processes; and (e) informs the process of termination, because all psychological services must eventually come to an end.

---

[3] Put differently: an opportunity to advance human understanding dies with them.

9.3   Core considerations in delivery and monitoring

Now that it is clear what is meant by delivery and monitoring, and the importance of these processes has been elucidated, we can consider the various options for delivering and monitoring psychological support. To a very large extent, the monitoring of effectiveness involves many of the same techniques involved in needs analysis (Chapter 5). However, it remains important to monitor exactly the things you are trying to influence, perhaps not always the same things that were evaluated during the original needs analysis. It is also important to monitor the effects in a way that is consistent with the philosophy and style being deployed. Measuring subjective enjoyment when a swimmer simply needs to produce faster times would require some pretty clear justification. But likewise, keeping a league table of mental toughness scores with a peewee's soccer team might be seen as overkill. With regard to delivering, there are different options we can consider: ranging from face-to-face meetings, video chat and phone sessions, workbooks and Web apps, and more. We also need to consider what we measure/monitor, and how. Further, one's delivery style can vary from instructional and prescriptive to Socratic and relatively hands-off (as per Chapter 3). Likewise, as noted throughout this book, the psychologist's underpinning philosophy and assumptions will have a significant influence on key aspects of delivery and monitoring. The following passages will review these key considerations so that the reader can become aware of the issues and able to construct their own coherent approach to applied practice.

9.3.1   Channels for the delivery and monitoring of service

Taking our previous definition of service delivery – carrying out support; monitoring effects or progress; monitoring client and stakeholder expectations; and ensuring that expectations match results – we need to consider the different media through which these tasks can be performed. Unlike many other types of psychological practice, sport psychology is rarely carried out in an office with comfy chairs and certificates on the wall. Likewise, the important tasks of delivering and monitoring are rarely constrained to 1-hour appointments, but instead they can take place at training, during travel, immediately before or after competitions or even at odd times via video calls as athletes travel to compete around the world. So when it comes to 'delivering', a sport psychologist is more challenged than many other psychologists in having to give careful consideration to exactly how 'delivery' will occur. The options, and their associated pros and cons, are listed here with view to informing such decisions. In each of the below examples remember we are attempting, ideally, to perform *all four* tasks from our definition of 'delivery/monitoring':

Face-to-face, formal appointments

It is difficult to beat the clear focus and attention one can offer in one-to-one meetings, and likewise this approach tends to be more consistent with people's assumptions about how psychology should be done. As such, there is a lot to be said for meeting face-to-face in formal appointments. It can also help you ensure a client is giving proper consideration to a question or questionnaire item, and there are important aspects of body language that are extremely difficult to detect in other situations. In a formal one-to-one meeting, the client's body language can only be a reaction to the psychologist, or perhaps some internal thought/feeling (likely generated by the conversation). This absence of 'noise' from other sources means that a skilled psychologist should find it quite straightforward to create and manage productive conversations in this setting, and to read and respond to the client's own input. However, athletes and coaches must frequently travel, and with busy training schedules their time is precious, so it can be very difficult to secure an hour in the same room as the psychologist. Such time is extremely valuable and we cannot afford to waste it or leave the client feeling the session wasn't quite right. There is also some consideration to be given about where and when such sessions can take place, as the athlete's absence may be noticed by coaches, other athletes or even family. Not all athletes will be happy for this to happen. Likewise, there is a balance to strike between creating a distance between the sessions and the training venue versus taking even more of the athlete's time (and money) in travel. There are many wonderful advantages of formal, focussed, face-to-face meetings, but in the world of sport, they can often be impractical and costly, meaning other options must be explored in order to deliver any sort of service at all.

Face-to-face, informal chats

Looking back over my career so far, many of my most effective moments as a sport psychologist happened in informal moments around training and competition. Athletes and players in teams I worked for would approach me at a key 'teachable moment', having just experienced something first hand – and possibly with an opportunity to go and test any advice immediately. As such, the athlete (or coach in some instances) may simply have been more receptive to psychological input in these moments. But further to this, there are athletes who would never have made a formal appointment to see me, despite it already being part of the service so no cost to them. Some athletes attach a certain stigma to being 'analysed' formally, but are happy to demand only what they want in these fleeting moments. In order for these moments to be possible, I had to adopt the approach of 'hanging out' (cf. Andersen, 2000): travelling to matches to film for analysis, attending post-match analysis and review sessions, even putting cones out at training, just to make myself available for such meetings. The clear benefit, to me, was being able to connect with athletes who would never have arranged to make a formal appointment for a 1-hour meeting. The clear disadvantage, of course, was that it substantially undermined the clear processes outlined in this book. Gaining ethical consent in a momentary chat was problematic (we ended up making it part of the joining pack for all new players). Performing a clear, separable intake and needs analysis, in sufficient detail, almost impossible. However, if I focused on creating good experiences in terms of relationship building, or simply listening, then I could gradually build up enough time and experience with a player to make reasonable recommendations. Of course, sometimes I was required to offer advice with nowhere near enough information to hand, and I quickly learned to qualify these recommendations such that people weren't disappointed if they didn't 'work' first time out. It is possible to operate in this way, but being self-aware and reflexive helps to mitigate any risks and ensure that the potential benefits are realized.

Video and telephone calls

As noted above, athletes and coaches regularly travel a lot, which often makes meeting in person, in a fixed location, quite challenging. Using video and telephone calls can be one way of overcoming this challenge. Like every channel outlined here, it comes with specific benefits and costs. For most ordinary practitioners, the psychologist will very rarely travel to competitions with their clients. This is because large distances and time commitments can be involved (I used to spend every Saturday travelling with the team). Video and telephone conversations allow a psychologist to provide their service immediately before, immediately after or between competitive events (or training and selection events). As such, video or phone calls can reduce costs and open up opportunities for support that might simply not have been available otherwise. However, we lose the level of 'control' that exists in a face-to-face formal meeting, such that athletes on a video call may also be checking social media, or on a phone call they could be driving or eating. By losing this control, the thoughts, emotions, body language, etc. cannot be guaranteed to be generated by 'the only other person in the room' – as there is no room to speak of. At present, video call, in particular, can be quite unreliable, and good Internet connections do not always exist in the places athletes train and compete (e.g., foreign countries, mountains, etc.). Phone calls over such distances can also be very expensive for both parties. Further still, there is no way of guaranteeing the client will chose a suitably private location to ensure confidentiality is maintained. However, it may be possible to plan such support in advance, and perhaps even have an agreement to switch off other phones, TV, social media, etc., and to only make the call from a quiet, private location.

Emails and private messaging

Electronic mail, as well the use of 'private messaging' functions in social media, has also become a vital way of keeping in touch with clients. On the one hand, it may be extremely difficult to perform the entire process from ethics and intake onwards using these channels, but once a relationship is established there may be real benefits to using these channels. For example, such messaging allows both the psychologist and client to respond in their own time, when they have had time to think and step away from other activities. Sometimes, it is possible to offer much more precise and considered responses in writing than 'in the moment'. Likewise, written responses can be saved and reviewed repeatedly – so if a particularly good or meaningful recommendation is made, the athlete can return and review it whenever they need to. Further still, given the use of written media is taking place over the Internet, it should also be possible to either attach worksheets and important forms very easily, as well as sending links to good papers, websites, videos, etc. Realistically, of course, the processes of billing and payment are very frequently performed by email too. By overcoming problems of limited time or long distances, emails and messaging are a worthwhile 'channel' for delivering psychological support, but not without risks. Here, more than ever, there is little or no way of being sure that either party is hearing what the other is saying, and many of us will have had email conversations where we think 'I said that in the last email..!' (even with friends). It is generally very difficult for either party to be sure exactly who is looking over their shoulder. By taking the interaction out of a formal meeting room and into one's real life, it becomes very easy for a window to be left open on a computer, or for a family member to see a phone screen just by sitting next to you. Then there is the mixed blessing of the 'waiting period'. Some people really appreciate taking their time over a response, but others need to know that they've been heard right away. I once heard a comedian using the [...] symbol to indicate someone is typing as a method of torture! It can certainly become excruciating to sit and wait, especially following an important question or statement. Overall, like all the channels discussed here, messaging comes with clear pros and cons, and the trick seems to be to maximize the pros whilst minimizing the cons.

Apps and monitoring software

Using the Internet and technology is increasingly becoming a practicable option for delivering sport psychology services (Dosil, Cremades, & Rivera, 2014), and has been found to be as effective as face-to-face contact in some instances (Zirri & Perna, 2002). Examples include: ingestible devices to measure core body temperature; intelligent clothing to support performance or monitor things like heart rate or sweat; digital video and biomechanical monitoring which can detect things like fatigue, depression or performance decrements; wearable devices such as accelerometers and heart monitors; and much more (Schack, Bertollo, Koester, Maycock, & Essig, 2014). With technology developing faster than many can comprehend, and wearable devices now complementing the capability of mobile phones. It is possible to both deliver and monitor with a client almost 24 hours a day. For example, a rugby team I once worked with sent players a reminder once a day to complete their training diary, including food intake, sleep hours and some psychological factors such as mood. The possibility for real-time monitoring and substantial amounts of data is extremely appealing to many, especially as compared to, for example, a fortnightly and highly subjective evaluation along the lines of 'I think it's going ok'. Realistically, however, individual psychologists may not always have the expertise to tailor-make apps and software for each client (or even as a tool offer to all clients), and gaining such expertise can be extremely expensive. Further, there is an added cost in safely storing the large amounts of data generated, and managing or analysing it efficiently. Then of course, we must consider the value of such data. Many companies are very keen to monitor people's movements, responses to certain experiences (e.g., adverts), daily habits, etc. This means that a psychologist bound by confidentiality may have to either tailor-make apps that never share the information with third parties, or at the very least gain informed consent from the client that they are happy for their data to be stored by the chosen app. There are many possible ways of such apps breaking and losing data. Further, many of the measurement techniques used do not reach scientifically publishable levels of reliability, in fact many do not even make public their validation processes – so it could be using a proverbial 'elastic tape measure'. However, the point here is that these technologies seem to be consistently improving, and it may not be long until some of the above issues of confidentiality and reliability are solved.

'Try it and get back to me if you need to'

As discussed in Chapter 8, there is sometimes an option to let a client 'work it out for themselves' – complete with fairly obvious pros and cons. Nonetheless, constraints on time, location, money, etc. (e.g., 'My club won't pay for any more sessions') can often leave the psychologist needing to leave an intervention or idea relatively unsupported, even after the client has agreed to the path chosen. Likewise, there comes a moment as we approach the termination of support where we are sometimes required to make an educated appraisal: 'I think you can take it from here'. In both instances, the option for monitoring is limited to only really detect that: (a) the advice/strategy has not worked; and (b) the client is self-aware enough to notice (and motivated to tell you). All options for the psychologist to monitor and influence progress and/or expectations are effectively abandoned. Of course, as noted above, there may be reasons for taking this risk, but the situation must be managed nonetheless. To minimize the risks, a psychologist may wish to explicitly set the client's expectations for progress without monitoring/support, as well as outlining the sort of circumstances that might require the athlete the get back in touch. The 'get back to be' strategy is arguably one of managed compromise: imperfect, but necessary on far more occasions that we realize. The lack of ability to monitor (in any detail), review or intervene is a notable concern but real-life considerations often necessitate the use of this 'channel'.

In the below passages, we hit upon some 'delivery' techniques that are, by definition, based on minimal needs analysis of the individual client.

'Putting it out there' – blogs, Web-resources, etc.

A number of sport psychology practitioners choose to offer advice, tools and worksheets on websites and blogs. In these instances, any individual reaching that site could choose to adopt the advice or resources on offer. To a very large extent, the possibility for any preceding needs analysis is missing in this approach, unless one adopts the stance that 'this advice will help most people, everybody needs to hear this'. It is, occasionally possible to 'monitor' any impacts using comments and feedback sections, or perhaps by getting people to sign up to regular participation in the activity (or app). Overall, however, relative to the other 'channels' discussed here, offering psychological advice by 'putting ideas out there' should probably be viewed more as a marketing technique. There can be no two-way discussion to obtain informed consent, and so ethically readers should not be encouraged to try things for themselves on the site. It is also very difficult to carefully discuss important decisions around philosophy and underpinning assumptions in this format – advice from a certaintist or a construalist might be treated very much the same by a casual reader. There are a number of problems with this 'channel', as noted, and regulated/registered psychologists are usually discouraged from adopting such an approach.

9.3.2 Delivering to groups and teams

Group workshops and presentations

Another way of generating new clients or introducing yourself to a new group of clients is through group presentations or workshops. In these examples, there is often very little opportunity for needs analysis, unless a coach or manager has requested help on a specific topic. Further, group work can become a regular part of working with teams, either delivering a pre-planned programme of sessions, or perhaps responding to team performances and recent observations. Many trainee psychologists have been asked to deliver generic sessions, for and the experiences and reflections that such a session can produce. A good friend of mine proposed a 'rule of thirds' for group sessions: a third will usually be very receptive; a third are 'convincible' and a third will remain resolutely resistant to anything to do with psychology. He insisted we should be happy, as a psychologist, to have reached two-thirds of our audience, and not expect to leave every group session with 100% of the audience 'won over'. However, real problems can occur if we are not keeping the interest of the 'convincibles', meaning less than half of the audience is 'on board'. Further, most sport psychologists can recall a session being ruined by one or two dissenting voices, especially if those voices are coaches or senior athletes in the team. Ultimately, by delivering pre-planned content to a large group of people, we can usually guarantee that there will be a small number of people who neither want nor need to be there.

The format for these sessions can vary from 'stand and deliver' – perhaps using slides and standing at the front of the room – right through to relatively 'hands-off' styles such as facilitating conversations and group decisions. The key tasks involved in delivery – carry out support; monitor progress; monitor expectations; and ensure expectations match results – can all be pursued through group work, but in quite different ways depending on style. A controlled and structured session can easily specify desired outcomes, deliver those and even measure effects, but this can involve delivering something the client may not want. To a large extent, the needs analysis could have been short-circuited. A facilitative and unstructured session can allow the clients to develop their own personally meaningful goals and outcomes, and empower them pursue these goals as a group. However, sometimes the skill of facilitation can go unnoticed leaving people asking 'Where was the psychology in that session?', or even 'Why did we need him there for that session?'. This issue harks back to the practitioner-led versus client-led styles, denoted in Chapter 3 (see also Keegan, 2010, 2014); except now applied at the group level. Do we want to appear as an expert in charge, or as a skilled facilitator? Culturally, we often expect a public speaker to be an expert who knows more than the audience and 'transmit' this information. However, this approach also pre-supposes that the audience do not know, and want/need to know, whatever is being said (or taught). Studying for many years to become an expert and then deliberately rejecting that position and asking 'dumb' questions can often be counter-intuitive, but may hold some positives (perhaps 'dumb' is unfair, but I often call them the '4-year-old's questions': But why... but why...?). Often, nobody else has ever asked the 'obvious' questions, and so their answers can become very insightful. Likewise, even when the answers do seem obvious, there can be an enormous difference between being told (as a listener) versus working it out for yourself. So mirroring the arguments made in Chapter 3, by trying to be less presumptuous and seek information from the audience we generate two very positive possibilities. First, the audience reach the same point you would have told them anyway, but because it was generated by them, it is more memorable and inspiring. Second, by not assuming that we know best and asking genuinely open questions, we create the possibility for the clients, or audience, to generate answers that are even better than the ones we would have given – if working from a prepared plan. These claims are both consistent with counselling theory (i.e., client-led approaches), and ultimately very consistent with my own 'lessons learned' from delivering to groups. As always, there is no 'correct' or 'perfect' way of working at the group level, but knowing the various options, their pros and cons, etc., arms the psychologist with the ability to make informed choices for delivering their services. In addition, knowing the pros and cons of each approach allows us to mitigate any risks or potential problems. For example, a psychologist delivering a stand-and-deliver presentation could mitigate the lack of needs analysis by incorporating opportunities to personalize key themes, or could encourage the audience to share their own experiences of the issues being discussed. Perhaps it might be possible to set a 'homework' of looking out for the influences of some key issue, or opportunities to use some new skill. Overall, having a language and classification system to define what we do when delivering allows us to understand what we did, why/how it worked (or not) and therefore facilitates reflection and improvement in the longer term.

Delivering through day-to-day coaching

There have been questions in the past about whether a coach is a suitable person to be delivering sport psychology. Brewer (2000) described the possibilities of dual-role conflicts (coaching performance versus supporting well-being) and, of course, most coaches are not trained in psychology to anywhere near the level of a registered psychologist (see also Ebert, 1997). However, the truth of the matter is that coaches do deal with psychological issues in every session – communicating clearly, building teams, managing confidence through feedback and much more. Likewise, every single coaching session is an opportunity to develop technique, tactical awareness, physical fitness and psychological 'fitness'. Psychologists frequently argue that almost every aspect of sport participation involves psychology – from preparation to execution to reviewing and reflecting. For most performers going through these processes, the coach is there the whole time. The coach is an integral part of the daily training environment (DTE) and the performance environment (PE – cf. Gould, Guinan, Greenleaf & Chung, 2002; Gould, Greenleaf, Chung & Guinan, 2002; Greenleaf, Gould & Dieffenbach, 2001; Gould, Guinan, Greenleaf, Medbery & Peterson, 1999). As such, the coach is arguably very well placed to reinforce important aspects of psychology, design training and preparation to develop and support good psychological approaches and to recognize any emerging issues that may require support from a psychologist (cf. Brewer, 2000; Burton & Raedeke, 2008). If there is any doubt around this, consider how hard a psychologist would have to work with a team if the coach was completely unaware of psychological factors, and frequently either neglected or even undermined mental preparations. Realistically, how many coaches would get very far without at least some awareness of how to motivate, communicate and organize?

Hence, perhaps one of the best ways of supporting a team, as a sport psychologist, is to assist the coach in creating DTEs and PEs that supports good psychology: either for performance, or well-being, or both. This is certainly a position being increasingly advocated in recent years (e.g., Dosil et al., 2014). Pragmatically, this approach allows us to support many more athletes per unit of the psychologist's time, and it can create benefits that persist even after the formal psychological support has ended. Probably the most important consideration in helping a coach create optimal DTEs and PEs is the ethical issue of competence: the coach must be able to recognize where her/his own expertise runs out and the psychologist should step in. Encouraging and facilitating things like confidence, motivation, appropriate focus, mental skills usage, etc., are probably all fine. But where there is a recognized issue that requires specific analysis, then the specific and nuanced expertise of the psychologist is required (e.g., needs analysis, case formulation, tailor-made intervention choices, planning individualized support, etc.). Further still, clinical issues may require referral to a clinical psychologist, or family issues (remembering many coaches are parents to at least one athlete) may require a referral to a family counsellor.

Overall, however, coaches can influence a lot of things in the DTE and PE, including: perceptions of pressure (competition for places, emphasizing importance); regret and remorse (e.g., punishing or dwelling on mistakes); his/her own emotional demeanour (e.g., nervous versus relaxed, angry versus tolerant); directing focus (e.g., play our own game versus game plans tailored to opposition); creating 'tough' competitive cultures versus supportive and friendly groups; staying aloof and authoritative versus approachable and accessible, and much more (Gould, Guinan et al., 2002; Gould, Greenleaf et al., 2002; Greenleaf et al., 2001). There is also growing recognition that the coach is a performer her/himself, and as such coaches depend on good psychology to reach peak performance and avoid choking (e.g., Feltz, Short & Sullivan, 2008).

As above, it should be theoretically possible to carry out support; monitor progress; monitor expectations; and ensure expectations match results when working 'through' the coach(es). Notably, when working through a coach, the psychologist's needs analyses, case formulations and planning processes should arguably recognize the 'layeredness' of working through an intermediary. This could be achieved by borrowing from family- and systems-based theories (as per Certaintism), or by constructing tailor-made models (as per Construalism). In either case, we are not dealing with an individual's psychology in isolation. However, given that the coach is likely to be defined as the 'client' in these instances, that is the person who you should work with to establish goals and expectations. Likewise, the coach is the person whose progress and expectations need to be monitored and managed. In this respect, the options remain similar to elsewhere in this chapter for delivering and monitoring, the difference being that one satisfied client, the coach, is likely to mean that you have also benefitted a large number of athletes – present and future. There are potential ethical issues of dual roles or conflict of interest if we choose to work with a coach *and* their respective athletes, and at the very least this would have to be recognized and carefully managed. Very few psychologists in other fields of psychology would find themselves working with an individual as well as their subordinates, and it is a problem that is relatively specific to sport and some occupational settings.

Embedded, on call or outsider

Finally, whilst this is not an exhaustive list of the 'channels' available, we must also consider whether a sport psychologist wishes to deliver as 'embedded', 'on call' or 'outsider'. Many trainees enter the field with a dream of becoming an integral staff member on a prominent sports team: travelling everywhere with them and always present at training, competitions, planning meetings, etc. This would be the *'embedded'* option, although it remains relatively rare, as few organizations are prepared to pay a full time wage for a sport psychologist. Even those that do tend to 'stretch' the psychologist across several squads, perhaps even competing in different sports (e.g., various national sports institutes or governing bodies). By being 'ever present' the psychologist has many and varied options to 'deliver and monitor' – being physically present to observe events in training, performance, analysis/reviews, travelling etc. In some respects, this can sometimes be quite overwhelming, as one's 'bandwidth' for capturing, analysing and recording important information may simply be unable to process such a constant stream of information. Further, being ever present also provides many more opportunities to make mistakes, in the same way than running numerous statistical tests increases our risk of reporting an incorrect finding. If there is always a small risk of making a mistake, then more opportunities will make the odd mistake inevitable. A team that is deeply sceptical of sport psychology might pounce on such a mistake and undermine or even terminate the provision of services. However, it is also highly unlikely that a team that is sceptical of sport psychology would ever want an embedded sport psychologist. Perhaps the message here is that we shouldn't necessarily push to become embedded if the team are not committed to the idea: that is, be careful what you wish for.

A sport psychologist who is *'on call'*, which is sometimes also referred to as being 'on retainer' does not necessarily follow the team to all events but rather waits for calls from coaches, athletes or other staff before becoming active. This psychologist would likely have an office away from the team's training facilities, and may work for other clients (either self-employed or as part of a wider organizational agreement to support several teams/squads). By not following a team to all events, the psychologist will obviously miss the 'behind the scenes' observations that can sometimes be highly informative. Instead, the psychologist must effectively wait for a problem to be identified. Problems, or rather 'support requirements' might be revealed either when an athlete or staff member notices that psychological support is needed, or perhaps if an ongoing monitoring process put in place by the psychologist suggests support is needed. For examples, if players keep regular diaries of sleep or anxiety levels and a certain threshold is breached then the psychologist may be called up. Likewise, I have reached successful arrangements in the past where physiotherapists make a referral of an injured player. In these instances, the 'monitoring' was achieved by simply discussing with the physiotherapist the sorts of signs and symptoms that might necessitate a referral to psychology. Overall, a psychologist who is 'on call' can be exceptionally passive and simply sit and wait, or s/he can leave a number of monitoring systems in place such that athletes and staff know when it is time to 'make that call' and bring in the psychologist.

Finally, there are occasions when a psychologist sits outside of a team or squad, but offers support to athletes (or coaches) on a one-off basis. In this instance, we can call this the *'outsider'* approach. Whilst his approach does not hold the advantages or good contact with the team, and familiarity with key gatekeepers (e.g., staff) or cultural norms, it is also a good option for building up a name for oneself and gradually building a client base. My first ever client recommended me to a friend, who recommended me to their team (one of several), who eventually recommended me to the entire organization. In this instance, even if the psychologist works with several players from the same team/squad, each client must be treated individually, making as few assumptions as possible about the team environment. The 'outsider' approach contrasts quite markedly with the 'embedded' approach, as we are working with one individual (or occasionally small sub-units and pairs) at a time as opposed to the whole group. It effectively casts the psychologist as offering relatively intensive support to the individual client, rather than influencing a lot of athletes a little at a time. In these situations, the delivery and monitoring would look a lot like regular one-to-one support, as described above.

9.3.3   Measurement and monitoring approaches

It is important to consider what monitoring techniques should be used, as well as the channels through which monitoring will occur. To a large extent, the same basic techniques are available as those discussed in Chapter 5: interviews; observations; questionnaires; performance profiling; performance statistics, etc. Having established clear goals for the support, one can also simply assess progress towards these goals. Another important consideration is the client's own subjective perception of whether things are improving, or whether the 'problem' is solved. When it comes to assessing any effects of the service delivery, it can be as simple as choosing appropriate monitoring techniques and deploying them appropriately. Perhaps the main consideration in assessing effects is to adopt techniques that are consistent with the philosophical assumptions being used, and consistent with the techniques used previously. For example, consider a psychologist who insisted that he was the authoritative expert and used validated questionnaires during intake and needs analysis. It might be quite noticeable to a savvy coach or athlete if such a psychologist then switched to relying on the client's subjective perceptions of progress: as this largely depends on the assumption that the client is best placed to enact and monitor changes. The sudden switch from 'practitioner-led' to 'client-led' might be quite jarring, especially if it is not clearly explained and managed. To be clear, without training in psychological practice, the client would be 'noticing' a slight feeling of dissonance, 'something isn't quite right here', rather than a clearly articulated insight. It is perfectly possible to 'forge through' such feelings with a bit of personality and charisma, but do we really want to? Likewise, a highly client-led practitioner suddenly deploying validated questionnaires with a focus on objectivity would also be a noticeable switch for a client. Perhaps the message is to only look for changes you are expecting to influence, and only do it in a way that is consistent with the expectations you have created.

Another key difference to the intake and needs analysis stages is that we are no longer looking at a broad array of potential attributes, but rather the specific areas that have been agreed as goals. Repeating the entire needs analysis process could be very time-consuming and wasteful. However, there may be times when it is important to see whether achieving the narrowly defined changes that were agreed has actually generated the broader benefits (e.g., those identified in the case formulation). For example, what if practitioner and client set out to develop some key skill or attribute with a view to enhancing performance, but once the skill was developed performance was unaffected? It would imply that either the case formulation was faulty, or that something else has changed in the meantime. Would achieving the goal of teaching the new skill/attribute be classed as 'success', or would it need to have impacted performance for a 'win' to be recorded? Again, perhaps the best solution to such questions is to have agreed the real goals with the client beforehand. Overall, there is an important issue within this discussion, as submissions from supervisees often fall into the trap of accepting any apparent benefit as proof of effective practice. If a doctor treating cancer seized onto the patient's recovery from an incidental cold and claimed it as success, you would be very suspicious. However, I have read submissions in sport psychology where the agreed aim of improving performance has not even been measured, but rather subjective reports of enjoying competition, or even the number of sessions attended, have been used to indicate 'success'.

An important difference to consider between needs analysis techniques and delivery and monitoring, as defined here, is that there are few (if any) agreed ways of measuring the client's expectations. Yet we are defining 'delivery' here as delivering to expectations, not just achieving a carefully specified goal that has subsequently become irrelevant. The two available solutions, therefore, are either to constantly check the client's expectations during each contact, and/or to constantly manage and influence their expectations. Realistically, both avenues are likely to be explored, as allowing inappropriate expectations to form and then meeting them would be unhelpful. To be clear though, meticulously delivering and measuring improvements in an area that the client does not expect or value would likely generate a poor outcome for all concerned.

As a final consideration, is it possible to fail in reaching the agreed outcomes, but still deliver good practice? For example, if a client chooses relatively uncontrollable or unethical outcomes (e.g., 'All I want is to knock him out in our next fight…'), is failing to deliver such an outcome a 'failure'? A more realistic example might be a client arguing 'I really thought, if I played along for long enough, you would just give me some trick to try that would fix everything'. Whereas the psychologist might never have agreed to this having declared a 'client-led' approach – awareness, reflexivity, empowerment – from the outset. To a large extent, delivering safe, ethical, evidence-based and coherent/logical practice could be claimed as success in terms of good *process*. In psychology, results are almost never guaranteed, and likewise people can often expect things that a psychologist cannot or should not deliver. I think most assessors of case studies would probably accept that good practice had been delivered even if the client was not happy with the outcome, if the psychologist could explain the discrepancies appropriately. It seems like sometimes we psychologists can be so caught up with trying to 'prove ourselves' that we are happy to claim selection for a team or event, or a couple of good performances, as success. In fact, it is arguably more important in the long run to deliver safe and effective practice: to create this expectation and to deliver to it.

9.3.4   Different traditions' approaches to delivery and monitoring

As a sport psychologist, there is an important decision to be made regarding whether you wish to take a principled stance and stick to it – only delivering what you consider a good service – or whether you are prepared to deliver whatever the client wants, even if it changes or seems inconsistent. Such considerations link directly to the type of philosophical assumptions one adopts (e.g., Chapter 3). 'Certaintist' assumptions would consider it best to stick to the certainty of the well-supported theory, even if the client felt differently. But likewise, a construalist approach would be quite strict in treating the client as a unique individual and developing tailor-made strategies for their specific world/experience – even if a client just wanted a one-size-fits-all type technique. Only a pure pragmatist would be extremely flexible in changing approaches whenever necessary because pragmatism is defined as doing whatever 'works' – and what works can be defined in the moment with the client. A highly cautious fallibilist approach would not place faith in the theory, nor research papers, nor in the method of treating each individual as unique. As such, there is scope for 'moving goalposts' within a fallibilist approach, but only after careful consideration. For example, is it really appropriate to change tact with this client, or should I try to correct his expectations instead? Is it ethical and safe to change what I am delivering to this client?

Overall, when we review Table 9.1, we can see that the assumptions made by 'certaintist' and 'pragmatist' philosophies are highly applicable across the full range of delivery and monitoring approaches. Certaintism involves adopting the role of an 'expert', which is almost always possible regardless of which 'channel' of delivery one is using. Pragmatism is, by nature, highly flexible, doing whatever it takes to 'get the job done'. So again, whichever channels are being used for delivery, a pragmatist approach should find a way. The assumptions of construalism are somewhat different, based on the idea that each individual's psychological reality is unique and 'constructed' around the individual. As such, any assumption of generalizable, universal truth would be ruled out, making apps and software an unlikely choice. Apps and software usually only ask specific, pre-considered questions and treat data in pre-programmed ways. Likewise, it would be extremely difficult to 'put ideas out there' or leave a client to try a particular technique on their own: purely because the ideas and techniques derived from 'construalist' approaches are so much more difficult to convey and 'package' than those from a more 'certaintist' approach. Finally, fallibilism, which is always careful to avoid or minimize errors, might be unwilling to tolerate the uncertainty and relative insensitivity of apps/software, leaving things to the client or releasing ideas into the wild without clear checks and nuances.

Table 9.1 Delivery channels

Available 'channels' for service delivery	Formal face-to-face sessions	Informal face-to-face chats	Video and telephone calls	Emails and private messaging	Apps and software	Try it and get back to me	Putting it out there	Group workshops and presentations	Through day-to-day coaching
Delivery and monitoring considerations									
Building on needs analysis and case formulation?	✓	✓	✓	✓	X	✓	X	?	✓
Performing the act of providing a service	✓	✓	✓	✓	✓	✓	✓	✓	✓
Monitoring progress towards goals	✓	✓	✓	✓	X	X	X	✓	✓
Monitoring client's expectations of service/progress	✓	✓	✓	✓	X	X	X	✓	✓
Ensuring matchup between outcomes and expectations	✓	✓	✓	✓	X	X	X	✓	✓
Monitoring / measuring techniques									
Interview method	✓	?	✓	X	X	X	X	?	?
Direct observation of training/performance	?	?	X	X	X	X	X	?	✓
Questionnaires	✓	?	X	✓	X	X	X	✓	✓
Performance profiling	✓	?	X	✓	X	X	X	✓	✓
Performance statistics	?	?	?	✓	X	X	X	✓	✓
Stakeholder analysis	?	?	?	?	X	X	X	✓	✓

(continued)

215

Table 9.1 Delivery channels (continued)

	Available 'channels' for service delivery	Formal face-to-face sessions	Informal face-to-face chats	Video and telephone calls	Emails and private messaging	Apps and software	Try it and get back to me	Putting it out there	Group workshops and presentations	Through day-to-day coaching
Overall delivery strategy	As an embedded psychologist/staff member	✓	✓	✓	✓	?	?	?	✓	✓
	As an on-call psychologist	✓	?	✓	✓	✓	?	?	✓	✓
	As an outside provider	✓	?	✓	✓	✓	✓	✓	✓	?
Philosophical Assumptions	Certaintist philosophy	✓	✓	✓	✓	✓	✓	✓	✓	✓
	Construalist philosophy	✓	✓	✓	✓	✗	?	?	✓	✓
	Pragmatist philosophy	✓	✓	✓	✓	✓	✓	✓	✓	✓
	Fallibilist philosophy	✓	✓	✓	✓	✗	?	✗	✓	✓
Practice style	Client-led style	✓	✓	✓	✓	✗	?	✗	✓	✓
	Practitioner-led style	✓	✓	✓	✓	✓	✓	✓	✓	✓

A fallibilist philosophy does not place 'total' faith in ideas – such that anybody will benefit from them – preferring to be sure that nobody will be harmed by them. For that reason, a fallibilist approach might shy away from leaving important aspects of delivery relatively unsupervised, as per these examples.

9.4   Conclusion

In summary, this chapter has detailed both the overall aims and goals of the delivery and monitoring processes, as well as detailing the core considerations within them. We have clearly positioned delivery and monitoring within the sport psychology service delivery process as the 'business end' of the role, where progress is made and recorded. Undeniably, delivery and monitoring depend heavily upon the preceding processes of intake, needs analysis, case formulation, intervention choices and planning. Likewise, delivery will depend heavily upon ethical considerations (as always), and on one's philosophical assumptions. Importantly, delivery and monitoring offer numerous opportunities to switch between philosophies, adopt new and different needs analysis tools, and even to override previous decisions around case formulation or intervention choices. On balance, this chapter argues that such temptations should be either avoided or given careful consideration: as only a pure 'pragmatist' philosophy would be prepared to move the goalposts in such a way (i.e., in order to score a 'win'). Delivery and monitoring, taken together, represents one of the least written-about aspects of the sport psychologist's role, even though it is arguably where we do most of our work and earn our just rewards. Hence, this chapter has offered an extensive – if not exhaustive – review of the various options available, their characteristics, strengths and weaknesses: all in relation to the core definitions of delivery and monitoring. By presenting all the options, and a comprehensive terminology that we can use to describe these processes, the clear aim of this chapter is to facilitate each practitioner's own development. Rather than having to operate, and learn, in a relative vacuum (What I call 'flying blind'), it is at least possible to give a common name to key issues, and to explore their relative merits. Different situations demand different responses, and none of the options presented here are offered as 'best' or 'true'. Rather, mirroring my own practice, the aim of this chapter (and book) is to help sport psychologists classify, analyse, reflect and improve. Adopting the terminology of this chapter, the ideas here are being presented in a 'try it and get back to me' format, with a view to creating psychologists who can 'work it out for themselves'. These are the constraints of writing a book, but also, consistent with the core aims of most regulatory bodies in sport psychology. There is rarely 'right' or 'wrong', meaning there is often a requirement to do the best we can in the given circumstances.

The relatively novel four-part definition of 'delivery and monitoring' offered here should at least help to avoid a number of bad experiences and perceived failures along the way. Do a good job, but make sure the client knows it too, and values it.

9.5   Ella's story: Part 9 – 'The goalposts are moving ... is that ok?'

Ella is writing up one of her clients as a case study, to support her application to complete supervision. The case study is based on work conducted with an international female golfer, Lisa. Lisa initially sought support after under-performing at several tournaments and missing the 'cut' (after 2 days of a 4-day tournament, players who are considered too far behind are 'cut' from the field). Travelling to tournaments and entry fees were mounting up, with very little in winnings, and so Lisa was having to make difficult financial decisions to keep competing. Lisa insisted that confidence was her main issue, following a season of injuries the previous year. Ella was initially content to work towards more robust confidence and improved performance, allowing Lisa, the client, to 'lead'. Over time, Ella noticed that Lisa was not committing to psychological work outside of the sessions and, if anything, seemed to expect Ella to provide a 'fix'. Ella noted phrases such as 'You're the expert' and 'I'll defer to you on this one, I can't explain what went wrong this week'. The first change, explicitly negotiated with Lisa, was to try and create improved self-awareness and empower Lisa to manage her own psychology, rather than to simply become more confident. Lisa agreed it would be better to proactively manage her own psychological approach, rather than being dependent on Ella, or a victim of circumstances.

As before, Lisa would display enthusiasm within sessions, but would carry out very little of the planned work in between sessions. Eventually, after several meetings where Ella tried to challenge this pattern, Lisa explained that she was thinking of starting a family, and could not commit to her golf and international travel given her new plans. In the end, Lisa and Ella agreed to work towards a managed transition out of elite sport, focussing on Lisa's welfare and support network, and the establishment of an identify beyond sporting success. This third approach was very successful, and Lisa was extremely happy with the support Ella offered her.

However, Ella's supervisor is concerned that these 'moving goalposts' may reflect badly on her in the final assessment of her competence. The supervisor is worried that Ella could be viewed as having 'failed' to get Lisa back to performing well at the elite level.

1. To what extent would you agree that Ella 'failed'? Can you justify your viewpoint?
2. Now adopt the opposite (or least an alternative) viewpoint. How would that be justified?
3. How could Ella write the case study to demonstrate that she competently delivered psychological support? What key points should she emphasize? What 'weak points' should she attempt to address?
4. The case study also requires critical reflections. How could Ella have handled this situation better, given Lisa only formed her plans several months into the relationship.

9.6   Review and reflect

1. What do we mean by 'delivery' and 'monitoring' in applied sport psychology support, and what is the relationship between these two concepts?
2. What other processes/stages, in our model of the sport psychology service delivery, influence the quality of delivering and monitoring? Which processes are most influential, and which are least?
3. What criteria would you look in order to qualify as an excellent service delivery in sport psychology? And what might a particularly bad service delivery look like?
4. What tools, cues and prompts could you use to try and ensure that your own delivery and monitoring are as strong as possible?
5. What options are available to you if the original 'deliverables' no longer seem appropriate, or achievable?

Quality Assurance Processes: Recording, Reflecting and Supervision

10

10.1 Introduction and overview

In addition to the core sport psychologist's roles outlined so far, there are also a number of important over-arching processes. Some of these processes are explicitly required by regulatory bodies, such as accurate record keeping, continued training throughout the career and supervision whilst under training. Others are more implicit requirements (or are only 'required' by certain countries' regulatory bodies). These might include being a reflective practitioner who evaluates their own practice, continuing supervision or mentoring once qualified and supervising other trainee psychologists. At their core, all of these activities can be considered part of a suite of *quality assurance processes*. First of all, we need to define quality assurance for sport psychology as follows. Overall, quality assurance is the maintenance of a desired level of quality in a service or product, especially by means of attention to every stage of the process of delivery (as suggested by the model in this book). Then we need to apply this concept to sport psychology. As a profession, we want to ensure that a minimum standard of competence is achieved through the training and qualification pathway we offer, but we also want to pursue continual improvement and 'best practice'. Remember that it is almost impossible to identify one true/right/best way of doing sport psychology, as evidenced in the previous nine chapters. Ensuring a minimum level of competence and ethical practice alongside continuing improvement are arguably our best options.

Fortunately, on the issues of reflective practice and supervision, there are increasing numbers of papers within sport psychology literature (e.g., see Cremades & Tashman, 2014). Regarding record keeping, there is very little written within sport psychology, but this book has specifically aimed to address this, at least partially, by offering worksheets and templates in every chapter. For the purpose of brevity, the following chapter will discuss 'mentoring' (between peers) alongside supervision (between a trainee and a qualified practitioner). Likewise, the act of performing supervision will be discussed alongside supervision, although obviously one accrues different benefits from supervising versus being supervised. It is also important to clarify the role of continuing professional development (CPD) within this quality assurance framework. CPD refers to the process of tracking and documenting the skills, knowledge and experience that we gain both formally and informally as we work, beyond any initial training. CPD can vary from attending formal courses and training, to changes implemented following supervision or reflection, to simply reading and keeping abreast of the evolving literature. In this way, CPD reflects the second part of our definition: to pursue continual improvement and 'best practice'. Hence, within this chapter we will treat CPD as 'moderator' – sitting between the detection processes of record keeping, reflective practice and supervision on the one side, and the outcomes of improved processes and outcomes on the other. For example, reflecting on a telephone conversation with an athlete may lead to the identification of the need to learn more about active listening skills. Such learning, CPD, should lead to a better demonstration of active listening in future phone consultations, and better outcomes (e.g., relationship, adherence, etc.). Importantly, however, once formal training is completed, CPD would need to be *actively pursued by the practitioner.* Even where regulatory bodies require a number of CPD hours

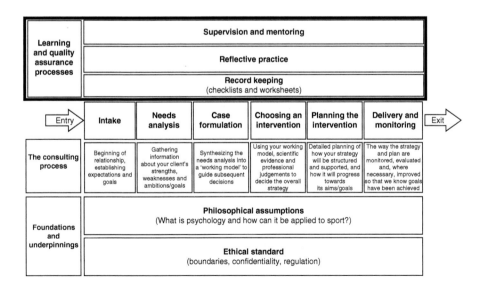

Figure 10.1 *Learning and quality assurance processes sit across every stage of the service delivery process and permeate every aspect of the role.*

to be completed, they rarely specify what (and rightly so). For such an active pursuit of learning to occur, we need some processes for evaluating practice. The two most obvious candidates are self-reflection and supervision. Then we simply need to 'fuel' those processes with good data: good record keeping.

The following section draws an analogy with a builder who designed a tall building herself and is now building it. Like many builder-architects, she keeps thinking of ways of making this building even better and taller. However, just to make things fun, let's imagine the building materials available keep changing as a result of some sort of mining crisis. In this analogy, the tall building itself represents learning – that is, the sport psychologist's development as a practitioner. It generates a constantly growing and improving model of service, capable of doing more, in different ways, in different contexts (all ethically!). The changing plans represent shifting understanding of what makes 'good psychological practice' as we grow and develop (noted in previous chapters and detailed by Tod & Bond, 2010). The changing availability of building materials represents the advances in scientific research, as well as the (relatively unrelated) changes in fashion and popular trends (some very popular techniques and approaches have no scientific grounding). To the interested reader, this is a deliberate (if slightly clumsy) attempt to draw on Vygotsky's (1978) conceptualization of learning as 'scaffolding'.

The analogy is appealing because it captures some of the unique problems of developing and quality assuring as a sport psychologist. After establishing the 'foundations' of formal training, the journey through supervised practice and beyond becomes increasingly self-driven (arguably this is a good thing, we want practitioners who are constantly striving to be as good as possible). Builder-architect reflects this nicely. The 'revised plans' aspect also seems a fair inclusion. If every sport psychologist sets out to only reflect what is promoted in core textbooks and undergraduate courses, the 'off-the-shelf' blueprint, we'd have a very limited profession. Clients would have an extremely limited choice, no new ideas or approaches would be developed, no discoveries could be made. A 'builder-architect' metaphor is useful here as it deliberately casts the psychologist as independent, empowered and driving the process. If all sport psychologists delivered exactly the same model of service regardless of situation, client and contextual demands, then a lot of clients could simply never be helped. People's psychological needs differ substantially, in the same way that we couldn't all live in identical houses. Finally, the changing availability of materials also forces our builder-architect to be self-aware, to make intelligent and informed decisions or else risk becoming a victim of these trends. 'Hmm, only concrete is available right now, how would that sit alongside the wood section I just built?' might equate to 'Hmm, there is a trend for Super-Neuro-OxyBrain-Wristbands at the moment, should I incorporate them into my practice and give one to every client?' A tower built to an outdated plan (or no plan) using whatever materials are to hand, would probably be very ugly, and at risk of falling down at any moment.

So how should the builder-architect proceed? She would need a clear idea of how the tower needs to look, where it needs grow next (upwards, mainly, but usually we need a wide base to support that). She would need to be able to stop work on building from time to time, step back, take pictures and compare them to the plans. She would need to be able to change the plans, in clever ways, for good reasons: either to accommodate new aims or new building materials. She would need to be able to critically evaluate progress, materials, effectiveness and more, all the time. Wherever she identified that she needed some new skill, she would need to go and learn it in order to keep building. If there were other builder-architects working on similar projects nearby, she might be able to save herself some real trouble by examining their work and learning from their successes and failures too. She could even ask them to appraise her progress and offer constructive advice. The frequent pausing and taking pictures can be equated to *keeping good records*. The constant appraisal and knowledge can be equated to *reflective practice*. The learning from others can be equated to *supervision and mentoring*. Finally, unmentioned so far but underlying all of this, we need to assume tremendous *intrinsic motivation* to constantly strive for a better/taller building (i.e., better learning, better capacity, more effective service delivery). Imagine a builder-architect with no ability to update the plans, or learn new building techniques, or spot problems and fix them. A pile of rubble seems an inevitable outcome (unless of course, the pre-existing blueprint is followed to the letter – but that creates a fixed building, that does not grow and leaves a lot of room for improvement).

The remainder of this chapter works on the assumption that good sport psychology emanates from a builder-architect approach, far more frequently and reliably than not. Like every other chapter, this chapter argues that post university (and hopefully during), the trainee sport psychologist becomes a 'builder-architect' *whether we admit it or not*. After that, you can either be a good one or a bad one – so for example, you could settle for developing a very limited but conformist model of practice and stop developing, but you would be of limited capacity/effectiveness as a result. I have even heard of a sport psychologist who left the profession after becoming bored of delivering the same service in the same way over and over. Arguably, the intrinsic motivation emphasized above would be missing in this approach. For constant development and quality assurance to occur: Reflection becomes the engine driving progress, fuelled by intrinsic motivation, which 'sucks in' information (from records and supervision) and turns it into increased capacity to deliver effective sport psychology. It seems important to try and capture that process neatly, as the relationships between reflective practice, supervision, record keeping, quality assurance and service capability have rarely been described.

It is important to note that once formal university-based training is completed, the four main factors listed here are all that remain to drive quality assurance: (a) record keeping; (b) self-reflection; (c) supervision/mentoring; and (d) an intrinsic desire for quality. In this chapter, let's assume (d) is in place already, or else you wouldn't be reading. Realistically, someone who goes through the arduous process of qualifying as a sport psychologist, with only extrinsic motivations (e.g., make money, be around sport, make parents proud) is unlikely to be engaging in constant improvement as described here. You can make (much more!) money, be around sport and make your parents proud a multitude of other (much easier) ways. The following sections focus on good record keeping, reflective practice and supervision – both in its legal formal sense as well as the more informal peer-mentoring and collegial sense.

10.2   Record keeping

There exists a reasonable range of articles and chapters regarding record keeping in psychological practice, and almost all of them base their argument heavily on legal arguments (Bradford & Stevens, 2013; Luepker, 2010; Soisson, VandeCreek, & Knapp, 1987). Even in 1987, Soisson et al. positioned the importance of record keeping as being 'A good defence in a litigious era' (p. 498): perhaps the litigious society is not such a recent occurrence after all. While there are legal and ethical imperatives to keep accurate records these are, of course, extrinsic factors. 'Keep good notes in case you get sued'. Notably, this approach seems to generate very little uptake, with both Luepker (2010) and Bradford and Stevens (2013) reporting very poor compliance with record keeping: both in quantity and quality. If we take a different attitude to record keeping, based on intrinsic motivation, we might begin to view it a different light. Record keeping can, instead, become a source of valuable information rather than a defence against litigation. Incidentally, it seems many sport psychologists are even less motivated by this threat, as they rarely work with clinical issues such as depression, schizophrenia or anxiety. As such, perhaps unofficially, many sport psychologists seem to believe they are at less risk of being investigated in relation to any issues around poor mental health. Given the prevalence of mental illness, such assumption seems rather risky. However, let's get back to viewing record keeping as a positive, empowering tool for quality assurance and development.

For roughly the first 4 years of their training, a sport psychologist will have received very structured training, neatly divided into discrete units/modules and formally assessed. Upon entering supervised practice, a lot of this structure is taken away (after all, the real world is not inherently structured into units/modules and assessed out of 100). Suddenly, there is nobody telling the trainee psychologist what is important, or how to approach things. If one clings desperately to the role of passive customer, we must perhaps wait for the next update of a textbook, or for a new technique to be discovered and promoted, or 'endorsed'. Perhaps we could wait for a supervisor or 'expert' to tell us what to learn next. There are real dangers with this approach – consuming more of the same, learning other (irrelevant) things, taking different perspectives on the same things – each of these is of limited practical use in enhancing the effectiveness of applied practice. Notably, each of these activities would appear at the lower end of Bloom's taxonomy (Bloom et al,. 1956) of learning: remembering, understanding or applying (in the sense of 'I can apply this thing I learned to this other thing', not necessarily 'applied practice').

Alternatively, we could become students of our own practice. We could observe and record what happens, analyse it, theorize about how to achieve better outcomes (more of the time) and then test those ideas. We could use record keeping as the raw materials for driving reflective practice, self-improvement and enhancing service capability. In the same way that people frequently bookmark/save blogs/articles and research articles to read later, what is wrong with viewing record keeping as a kind of 'hoarding' of experiences. Importantly, the experiences being collected and collated are highly personal and relevant. Using these as raw materials may be much more meaningful than reading abstract theoretical ideas or even someone else's experiences. Some experiences will feel like they need to be analysed and understood straight away. Others may not seem important at the time, but suddenly gain relevance later on. Imagine having detailed accurate records when the time comes to go back and understand why a former client quietly terminated the relationship after five sessions. Most models of reflective practice begin with a section describing what happened, followed by sections analysing and drawing out key lessons (e.g., Gibbs, 1988; Johns, 1995; Kolb, 1984; Rolfe, 2001). Fundamentally, record keeping can simply fulfil this first step without necessitating that we continue to critically analyse every experience. It could be viewed as an investment so that if and when we need to analyse and reflect, we have captured accurate details from which to start the analysis. In addition, this distinction would help to delineate between 'description' and 'reflective practice'. When acting as a reviewer, I frequently see trainees presenting narrative description in place of critical analysis. However, one is clearly capturing information for the purpose of record keeping, the other is a deliberate attempt to extract learning and improve practice. In the vast majority of cases, higher learning and deeper learning do not automatically follow from narrative description. With a little analysis, evaluation and critical thinking, such insight can be generated (of course, pausing to critically examine our own practice is not always the most pleasurable experience, but the benefits far outweigh the 'cost' of discomfort or damaged egos).

What things need to be recorded? Bradford and Stevens (2013) and Luepker (2010) offer simple and effective guidelines on what to record. In a word: everything. But more specifically we should be accurately recording:

- Referral information (where relevant).
- Informed consent (perhaps subdivided for data storage, goals/aims, style adopted, etc.)
- Agreement over fees.
- Client contact details.
- Next of kin details.
- Any other services being received (sport or psychology or medical).
- Full details of intake and any decisions regarding progress. Screening information. Case history.
- Details of close social network – family, peer group, work details.
- Context of each record – what happened, but also what events preceded or followed that may have 'framed' the content of the record.
- All needs analysis data and interpretations.
- Case formulations (including alternatives or areas of uncertainty).
- Choices of support or intervention (with justification and alternatives).
- Support plan (progression, milestone, end-point, alternatives).
- Delivery decisions – methods channels, styles.
- Summary details of each meeting and interaction (including phone, email, etc.).
- Progress reports – any measures of progress towards goals, or reasons for changing goals.
- Records of supervision and mentoring (see below).
- Any authorizations for release of information (e.g., to coaches, parents, other psychologists, etc.)
- Any disclosures made – mandatory (e.g., legally obliged) or voluntary (as above).
- Closing summary or discharge summary – date, nature (mutually agreed or not, expected or sudden) reasons for termination of support.
- Any modifications made to records, with justification.

Luepker (2010) is also instructive in offering key guidelines for ensuring good record keeping. Records should: be legible; focussed and relevant; reliable (i.e., avoiding personal opinion or speculation); transparent (What, where, when, with who, etc.); logical (i.e., could another psychologist 'follow your workings' if required, without making any leaps of faith or assumptions); chronological (in order); concise (we don't need essays). Remember, record keeping can be mainly about accurate and reliable description, not deep analysis which can be performed afterwards as part of reflective practice.

In addition to the above list, we should also consider recording the way we analyse, reflect on and learn from these experiences. So whilst recording, the above-listed activities might be viewed as a bare minimum – photographing the project in progress – we also need to analyse, evaluate, reflect and receive feedback (i.e., supervision/mentoring); all with a view to constantly improving and building capability. When performing these activities, we also need to keep accurate records of them. Many qualification processes require evidence of reflective practice and supervision. Equally, it may be beneficial to record reflections or key insights with a view to avoiding repetition (of mistakes, mainly). It can also be instructive to review records from reflections and perform a kind of meta-reflection: comparing our thinking then versus now, contemplating what might have caused any changes and whether we are comfortable with that. Likewise, if nothing has changed in one's thinking over a protracted period, then that might warrant a degree of critical self-reflection. I have certainly found this process instructive, although it has produced in me the annoying habit of preceding certain statements with: 'At this stage in my career, and this could change over time, I think... [insert idea here]'. The same applies to supervision and peer mentoring: We should record as much as possible at the descriptive/observational level as an investment in future learning. Sometimes a comment can be made (and recorded) that makes no sense or holds little relevance in the immediate moment. However, if it is recorded, then at a later date we might be reflecting and self-evaluating with new questions and issues in mind, and suddenly it could be very significant. 'I didn't even realize I have this quirk, but look, my supervisor picked up on it 5 years ago. I just didn't hear her'.

Remember, all the considerations listed here for recording are legally mandated in most countries: We must be recording them in order to maintain our ethical and legal obligations to our regulatory bodies. However, we can do a lot better than that. We can record and observe everything as accurately and reliably as possible, even when it appears insignificant, *with a view to one day analysing it and learning from it.* It can be viewed as a present to our future selves, to help us solve some future problem we don't even know we'll experience (and couldn't possibly anticipate). In this way, keeping good records is also a positive investment for our future clients, and the future of our profession. There are forms and worksheets throughout this book that might be used for recording events, reflections and feedback.

10.3   Reflective practice

If we have practitioners with the intrinsic motivation to fuel the engine of development, and our record keeping gives us the raw materials to feed into that engine, what does the engine actually look like? Records, experiences and observations go in one end, and there is a cyclical and iterative process spinning away in the middle. Emerging from the other end, fundamentally, is learning – in the form of enhanced capability, increased contextual sensitivity and self-regulation. Learning which, in the end, makes us better sport psychologists who are exposed to fewer and fewer risks (*primum non nocere*), yet able to help a wider variety of clients with different needs and in different situations (and more reliably). Reflective practice can be defined as 'the capacity to reflect on action so as to engage in a process of continuous learning' Schön, 1983, p. 168). It involves '...paying critical attention to the practical values and theories which inform everyday actions, by examining practice reflectively and reflexively... [leading to] developmental insight' (Bolton, 2010, p. xix).

A number of authors have advocated the use of reflection as a tool for practitioners to self-evaluate and improve their understanding of the effectiveness of their own practices (e.g., Anderson et al., 2002; Cropley, Miles, Hanton, & Niven, 2007; Cropley, Hanton, Miles, & Niven, 2010; Simons & Andersen, 1995). Likewise, authors across the 'helping professions' have consistently highlighted the benefits of reflective practice in personal and professional development (e.g., sport psychology, Cropley et al., 2007, 2010; coaching, Knowles, Gilbourne, Borrie, & Nevill, 2001; education, Crockett, 2002; nursing, Williams, 2001). Consequently, a developing body of literature has reported the reflective practices of sport psychology practitioners (e.g., Andersen, 2000; Cropley et al., 2007, 2010; Holt & Strean, 2001; Tod, 2007). Cropley et al. (2007) summarize the core arguments neatly: *'Reflection is thought to afford practitioners the opportunity to examine their own practices and the thoughts and feelings that are associated with their actions in the particular context in which they occur. Thus, reflection results in the generation of knowledge and self-awareness that can be used to inform and improve future behaviour. It is thought that reflection creates a link between the application of professional knowledge and practice' (p. 477), ... [and later on page 491]... reflection presents a method to access, make sense of, and learn through experience (Johns, 1994)... This is supported by Ghaye et al. (1996), who suggested that reflective practice allows a person to 'look back and make sense of practice, learning from this and using this learning to affect future action. It is about making sense of your professional life' (p. 2).*

When we delve deeper into this process whereby reflection and thinking after the moment can subsequently inform our thinking in the moment, we meet an important distinction, drawn by Schön (1987). Reflection on action can occur after the event, ideally *drawing on accurate records* of what happened, in what context, for what reasons. Reflection on action can begin to sensitize the practitioner to future similar or comparable moments and inform their in-the-moment decision-making. This is termed reflection in action or *in vitro* reflection. Schön (1987) argued that knowledge in action and reflection in action are pivotal to effective professional practice as they guide practitioners in dealing with complex practical situations in which it is insufficient to simply apply theory to practice. Certainly in my own experience, reflection in action has allowed me to 'notice' when a session is not going right for some reason, even if I am doing everything that normally seems to 'work'. Not only that, I have been able to reflect on how/why things are amiss, and take corrective action without anybody noticing (Okay, perhaps there are occasional hesitations!). I do not believe for one moment I would have been able to do this without having a carefully developed a very efficient 'reflective engine', that is able to work very quickly and without intruding into my listening and responding with the client. There remains, of course, the longer game, where reflecting on action creates the opportunity to explore good practice, identify areas for improvement and formulate ideas for change (Knowles et al., 2001). Reflective practice provides the opportunity to become aware of what is effective within our practice, identify current levels of competence in key areas, consider different ways of improving competence in those areas and ultimately become a more effective practitioner. Armed with an ever-increasing awareness of what works, with who, in what situations and for what reasons, a sport psychologist becomes increasingly empowered to generate positive outcomes (Petitpas, Giges, & Danish, 1999; Simons & Andersen, 1995). Further still, this may be quite unique to each practitioner, as s/he is perhaps the most important determinant of success in the relationship. We, as the psychologist, are the main 'tool of the trade' and so we must learn how to use this tool even as it develops and changes. As such, the 'reflective practitioner' may not be developing universal rules that apply to everyone, but rather, an awareness of how s/he generates different outcomes in different contexts (Petitpas et al., 1999; Simons & Andersen, 1995).

The problem, for many practitioners, is that reflective practice can be very time-consuming and effortful: deliberately writing about experiences and fitting them into some sort of structured template (cf. Andrews, Gidman, & Humphreys, 1998; Gil-Garcia & Cintron, 2002; Price, 2004). Added to that, many practitioners feel they already reflect, and are reflective people generally, in which case why do it so formally? Perhaps related to this, it is uncomfortable to face the possibility that the service we deliver may not be perfect in every instance – especially after such lengthy and expensive training – so many psychologists dislike the idea for that reason (Price, 2004). *If I must constantly reflect and be self-critical, then I will never get to feel like I've made it.*

As summarized by Faull and Cropley (2009, p. 337): 'ASP [Applied Sport Psychology] Practitioners need to be convinced of the value and worth of reflection'. Further still, reflective practice can be difficult, as we are taking something we do quite naturally and trying to bring a structure to it. Likewise, reflective practice in the sense being used here – as a mechanism driving learning and improvement – must itself be developed and refined over time, like any other skill. 'Another thing to learn? No thanks!'. But without this learning of the skill, reflective practice will likely be quite ineffective or unreliable in generating meaningful improvements for the psychologist's practice. Hence it would be understandable, but not correct, to feel that we do some form of reflection already; it is hard to learn, seems to generate mixed results, and it might just be viewed as being pointlessly picky.

In contrast, this chapter is positioning reflective practice as the engine that drives almost all learning and improvement once we exit formal education settings. In fact, reflective students in university and school arguably fare much better here too, as higher education places a heavier emphasis on independent learning as opposed to directive instruction. Where a passive learner may ask, 'What is the point of learning X?' a reflective learner will have their 'blueprint' in hand, compare their current understanding to the blueprint and evaluate the new 'materials' on offer using that information. In a formal training setting, the reflective learner should be better placed to either perceive or create relevance in whatever is being offered – and therefore be more motivated. Post university, a reflective learner is empowered to deliberately go looking for new materials, to revise and change the blueprint and to reject materials or plans that are not suitable. Metaphorically, learning the skill of reflective practice can be compared to building the engine that will drive our development long after we finish formal training. Better still, as the engine becomes faster and more efficient – requiring less cognitive effort to function – it can begin to run in the background while we work, spotting opportunities and preventing problems that could easily be missed. By driving long-term learning (reflection on action) and feeding into live, in-the-moment actions (reflection in action), the skill of reflective practice becomes one of the most valuable tools a psychologist will ever have.

Before we spend a few moments explaining how we might approach reflective practice, there remains a little question of how to develop it. How would a psychologist know how good or bad s/he is at reflective practice? Two immediate answers come to mind. First, this is a vital aspect of supervision and mentoring, which we shall discuss shortly. Supervisors should generally have much more experience than their supervisees, and this should have led to additional insights and learnings. So a supervisor can, as a minimum, convey such learnings, but better still they can seek to encourage the supervisee to generate their own insights, based on experiences. As the trainee improves, there should be less 'Here is what I would do?' And much more "What would you do differently next time?' (Sound familiar? Practitioner-led versus client-led?). Further still, given that both the raw materials (records) and reflections themselves should have been recorded, the supervisor can monitor and 'tweak' the reflective process, almost as it happens, ensuring that it develops in a suitable way. This could vary from offering formal guidelines such as Gibbs (1988) or Johns (1994) right through to becoming a 'critical friend' and challenging key themes and ideas during and after reflective practice. To me, one of the most valuable aspects of recording reflective practice is that it allows practitioners to demonstrate their level of development – both regarding the subject of reflection (e.g., practice style) as well as in the skill of reflecting. Remembering that a key motivation of this book was to help practitioners 'demonstrate competence', recording reflective practice is one very suitable approach. Second, and perhaps more difficult, is what might be called 'meta-reflection': reflecting upon one's ability to reflect. Is it generating meaningful insights and lessons for me? How easy or hard do I find it? How do I feel about reflective practice, emotionally? How automatic and effortless is my reflective practice, can I do it 'in the moment' as well as after the moment'? What might I need to do to improve the quality of my reflective practice, and make it more valuable as a tool? Remembering, of course, that the answers to these questions will not be in a textbook or lecture, because this skill will likely become much more relevant after formal textbook-based learning has finished. As noted above, the practitioner performing meta-reflection is asking all these questions in relation to her/himself. How do *I* use it? How can *I* get more value and benefit from *my* reflective practice? Different practitioners at different stages of development will arrive at very different answers. However, if there is to be a 'general direction' of improvement and learning generated by reflective practice, Bloom's (1956) taxonomy appears to be a good frame of reference. The six levels are as follows:

- Level 1 – Remember and recall: recognizing, listing, describing, identifying, retrieving, naming, locating and finding
- Level 2 – Understand and describe: interpreting, comprehending, summarizing, inferring, paraphrasing, classifying, comparing, offering examples
- Level 3 – Application: implementing, carrying out, using, executing
- Level 4 – Analysis: comparing, organizing, deconstructing, attributing, structuring, integrating
- Level 5 – Evaluation: checking, hypothesizing, critiquing, experimenting, judging, testing, detecting, monitoring (Bloom, 1956) .

When it comes to evaluating the effectiveness of almost all the key psychologists' roles/processes outlined in this book, we are dealing with skills higher up the learning taxonomy. The reason for this is simply that we are in the business of applying knowledge in the real world, applied practice, which is extremely different from understanding a theory and noting that it is 'applicable'. In fact, there is an extremely important distinction between being able to identify 'applicability' – which occurs midway up the learning taxonomy – versus performing applied practice by assessing, evaluating, synthesizing, theorizing, hypothesizing, planning, designing, etc. All of these characterize applied practice, as described in this book, and all of them are completely different skills to 'being able to state how an idea is applicable'. Application is described in the taxonomy as 'implementing, carrying out, using, executing' – which could simply mean following instructions – and we need to carefully delineate that from 'applied practice'. If we truly believed being a sport psychologist was about carrying out clear instructions as dictated by some expert, and nothing more, then we would have an extremely homogeneous profession of very limited capacity to help people. In contrast, by never proffering a 'true and correct' way of approaching any of the sport psychologist's processes – intake, needs analysis, case formulation, deciding a support programme, planning it and delivering and monitoring our support – reflective practice and reflexivity become paramount. Applied practice is about generating the best (or least bad) outcomes in any given situation, even very unpredictable or unclear ones. Application, as described in the Bloom taxonomy, is about matching concepts: 'Align Part A to Part B and twist until you hear a click'.

So how do we improve in the skills specified at the higher end of Bloom's taxonomy? How can we know if one 'act of creation' is better than another, or if one evaluation is better than another (e.g., when delivering applied sport psychology)? If a reflective practitioner is able to keep in mind the intended outcomes, the processes followed, the information that was available when key decisions were made and more, then that practitioner is able to evaluate and improve those processes. If we cast our mind backs to the Chapter 9, the 'science-versus-craft' debate does not mean that we can simply be 'creative' as we like, but rather we are 'creating' within the bounds of a scientific process. As comedian Dara O'Briain famously said: 'Science knows it doesn't know everything; otherwise, it'd stop. But just because science doesn't know everything doesn't mean you can fill in the gaps with whatever fairy tale most appeals to you'. Applied practice remains a scientific process, but where unique needs and contexts are inevitably encountered, we must use creativity to generate scientifically justifiable and testable solutions[1]. That requires constant and sophisticated reflective abilities, to analyse our own creative process and attempt to constantly refine it.

---

[1] Remembering that 'scientific' will be defined within the particular philosophy adopted – the ontological and epistemological assumptions made.

What this means, then, is that the 'direction of travel' when we switch on our reflective engine should be upwards in relation to Bloom's taxonomy. Importantly, we should also note that the 'lower' skills need to be in place first, as these form the foundations upon which the rest is built. It fits neatly with our 'building' metaphor, based on Vygotsky's (1978) scaffolding theory, that foundations need to be in place, and that developments in some areas support improvements in related conceptual areas. The builder-architect, analogized to a reflective practitioner, manages the whole process so that 'progress' is upwards, building a taller tower (i.e., becoming more capable as a practitioner) on firm foundations, with reliable materials. The process is effectively, never ending, but to paraphrase Dara O'Briain's routine about good science (versus pseudo-science): The reflective practitioner knows she doesn't know everything; otherwise, she would stop! Presumably, a practitioner who did think they knew everything would stop practising and write it all into a book entitled: 'Stop wasting your money on sport psychologists and just do what I say'.

10.3.1   How can we undertake reflective practice?

There are models that attempt to offer structure and guidance on how to perform reflective practice, such as Gibbs (1988) and Johns (1995). Many practitioners choose to simply write unstructured notes, or to record a stream of consciousness, and others may simply rely on unrecorded quiet pondering. As an assessor and reviewer of trainee psychologists, the less recorded (i.e., pondering) and the less clear/structured reflections are, the less easy it is to assess the practitioner's competence. Hence, one key reason for using structure in reflective practice is to facilitate the demonstration of competence – either the subject of the reflections or the reflections themselves – so that a supervisor or assessor can access them. Another good reason to use some kind of structure is simply that it forces or steers us towards generating productive outcomes – describe, analyse, conclude, enact (or perhaps a variation of plan do review). Without such structure, it is possible to simply remember and replay key moments, without analysing them for meaningful opportunities to learn and improve. My own reflection on using models of structured reflective practice (a meta-reflection?) is that it sometimes feels like I am being forced to 'isolate' one key even from the others that may have happened around it. For example, the questions often refer to one moment, or one 'thing', and there is not enough space to fit in the full history of events on one page. However, I began to view this act of isolating key events as analogous to the way we sometimes perform experiments in a lab or petri-dish, away from the 'noise' of the real world. The context can be lost, but only if I allow it to be lost. With the ability to hyperlink between documents and index reflections a number of ways using tagging systems, it is possible to retain

Table 10.1 *A comparison of Gibbs (1988) Learning by doing: A guide to teaching and learning methods, and Johns (1994) Nuances of reflection*

Gibbs (1988) Learning by doing: A guide to teaching and learning methods. Further Education Unit, Oxford Brookes University, Oxford	Johns (1994) Nuances of reflection. *Journal of Clinical Nursing* 3 71–75
Description: 'What happened? Don't make judgements yet or try to draw conclusions; simply describe.'	**Description** Write a description of the experience. What are the key issues within this description that I need to pay attention to?
Feelings: 'What were your reactions and feelings? Again don't move on to analysing these yet.'	**Reflection** What was I trying to achieve? Why did I act as I did? What are the consequences of my actions? For the patient and family For myself For people I work with
Evaluation: 'What was good or bad about the experience? Make value judgements.'	How did I feel about this experience when it was happening? How did the client feel about it? How do I know how the patient felt about it?
Analysis: 'What sense can you make of the situation? Bring in ideas from outside the experience to help you.' 'What was really going on?' 'Were different people's experiences similar or different in important ways?'	**Influencing factors** What internal factors influenced my decision-making and actions? What external factors influenced my decision-making and actions? What sources of knowledge did or should have influenced my decision-making and actions?
Conclusions (general): 'What can be concluded, in a general sense, from these experiences and the analyses you have undertaken?'	**Alternative strategies** Could I have dealt better with the situation? What other choices did I have? What would be the consequences of these other choices?
Conclusions (specific): 'What can be concluded about your own specific, unique, personal situation or way of working?'	
Personal action plans: 'What are you going to do differently in this type of situation next time?' 'What steps are you going to take on the basis of what you have learnt?	**Learning** How can I make sense of this experience in light of past experience and future practice? How do I NOW feel about this experience? Have I taken effective action to support myself and others as a result of this experience? How has this experience changed my way of knowing in practice?

and even learn from the context – even if each structured cycle tends to address one thing. It may even be possible to build a layered 'nest' of reflections: some capturing individual aspects of the situation, and others building from those and extracting recurring themes or issues to further analyse. For example, Van Manen (1977) proposes three major hierarchical levels at which reflection may take place (as do Lasley, 1992; Grimmett, Erickson, MacKinnon, & Riecken, 1990; Valli, 1997). You will notice that many of the worksheets offered in this book are based around the model of Gibbs (1988), purely because this is the model I have found most useful (I am not aware of any research showing one model of reflection is better than another). Remember, when choosing whether to adopt (or even create) a model of reflective practice that what you do 'formally' after the moment is likely training what you do informally, in the moment. So if you explicitly reflect in a disordered manner, or in a manner that does not progress towards solutions and outcomes, the chances are that you are training your *in vitro* reflective processes to be the same. Table 10.1 contains two of the most prominent models of structured reflective practice, that may be of assistance to those beginning formal reflection or seeking additional guidance on how to reflect. Notice that both models are based upon a cyclical process: describe, analyse, learn/improve. This is arguably the very heart of what structured reflective practice comes down to, but that is not to say that important insights cannot be gained through other, less structured, approaches.

The preceding section has made the case for engaging in reflective practice as part of a strong quality assurance process. We adopted the metaphor of a builder-architect, who must both do the work of building, but also step back and take stock of progress. To acknowledge the difficulties of practising in the real world, we introduced ideas of a constantly changing blueprint, as the architect becomes more ambitious, and constant changes in the availability of building materials, as new ideas and findings emerge. To address the problem, our builder-architect has one key tool, a spinning engine of reflective practice, that has been built and developed over time. With this magical tool, whatever new blueprint the architect wants can be enacted, and whatever new materials are available can be incorporated. Similarly, by carefully developing the engine of reflective practice, a sport psychologist can pursue increased capability and incorporate new concepts and ideas deliberately, and ensuring that progress is always in the right direction. As noted earlier, however, it is not easy to develop such a fantastic machine offering us a lifelong skill of learning and adapting. As such, one of the best options when we need to develop this capacity is to seek help from one of the very few individuals who has also managed the task. An experienced and effective sport psychologist. A supervisor.

10.4 Supervision and mentoring

At the point where a trainee psychologist exits formal education – based on lectures, books and structured content – the usual progression towards becoming fully qualified is to undergo 'supervised practice'. As such, the trainee will be able to practice with real clients, but must be supervised in some capacity – for example, sharing case notes from each client, planning assessment portfolios and competency development, reflecting on service effectiveness or ethical considerations and more. Supervision can be defined as a long-term interpersonal relationship designed to foster the growth and development of a trainee's skills as a professional (Van Raalte & Anderson, 2000; Watson, Zizzi, Etzel, & Lubker, 2004). Van Raalte and Anderson (2014) extended this to specify that supervision is an ongoing and iterative process with the purpose of ensuring that clients' interests are the focus of service provision, and that clients are receiving the best possible service: ongoing iterative quality assurance – just like reflective practice. Elsewhere, Hutter, Oldenhof-Veldman, and Oudejans (2015; p.1) explained that: 'Learning in supervision can be defined as learning on the basis of reflective practice with a supervisor. Supervision should develop self-directed learning by the supervisee' (i.e., supervision should develop reflective practice skills – see also: Holt & Strean, 2001). Supervision should offer the trainee practitioner a greater sense of self-knowledge and a clearer understanding of the therapeutic process, through close/regular contact and frequent two-way communication with a skilled professional (Van Raalte & Anderson, 2004). The supervisor arguably focuses on two things: the quality of service received by the trainee's current clients, and the development of the trainee into a competent and ethical practitioner (Van Raalte & Anderson, 2000; Watson, McAlarnen, & Shannon, 2014). As such, the supervisor affects the outcomes and experiences of very many clients, right through the remainder of the young trainee's career (cf. Watson et al., 2014): it is an important role!

There have been many models of how supervision relationships develop and play out, frequently offering descriptive stage models where the trainee is initially in need of formal instruction, but ultimately becomes empowered and independent (e.g., Stoltenberg, 1981; Hess, 1986; Vosloo, Zakrajsek, & Grindley, 2014). Effectively, this would mean the supervisor gradually transitioning from 'practitioner-led' to become more 'client-led', in a pleasing echo of the way psychologists appear to develop in the first place (e.g., Tod & Bond, 2010). For example, the framework offered by Vosloo et al. (2014) outlines a progression of supervisory relationships in three phases: Phase 1 – build rapport and establish a safe environment; Phase 2 – structure progression and build autonomy; Phase 3 – transition to self-evaluation and reflection, without need for supervision. Understanding the transition from dependence and guidance to independence and autonomy is a common feature of supervision models and psychological practice alike. However, when it comes to the core issues that are covered during supervision, Hutter et al. (2015) sought to establish what trainees want/need to know, by analysing the notes they prepared before supervision meetings. This paper is highly relevant as the analysis is *specific to sport psychology* supervision practices. The themes that were identified were broken down into 'Know-how' (how to do the job) and 'Professional development' (reflective practice, ethical dilemmas and philosophical issues). If we compare the themes identified in this study to the service delivery model introduced in this book, or the topics of Chapters 2–10, we see that trainee sport psychologists seek supervisory guidance covering all of these topics. Bearing in mind this book was first proposed in 2012, it's an incredible coincidence – or at least, a 'reassuring convergence'. In this study, trainee psychologists sought advice from their supervisors regarding: (a) ethical dilemmas and boundaries (i.e., Chapter 2); (b) 'working principles' such as practice style and philosophy (i.e., Chapter 3); (c) the intake process (i.e., Chapter 4); (d) needs analysis methods and interpretation/reporting (i.e., Chapter 5); (e) treatment goals and justification (i.e., case formulation, Chapter 6); (f) choosing interventions and service options (e.g., Chapter 7); (g) 'treatment planning' (i.e., Chapter 8); (h) evaluating, adapting plans and terminating service (i.e., delivery and monitoring, Chapter 9); and (i) reflection and personal development (this Chapter). Whilst different words may be used, the semantic similarities are striking, and tell us that trainee sport psychologists encounter broadly similar issues in their 'post-university' development. To be clear, very similar concepts were raised by the participants in Stambulova and Johnson (2010) as 'lessons learned' from supervision (e.g., professional philosophy, interventions/tools, practice style/skills). Likewise, the model offered by Poczwardowki, Aoyagi, Shapiro, and Van Raalte (2014) covers extremely similar themes (e.g., theoretical approach, interventions/techniques available). In the latter two instances, the themes were coded or presented is a manner that is less compatible with the approach taken in this book. However, the semantic overlaps remain clear and the 'content' of the sport psychologist's role is increasingly well described. As such, once we understand the aims of supervised practice, the likely progression and the topics that are likely to be covered, we can begin to consider how this support is provided.

10.4.1   How can we undertake supervised practice?

One thing that starts to stand out when studying the role of supervision is that there are distinct similarities to the role of the psychologist, modelled in this book. Supervision will usually involve: (a) an initial conversation about whether the supervisor and trainee can work together (intake); (b) an evaluation of the trainee's current competence and learning needs (needs analysis and case formulation); (c) a deliberate planning out of the trainee's development over the supervision period (planning progress and choosing activities/'interventions'); and (d) an ongoing process of monitoring progress (delivery and monitoring); leading to (e) termination. The most striking difference, however, is that while a sport psychologist may work with a client to address one issue, often in a short time frame, supervisors will work with trainees to address multiple developmental needs over a long time frame. Hence, a significant advantage of this arrangement is that the supervisor should already be extremely well suited to delivering these roles, having already done something very similar throughout her/his own practice. A potential disadvantage is that the supervisor may choose to approach supervision using the same philosophical assumptions s/he uses with athletes, without assessing their suitability for use in supervision (or, e.g., with this particular trainee).

A useful guideline for the selection of supervisors comes from Hutter (2014), who proposed a list of competencies a supervisor should demonstrate. Core supervisory competencies include: (a) creating a productive working alliance with the supervisee; (b) dealing with the diversity and individuality of supervisees; (c) structuring the learning experience into meaningful phases; (d) creating an effective learning environment; (e) ensuring boundaries are maintained within the supervisory relationship; (f) the administration of supervisory responsibilities; (g) being able to explicate and justify one's own actions as a supervisor; and (h) shaping her/his own professional development as a supervisor. This list could be used by trainees seeking a supervisor, neophyte supervisors assessing their suitability to deliver the role (cf. Cropley & Neil, 2014); or organizations seeking to employ a supervisor for the training of sport psychologists. Hutter et al. (2015) offer illustrative examples of these competencies, such as: clarifying expectations within the supervision; adding structure to the overall supervision trajectory; managing the rhythm of individual meetings/sessions; directing reflections and developing the supervisee's reflective capability; demonstrating and role modelling service delivery; performing accurate and honest evaluations of progress and performance, amongst many other things. In many instances, there are clear analogies between the supervisor–supervisee relationship and the psychologist–client relationship, as many of the above competencies and behaviours could easily be expected of a practitioner too. Overall, if the case for the importance of supervision has been successfully made, then it must therefore be important to both access good supervision and to get the most out of the process.

While the above list is useful in helping to select a good supervisor, there remains the issue of making sure that the process delivers the key outcomes of helping the trainee to become able to practice independently.

Adapting our definition of 'delivery' from Chapter 9, supervision may be expected to: (a) perform, instigate or support the activities that will lead to the capacity for independent psychological practice; (b) monitor any effects or progress of these activities; (c) monitor the expectations of the trainee and any stakeholders in the trainee's development (e.g., regulatory bodies, employers, clients); and (d) constantly attempt to ensure the best possible overlap between the trainee's expectations and the progress/competence demonstrated. To a very large extent, the trainee plays pivotal roles in all of these delivery considerations – performing the majority of the work involved in developing her/himself as a practitioner, recording and reflecting upon the effects of this work, holding personal expectations and managing the expectations of key stakeholders and discussing/agreeing expectations (goals, current competence, etc.) with the supervisor. One example I can recall regarding stakeholder involvement was a supervisee who persistently told their employer that they were about to qualify and become registered. Unfortunately, the documentary evidence they provided to the regulatory body (checked by the supervisor) could not support a case for being 'ready'. Of course, this could be due to a lack of practical competence, but it is more often a difficulty in ensuring that the evidence and documents submitted *demonstrate* competence. Weirdly, this led to pressure being put on the assessors reviewing the trainee's progress to 'be lenient', as 'people's careers depend on this'. Several years later, I would reflect that, instead, it is the supervisor's role to accurately appraise the trainee *and documentation*, challenge any over claims or divergent expectations and implement a development plan to gain competence as needed. It is arguably not the supervisor's role to 'advocate' for a trainee who may be applying to complete supervision. It was troubling that any trainee, or trainee–supervisor dyad, would allow such conflicting expectations to evolve in the first place. Hence, the emphasis on managing expectations remains extremely important, again mirroring the 'delivery' of service to clients, in Chapter 9. Overall, we can infer that, the trainee psychologist has the most to gain from the supervisory process, and therefore undeniably is required to invest the most time, effort and energy (and often money too). While we place an important emphasis on the skills and approach of the supervisor, s/he is also managing a challenging balancing act: supporting the trainee on the one hand and yet enforcing a level of quality assurance on the other. Overall, the person who stands to gain the most from the process must, arguably, be the one who takes responsibility for its success or otherwise. If anything ever were to go wrong, post supervision, it would be extremely difficult to blame your former supervisor. The builder-architect must live with the consequences if s/he builds a faulty tower, and the reflective psychologist must also take responsibility for her/his own development.

So what should a trainee undergoing supervision be doing? Each regulatory body offers rules about how supervision should proceed, ranging from the number of hours of supervision (and the proportion that must be face-to-face), the duration of supervised training (2–6 years in most cases) and, of course, the competencies that must be developed. However, the above anecdote also leads to the first of several unofficial 'golden rules' for trainees undergoing supervised practice: *don't rush the process*. If official rules specify 2 years or 1000 hours, there is no guarantee that the trainee will be completely ready to 'go it alone' just because of the passing of time. In fact, I often evaluate students and trainees on their responsiveness to experience, which presumably is driven by reflective practice (making the most of the available materials to increase capacity/leaning). However, if someone passively completed the time without also reflecting and learning from the experience, it's possible that the 'minimum time' would not have made them ready to qualify. Further, a psychologist may never have such a strong and understanding support network in place as when they are under supervision, so why seek to break free of it so quickly?

A second golden rule might be to *drive the process yourself*, rather than waiting to be told what do. Of course, this does not mean simply dive into difficult situations and ask questions afterwards. It may, however, be possible to ask the supervisor when you might be ready to take on a particular task, or to perhaps set up opportunities to practice a new skill. If you're unsure about how to approach a particular situation, ask. This demonstrates reflective self-awareness, and even ethical sensitivity. Further, a proactive and motivated trainee is much more rewarding to supervise than an 'expectant customer', even if you are paying to receive supervision. The metaphor of going to the gym may be applicable here – you're not paying to simply get strong, lose weight or get qualified, you're paying for the opportunity to train and develop.

Third, given the importance of the reflective practice 'engine' for taking experiences and turning them into increased capacity, we might urge trainees to *value reflective practice and deliberately develop it* from the outset. Research in nursing suggests that those who scored better on reflective ability in assignments also went on to receive better scores on practice placements; that is, the quality of their practice was enhanced (Embo, Driessen, Valcke, & Vleuten, 2014).

Fourth, linked to the above, supervisees might be well advised to *keep excellent records*, and to emphasize not only submitting forms when requested, but actually ensuring that all forms, case studies, etc. clearly demonstrate the exact competencies required (either by the regulatory body or supervisor).

Fifth, perhaps most importantly, those undergoing supervised practice in sport psychology will need to *forget about having an ego*. Despite having completed 3–4 years of university-based training, you must assume you are not ready yet, and accept that there will be areas where you do not know everything (in fact, this is the entire assumption of the 'fallibilist' philosophical tradition in Chapter 3). Some clients may expect you to work for free or at a reduced rate. While there are good arguments not to 'under sell' your services, it may be that the experiences and learning on offer outweigh the financial cost. Other clients will toss you a camera and ask you to film for analysis, or perhaps ask you to help at training by putting out cones. Again, though, valuable experiences might be lost if we simply refused to participate when our services appeared undervalued. In fact, how else do we get to prove to some people that sport psychology is, in fact, useful? Certainly in my own experiences, even long after completing supervision, reducing or rejecting one's own ego is probably more advisable for someone in a helping profession.

Related to the above, but sixth, we might suggest that an *extra-mile mentality* is more beneficial. Obviously, this does not mean you should attempt to operate beyond your current capability, that's a key ethical principle. However, occasionally we might be asked to undertake a task that isn't as glorious as working with the national squad as they travel the world, or to go over an area that we consider we've already learned well. However, there is always something to be gained from each experience, even if it's simply observing and evaluating our own reaction, and perhaps challenging our own assumptions about how to approach a familiar problem. A good reflective practice engine can usually extract these lessons, whereas an unreflective trainee will likely be too preoccupied complaining to actually learn.

Finally, we could suggest one last golden rule: *finishing supervision does not mean you're infallible.* It simply means the support rods and scaffolding have been kicked away and it's time to stand, or fall, on your own. In the end, this emphasizes the importance of firm foundations, an efficient engine for continual building and rebuilding (i.e., learning/capability), the ability to draw and redraw blueprints for your development and future capabilities and to evaluate overall progress towards these plans. Once you finish supervised practice, nobody will be doing this for you: it's all on you. And being incomplete in any of these areas would place you at great risk of either being ineffective or unethical in your applied practice. For example, if you were unable to understand your current capabilities as a practitioner, it would be quite easy to take on a client or set goals with a client that were simply beyond your competence to deliver: a big ethical no no.

Overall, supervision achieves a number of key roles, one of which is ensuring that the trainee reaches a point where they are safe to practice unsupervised as well as able to continue learning and improving their practice. Many positive aspects of supervision can be maintained after the completion of supervised practice, by seeking peer supervision or mentoring (e.g., Yambor & Thompson, 2014; Titkov, Bednarikova, & Mortensen, 2014). Some regulatory bodies actually require this, whereas others merely recommend it. It is possible, in some counties, that supervision may be minimal once a sport psychologist is qualified and registered, in which case, the main quality assurance mechanisms left will be record keeping and reflective practice. Overall, however, this chapter has presented the three strategies as a coherent whole for quality assurance. Raw materials in the form of accurate record keeping, a 'reflective practice engine' driving increased capability and improved service and a supervisory process that guides, refines and tunes that engine. We have equated an ever-growing tower to the psychologist's capability, and the psychologist to a 'builder-architect' who both designs and builds the tower, but also constantly revises plans and responds to new materials becoming available. Formal training develops strong foundations, and supervised practice develops a basic building as well as the builder-architect. When we strip away that support and input, we should have a very capable sport psychologist but not only that. Our psychologist will self-monitor, find and fix any faults and thus keep getting better by eliminating more and more imperfections.

10.5   Conclusions

In this chapter, we have reviewed some of the main quality assurance processes available to a sport psychologist: record keeping, reflective practice and supervision. It should be clear that other processes are available, such as CPD, peer mentoring, auditing by regulatory bodies and in some organizations, employee performance appraisals. Overall, the main aim of quality assurance is the maintenance of a desired level of quality in the psychological services we offer, by means of attention to every stage of the process. Of course, this can be time-consuming or tedious, and I can distinctly remember times in my early career where I desperately wanted to just 'get on and do the job'. It is only now that my own 'reflection engine' is suitably powerful and tuned that I can look back on those times, with a little remorse, and wish I had appreciated the learning opportunities available. In this chapter, we have focussed on three core processes, the ones that are most likely to be used by any and every sport psychologist. Post university, CPD courses, workshops or online-contents are often a 'free market' where practitioners can choose what content to engage with. Peer mentoring carries many of the benefits of supervision, without the (usually) legal obligations around safeguarding current clients. Likewise, peer mentors are not under any pressure to 'get you qualified'. However, not all sport psychologists are lucky enough to be working in close proximity to others. In the current climate, very few sport psychologists are employed in large organizations where annual performance reviews might take place, and almost certainly no psychologist would welcome being audited by their respective regulatory body. Hence overall, the most reliable choices for quality assurance, available to all sport psychologists, are: record keeping, reflective practice and supervision.

It is worth closing with the reasons that quality assurance is important. Arguably, the same reasons you are reading this book. *We want to give our clients the best possible service.* Unfortunately, 'delivering guaranteed performance results' is extremely difficult, and promising such outcomes may do more harm than good. Instead, we tend to seek two things in quality assurance: ethical practice and competent practice. Upon reading this chapter, and this book, we might be reassured that ethical practice is rarely black and white, and there can be many situations – particularly in sport – that a practitioner cannot anticipate or simply avoid. Likewise, we might have moved away from any idea that a sport psychologist can train to a level where s/he is the 'finished' product, and unable to learn anything else that might improve their capability to deliver effective support. As explained earlier, we seek to establish a minimum standard, and then a perpetual pursuit of improvement and development. We require the practitioners themselves to both be aware of how to manage key tensions within their service as well as managing their own development and learning.

These considerations lead to several other important justifications of quality assurance. First, it should help sport psychologists to be ethical, and never leave clients or the public with doubts or bad experiences as a result of poor ethical practice. Second, it should help sport psychologists accurately deliver to expectations, leaving clients and stakeholders content that the support actually helped. Third, this should create an ever-growing collection of satisfied customers, both for the individual and for the profession as a whole. Effective quality assurance focussing on excellent processes, as described in this book, should minimize the number of clients who feel they were not helped by a sport psychologist (or have even worse things to say). Fourth, as we continue to understand what effective practice is, by focussing on quality assurance and not just 'doing the job', we can begin to capture, record, study and communicate the central considerations. For one thing, this may assist in the training of future sport psychologists, informing trainees, supervisors and training institutions of how best to approach the process. Further, such understanding may enable the more accurate marketing/'selling' of sport psychology, both in terms of the aims of sport psychology and what really represents a 'world-class' sport psychologist. Perhaps in future, we will not judge a sport psychologist by the fame or success of their clients, or the size of their wallet, but rather by the quality of the processes they follow. As argued in Chapter 1, we can deliver world-class sport psychology to a children's team, or very poor sport psychology to a world champion. At the moment, it's not always clear how those receiving (or funding) the service would know the difference, so we as a profession must tell them – once we agree what effective practice really means. Further, by evaluating our psychological practice we may also feed back into the scientific research that we draw on. In this book, we have defined sport psychology as a scientific endeavour, and that means we must also communicate important findings from our activities. Whether we communicate them amongst ourselves (between supervisor and trainee), to the public (e.g., here is an example of effective practice) or to researchers: 'Without publication, science is dead' (Gerard Piel – Editor of Scientific American). Practitioners of applied sport psychology should demand relevant research that actually informs their practice, and criticize abstract conceptual research that does nothing to assist practitioners, athletes or coaches. Practitioners should also demand higher quality research, to ensure that their practice is informed by the best quality evidence available. Perhaps by writing and publishing a little more, practitioners might also overcome the mindset that 'published = true or gospel', which seems to lead to disillusionment when contradictory findings emerge. Realistically, research being published simply means it is fit to be evaluated by others, but they may still choose to reject or ignore the claims/findings.

Overall, however, quality assurance in sport psychology has much more potential than to simply be a 'stick' to scare people and enforce standards. Done well, and communicated properly, quality assurance could improve the practice of thousands, change the expectations of millions and stimulate new ideas and studies that could change the entire field of psychology. Sport psychology does something quite unique, often working with amazing individuals, in unique contexts. As others have already argued, the time has come to be proud of this, and start promoting the ideas and processes that emerge from working in this unique and wonderful area.

10.6   Ella's story: Part 10 – 'Go forth and prosper'

Ella is approaching the end of her supervised experience, and faced with the challenge of submitting documentation that clearly documents her competence to anonymous 'examiners'. In particular, Ella has been struggling to demonstrate her reflective awareness and processes in document format. Ella's supervisor steps in with some 'assignments' that will force her to put all her experience and tacit knowledge into words.

1. First, Ella is challenged to define what reflective practice is, and illustrate its importance and relevance to sport psychology. How could she respond to these questions in a way that demonstrates deep knowledge?
2. Second, Ella is challenged to identify and capture examples of instances where reflective practice has improved the outcomes for her clients. However, she is concerned that her records from the time are not reflective

enough. How could Ella explicitly demonstrate her reflective processes to an outsider, assessing her competence on paper and electronic documents?

3. Third, the registration process requires that Ella demonstrate reflection across a variety of settings and situations, yet the supervisor is concerned that Ella's first draft of the submission contains too many examples from one-to-one client meetings. What other types of activities could Ella reflect on in order to demonstrate this breadth of application?

4. Finally, Ella is challenged to demonstrate 'meta-reflections' – reflecting on the quality of her own reflective process. What type of criteria could she use to evaluate her competence? How might she be able to demonstrate such meta-reflections?

Only 1 year after successfully competing her training, Ella is approached to be a supervisor by a colleague who would much rather work with her than a stranger. She completes the necessary training course, but when filling in the forms to become Simon's supervisor, she is gripped by doubt. Feeling reflective, Ella decides to reflect on what type of supervisor she wants to be.

5. What are the core roles and responsibilities of a supervisor, in relation to sport psychology practice?

6. What are the options for Ella regarding style, approach or philosophy? Having followed her journey through this book, what style do you feel might suit her best? Try to explain your answers.

7. Ella and Simon would likely be asked to work for the same organization, providing support to a range of athletes as they transition from elite juniors to national and international competitors. What issues might this raise for the pair (ethical, practical etc.), and how might they be managed?

10.7   Review and reflect

1. What do we mean by 'quality assurance' in applied sport psychology support, and why is it important to (a) clients, (b) practitioners and (c) the profession as a whole?

2. What other processes/stages, in our model of sport psychology service delivery, are subject to being quality assured through reflection, supervision and documentation? Which processes are most important to quality assure, and which are less so?

3. What criteria would you look for in order to qualify as an excellent quality assurance process from a sport psychologist? And what might a particularly bad process look like?

4. What tools, cues and prompts could you use to try and ensure that your own quality assurance processes are as strong as possible?

Worksheet 10.1 Sport psychology checklist

	Do I have accurate records stored securely?	Have I already reflected on this, and what are my current reflections?	What specific questions do I want to ask of my supervisor?	Following supervision, what specific actions do I want to take, in the short or long term?
Ethical considerations				
Philosophy – aims, ontology or style				
Intake processes (including ethical marketing of services)				
Needs analysis techniques and interpretation				
Case formulations				
Choosing ways forwards and interventions				
Planning the delivery of service				
Delivering, monitoring and terminating services				
Reflective practice (what, why, how, when?)				
Supervision and overall development				

Learning Aids – Individual Case Studies for Discussion

Seb – Part 1

Seb is an excellent golfer, making appearances on both the US and European tours. Capable of top-10 ranking at international level. However, he is yet to win a major tournament. Twenty-eight years old, from Toulon, in he turned professional at 19 years old. When he first turned professional, he had an unorthodox swing with a loop and large lag, and so he worked towards making his swing more conventional.

In his early years, he repeatedly gripped, released and re-gripped his hands on the club handle before finally taking a shot. He has been observed taking over a minute to hit a shot after addressing the ball, and commentators labelled him as being 'unable to make a swing'. Responding to criticism of his swing, he said, 'My swing works for me, so why should I change it? I prefer to have a natural swing and play well rather than a perfect swing and not be able to play with freedom'. This inconsistency – in both the swing and its results – appears to have slowly undermined Seb's game, and even his outgoing personality is now much more reserved.

Seb also tends not to take responsibility for his own mistakes and failings (e.g., thinking his swing is 'natural'). After losing a tournament that he appeared to have 'in the bag', his post-match conference seemed to suggest that bad luck had cost him the championship. On the 16th hole, his tee shot hit the flag stick but then bounced 20 feet meaning he could not convert for birdie. 'It's not the first time, unfortunately', he stated. 'I'm playing against a lot out there, more than just the other golfers.' Commentators and pundits note how Seb makes external attributions for both success and failure.

Seb is known for being hot headed and temperamental. This has won him some fans but also made him 'fragile' on the course – as a single mistake can 'snowball' when he tries to 'make up for it'.

When he was a rookie, Seb was an assertive putter, never leaving it short and often making long putts. In recent times, he has become much more tentative, often leaving the ball well short and even carrying two putters in his bag.

Many golf fans feel that this is by far his biggest weakness, as he often strikes the ball well despite his swing faults, whereas his putting has become an obvious and consistent issue.

Seb has now reached crisis point, after becoming increasingly frustrated by his failure to win a major combined with his unpredictable performances. He has taken a break from playing and is even considering retiring from the game. His conduct and demeanour on the course are flat, low and subdued, yet he interviews well, and acts as a commentator.

- What signs are there in this profile of Seb's current psychological needs?
- What evidence is there of a link between Seb's psychology and his on-course performances?
- What theories from the literature appear relevant to Seb's situation?
- What interventions appear most relevant to Seb?
- What steps could you take to start improving Seb's psychological approach? (and therefore, in theory, his game).
- Justify your decisions as clearly as possible.

Seb – Part 2

Shaken by recent performances, Seb tried to make a series of changes to his swing and putting stroke. Training obsessively, Seb has effectively destroyed his own game and, as a consequence, he recently held a press conference to announce an 'indefinite' break from the game.

During the press conference, Seb spoke of the new breed of players coming through, who seemed to hit further than him, putt better and several of whom had already picked up majors while he grew increasingly frustrated waiting for his first major win. He said he didn't want to become a 'dinosaur' of the game, or to keep having to answer questions about what 'could have been'. He said he could no longer compete with this new breed of super-competitive and super-fit 'athlete-golfers' ('They even lift bigger weights bigger than me', he joked) – and that he does not like losing every week: 'So why keep coming back for more?'

In recent months, Seb has also become isolated from his fellow professionals, declining invitations to 'Players' Dinners' before and after key tournaments, and appearing to make very little conversation with players whilst out on the course. Serge also reacted angrily to criticisms of his swing, and his attempts to change it, criticism which seems to have come from players and pundits alike. He felt his peers and colleagues had effectively 'turned against him'. The final straw was when his decision to 'take a break' was also questioned, at which point he refused to give media interviews and has returned home to France to stay with his parents.

Also during his press conference, Seb said he had made a mistake in trying to change his natural game, and that he felt like he had created his own bad luck by questioning his 'God-given ability'. He made repeated references to luck, fate and concluded that he currently felt 'destined' to never win a major.

Finally, Seb has abandoned all practice at this time. When you speak on the phone, he tells you that he feels practice is only making him worse and he is sick of failing to meet his own expectations, even on the driving range. 'If I cannot put it within 10 feet of my target after maybe two or three attempts, I just give up ... I just leave the whole bucket of balls there for someone else ... It's got to the point where I think 'Why go? Why prove to myself that I have lost my ability?'

- What signs are there in this profile of Seb's current psychological needs?
- What evidence is there of a link between Seb's psychology and his recent behaviours?
- What theories from the literature appear relevant to Seb's situation?
- What interventions appear most relevant to Seb?
- What steps could you take to start improving Seb's psychological approach? (and therefore, in theory, his game).
- Justify your decisions as clearly as possible.

Helene – Part 1

Twenty-four-year-old professional women's tennis player. Ranked between 30 and 80 in the world in recent years (has gone up as well as down the rankings). Last year, she dropped to her lowest ranking (80th), failing to convert match points and openly weeping on court. A TV documentary on her labelled her as 'a bit of a perfectionist' after it appeared that she puts a lot of pressure on herself in training.

In the early round of tournaments, Helene has beaten many of the world's top players, even world number ones. However, she has never progressed beyond the semi-finals at a major tournament, and more often the quarter-finals represent a decent result for her.

Her inconsistent performances, and a tendency to 'fall apart' at key moments in matches (often when leading) – along with her diminutive stature and quiet voice, have led people to think of her as too 'fragile' to succeed on the women's tour. She often struggles in longer matches, and has a very poor record in third sets.

Helene has started making more unforced errors, leading to her becoming visibly frustrated and upset on court. The nature of the errors she makes is often completely out of step with the way she has played up to that point, but once these mistakes occur they tend to become more frequent, and severe ('wayward').

In interviews, Helene attributes many of her defeats to factors outside her control – her fitness levels, physical strength, injuries or, at one point, the break-up of her parents. However, she is also her own strongest critic and sets very high standards for herself. Unfortunately, after several years of falling below her own high standards, she has started to become disheartened.

Helene has shown excellent commitment levels throughout her career, refraining from pursuing romantic relationships and generally committing all her time to training and preparing for matches. She has no hobbies, and her tour/training schedule means she has a highly limited social life. Her coach is from Russia and 'does not believe in being friends' with his athletes.

- What signs are there in this profile of Helene's psychological needs?
- What evidence is there of a link between Helene's psychological approach and her on-court performances?
- What theories from the literature appear relevant to Helene's situation?
- What interventions appear most relevant to Helene?
- What steps could you take to start improving Helene's psychological approach? (and therefore, in theory, her game).
- Justify your decisions as clearly as possible.

Helene – Part 2

You are brought in to act as Helene's 'coach–psychologist', after her previous coach resigned saying he could no longer work with her. She makes no effort to contact you and it is only by speaking to her agent that you are able to arrange a meeting. When you speak, Helene feels there is nothing more to improve in her game and she must simply wait for her luck to change. Helene lives a very comfortable life, as her regular appearances at Tour events continue to pay the bills. However, her endorsements and modelling contracts far exceed any prize money she wins at the moment.

Helene reports that she needs to take a break from her 'obsessive ways' and her super-competitive approach, which have led to emotional outbursts, so she has reduced her training to simply maintain her fitness and nothing more. She is also glad her coach has left as she feels he was pushing her too hard and, in fact, since he left she feels she is 'On her first real holiday ever … 10 years of being told what to do and when by the same guy. And before that it was my parents telling me what to do. I haven't gone to the beach, but this is a holiday right now.'

The problem appears to be that her coach was the main 'driving force' behind Helene for some time, and in his absence there is no 'drive' left. Helene did not contact you because she is suspicious of all people at the moment; she has stopped all but her immediate family from coming to see her. 'You just cannot trust people when you're famous. Since I made it as a player, all these family members and old friends have just come out of the woodwork. They come and visit, wanting to get in pictures with me, eat and drink at my expense, even using my house as a sort of free holiday villa. They are not real friends. They would not care about me if I wasn't famous.'

Your analysis of Helene's game suggests several changes that could really help. Upper body strength, a firmer base for her forehand and a more consistent serve are all obvious areas for improvement.

However, you are unsure about raising these issues with her at this first meeting, and you leave wondered if you should raise them at all. Helene seems happy simply coasting, and if you come in with these recommendations, you worry she may ignore or even sack you.

- What signs are there in this profile of Helene's psychological needs?
- What evidence is there of a link between Helene's psychological approach and her on-court performances?
- What theories from the literature appear relevant to Helene's situation?
- What interventions appear most relevant to Helene?
- What steps could you take to start improving Helene's psychological approach? (and therefore, in theory, her game).
- Justify your decisions as clearly as possible.

Jordan – Part 1

A talented soccer player, Jordan was hyped as the most exciting player to emerge from the academy in years, 'the complete package' of skills, fitness and 'natural ability'. Six goals from midfield in his first season with the first team led to him being sold to a Premiership team for £5m.

After an impressive first season, in which he won the 'Young Player of the Year' award, he failed to repeat his early promise and the two subsequent seasons were disappointing. After developing a reputation for being strong 'box to box', these two seasons were surprisingly bland and nondescript – leading to 2 goals in 48 appearances (but the number of starts also decreased).

In media reports, Jordan reported feeling he was living life in a 'goldfish bowl' – constantly on public display with every mistake and misdemeanour magnified for all to see. In light of this 'unhappiness' – he was sold to another premiership club for £7m, after 8 goals in 90 appearances.

At his new team, Jordan's form is still decidedly up and down. He flourished under one manager who showered Jordan with personal words of encouragement. He also scored the team's winning goal in a vital match, just hours after being named the new vice-captain.

However, he is capable of 'vanishing' from a game – making only short passes, 'hiding' from the ball and shying away from making tackles. Several persistent injuries have also interrupted Jordan's development. His talent remains unquestioned, and in a fun 'cross-bar challenge' for TV he was the only player from his team to succeed. Labelled the 'elegant pretender' by one newspaper, the problem remains whether Jordan can display this full talent every week.

Jordan is acutely aware of the media coverage of him. 'I can understand the fans' frustrations', Jordan says of his patchy performances, 'but hopefully now I have run into a bit of form, scored a couple of goals, I can just keep playing my football – scoring has given me that extra boost that was maybe lacking', admits Jordan. 'And I've settled down into the position I've been asked to play.' Jordan's natural ability has led to him being asked to play several positions and he feels this has also restricted his performance.

- What signs are there in this profile of Jordan's psychological needs?
- What evidence is there of a link between Jordan's psychological approach and his on-court performances?
- What theories from the literature appear relevant to Jordan's situation?
- What interventions appear most relevant to Jordan?
- What steps could you take to start improving Jordan's psychological approach? (and therefore, in theory, his game).
- Justify your decisions as clearly as possible.

Jordan – Part 2

A talented soccer player, Jordan has been playing tentatively and failing to influence games. In the midst of this 'slump', Jordan was injured when an opposing midfielder tackled him hard in the first 10 minutes of a game. Ankle ligament damage is likely to keep Jordan off the pitch for at least 3 months, after which he is likely to face stern competition to get back into the starting XI, because the coach bought several new players in the summer. Jordan has had several injuries in recent years, but he seems more upset than in previous instances.

The physio has been able to recommend a fairly comprehensive regime of rehab exercises, but Jordan complains that the sessions are long and boring, and he feels isolated in the gym on his own (e.g., balancing on leg, throwing a ball against the wall or standing on wobble board), and gym staff have reported Jordan has not been attending his rehab. When challenged, Jordan said he felt that the physiotherapist's 'magic tricks' (ultrasound, massage) should do the trick, but both the physio and doctor have told him that this not doing his exercises could double his recovery time.

Following his injury, Jordan has lost almost all contact with his friends in the first team squad, training at different times of day, not travelling to matches and generally having to 'rest' between rehab sessions (ice packs, etc.). He complained about this for a while, but now he has simply become isolated and withdrawn.

The coaches, physio and team doctors have all told Jordan exactly what he ought to be doing, how many times and days and even recommended a special diet to aid recovery and avoid weight gain. It is clear, though, that Jordan is simply not following this advice. The manager sent a letter to Jordan asking him to attend home matches but he has not responded. The physio has also shown Jordan charts of how other players with similar injuries have recovered fast by following his advice, but again this just seemed to annoy Jordan. In response, the management has decided to fine Jordan for every rehab session he misses, which at present has reduced his weekly payments to almost nothing, but he says he is fine financially and can live without the money being lost in fines.

The crisis point has now been reached as Jordan has not attended for several weeks, he is not responding to phone calls, texts or emails, and media reports suggest he is gaining weight, whilst still needing crutches several weeks after the physio said he could come off them. He has also hired a new physio who visits Jordan privately at his house.

- What signs are there in this profile of Jordan's psychological needs?
- What evidence is there of a link between Jordan's psychological approach and his on-court performances?
- What theories from the literature appear relevant to Jordan's situation?
- What interventions appear most relevant to Jordan?
- What steps could you take to start improving Jordan's psychological approach? (and therefore, in theory, his game).
- Justify your decisions as clearly as possible.

References

Abernathy, B., Kippers, V., Mackinnon, L., Neal, R., & Hanrahan, S. (1997). *The biophysical foundations of human movement*. Melbourne: Macmillan.

Acierno, R., Hersen, M., & Van Hasselt, V. (1995). Accountability in psychological treatment. In V. B. Van Hasselt, & M. Hersen (Eds.), *Sourcebook of psychological treatment manuals (volume II): Adult disorders* (pp. 3–20). New York, NY: Wiley.

Albee, G. W. (2000). The Boulder model's fatal flaw [Journal Article] *American Psychologist, 55*(2), 247–248. American Psychological Association, US.

Aldrich, J. (1995). Correlations genuine and spurious in Pearson and Yule. *Statistical Science, 10,* 364–376.

American Psychological Association (2010). Ethics Principles of Psychologists and Code of Conduct. Washingon DC: Author. Retrieved from http://www.apa.org/ethics/code/

American Psychological Association – Committee on Training in Clinical Psychology. (1947). Recommended graduate training program in clinical psychology. *American Psychologist, 2,* 539–558.

Anatasi, A., & Urbina, S. (1997). *Psychological testing* (7th ed.). Upper Saddle River, NJ: Prentice Hall.

Andersen, M. B. (1994). Ethical considerations in the supervision of applied sport psychology graduate students. *Journal of Applied Sport Psychology, 6,* 152–167.

Andersen, M. B. (2000). *Doing sport psychology*. Champaign, IL: Human Kinetics.

Andersen, M. B. (2004). The evolution of training and supervision in sport psychology. In T. Morris, & J. J. Summers (Eds.), *Sport psychology: Theory, applications and issues* (2nd ed., pp. 452–469). Brisbane, Australia: Wiley.

Andersen, M. B. (2005) 'Yeah, I worked with Beckham': Issues of confidentiality, privacy and privilege in sport psychology service delivery. *Sport and Exercise Psychology Review, 1*(2), 5–13.

Anderson, A. G., Miles, A., Mahoney, C., & Robinson, P. (2002). Evaluating the effectiveness of applied sport psychology practice: Making the case for a case study approach. *The Sport Psychologist, 16*(4), 432–453.

Andrews, M., Gidman, J., & Humphreys, A. (1998). Reflection: Does it enhance professional nursing practice? *British Journal of Nursing* (Mark Allen Publishing), *7,* 413–417.

Annas, G. J., & Grodin, M. A. (1992). *The Nazi doctors and the Nuremburg code: Human rights in human experimentation*. New York, NY: Oxford University Press, Inc.

Aoyagi, M. W., & Portenga, S. T. (2010). The role of positive ethics and virtues in the context of sport & performance psychology service delivery. *Professional Psychology: Research and Practice, 41,* 253–259.

Asch, S. E. (1951). Effects of group pressure on the modification and distortion of judgments. In H. Guetzkow (Ed.), *Groups, leadership and men* (pp. 177–190).

Assay, T. P., & Lambert, M. J. (1999). The empirical case for the common factors in therapy: Quantitative findings. In M. A. Hubble, B. L. Duncan, & S. D. Miller (Eds.), *The heart and soul of change: What works in therapy* (pp. 33–56). Washington, DC: American Psychological Association.

Association for Applied Sport Psychology (2013). *Speaker Guidelines for Conference Presentations. AASP 28th Annual Conference*, October 2–5, New Orleans, LA. Retrieved from http://appliedsportpsych.org/files/AASPGuidelines2013.pdf

Australian Psychological Society (2010). [online] Retrieved 20 October 2011, from http://www.psychology.org.au/Assets/Files/APS-Code-of-Ethics.pdf

Bacon, F. (1627). *The new Atlantis*.

Bacon, F. (1859). Essays. In B. Montagu (Ed.), *The works of Francis Bacon, Lord Chancellor of England*. Philadelphia, PA: Parry and McMillan.

Bandura, A. (1977). Self-efficacy: Toward a unifying theory of behavioral change. *Psychological Review, 84*(2), 191–215.

Barker, J., McCarthy, P., Jones, M., & Moran, A. (2011). *Single-case research methods in sport and exercise*. London: Routledge.

Barker, J. B., Mellalieu, S. D., McCarthy, P. J., Jones, M. V., & Moran, A. (2013). A review of single case research in sport psychology 1997–2012: Research trends and future directions. *Journal of Applied Sport Psychology, 25*(1), 4–32.

Baron, J. (2000). *Thinking and deciding*. Cambridge, UK: Cambridge University Press.

Bedi, R., Davis, M., & Arvay, M. (2005). The client's perspective on forming a counselling alliance and implications for research on counsellor training. *Canadian Journal of Counselling, 39*, 71–85.

Belar, C. D. (2000). Revealing data on education and training. *Clinical Psychology: Science and Practice, 7*(4), 368–369.

Belar, C., & Perry, N. W. (1992). National conference on scientist-practitioner education and training for the professional practice of psychology. *American Psychologist, 47*, 71–75.

Benjamin, L. T., & Baker, D. B. (2000). Boulder at 50: Introduction to section. *American Psychologist, 55*, 233–236.

Bergner, R. (1998). Characteristics of optimal clinical case formulation. *American Journal of Psychotherapy, 52*(3), 287–301.

Bernieri, F. J., & Petty, K. N. (2011). The influence of handshakes on first impression accuracy. *Social Influence, 6*, 78–87. doi:10.1080/15534510.2011.566706

Beutler, L. E. (2009). Making science matter in clinical practice: Redefining psychotherapy. *Clinical Psychology: Science and Practice, 16*, 301–317. doi:10.1111/j.1468-2850.2009.01168.x

Beutler, L. E., & Malik, M. L. (2002a). Diagnosis and treatment guidelines: The example of depression. In L. E. Beutler, & M. L. Malik (Eds.), *Rethinking the DSM (251–278)*. Washington, DC: American Psychological Association.

Beutler, L. E., & Malik, M. L. (Eds.). (2002b) *Rethinking the DSM (3–16)*. Washington, DC: American Psychological Association.

Bhaskar, R. (1975). *A realist theory of science* (2nd ed.). London: Verso.

Bhaskar, R. (1979). *The possibility of naturalism: A philosophical critique of the contemporary human sciences* (3rd ed.). London: Routledge.

Bhaskar, R. (1989). *'Rorty, realism and the idea of freedom', reading Rorty*, A. Malachowski (Ed.), Oxford: Blackwell.

Blaikie, N. W. H. (1993). *Approaches to social inquiry*. Cambridge, MA: Policy Press.

Bolton, G. (2010). *Reflective practice: writing and professional development* (3rd ed.). Los Angeles: Sage Publications (p. xix). ISBN 9781848602113.

Botterill, C. (1990). Sport psychology and professional hockey. *The Sport Psychologist, 4*(4), 358–368.

Boutcher, S. H., & Rotella, R. J. (1987). A psychological skills educational program for closed skill performance enhancement. *The Sport Psychologist, 1*, 127–137.

Bouvy, M. L., Heerdink, E. R., Urquhart, J., Grobbee, D. E., Hoes, A. W., & Leufkens, H. G. (2003). Effect of a pharmacist-led intervention on diuretic compliance in heart failure patients: A randomized controlled study. *Journal of Cardiac Failure, 9*(5),404–411.

Boyce, B. A., & Bingham, S. M. (1997). The effects of self-efficacy and goal setting on bowling 2 performance. *Journal of Teaching in Physical Education, 16,* 312–323.

Boyer, L., Antoniotti, S., Sapin, C., Doddoli, C., Thomas, P. A., Raccah, D., & Auquier, P. (2003). The link between satisfaction and quality of care for inpatients [French]. *Journal d'Economie Medicale, 21*(7–8), 407–418.

Bradford, L., & Stevens, B. (2013). What's in the file? Opening the drawer on clinical record keeping in psychology. *Australian Psychologist,* doi:10.1111/j.1742-9544.2012.00080.x

Braithwaite, J. (1999). Accountability and Governance under the New Regulatory State. *Australian Journal of Public Administration, 58,* 90–93.

Breen, L., & Darlaston-Jones, D. (2008). *Moving beyond the enduring dominance of positivism in psychological research: An Australian perspective.* Paper presented at the 43rd Australian Psychological Society Annual Conference.

Brewer, J. D. (2000). *Ethnography.* Buckingham: Open University Press.

Brown, J. L., & Cogan, K. D. (2006). Ethical clinical practice and sport psychology: When two worlds collide. *Ethics and Behavior, 16*(1), 15–23.

Brustad, R. J., & Ritter-Taylor, M. (1997). Applying social psychological perspectives to the sport psychology consulting process. *The Sport Psychologist, 11*(1), 107–119.

Bull, S. J. (1995). Reflections on a 5-year consultancy program with the England women's cricket team. *The Sport Psychologist, 9,* 148–163.

Burton, D., & Raedeke, T. D. (2008). *Sport psychology for coaches.* Champaign, IL: Human Kinetics.

Butler, R. J., & Hardy, L. (1992). The performance profile: Theory and application. *The Sport Psychologist, 6,* 253–264

Cameron, S., & Turtle-Song, I. (2002). Learning to write case notes using the SOAP format. *Journal of Counseling and Development, 80*(3), 286–292.

Carnap, R. (1950). Empiricism, semantics and ontology. *Revue Intern de Phil, 4,* 20–40 (Reprinted in the second edition of Carnap 1947, pp. 2052–2221).

Carver, C. S. (2003). Pleasure as a sign that you can attend to something else: Placing positive feelings within a general model of affect. *Cognition and Emotion, 17,* 241–261.

Carver, C. S., & Scheier, M. F. (1998). *On the self-regulation of behavior.* New York: Cambridge University Press.

Carver, C. S., & Scheier, M. F. (2002). Control processes and self-organization as complementary principles underlying behavior. *Personality and Social Science Psychology Review, 4,* 301–315.

Chambless, D. L., Baker, M. J., Baucom, D. H., Beutler, L. E., Calhoun, K. S., Crits-Christoph, P., ... Woody, S. R. (1998). Update on empirically validated therapies, II. *The Clinical Psychologist, 51*(1), 3–16.

Chambless, D. L., & Ollendick, T. H. (2001). Empirically supported psychological interventions: Controversies and evidence. *Annual Review of Psychology, 52,* 685–716.

Chen, S., Duckworth, K., & Chaiken, S. (1999). Motivated heuristic and systematic processing. *Psychological Inquiry, 10*(1), 44–49.

Chwalisz, K. (2003). Evidence-based practice: A framework for twenty-first century scientist-practitioner training (major contribution). *The Counseling Psychologist, 31*(5), 497–528.

Collins, R., Evans-Jones, K. and O'Connor, H. (2013) Reflections on three neophyte sport and exercise psychologists' developing philosophies for practice. *The Sport Psychologist, 27*(4), 399–409.

Corrie, S., & Callahan, M. M. (2000). A review of the scientist-practitioner model: Reflections on its potential contribution to counselling psychology within the context of current health care trends. *British Journal of Medical Psychology, 73,* 413–427

Cremades, G. J., & Tashman, L. S. (2014). Becoming a sport, exercise, and performance psychology professional: A global perspective. London: Routledge (Taylor and Francis)

Crits-Christoph, P., Barber, J., & Kurcias, J. (1993). The accuracy of therapists' inter-pretations and the development of the therapeutic alliance. *Psychotherapy Research, 3*, 25–35.

Crits-Christoph, P., Cooper, A., & Luborsky, L. (1988). The accuracy of therapists' interpretations and the outcome of dynamic psychotherapy. *Journal of Consulting Clinical Psychology, 56*, 490–495.

Crockett, M. D. (2002). Inquiry as professional development: Creating dilemmas through teachers' work. *Teaching and Teacher Education, 18*, 609–624.

Cropley, B., Hanton, S., Miles, A., & Niven, A. (2010). Exploring the relationship between effective and reflective practice in applied sport psychology. *The Sport Psychologist, 24*, 521–541.

Cropley, B., Miles, A., Hanton, S., & Anderson, A. (2007). Improving the delivery of applied sport psychology support through reflective practice. *The Sport Psychologist, 21*, 475–494.

Cropley, B., & Neil, R. (2014). The neophyte supervisor: what did I get myself into? In G. Cremades and L. Tashman (Eds.) *Becoming a sport. execirse, and performance psychology professional: A global perspective* (pp. 219–227). London: Routledge.

Crowne, D. P., & Marlowe, D. (1960). A new scale of social desirability independent of psychopathology. *Journal of Consulting Psychology, 24*, 349–354.

Darley, J. M., & Gross, P. H. (1983). A hypothesis-confirming bias in labeling effects. *Journal of Personality and Social Psychology, 44*(20),33.

Dawes, M., Summerskill, W., Glasziou, P., Caartabellota, A., Martin, J., Hopayian, K., ... Osborne, J. (2005). Sicily statement on evidence-based practice. *Biomed Central Medical Education, 5*(1), 1–7.

Deal, T. & Kennedy, A. (1982). *Corporate Cultures: The rites and rituals of corporate life.* Addison-Wesley

Descartes, R. (1954). *Philosophical writings.* Ed. and Trans. by G. E. M. Anscombe, & P. T. Geach. Edinburgh: Nelson.

Descartes, R. (1970). *Philosophical letters.* Ed. and Trans. by A. Kenny. Oxford: Clarendon Press.

Dewey, J. (1916). *Democracy and education. An introduction to the philosophy of education* (1966 ed.). New York, NY: Free Press.

Dewey, J. (1929). *Experience and nature.* New York, NY: Dover. (Dover edition first published in 1958). Explores the relationship of the external world, the mind and knowledge.

Dewey, J., & Bentley, A. (1949). *Knowing and the known.* Boston, MA: Beacon Press.

Dosil, J. J., Cremades, G., & Rivera, S. (2014). *Psychological skills training and programs. Fundamental concepts in sport and exercise psychology* (pp. 327–342). London: Taylor & Francis.

Doyle, J., & Parfitt, G. (1996). Performance profiling and predictive validity. *Journal of Applied Sport Psychology, 8*(2), 160–170.

Drabick, D. A., & Goldfried, M. R. (2000). Training the scientist–practitioner for the 21st century: Putting the bloom back on the rose. *Journal of Clinical Psychology, 56*, 327–340.

Eassom, S. (1994). *Critical reflections on the Olympic ideology.* Ontario: The Centre for Olympic Studies.

Ebert, B. W. (1997). Dual-relationship prohibitions: A concept whose time never should have come. *Applied and Preventive Psychology, 6*, 137–156.

Eells, T. D., Kendjelic, E. M., & Lucas C. P. (1998). What's in a case formulation? Development and use of a content coding manual. *Journal of Psychotherapy Practice Research, 7*,144–153.

Elliott, K. M., & Shin, D. (2002). Student satisfaction: An alternative approach to assessing this important concept. *Journal of Higher Education Policy and Management, 24*(2), 199–209.

Ellis, A. (1994). *Reason and emotion in psychotherapy: comprehensive method of treating human disturbances: Revised and updated.* New York, NY: Citadel Press.

Ellis, A. (2004). *Rational emotive behavior therapy: It works for me—it can work for you.* Amherst, NY: Prometheus Books.

Embo, M. P. C., Driessen, E., Valcke, M., & Van Der Vleuten, C. P. M. (2014). Scaffolding reflective learning in clinical practice: A comparison of two types of reflective activities. *Medical Teacher, 36*(7), 602–607.

ESPN Sport Media Ltd. (2013). *Woodward slams England's open door policy.* Retrieved 21 March 2013, fromhttp://en.espn.co.uk/england/rugby/story/179118.html

Etcoff, N. L., Stock, S., Haley, L. E., Vickery, S. A., & House, D. M. (2011). Cosmetics as a feature of the extended human phenotype: Modulation of the perception of biologically important facial signals. *PLoS ONE, 6*(10), e25656. doi:10.1371/journal.pone.0025656

Evans, J. St. B. (2006). The heuristic-analytic theory of reasoning: Extension and evaluation. *Psychonomic Bulletin & Review, 13*(3), 378–395.

Evetts, J. (2001). New directions in state and international professional occupations: Discretionary decision-making and acquired regulation. Paper presented at SASE 13th Annual Meeting on Socio-Economics Knowledge: The New Wealth of Nations, University of Amsterdam, The Netherlands.

Eysenck, H. J. (1949). Training in clinical psychology: An English point of view. *American Psychologist, 4*, 173–176.

Faulkner, M. A., Wadibia, E. C., Lucas, B. D., & Hilleman, D. E. (2000). Impact of pharmacy counseling on compliance and effectiveness of combination lipid-lowering therapy in patients undergoing coronary artery revascularization: A randomized, controlled trial. *Pharmacotherapy, 20*(4), 410–416.

Faull, A., & Cropley, B. (2009). Reflective learning in sport: A case study of a senior level triathlete. *Reflective Practice, 10*, 325–339.

Feigl, H. (1974). Positivism in the twentieth century, logical empiricism. Dictionary of the history of ideas, vol. 3. Charlottesville, VA: Elektronic Text Center.

Feltham, C., &Dryden, W. (1993). *Dictionary of counselling.* London: Whurr.

Feltz, D., Short, S., & Sullivan, P. (2008). Self-efficacy in sport: Research and strategies for working with athletes, teams, and coaches. Champaigne, IL: Human Kinetics.

Fifer, A., Henschen, K., Gould, D., & Ravizza, K. (2008). What works when working with athletes. *The Sport Psychologist, 22*, 356–377.

Friedman, R. H., Kazis, L. E., Jette, A., Smith, M. B., Stollerman, J., Torgerson, J., Carey, K. (1996). A telecommunications system for monitoring and counseling patients with hypertension. Impact on medication adherence and blood pressure control. *American Journal of Hypertension, 9*(4), 285–292.

Fulero, S. M., & Wilbert, J. R. (1988). Record-keeping practices of clinical and counseling psychologists: A survey of practitioners. *Professional Psychology: Research and Practice, 19*(6), 658–660.

Gardner, M. (1959). Mathematical games. *Scientific American,* November, p. 188.

Gardner, F. L., & Moore, Z. E. (2006). *Clinical sport psychology.* Champagne, IL: Human Kinetics.

Gaudiano, B. A., & Statler, M. A. (2001). The scientist-practitioner gap and graduate education: Integrating perspectives and looking forward. *The Clinical Psychologist, 54*(4), 12–18.

Ghaye, T., Danai, K., Cuthbert, L., & Dennis, D. (1996). *Introduction to learning through critical reflective practice.* Newcastle-Upon-Tyne: Pentaxion.

Gibbs, G. (1988). *Learning by Doing: A guide to teaching and learning methods.* Oxford: Further Education Unit, Oxford Brookes University.

Gil-Garcia, A., & Cintron, Z. (July 2–5 2002). *The reflective journal as a learning and professional development tool for teachers and administrators.* Paper presented at the World Association for Case Method Research and Application Conference, Germany.

Gill, D. L. (1995). Gender issues: A social-educational perspective. In S. M. Murphy (Ed.), *Sport psychology interventions* (pp. 205–234). Champaign, IL: Human Kinetics.

Gillies, D. (1998). *The Duhem thesis and the Quine thesis.* In M. Curd & J. Cover (Eds.), Philosophy of science: The central issues (pp. 302–319).

Gipson, M., McKenzie, T. L., & Lowe, S. (1989). The sport psychology program of the USA Women's National Volleyball Team. *The Sport Psychologist, 3,* 330–339.

Glaser, B. (1978). *Theoretical sensitivity.* Mill Valley, CA: Sociology Press.

Glaser, R. (1996). Changing the agency for learning: Acquiring expert performance. In K. A. Ericsson (Ed.), *The road to excellence: The acquisition of expert performance in the arts and sciences, sports and games* (pp. 1–50). Mahwah, NJ: Erlbaum.

Goedeke, S. (2007). Teaching psychology at undergraduate level: Rethinking what we teach and how we teach it. *New Zealand Journal of Teacher's Work, 4*(1), 48–63.

Gordin, R. D., & Henschen, K. P. (1989). Preparing the USA women's artistic gymnastics team for the 1988 Olympics: A multimodel approach. *The Sport Psychologist, 3,* 366–373.

Gordon, S. (1990). A mental skills training programme for the Western Australian state cricket team. *The Sport Psychologist, 4,* 386–399.

Gould, D., Eklund, R. C., & Jackon, S. A. (1992). 1988 US Olympic wrestling excellence II: Thoughts and affect. *The Sport Psychologist, 6,* 383–402.

Gould, D., Greenleaf, C., Chung, Y. C., & Guinan, D. (2002). A survey of US Atlanta and Nagano Olympians: Variables perceived to influence performance. *Research Quarterly for Exercise and Sport, 73,* 175.

Gould, D., Guinan, D., Greenleaf, C., Medbery, R., & Peterson, K. (1999). Factors affecting Olympic performance: Perceptions of athletes and coaches from more and less successful teams. *The Sport Psychologist, 13,* 371–394.

Gould, D., & Pick, S. (1995). Sport psychology: The Griffith era, 1920–1940. *The Sport Psychologist, 9,* 391–405.

Greenleaf, C. A., Gould, D., & Dieffenbach, K. (2001). Factors influencing Olympic performance: Interviews with Atlanta and Nagano U.S. Olympians. *Journal of Applied Sport Psychology, 13,* 154–184.

Grimmett, P. P., Erickson, G. L., Mackinnon, A. A., & Riecken, T. J. (1990). Reflective practice in teacher education. In R. T. Clift, W. R. Houston, & M. C. Pugach (Eds.), *Encouraging reflective practice in education: An analysis of issues and programs* (pp. 20–38). New York, NY: Teachers College Press.

Groth-Marnat, G. (1999/2000). Financial efficacy of clinical assessment: Rational guidelines and issues for future research. *Journal of. Clinical Psychology, 55,* 813–824.

Grove, W. M., Zald, D. H., Lebow, B. S., Snitz, B. E., & Nelson, C. (2000). Clinical versus mechanical prediction: A meta-analysis. *Psychological Assessment, 12,* 19–30.

Guadagno, R. E., & Cialdini, R. B. (2007). Gender differences in impression management in organizations: A qualitative review. *Sex Roles, 56,* 483–494. doi:10.1007/s11199-007-9187-3

Gucciardi, D. F., & Gordon, S. (2009). Revisiting the performance profile technique: Theoretical underpinnings and application. *The Sport Psychologist, 23*(1), 93–117.

Haberl, P., & Peterson, K. (2006). Olympic-size ethical dilemmas: Issues and challenges for Sport Psychology consultants on the road and at the Olympic games. *Ethics and Behavior, 16*(1), 25–40.

Halliwell, W. (1989). Delivering sport psychology services to the Canadian sailing team at the 1988 Summer Olympic Games. *The Sport Psychologist, 3,* 313–319.

Halliwell, W. (1990). Providing sport psychology consulting services in professional hockey. *The Sport Psychologist, 4,* 369–377.

Hardy, L. (2012). Comment. *Sport and Exercise Psychology Review, 8*(2), 17–18.

Harwood, C. G., Keegan, R. J., Smith, J. J., & Raine, A. (2015). A systematic review of the intrapersonal correlates of motivational climate perceptions in sport and physical activity. *Psychology of Sport and Exercise, 18,* 9–25.

Hawking, S. (1988). *A brief history of time.* New York: Bantam Dell Publishing Group.

Hayes, S. C., Strosahl, K., & Wilson, K. G. (1999). *Acceptance and commitment therapy: An experiential approach to behavior change.* New York, NY: The Guilford Press.

Hays, K. F. (2006). Being fit: The ethics of practice diversification in performance psychology. *Professional Psychology: Research and Practice, 37*, 223–232.

Health and Care Professionals Council (2008). Standards of conduct, performance and ethics. London: HCPC. [online] Retrieved from http://www.hcpcuk.org/assets/documents/10003B6EStandardsofconduct,performanceandethics.pdf

Henriksen, K., Stambulova, N., & Roessler, K. K. (2010). Holistic approach to athletic talent development environments: A successful sailing milieu. *Psychology of Sport and Exercise, 11*, 212–222.

Hess, A. K. (1986). Growth in supervision: Stages of supervisee and supervisor development. *The Clinical Supervisor, 4*, 51e67.

Hill, K. L. (2001). Frameworks for sport psychologists. Champaign IL: Human Kinetics.

Holmes, P. S., & Collins, D. J. (2010). The PETTLEP approach to motor imagery: A functional equivalence model for sport psychologists. *Journal of Applied Sport Psychology, 13*(1), 60–83. doi:10.1080/10413200109339004

Holt, N. L., & Strean, W. B. (2001). Reflecting on initiating sport psychology consultation: A self-narrative of neophyte practice. *The Sport Psychologist, 15*, 188–204.

Hutter, R. I., Oldenhof-Veldman, T., & Oudejans, R .R. D. (2015). What trainee sport psychologists want to learn in supervision. *Psychology of Sport and Exercise, 16*, 101–109. doi:10.1016/j.psychsport.2014.08.003

Johns (1994). Nuances of reflection. *Journal of Clinical Nursing, 3*, 71–75.

Kahneman, D. (2011). *Thinking fast and slow*. New York: Macmillan. ISBN 978-1-4299-6935-2.

Kahneman, D., & Klein, G. (2009). Conditions for intuitive expertise: A failure to disagree. *American Psychologist, 64*(6), 515–526.

Kahneman, D., & Tversky, A. (1974). Judgment under uncertainty: Heuristics and biases. *Science, 185*, 1124–1131.

Kahneman, D., & Tversky, A. (1979). Prospect theory: An analysis of decision under risk. *Econometrica, 47*(2), 263–291.

Kanfer, R. (1990). Motivation theory and industrial and organizational psychology. In M. D. Dunnerre (Ed.), *Handbook of industrial and organizational psychology* (Vol. 1, 2nd ed., pp. 75–130). Palo Alto, CA: Consulting Psychologists Press.

Katz, J., & Hemmings, B. (2009). *Counselling Skills Handbook for the Sport Psychologist*. London: British Psychological Society.

Kazdin, A. E. (1998). *Research design in clinical psychology* (3rd ed.). Boston, MA: Allyn and Baco.

Keegan, R. J. (2010). Teaching consulting philosophies to neophyte sport psychologists: Does it help, and how can we do it? *Journal of Sport Psychology in Action, 1*, 42–52.

Keegan, R. J. (2014). Developing a philosophy and theoretical framework. In. L. S. Tashman, & G. Cremades (Eds.), *Becoming a sport, exercise, and performance psychology professional: International perspectives*. London: Routledge/Psychology Press.

Keegan, R. J., Harwood, C. G., Spray, C. M., & Lavallee, D. E. (2010). From motivational climate to motivational atmosphere: A review of research examining the social and environmental influences on athlete motivation in sport. In B. D. Geranto (Ed.), *Sport psychology*. Hauppauge NY: Nova Science Publishers. ISBN 9781617289323.

Keegan, R., & Killilea, J. (2006). Entering sport cultures as a supervised practitioner: What am I getting myself into? *The Sport and Exercise Scientist, 1*(7), 22–23.

Kelly, G. A. (1955). *The psychology of personal constructs*. New York, NY: Norton.

Kendjelic, E. M., & Eells, T. D. (2007). Generic psychotherapy case formulation training improves formulation quality. *Psychotherapy, 44*, 66–67.

Kenrick, D. T., Griskevicius, V., Sundie, J. M., Li, N. P., Li, Y. J., & Neuberg, S. L. (2009). Deep rationality: The evolutionary economics of decision making. *Social Cognition, 27*, 764–785.

Klein, G. (1998). *Sources of power: How people make decisions*. Cambridge, MA: MIT Press.

Knowles, Z., Gilbourne, D., Borrie, A., & Nevill, A., (2001). Developing the reflective sports coach: A study exploring the processes of reflective practice within a higher education coaching programme. *Reflective Practice, 1*, 924–935.

Koestler, A. (1976). *The act of creation.* London: Penguin Publishers.

Kolb, D. A. (1984). *Experiential learning: Experience as the source of learning and development.* Englewood Cliffs, NJ: Prentice Hall.

Kontos, A. P., & Feltz, D. L., (2008). The nature of sport psychology. In T. Horn (Ed.), *Advances in sport psychology* (3rd ed., pp. 3–14).

Krauss, S., & Wang, X. T. (2003). The psychology of the Monty Hall problem: Discovering psychological mechanisms for solving a tenacious brain teaser. *Journal of Experimental Psychology, 132*(1), 3–22.

Kuhn, T. S. (1962/1970). *The structure of scientific revolutions* (2nd ed.). Chicago, IL: University of Chicago Press.

Kutz, M. R. (2008). Toward a conceptual model of contextual intelligence: A transferable leadership construct. *Leadership Review, 8*, 18–31.

Kuyken, W., Fothergill, C. D., Musa, M., & Chadwick, P. (2005). The reliability and quality of cognitive case formulation. *Behaviour Research and Therapy, 43*, 1187–1201.

Lakatos, I. (1970). *The changing logic of scientific discovery* [self-published].

Landers, D. M., (1983). Whatever happened to theory testing in sport psychology? *Journal of Sport Psychology, 5*, 135–151.

Lasley, T. (1992). Promoting teacher reflection. *Journal of Staff Development, 13*(1), 24–29.

Leibniz, G. W. (1969). Philosophical papers and letters. Trans. and Ed. by L. E. Loemker. Dordrecht: Reidel Publishing.

Lerner, B. S., Ostrow, A. C., Yura, M. T., & Etzel, E. F. (1996). The effects of goal-setting and imagery training programs on the free-throw performance of female collegiate basketball players. *The Sport Psychologist, 10*, 382–397.

Levi-Strauss, C. (1966). *The savage mind.* Chicago, IL: University of Chicago Press.

Lewin, K. (1951). Problems of research in social psychology. In D. Cartwright (Ed.), *Field theory in social science: Selected theoretical papers* (pp. 155–169). New York, NY: Harper & Row.

Lidor, R., Morris, T., Bardoxaglou, N., & Becker, B. (2001). The world sport psychology sourcebook (3rd ed.). Morgantown, WV: Fitness Information Technology.

Likert, R. (1932). A simple and reliable method of scoring the Thurstone attitude scale. *Journal of Social Psychology, 5*, 228–238.

Little, G., & Harwood, C. (2010). Enhancing our understanding of the potential violation of sexual boundaries in sport psychology consultancy. *Journal of Clinical Sport Psychology, 4*, 302–311.

Locke, J. (1690). *An essay concerning human understanding* (1st ed.). New York, NY: Dover Publications (1959).

Locke, J. (2009).*Two treatises on government: A translation into modern English.* London: Industrial Systems Research.

Loehr, J. E. (1990). Providing sport psychology consulting services to professional tennis players. *The Sport Psychologist, 4*, 400–408.

Lord, C. G., Ross, L., & Lepper, M. R. (1979). Biased assimilation and attitude polarization: The effects of prior theories on subsequently considered evidence. *Journal of Personality and Social Psychology* (American Psychological Association), *37*(11), 2098–2109. doi:10.1037/0022-3514.37.11.2098

Luepker, E. T. (2010). Records: Purposes, characteristics and contents. In Hanrahan S. J., & Andersen, M. B. *Handbook of Applied Sport Psychology.* London: Routledge.

Lukas, S. R. (1993). *Where to start and what to ask: An assessment handbook.* New York, NY: Norton.

Maehr, M. L., & Nicholls, J. G. (1980). Culture and achievement motivation: A second look. In N. Warren (Ed.), *Studies in cross-cultural psychology: Vol. 3,* (pp. 221–267). New York, NY: Academic Press.

Malik, M. L., & Beutler, L. E. (2002). The emergence of dissatisfaction with the DSM. In L. E. Beutler, & M. L. Malik (Eds.), *Rethinking the DSM (3–16)*. Washington, DC: American Psychological Association.

Marchant, D. (2010). Psychological assessment: Objective/self-report measures. In M. A. Andersen, & S. Hanrahan (Eds.), *Handbook of applied sport psychology for practitioners*. Abingdon: Routledge Press.

Marewski, J. N., & Gigerenzer, G. (2012). Heuristic decision making in medicine. *Dialogues Clinical Neuroscience, 14*, 77–89.

Martens, R., (1979). About smocks and jocks. *Journal of Sport Psychology, 1*, 94–99.

Martens, R. (1987). *Coaches' guide to sport psychology*. Champaign, IL: Human Kinetics.

Martens, R., Vealey, R. S., & Burton, D. (1990). *Competitive anxiety in sport*. Champaign, IL: Human Kinetics.

Martindale, A., & Collins, D. (2005). Professional judgment and decision making: The role of intention for impact. *The Sport Psychologist, 19*, 303–317.

Martindale, A., & Collins, D. (2012). A professional judgment and decision making case study: Reflection-in-action research [Special issue]. *The Sport Psychologist, 26*, 500–518.

Martindale, A. & Collins, D. (2013). The development of professional judgment and decision making expertise in applied sport psychology. *The Sport Psychologist, 27*, 390–398.

Maslow, A. H. (1968). *Toward a psychology of being* (2nd ed.). New York: Van Nostrand.

May, J. R., & Brown, L. (1989). Delivery of psychological services to the U.S. alpine ski team prior to and during the Olympics in Calgary. *The Sport Psychologist, 3*, 320–329.

Meadows, D. H. (2008) *Thinking in systems – A primer*. London: Earthscan.

Meyers, A. W., Whelan, J. P., & Murphy, S. M. (1996). Cognitive behavioral strategies in athletic enhancement. In M. Hershen, R. M. Eisler, & P. M. Miller (Eds.), *Progress in behavior modification* (Vol. 30, pp. 137–164). Pacific Grove, CA: Brooks/Cole.

Milne, D., & Paxton, R. (1998). A psychological re-analysis of the scientist- practitioner model. *Journal of Clinical Psychology and Psychotherapy, 5*, 216–230.

Moore, Z. E. (2003). Ethical dilemmas in sport psychology: Discussion and recommendations for practice. *Professional Psychology: Research and Practice, 34*(6), 601–610.

Morgan, W. P. (1980). The trait psychology controversy. *Research Quarterly for Exercise and Sport, 51*, 50–76.

Mosby's Medical Dictionary, 8th edition. (2009). Retrieved July 15 2014, from http://medical-dictionary.thefreedictionary.com/treatment+plan

Munz, P. (1985). *Our knowledge of the growth of knowledge: Popper or Wittgenstein.* London: Routledge & Kegan Paul.

Murphy, S. M., & Ferrante, A. P. (1989). Provision of sport psychology services to the US team at the 1988 summer Olympic games. *The Sport Psychologist, 3*, 374–385.

Nathan, P. E., & Gorman, J. M. (2002). *A guide to treatments that work* (2nd ed.). London: Oxford University Press.

Naumann, L. P., Vazire, S., Rentfrow, P. J., & Gosling, S. D. (2009). Personality judgments based on physical appearance. *Personality and Social Psychology Bulletin, 35*, 1661–1671. doi:10.1177/0146167209346309

Neff, F. (1990). Delivering sport psychology services to a professional organization. *Sport Psychologist, 4*(4), 378–385.

Nezu, A. M., Nezu, C. M., & Lombardo, E. (2004). *Cognitive-behavioral case formulation and treatment design: A problem-solving approach*. New York, NY: Springer.

Nickerson, R. S. (1998). Confirmation bias: A ubiquitous phenomenon in many guises. *Review of General Psychology, 2*(2): 175–220.

Nickerson, R. S. (2004). The production and perception of randomness. *Psychological Review, 109*(2), 330–357.

Nickerson, R. S. (2005). Bertrand's chord, Buffon's needle, and the concept of randomness. *Thinking and Reasoning, 11*(1), 67–96.

Nideffer, R. M. (1989). Theoretical and practical relationships between attention, anxiety, and performance in sport. In D. Hackfort, & C. D. Spielberger (Eds.), *Anxiety in sport: An international perspective* (pp. 117–136). New York, NY: Hemisphere Publishing.

Norcross, J. C. (Ed.). (2011). *Psychotherapy relationships that work* (2nd ed.). New York, NY: Oxford University Press.

O'Gorman, J. (2001). The scientist-practitioner model and its critics. *Australian Psychologist, 36*(2), 164–169.

Ogedegbe, G., Chaplin, W., Schoenthaler A., Statman, D., Berger, D., Richardson, T. ... Allegrante, J. P. (2008). A practice-based trial of motivational interviewing and adherence in hypertensive African Americans. *American Journal of Hypertension ,21*(10), 1137–1143.

Orlick, T. (1989). Reflections on sport psych consulting with individual and team sport athletes at summer and Winter Olympic Games. *The Sport Psychologist, 3,* 358–365.

Orlick, T., & Partington, J. T. (1988). Mental links to excellence. *The Sport Psychologist, 2,* 105–130.

Page, A. (1996). The scientist-practitioner model: More faces than Eve. *Australian Psychologist, 31*(2), 103–108.

Page, A., Stritzke, W., & Mclean, N. (2008). Toward science-informed supervision of clinical case formulation: A training model and supervision method. *Australian Psychologist, 43*(2), 88–95.

Patrick, T. D., & Hrycaiko, D. W. (1998). Effects of a mental training programme on endurance performance. *The Sport Psychologist, 12,* 283–299.

Pavlov, I. P. (1927). *Conditional reflexes.* New York, NY: Dover Publications (Retrieved from http://psychclassics.yorku.ca/Pavlov/)

Peirce, C. S. (1881). On the logic of number. *American Journal of Mathematics, 4,* 85–95.

Peirce, C. S. (1885). On the algebra of logic: A contribution to the philosophy of notation. *American Journal of Mathematics, 7,* 180–202.

Perkinson, R. R. (2007). *Chemical dependency counselling: A practical guide.* Thousand Oaks, CA: Sage Publications.

Petitpas, A. J., Giges, B., & Danish, S. J. (1999). The sport-athlete relationship: Implications for training. *The Sport Psychologist, 13,* 344–357.

Plous, S. (1993). The psychology of judgment and decision making. New York, NY: McGraw-Hill. (Hardbound edition concurrently published by Temple University Press.)

Poczwardowski, A., Aoyagi, M. W., Shapiro, J. L., & Van Raalte, J. L. (2014). Developing professional philosophy for sport psychology consulting practice. In A. Papaioannou & D. Hackfort (Eds.), *Routledge companion to sport and exercise psychology: Global perspectives and fundamental concepts* (pp. 895–907). London: Routledge.

Poczwardowski, A., Sherman, C. P., & Ravizza, K. (2004). Professional philosophy in the sport psychology service delivery: Building on theory and practice. The Sport Psychologist, 18, 445–463.

Pope, K. S., & Vasquez, J. T. M. (1998). *Ethics in psychotherapy and counselling* (2nd ed.), San Francisco, CA: Jossey-Bass.

Popper, K. R. (1959). *The logic of scientific discovery.* New York, NY: Harper.

Popper, K. R. (1969). *Conjectures and refutations: The growth of scientific knowledge.* London: Routledge & Kegan Paul.

Popper, K. R. (1972). *Objective knowledge: An evolution approach.* Oxford: Oxford University Press.

Price, A. (2004). Facilitating reflection and critical thinking in practice. *Nursing Standard* 18(47), 46–52.

Prochaska, J. O., & DiClemente, C. C. (1983). Stages and processes of self-change of smoking: Toward an integrative model of change. *Journal of Consulting and Clinical Psychology, 51,* 390–395.

Rachman, S. (1997). The evolution of cognitive behaviour therapy. In D. Clark, C. G. Fairburn, & M. G. Gelder. *Science and practice of cognitive behaviour therapy* (pp. 1–26). Oxford: Oxford University Press. ISBN 0-19-262726-0.

Raimy, V. (Ed.) (1950). *Training in clinical psychology*. New York, NY: Pentice Hall.

Raki, T., Steffens, M. C., & Mummendey, A. (2011). When it matters how you pronounce it: The influence of regional accents on job interview outcome. *British Journal of Psychology, 102*, 868–883. doi:10.1111/j.2044-8295.2011.02051.x

Ravizza, K. (1988). Gaining entry with applied personnel for season-long consulting. *The Sport Psychologist, 2*, 243–245.

Ravizza, K. (1990). Sportpsych consultation issues in professional baseball. *The Sport Psychologist, 4*, 330–340.

Ravizza, K. (2001). Reflections and insights from the field on performance enhancement consultation. In G. Tenembaum (Ed.), *The Practice of Sport Psychology* (pp. 197–216). Morgantown, WV: Fitness Information Technology.

Redgrave, S. & Townsend, N. (2004). *A golden age: Steve redgrave – The autobiogaphy*. Chatham: BBC Books.

Reeve, J., Jang, H., Hardre, J., & Omura, M. (2002). Providing a rationale in an autonomy-supportive way as a strategy to motivate others during an uninteresting activity. *Motivation and Emotion, 26*(3), 183–207.

Reyna, V. (2008). A theory of medical decision making and health: Fuzzy trace theory. *Medical Decision Making, 28*, 850.

Roberts, G. C. (1989). When motivation matters: The need to expand the conceptual model. In J. S. Skinner, C. B. Corbin, D. M. Landers, P. E. Martin, & C. L. Wells (Eds.), *Future Directions in Exercise and Sport Sciences* (pp. 71–83). Champaign, IL: Human Kinetics.

Robinson, B. (2009). When therapist variables and the client's theory of change meet. *Psychotherapy in Australia, 15*(4), 60–65.

Rogers, C. (1957). The necessary and sufficient conditions of therapeutic personality change, *Journal of Consulting Psychology, 21*(2), 95–103.

Rogers, C. (1961). On becoming a person: A therapist's view of psychotherapy. New York, NY: Constable.

Rolfe, G. Freshwater, D., & Jasper, M. (2001). *Critical reflection for nursing and the helping professions: a user's guide*. Houndmills, Basingstoke, Hampshire; New York: Palgrave. ISBN 0333777956.

Rotella, R. J. (1990). Providing sport psychology consulting services to professional athletes. *The Sport Psychologist, 4*, 409–417.

Roth, A., & Fonagy, P. (1996). *What works for whom? A critical review of psychotherapy research*. New York, NY: Guilford Press.

Sacket, D. L., Rosenberg, W. M. C., Gray, J. A. M., & Richardson, W. S. (1996). Evidence based medicine: what it is and what it isn't. *British Medical Journal, 312*, 71–72.

Salmela, J. H. (1989). Long-term intervention with the Canadian men's Olympic gymnastics team. *Sport Psychologist, 3*, 340–349.

Schack, T., Bertollo, M., Koester, D., Maycock J., & Essig, K. (2014). Technological advancements in sport psychology. In A. G. Papaioannou & D. Hackfort (Eds.), *Routledge companion to sport and exercise psychology* (pp. 895–908). London: Routledge Taylor and Francis.

Schön, D. A. (1983). *The reflective practitioner: how professionals think in action*. New York: Basic Books. ISBN 046506874X.

Schön, D. A. (1991). *The reflective turn: Case studies in and on educational practice*. New York, NY: Teachers Press, Columbia University.

Scott, C. (2000). Accountability in the Regulatory State. *Journal of Law and Society, 27*, 38–60.

Selvin, S. (1975a). On the Monty Hall problem (letter to the editor). *American Statistician, 29*, 134.

Selvin, S. (1975b). A problem in probability (letter to the editor). *American Statistician, 29*, 67.

Shanteau, J. (1992). The psychology of experts: An alternative view. In G. Wright, & F. Bolger (Eds.), *Expertise and decision support* (Vol. 66506, pp. 11–23). New York, NY: Plenum Press.

Shapiro, M. B. (1955). Training of clinical psychologists at the Institute of Psychiatry. *Bulletin of the British Psychological Association, 8*, 1–6.

Shapiro, D. (2002). Renewing the scientist practitioner model. *The Psychologist, 15*, 232–234.

Silberschatz, G., Curtis, J. T. (1993). Measuring the therapist's impact on the patient's therapeutic progress. *Journal of Consulting and Clinical Psychology, 61*, 403–411.

Simon, H. A. (1992). What is an explanation of behavior? *Psychological Science, 3*, 150–161.

Simons, J. P., & Andersen, M. B. (1995). The development of consulting practice in applied sport psychology: Some personal perspectives. *The Sport Psychologist, 9*, 449–468.

Skynner, A. C. (1984). Group analysis and family therapy. *International Journal of Group Psychotherapy, 34*, 215–224.

Smith, D., & Bar-Eli, M. (Eds.). (2007). *Essential readings in sport and exercise psychology*. Champaign, IL: Human Kinetics Publishing.

Soisson, E. L., VandeCreek, L., & Knapp, S. (1987). Thorough record keeping: A good defense in a litigious era. *Professional Psychology: Research and Practice, 18*, 498–502.

Speck, R. V., & Attneave, C. (1972). *Family networks*. New York, NY: Pantheon.

Stambulova, N., & Johnson, U. (2010). Novice consultants' experiences: lessons learned by applied sport psychology students. *Psychology of Sport and Exercise, 11*, 295–303.

Stambulova, N. B., Wrisberg, C. A., & Ryba, T. V. (2006). A tale of two traditions in applied sport psychology: The heyday of Soviet sport and wake-up calls for North America. *Journal of Applied Sport Psychology, 18*, 173–184.

Stanovich, K. E., West, R. F., & Toplak, M. E. (2013). Myside bias, rational thinking, and intelligence. *Current Directions in Psychological Science, 22*(4), 259–264. doi:10.1177/0963721413480174

Stapleton, A. B., Hankes, D. M., Hayes, K. F., & Parham, W. D. (2010). Ethical dilemmas in sports psychology: A dialogue on the unique aspects impacting practice. *Professional Psychology: Research and Practice, 41*(2), 143–152.

Sternberg, R. J. (1985). *Beyond IQ: A triarchic theory of human intelligence*. New York, NY: Cambridge University Press.

Sternberg, R. J. (1997). *Successful intelligence*. New York, NY: Plume.

Stoltenberg, C. (1981). Approaching supervision from a developmental perspective: the counsellor complexity model. *Journal of Counselling Psychology, 28*, 59–65.

Stoltenberg, C., Pace, T. M., Kashubeck-West, S., Biever, J. L., Patterson, T., & Welch, I. D. (2000). Training models in counseling psychology: Scientist-practitioner versus practitioner-scholar. *The Counselling Psychologist, 28*, 622–640.

Stoner, G., & Green, S. (1992). Reconsidering the scientist-practitioner model for school psychology practice. *School Psychology Review, 21*, 155–167.

Strasburger, L. H., Jorgenson, L., & Sutherland, P. (1992). The prevention of psychotherapist sexual misconduct: Avoiding the slippery slope. *American Journal of Psychotherapy, 46*, 544–555.

Stricker, G. (1997). Are science and practice commensurable? *American Psychologist, 52*, 442–448.

Stricker, G. (2000). The scientist-practitioner model: Gandhi was right again. *American Psychologist, 55*, 253–254.

Strong, S. R., & Claiborn, C. D. (1982). *Change through interaction: Social psychological processes of counseling and psychotherapy*. New York, NY: Wiley.

Svenson, O. (1981). Are we less risky and more skillful than our fellow drivers? *Acta Psychologica, 47*, 143–151.

Taylor, J. (1995). A conceptual model for integrating athletes' needs and sport demands in the development of competitive mental preparation strategies. *The Sport Psychologist, 9*, 339–357.

Taylor, J., & Schneider, B. (1992). The Sport-Clinical Intake Protocol: A Comprehensive Interviewing Instrument for Applied Sport Psychology. *Professional Psychology: Research and Practice, 23*(4), 318–325.

Terry, P. C., Mayer, J. L., & Howe, B. L. (1998). Effectiveness of a mental training program for novice scuba divers. *Journal of Applied Sport Psychology, 10*, 251–267.

The British Association of Sport and Exercise Sciences (2006). [online] Retrieved from http://www.bases.org.uk//CoreCode/DownLoad.aspx?id=3208

The British Psychological Society (2009). [online] Retrieved from http://www.bps.org.uk/sites/default/files/documents/code_of_ethics_and_conduct.pdf

Thomas, E. H., & Galambos, N. (2004). What satisfies students? Mining student-opinion data with regression and decision-tree analysis. *Research in Higher Education, 45*(3), 251–269.

Thomas, P., Murphy, S., & Hardy, L. (1999). Test of performance strategies: Development and preliminary validation of a comprehensive measure of athletes' psychological skills. *Journal of Sports Sciences, 17*, 697–711.

Titkov, A., Bednarikova, M., & Mortensen, J. R. (2014). Peer mentoring and peer supervision: Nordic experiences. In G. Cremedes, & L. Tashman (Eds.), *Becoming a sport, exercise, and performance psychology professional: A global perspective*. New York, NY: Psychology Press.

Tod, D. (2007). Reflections on collaborating with a professional rugby league player. *Sport and Exercise Psychology Review, 3*(1), 4–10.

Tod, D., Andersen, M. B., & Marchant, D. B. (2009). A longitudinal examination of neophyte applied sport psychologists' development. *Journal of Applied Sport Psychology, 21*, S1–S16.

Tod, D., Andersen, M. B., & Marchant, D. B. (2011). Six years up: Applied sport psychologists surviving (and thriving) after graduation. *Journal of Applied Sport Psychology, 23*, 93–109.

Tod, D., & Bond, K. (2010). A longitudinal examination of a British neophyte sport psychologist's development. *The Sport Psychologist, 24*, 35–51.

Trice, H. M., & Beyer, J. M. (1984). Studying organizational cultures through rites and rituals. *Academy of Management Review, 9*(4), 653–669.

Triplett, N. (1898). The dynamogenic factors in pacemaking and competition. *American Journal of Psychology, 9*, 507–533.

Uleman, J. S., Saribay, S. A., & Gonzalez, C. M. (2008). Spontaneous inferences, implicit impressions, and implicit theories. *Annual Review of Psychology, 59*, 329–360. doi:10.1146/annurev.psych.59.103006.093707

Vaillant, G. E. (2003). A 60-year follow-up of alcoholic men. *Addiction, 98*(8), 1043–1051. PMID: 12873238

Valli, L. (1997). Listening to other voices: A description of teacher reflection in the United States. *Peabody Journal of Education, 72*(1), 67–88.

Van Audenhove, C., & Vertommen, H. (2000). A negotiation approach to intake and treatment choice. *Journal of Psychotherapy Integration, 10*, 287–299.

Van Deurzen-Smith, E. (1990). What is existential analysis? *Journal for Existential Analysis, 1*. London.

Van Manen, M. (1977). Linking ways of knowing to ways of being practical. *Curriculum Inquiry, 6*, (3), Spring.

Van Raalte, J. L., & Andersen, M. B. (2000). Supervision I: From models to doing. In M. Andersen (Ed.), *Doing sport psychology* (pp. 153–165). Champaign, IL: Human Kinetics.

Van Raalte, J. L., & Andersen, M. B. (2014). Supervision. In R. C. Eklund, & G. Tenenbaum (Eds.). *Encyclopedia of sport and exercise psychology*. Thousand Oaks, CA: Sage.

Vazsonyi, A. (1999). Which door has the Cadillac? *Decision Line*, *19*, 17–19.

vos Savant, M. (1996). *The power of logical thinking*. New York, NY: St. Martin's Press.

vos Savant, M. (1990). "Ask Marilyn". *Parade Magazine* (9 September) p. 16.

Vosloo, J., Zakrajsek, R., & Grindley, E. (2014). From mentee to mentor: Considerations for the neophyte supervisor. In G. Cremedes, & L. Tashman (Eds.), *Becoming a sport, exercise, and performance psychology professional: A global perspective*. New York, NY: Psychology Press.

Vygotsky, L. S. (1978). *Mind in society: Development of higher psychological processes*, p. 86.

Wakefield, C. J., & Smith, D. (2012). Perfecting practice: Applying the PETTLEP model of motor imagery. *Journal of Sport Psychology in Action*, *3*, 1–11.

Wakefield, C. J., Smith, D., Moran, A., & Holmes, P. (2013). Functional Equivalence or Behavioural Matching? A Critical Reflection on 15 years of Research Using the PETTLEP Model of Motor Imagery. *International Review of Sport and Exercise Psychology*, 6, 105–121.

Wampold, B. E. (2001). *The great psychotherapy debate: Models, methods and findings*. Hillsdale, NJ: Erlbaum.

Watson, J. C. (2002). Re-visioning empathy. In D. J. Cain (Ed.), *Humanistic psychotherapies: Handbook of research and practice* (pp. 445–471). Washington, DC: American Psychological Association.

Watson II, J. C., MacAlarnen, M. M., & Shannon, V. (2014). Facilitating our future: Roles, responsibilities, and the development of the sport, exercise, and performance supervisor. In G. Cremedes, & L. Tashman (Eds.), *Becoming a sport, exercise, and performance psychology professional: A global perspective*. New York: Psychology Press.

Watson II, J., & Shannon, V. (2010). Individual and group observations: Purposes and processes. In M. Andersen, & S. Hanrahan (Eds.), *Routledge handbook of applied sport psychology*. London: Routledge Publishing.

Watson, J. C., Zizzi, S. J., Etzel, E. F., & Lubker, J. R. (2004). Applied sport psychology supervision: A survey of students and professionals. *The Sport Psychologist*, *18*, 415–429.

Weber, M. (1949). *The methodology of the social sciences*. Trans. & Ed. by E. A. Shills and H. A. Finch. Glencoe, IL: Free Press.

Weber, M. (1962). *Basic concepts in sociology*. New York, NY: The Citadel Press.

Weimar, D., & Wicker, P. (2014). Moneyball revisited effort and team performance in professional soccer. *Journal of Sports Economics* (online pre-print) 1527002514561789.

Weinberg, R. (2010). Making goals effective: A primer for coaches. *Journal of Sport Psychology in Action*, *1*(2), 57–65.

Weinberg, R. S. (1989). Applied sport psychology: Issues and challenges. *Journal of Applied Sport Psychology*, *1*, 181–195.

Weinberg, R., & Gould, D. (1995). *Foundations of sport and exercise psychology*. Champaign, IL: Human Kinetics.

Weiss, M. R. (1995). Children in sport: An educational model. In S. M. Murphy (Ed.), *Sport psychology interventions* (pp. 36–69). Champaign, IL: Human Kinetics.

Weiss, M. R., & Gill, D. L. (2005). What goes around comes around: Re-emerging themes in sport and exercise psychology. *Research Quarterly for Exercise and Sport*, *76*(Supplement), S71–S87.

Westen, D., Blagov, P. S., Harenski, K., Kilts, C., & Hamann, S. (2006). Neural bases of motivated reasoning: An fMRI study of emotional constraints on partisan political judgment in the 2004 U.S. presidential election. *Journal of Cognitive Neuroscience* (Massachusetts Institute of Technology), *18*(11), 1947–1958. doi:10.1162/jocn.2006.18.11.1947

Weston, N. J. V., Greenlees, I. A., & Thelwell, R. C. (2011a). Athlete perceptions of the impacts of performance profiling. *International Journal of Sport and Exercise Psychology, 9*(2), 173–188.

Weston, N. J. V., Greenlees, I. A., & Thelwell, R. C. (2011b). The impact of a performance profiling intervention on athletes' intrinsic motivation. *Research Quarterly for Exercise and Sport, 82*(1), 151–155. doi:10.1080/02701367.2011.10599733

Weston, N. J. V., Greenlees, I. A., & Thelwell, R. C. (2013). A review of Butler and Hardy's (1992). performance profiling procedure within sport. *International Review of Sport and Exercise Psychology, 6*(1), 1–21.

Weston, N., Greenlees, I., & Thelwell, R. (2010). Applied sport psychology consultant perceptions of the usefulness and impacts of performance profiling. *International Journal of Sport Psychology, 41*(4),360–368. ISSN 0047-0767

Wiers-Jenssen, J., Stensaker, B., & Grogaard, J. B. (2002) Student satisfaction: Towards an empirical deconstruction of the concept. *Quality in Higher Education, 8*(2), 183–195.

Williams, B. (2001). Developing critical reflection for professional practice through problem based learning. *Journal of Advanced Nursing, 34*, 27–34.

Wittgenstein, L. (1922/1961). *Tractatus logico-philosophicus*. D. F. Pears, & B. F. McGuinness (Trans.), New York, NY: Humanities Press.

Wylleman, P., Alfermann, D., & Lavallee, D. (2004). Career transitions in sport: European perspectives. *Psychology of Sport and Exercise, 5*, 7–20.

Yambor, J., & Connelly, D. (1991). Issues confronting female sport psychology consultants working with male student-athletes. *The Sport Psychologist, 5*, 304–312.

Yambor, J., & Thompson, M. (2014). A supervision model utilizing peer mentoring and consultation teams in the provision of applied sport psychology services. In G. Cremedes, & L. Tashman (Eds.), *Becoming a sport, exercise, and performance psychology professional: A global perspective*. New York, NY: Psychology Press.

Yates, J. F., & Tschirhart, M. D. (2006). Decision making expertise. In K. A. Ericsson, N. Charness, P. J. Feltovich, & R. R. Hoffman (Eds.), *Cambridge handbook of expertise and expert performance* (pp. 421–438). New York, NY: Cambridge University Press.

Yerkes, R. M., & Dodson, J. D. (1908). The relation of strength of stimulus to rapidity of habit-formation. *Journal of Comparative Neurology & Psychology, 18*, 459–482.

Young, T. J. (1990). Sensation seeking and self-reported criminality among student-athletes. *Perceptual and Motor Skills, 70*, 959–962.

Zajonc, R. B. (1965). Social facilitation. *Science*, 149, 269–274.

Zirri, S. J., & Perna, F. M. (2002). Integrating web pages and e-mail into sport psychology consultations. *The Sport Psychologist, 16*(4), 416–431.

Index